Counterpublic is a civic exhibition that weaves contemporary art into the life of St. Louis for three months every three years in order to reimagine civic infrastructures toward generational change. Counterpublic's second edition will run from April 15 to July 15, 2023.

Actively engaged with both its neighbors in St. Louis and national conversations on the role of contemporary art, Counterpublic aims to be a beacon of creative thinking and community engagement—an inclusive art platform that expands social, political, and civic horizons.

Working in public places, cultural institutions, historic houses, and community gathering spaces, Counterpublic commissions dozens of artists, collectives, and community organizers to make and present works in St. Louis that engage the city's histories and imagine new futures. The three-month exhibition also includes active education, research, residencies, performances, publications, public projects, and commissions.

COUNTERPUBLIC 2023

Counterpublic 2023 engages the complex histories, charged present, and many possible futures of St. Louis from April 15 to July 15, 2023. Counterpublic 2023 brings together thirty-plus leading and emergent artists, architects, collectives, and community organizers to reimagine civic infrastructures toward generational change.

Following a year-long process of community engagement in which over 800 neighbors in St. Louis were invited to reflect upon the most urgent needs facing their communities in order to shape the theme of the exhibition, Counterpublic determined to focus its 2023 edition on public memory and reparative futures—how our history is told, held, and healed, and how our future is envisioned collectively toward new liberated lifeways.

LAND RECOGNITION

We want to respectfully acknowledge that we are on the traditional, ancestral, and unceded territory of the Osage, Missouri, and Illini people, who have stewarded this land throughout the generations. We ask you to consider the many legacies of violence, displacement, migration, and settlement that bring us to this community today, and the ways in which we may work to care for and repair these legacies in the present.

Beyond recognition of the land, we are committed to supporting the Osage Nation's efforts to rematriate Sugarloaf Mound, the last remaining intact mound and oldest man-made structure in the city of St. Louis, in accordance with the Osage Nation's Sugarloaf Mound Management Plan.

Table Of Contents

RISA PULEO

JAMES MCANALLY

KATHERINE SIMÓNE REYNOLDS

DIYA VIJ

ST. LOUIS A CITY OUT OF TIME

If a city
takes its rhythms
from the river
that cuts through it
the pulse of the Mississippi
has torn this city
apart.

St. Louis is
somebody's home
and not answering
was nobody shovels snow
because spring will come
some day.

People who live
by rivers   dream
they are immortal.

Audre Lorde, 1971

ACTS OF FUTURING:

An Introduction to Counterpublic 2023

By
James McAnally

St. Louis is, for better and worse, at the crux of American history. As "the heart of the heart of the country,"[1] St. Louis, like the nation it sits in the center of, is all too often stuck in its accumulated histories. In his 2020 book *The Broken Heart of America*, Walter Johnson compellingly posits the city as a kind of historical hinge, not just between the East and West Coasts, as it is typically seen, but also for different Americas.[2] The city takes its rhythms from the confluence of the two largest waterways on the continent, the flows of the city unsettling the sediments of American Empire that move through its muddy waters, compelling us to consider what we do with the weights of history and how to imagine other futures.

As an ancient city of the Americas, St. Louis has been an important gathering point for more than a millennium. Cahokia was the largest center of influence on the pre-Columbian continent as a trade route connecting Native peoples along the length of the rivers and well beyond. Following European settlement, the region remained strategically important for the imperial project such that by the peak of its influence at the turn of the twentieth century, the city was for a time proposed to become the new national capital. Beneath this line of expansion and influence, St. Louis has also been a crucible in which the violent advancement of Western settlement and displacement of Native peoples was authored as well as a focal point of centuries of racial tensions, of violence and mapped decline.[3] Counter to these simmering histories, the city has equally been the seedbed of some of the most significant resistance movements in the nation. From the first general strike in the United States and early tenant unionizing to the eruption of the Black Lives Matter movement in neighboring Ferguson, the actions of St. Louis organizers have often defined their time. Whatever cross-section is observed, St. Louis continually intersects with the recurring histories haunting the entire nation. Likewise, the futures born here seed new ways of being that have a rippling impact outward in the world.

As a curator, editor, and founder of St. Louis-based artist space The Luminary, and now as the Executive and Artistic Director of Counterpublic, I came to this exhibition out of a time in which it seemed to me that exhibition-making was not keeping pace with the urgencies that were continually arising around us. While both participating in and learning from the organizing around St. Louis in and after the 2014 Ferguson Uprising, alongside the reconsiderations of monuments and museums alike arising throughout the 2020 pandemic and beyond, I have found myself increasingly at odds with the pace and methods employed within most contemporary art exhibitions, and biennials in particular.

[1] St. Louis-based novelist William H. Gass coined this phrase as the title of a collection of five short stories published in 1968 reflecting on writing and living in the Midwest.

[2] Walter Johnson, *The Broken Heart of America: St. Louis and the Violent History of the United States* (New York: Basic Books, 2020).

[3] Colin Gordon's *Mapping Decline: St. Louis and the Fate of the American City* (Philadelphia: University of Pennsylvania Press, 2008) looks to St. Louis as a central example of the failed policies inscribed in trends of white flight and urban renewal as a way to actively map American cities' evolutions through the twentieth century. The accompanying web project is available at: http://mappingdecline.lib.uiowa.edu/.

An enormous amount of energy is spent to realize increasingly ambitious exhibitions that use the aesthetics and content of these mass movements but rarely engage in any kind of material change these movements directly demand. At most, individual artists and curators call for these changes but are frustrated, delayed, or denied outright by the structures within which they work. In other words, despite the altered world around us, the art world has attempted to keep its course. This is an exhibition emerging from frustration at the limitations of an anemic art world met with concrete possibilities for more liveable worlds experienced in grassroots organizing in St. Louis, as well as a deep care for a place I have committed much of my adult life to seeing flourish, despite witnessing its legacies of harm, fragmentation, and structural inequities firsthand. In envisioning the exhibition, I aimed for something altogether different—a triennial that allied itself with generational, cultural, economic, and civic change; a post-pandemic, post-uprising exhibition demanding that we, as arts workers and artists, do more to repair our broken world.

From this ground, we grew Counterpublic 2023, the second edition of a triennial civic exhibition I co-founded in 2019. Counterpublic was conceived as a *triennial civic exhibition* and both adopts and adapts the understood forms of cyclical exhibition-making toward other uses. As a *triennial*, we aim to consider alternate approaches to time as a core part of our form. As a *civic exhibition*, we attempt to propose a more concrete working theory of how art can be allied with change. "Ennial" exhibitions, in their most superficial sense, share only an approach to time: they happen cyclically, swelling and receding on a set schedule that nests into the hums of institutional movements and the thrumming activities of other art worlds. They occur every two, three, five years, each in succession, and constantly converging.[4] In our formation, we asked, instead, what possibilities exist for the triennial to reimagine relations to the world, working to answer how a cyclical exhibition can use its time to both slow down and deepen relations to place, to process, to multiple communities and (counter)publics. We worked to consider our own temporariness and position as a non-institution as an opportunity to be better collaborators and conveners—to gather rather than to compete—and to leverage our assets and multiyear time span to create a focused approach toward generational change.

Embedded in our name and concept equally is an understanding that we must speak concretely to the fissured publics we engage.[5] Counterpublics are a divergent set of publics typically at odds with dominant ideology; they are formed through a temporal and intentional gathering around a space, text, or, in this case, an exhibition. In anthropologist Michael Warner's words, a "public is poetic world-making" and all cultural activity addressed to a public "must characterize the world in which it attempts to circulate, projecting for that world a concrete and livable shape, and attempting to realize the world through address."[6] Counterpublics create those liveable shapes for specific communities or contexts that are often resistant to being seen together as one. These publics have specific needs, specific spaces, specific means of expression and engagement not always confluent with broader desires or top-down processes that public art often employs.

[4] In 2022, for example, documenta, Prospect New Orleans, FRONT International, Venice Biennale, Manifesta, Toronto Biennial of Art, and numerous others overlapped with divergent formats and interests.

[5] "Counterpublic" comes to us as a readymade with multiple meanings. It was first circulated in feminist theory by Nancy Fraser and later expanded upon in Michael Warner's "Publics and Counterpublics." Fraser describes counterpublics as "where members of subordinated social groups invent and circulate counter discourses to formulate oppositional interpretations of their identities, interests, and needs." Nancy Fraser, "Rethinking the Public Sphere: A Contribution to the Critique of Actually Existing Democracy," in *Habermas and the Public Sphere, ed. Craig Calhoun* (Cambridge, MA: MIT Press, 1992), 123. Throughout these writings, counterpublics are seen as a means to rethink participatory publics that emerge from marginalized social spaces and communities as counter to dominant forms of power and capital.

[6] Michael Warner, "Publics and Counterpublics," *Public Culture* 14, no. 1 (Winter 2002): 49–90.

St. Louis is a poster example of fragmentation, from its fractured histories to geographic and geopolitical boundaries that hem in the experience of the city. Questions of how to consider divergent publics together are essential here as well as in an American experience presently defined by discord.

The universalization of a general public typically spoken to through public art is itself a mode of erasure that tends to uplift those already visible within historical narratives and normative power. To address the counterpublics of St. Louis is to enter into relation with multiple, overlapping narratives and neighbors that do not have to come to consensus. Yet, we hope through our work these counterpublics may be able to see in one another some collectivity of parts and people. We are attempting to conjure liveable shapes for the city through the convening of artist commissions and programs, publications and performances, education and curriculum-building, community and civic partnerships at all scales of operation, and, perhaps most of all, in the innumerable interactions among audiences, artworks, sites, histories, and neighborhoods throughout the three-month run.

This converging non-consensus is evident in our embrace of the ensemble—a word that means *parts of a whole, taken together*—as our organizing principle. We are attempting to respond to, speak with, and experiment alongside the publics of St. Louis to start to build toward a whole. For Counterpublic 2023, we have invited a curatorial ensemble of three curators, Allison Glenn, Diya Vij, and Risa Puleo, alongside Associate Curator and artist Katherine Simóne Reynolds and an artist collective and "public secret society," New Red Order.[7] Within our team, we are always multiple and resistant—sometimes reflective of our publics and also divergent from them, finding our own ways toward a more compelling mode of exhibition-making. Together, this ensemble worked over the course of two years to respond to the histories, presents, and futures of St. Louis in order to reimagine relations between the city, the land, and the times we have inherited.

Through every aspect of Counterpublic 2023's emergence, we have posed these questions to ourselves: *What will have changed because of our work? What new paths become possible, not only in St. Louis, but for artists and arts organizations more broadly to ally with and initiate concrete change?*

[7] The architecture collaborative Dream the Combine was a formational part of the curatorial ensemble but had to step away from their curatorial contribution in 2022.

Creating an exhibition at the scale of Counterpublic *now* calls for a different urgency and commitment. We defined a set of goals for how we would enact this vision before we began:

- COMMUNITY-LED: Counterpublic starts with a robust community engagement process to determine how and where we work, what is needed now, and what is needed next in direct dialogue with our neighbors through a year-long community process. Our first hire was community engagement and our last act in each edition will be evaluation of impact.

- INTENTIONAL INVESTMENT: Counterpublic focuses resources on existing community anchors, sustaining and expanding under-resourced partners toward lasting impact. Over 50 percent of our budget goes directly toward long-term assets owned by the community, resisting the tendency of biennials to disappear with no lasting impact in their communities and contexts.

- COLLABORATION x CONNECTION: Counterpublic connects leading artists and curators to initiate transformative projects alongside civic, cultural, and community partners, building up an ecosystem of collaboration and connection at all scales of operation.

- REPARATIVE FUTURES: A foundational vision for Counterpublic is to initiate and lead acts of repair, reparations, and repatriation/rematriation within St. Louis that create possibilities for reparative relations to both the past and future.

We initiated this edition with an intensive community-engagement process documented in a community report (included in this catalog) that gathered responses from over 800 neighbors and stakeholders in our immediate footprint. The report points to a reality we already knew: that art has more often than not been allied with normative power and siloed from emergent community work. Using the word "future" itself can be language that at first feels hopeful, but it holds on as a bitter reminder of how *future* has been used as a weapon, an engine of power and capital that has been used to tear down entire neighborhoods and ask their residents to forget and move forward without attending to that hurt. Finally, that the public narratives of St. Louis are partial, and our monuments and memorials reinscribe its histories of settlement and displacement while many communities' histories are ignored, or actively forgotten. The report made clear that acknowledging these histories in public is essential to start to respond and repair all that has been done.

With Counterpublic 2023, we aim to open a doorway between our inherited pasts and the present crises we see all around to understand what changes when we hold the past with honor, when we tell the truth with care, when we look to the future only after earning the right to do so through repair. This text, and the exhibition it frames, is not about meditating on the past as a means to trace what has gone wrong. It instead aims to look for means of both acknowledging and unsettling the histories of the city in order to open up concrete means of repair and to reenvision liberatory lifeways with and alongside our neighbors. This is not only a question for St. Louis, but is, I believe, a central project of our time. *With so many accumulated harms, how do we move forward? In a city out of time, how do times change?*

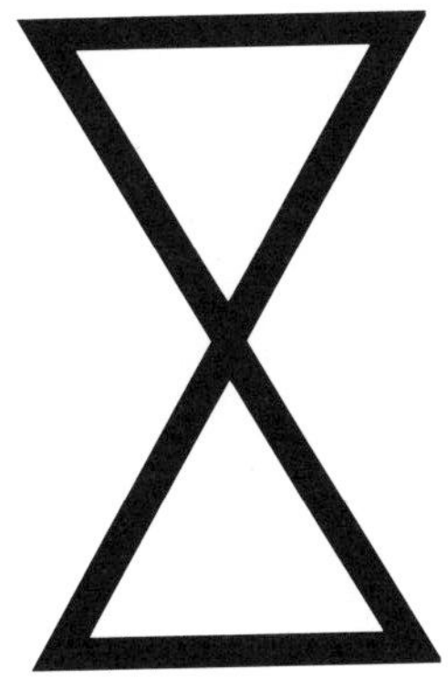

For Counterpublic 2023, we are looking to St. Louis as the narrowed flute between the two ends of an hourglass through which the flows of American experience have filtered. This hourglass symbol recurs throughout the exhibition, suggesting alternate temporalities—an overfull past, an unknown future, and a narrow passage through a complex present. However, it is this symbol's other meanings that start to open onto the exhibition's embodied practices.

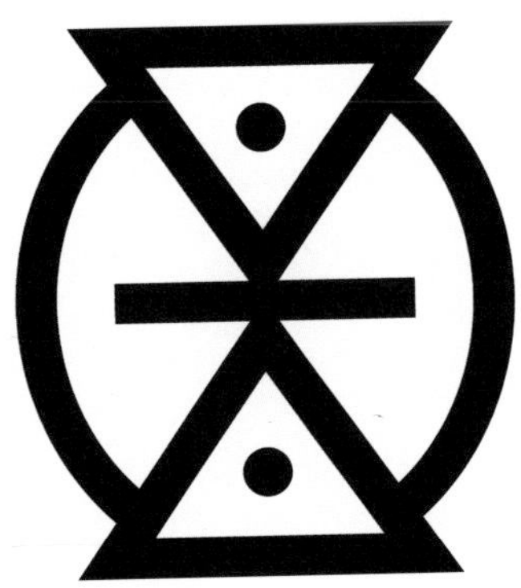

The Adinkra symbol *Mmere Dane* translates as both "time changes" and "times change." The symbol, an hourglass bisected by a line and set into a circle that connects both past and future, appears often in Counterpublic 2023 participating artists Black Quantum Futurism's practice, which attempts to reclaim Black temporalities and self-sovereignty through an engagement in time and land alike. In Lakota (and other Native) cosmology, the symbol *Kapemni* is an "X," or two triangles reflected—suggesting a portal or doorway between the physical and the spiritual worlds, a reflection of earth and sky, and an image of the world itself. The symbol likewise appears throughout Osage sacred sites around the St. Louis region and beyond. While on a site visit to St. Louis, Osage artist Anita Fields, unaware of our other reflections on the hourglass, sketched the symbol in her notebook as she, curator Risa Puleo, and I discussed the presences and erasures of Osage land and people in the region, as well as the persistent memory held in the land and stone. We asked in that conversation: *What have the mounds seen? What does the river remember?* Now, we may ask, what are we offering to this long history in realizing this exhibition?

As Artistic Director, I oriented Counterpublic 2023 as a durational exhibition that invites us to think ancestrally and infrastructurally: to respond both to what has brought us here and what we will leave behind. The curators, artists, and collaborators who came to shape the exhibition were invited to consider this moment as a confluence of times, proposing what agency an artistic platform can have toward reimagining complex pasts, conflictual presents, and reimagined futures for the land and those living on it. Together, we conceived of an exhibition that operates at every timescale in a city too often trapped in its past. Counterpublic is an intentional intervention into St. Louis and its histories that is meant to offer an opening to new ways of exhibition-making. Artist commissions reach back as a balm to centuries-old wounds, attempting to hold historic harms with agency in order to allow for other reparative futures. Other aspects of the exhibition attempt to place those futures in motion directly through "land back" efforts, community housing labs, responsive new monuments, and curricula embedded directly in schools around the region.

Arising out of this early work, the exhibition has been organized as a timeline, tracing histories of displacement and marking out acts of repatriation/rematriation, reparations, reimagined inhabitations, and reparative futures. Using the six-mile length of a major arterial street, Jefferson Avenue, as our organizing principle, the exhibition moves through the length of the city across thirteen neighborhoods, threading together a series of sites key to St. Louis's history and future.

We start, both physically and conceptually, with Sugarloaf Mound on Counterpublic 2023's southernmost terminus, the last remaining Mississippian mound and the oldest human-built structure in the city of St. Louis. As the seat of the Mississippian peoples, Cahokia formed the largest city in the present-day United States, rivaling London at its height before its sudden and still unexplained collapse. The most evident mark of this advanced society is in the earthen mounds that reshaped the terrains of the region, from the largest earthwork in the Americas at Monks Mound across the Mississippi through the prominent twinned mounds on the St. Louis riverfront in Big Mound to Sugarloaf Mound and the hundreds of other mounds that were spread throughout the region.[8] In the city of St. Louis, of these, only Sugarloaf Mound remains in public view, a reminder of the violent dispossessions and destruction of the mounds and an image of occupation of Native land as it has been lived on, dug at, and overlooked in the long last several centuries. Persistent through this history, the mound remains a foothold for the preservation of one of the most sacred sites remaining for the Osage people, one of the extant tribes that are the ancestors of the mound builders.

Sugarloaf has been unevenly occupied since 1928 by three private homes and shorn away by quarries and highway construction that have reduced its footprint by at least half in that time period. The homes were part of a small neighborhood and were at least partially built by prison labor[9] plotted out by the warden of the adjacent Workhouse, a medium-security prison that has since relocated but remains a central locus in the imaginary of hostile policing practices in the city.[10] So named due to an 1840s city ordinance that allowed forced labor as a punishment for sentenced criminals who couldn't pay their fines, the Workhouse was intrinsically connected to the occupation of the mound.

[8] See Andrea Hunter and Andrew Weil, "Saving Sugarloaf Mound in St. Louis, Missouri," *CRM: The Journal of Heritage Stewardship* 7, no. 1 (Winter 2010): https://www.nps.gov/crps/CRMJournal/Winter2010/research3.html/ and also included in this catalog on page 60.

[9] As told to the author by the owner of 4414 Ohio Avenue on the second tier of the mound, and as it is recorded in her family scrapbook. For more information see Jennifer Colten and Jesse Volger, "Commingling, or the Mound Called Sugarloaf," on page 66.

[10] The Workhouse is a medium-security institution (MSI) that was originally located near the southern riverfront near Sugarloaf Mound. It later moved to a site on the northern riverfront and has been the focus of sustained high-profile efforts to close and reimagine the site. More information available at: closetheworkhouse.org.

Prisoners forcibly molded stone retaining walls, framed foundations, and dug at this sacred site on orders from the warden, who owned the rights to the land and saw in it only a cheap building site near a "Hooverville" beneath the bluffs. This confluence of violences inherent in the project of construction is a reminder of Ruth Wilson Gilmore's assertion that abolition is always intersectional, requiring more profound imaginings in which both these walls and histories are undone through acts of futuring.

The sacred mound has been partially reclaimed by the Osage Nation, its summit purchased in 2009 when it was advertised by its realtors for would-be buyers to "own a piece of ancient history." In subsequent years, the Osage have stabilized this section of the mound, including unrooting a tree gripping into the ground and fencing off the mound to protect it from artifact seekers (much like Big Mound, its sister earthwork further up the Mississippi River north of downtown St. Louis, which was consumed piece by piece by settlers and levelers throughout the nineteenth century). Yet, as of the time of this writing, two homes still remain on the mound: one lived in and owned for three generations by the Heckenberg family and the other by Kappa Psi, a pharmaceutical fraternity affiliated with Saint Louis University.

Our goal in engaging Sugarloaf Mound goes beyond the understood and limited mechanics of art toward a deeper and more powerful outcome: the comprehensive repatriation/rematriation of this sacred land to its rightful stewards, the Osage Nation, and the mobilization of a localized "land back" movement in St. Louis. To enter into relation with this mound and these entangled histories meant for us to enter into relation with the Osage Nation Historic Preservation Office and Traditional Cultural Advisors for permission to engage Sugarloaf through artistic and public actions. We attempt to respond directly to the Osage Nation's preservation plan for Sugarloaf Mound—for the Osage to steward the full footprint of this site that is considered one of their most sacred and to move toward the creation of an interpretive center adjacent to the mound.[11] Counterpublic 2023, in engaging Sugarloaf Mound, explicitly aims to go beyond artistic activation or symbolic gesture, to consider more concrete outcomes that the exhibition's confluence of intent, energies, resources, and attention could help to make happen.

[11] More information available at: https://www.osageculture.com/culture/geography/sugarloaf-mound.

I have undertaken this work alongside curatorial ensemble members New Red Order and Risa Puleo, who each in their own ways address the mound as a point of departure. New Red Order, through a new film commission, a series of film- and performance-based programs, as well as a multi-modal "land back" marketing effort, attempt to call in settler imaginaries to a non-metaphorical decolonization of Native life and land. New Red Order closes the exhibition with a full weekend series of performances, screenings, and programs.

Moving north along Jefferson, Puleo's curatorial contribution imaginatively responds to the geographies between Sugarloaf Mound and Arsenal Street. Arsenal, so named because it housed the United States Army arsenal that armed the Plains Wars, using St. Louis as the departure point for the violent settlement of the West. Puleo sees in these sites successive entanglements of repatriation and rematriation, Native vs. settler mounds, and, with a commissioned painting by Jaune Quick-to-See Smith, considers the ways in which the names of the street grid itself mark out a history of settlement and displacements. Streets with state names (such as Tennessee) intersect with streets named after Native nations (such as Cherokee) eight times throughout her project footprint. These intersections are addressed with permanent sign markers naming and bringing attention to often invisible histories that are entangled in our infrastructure.

Elsewhere, Puleo engages Indigenous futures with Cannupa Hanska Luger's first augmented reality monument, a ritual performance that encircles the St. Louis horizon with seven figures dancing in Luger's designed regalia. Raven Chacon installs a public sound sculpture in Benton Park, *Music for 13 Paths*, that unsettles the twelve tones foundational to Western music, the performance of which opens the exhibition.

With General Sisters, Juan William Chávez, and jackie sumell, Puleo finds in the dirt and clay, the bricks and bees, a more-than-human brimming of life and lineage along Jefferson Avenue through guided walks, a native bee hub, and a garden using rematriated clay, respectively. With *(a river) will flow*, X returns the footpaths of the street back to the Mississippi River, imaginatively connecting us to the water through a reflective analog "projection" draped over the river bluffs. Anita and Nokosee Fields work adjacent to the mound with a set of ceremonial platforms inscribed with Osage designs. Entitled *WayBack*, I see this work as an act of deep futurity. This land, these platforms, are ready for the ceremonies to come after repatriation/rematriation, reaching back and forward, while offering our bodies, now, a welcome.

The second heart of the exhibition forms around several entangled sites focused on legacies of Black life and its erasures in St. Louis—from the former site of Mill Creek Valley, a neighborhood that was home to 20,000 predominantly Black residents at the time of its demolition in 1959, past Pruitt-Igoe, a notorious public housing project open for only twenty-two years, to a series of Black historic houses and history museums, including the George B. Vashon Museum of African American History, the Scott Joplin House State Historic Site, the currently closed Frederick Douglass Museum of African American Vernacular Images, and The Griot Museum of Black History.

Rooted in specific histories of Black displacement, this vein of the exhibition continues Walter Johnson's singular thesis in *The Broken Heart of America* that the city's template of removal inaugurated through the Native displacements that departed from St. Louis has been extended to numerous Black communities in the city. These histories manifest in the present as eminent domain; redlining and conscious abandonment mark many of the adjacent neighborhoods north of Delmar.[12] In an act of affirmative resistance, it is in these same places that emergent Black institutions intent on memory-keeping and community formation have sprung up to resist erasure and insist on Black futurity. These sites form multiple anchor points in the northern section of the exhibition.

As Artistic Director, I curated a number of artists engaging these sites in order to stitch these essential histories together with a rooted local knowledge. In tandem with Great Rivers Greenway's Brickline project, St. Louis CITY SC, Harris-Stowe State University, and the City of St. Louis, we commissioned artist, activist, and polymath Damon Davis to create a mile-long permanent monument to the residents of Mill Creek Valley. Davis's sculptural installation *Pillars of the Valley* is a major focal point of Counterpublic 2023 and will continue to expand along Market Street in subsequent years to Harris-Stowe State University, an Historically Black University (HBCU) whose campus contains some of the only remaining buildings original to Mill Creek Valley. Taking an abstracted hourglass form, the sculptures embed quotes from residents of the neighborhood along with maps of Mill Creek Valley and markers of the site of former homes, outlining its sheer scale with specific sites and stories returning into public view for the first time since the neighborhood's demolition. Echoing the multiple meanings of the hourglass described above, Davis has described these pillars as portals, giving a filtered view back to the thriving time of Mill Creek Valley, but also toward futures that imagine Black life in its varied forms back in these same streets.

Black Quantum Futurism traces a history of freedom seekers who moved through the caves beneath St. Louis along the Underground Railroad, seeing a subaltern/subterranean history to enshrine and creating a portal to this nonlinear time of resistance and freedom of movement. Along Dr. Martin Luther King Drive at La Rose Room Cocktail Lounge, they respond again to the hourglass form in a gate outside of the bar, seeing in it an invitation to change the times.

[12] St. Louis's infamous "Delmar Divide" demarcates a clear boundary between the well-resouced central corridor and the deeply disinvested North St. Louis, which is over 90 percent Black. See Chico Harlan, "In St. Louis, Delmar Boulevard is the line that divides a city by race and perspective," *Washington Post*, August 22, 2014, https://www.washingtonpost.com/national/in-st-louis-delmar-boulevard-is-the-line-that-divides-a-city-by-race-and-perspective/2014/08/22/de692962-a2ba-4f53-8bc3-54f88f848fdb_story.html.

At The Luminary, Black Quantum Futurism places the histories of dispossession of Black and Brown people in St. Louis into a space of active organizing, bringing together regional tenants' rights organizations and housing advocates to document community histories in a recording booth, hosting workshops on tenant organizing, and mapping out direct forms of action in their community futures lab.

Tim Portlock addresses the charged site of Pruitt-Igoe from the vantage point of oral histories from former residents of the housing complex. Across a series of interviews, participants described their apartments and the surrounding buildings in detail according to their own memories. Using special effects software, Portlock builds detailed renderings of their memories, crucially without referencing the overly circulated images of the Minoru Yamasaki-designed buildings. The project creates a subjective, faulty, but ultimately more intimate view of how this space lives on in memory, and how these memories and the legacies of Pruitt-Igoe do not have to (and will never) coalesce into a unified narrative. Portlock's work is complemented by a series of programs with artist Robert E. Green, who grew up in Pruitt-Igoe and still lives near the site in the St. Louis Place neighborhood. His studio and artwork, which he will open for a series of tours and conversations throughout Counterpublic 2023, are a living history of the neighborhood, and his continued organizing in the neighborhood points to shapes still to come.

Torkwase Dyson's imaginative response to Scott Joplin positions the ragtime inventor as an example of Black spatial liberation. Engaging the neighborhoods in which Joplin lived and first performed ragtime, a musical precursor of jazz many consider the first truly American art form through its melding of African rhythms with classical technique, Dyson creates a massive, immersive, syncopative architectural space that advances her own hybrid new forms merging painting, architecture, sculpture, sound, and performance into new dimensions.

Further, Seitu Ken Jones realizes a series of installations along the Metro bus system featuring family recipes and collard greens designs wrapping around active buses and bus shelters along Jefferson Avenue. Placing the collard greens along the bus systems that act as a primary means of movement through the city offers an alternate record of survivance and nourishment, a persistence of Black life and tradition stretching back centuries, and a proposition to the future health of the many communities the work moves through.

Curators Diya Vij, Katherine Simóne Reynolds, and Allison Glenn, in divergent ways, each respond to this terrain with their own curatorial contributions. Vij, working with Steffani Jemison, considers the Black performance spaces of Mill Creek Valley alongside the city's refusals of Black creativity, most centrally through the words and legacy of iconic expatriate Josephine Baker, who "ran away from St. Louis, and then . . . ran away from the United States of America, because of that terror of discrimination."[13] Through a monumental sculpture composed of decommissioned theater drapes, a functioning penny press, and a set of sound compositions created in collaboration with Glen "Papa" and Jackie Wright, Jemison activates the historic departure point of Union Station.

[13] Quoted from Josephine Baker's speech in St. Louis on February 3, 1952 (Josephine Baker Homecoming Day), her first visit back to the city since her flight. Source: UMSL Black History Project, available at: http://umsl.edu/~virtualstl/phase2/1950/events/perspectives/documents/jbhomecoming.html.

With Jordan Weber and virgil b/g taylor, Vij engages the streams out of Mill Creek to look at legacies of water and environmental apartheid to rebuild resilient spaces for Black and Brown communities in North St. Louis. Anchored at the Metropolitan Sewer District built in the center of the Mill Creek Valley footprint at Jefferson Avenue and Market Street, their work traces the ways this River City is codetermined by water, what it receives and what it sends downstream along the Mississippi. Weber's work, as a culmination of multiple years of community engagement efforts, manifests fully in the creation of a permanent park and wetland at Peace Park in collaboration with the Green City Coalition, Washington University in St. Louis, and a community-led land trust that will maintain the park in the only city neighborhood without one.

Associate Curator Katherine Simóne Reynolds has woven punctuated performances and reimagined engagements with the localized landscape through her contributions. Will Rawls's four-channel film documents a series of performances by Katherine Dunham-certified dancer Heather Beal that consider the anti-Black formation of American cities, creating an alternate temporality through stop-motion filmmaking. Ralph Lemon likewise presents a performative intervention at the site of Josephine Baker's childhood home, which is now disappeared by the waves of demolition that have radiated out from Mill Creek Valley.

Vincent Stemmler takes a more immediate approach to history, making casts and impressions from the buildings surrounding the confluence of Jefferson Avenue, South Broadway, and Chippewa Street, inserting material histories of the neighborhood into a public park and fountain. Yvonne Osei adorns the public spaces of the city with collaged photographs of nearby laborers' hands, posing the question as to who upholds the infrastructures of the city. Simiya Sudduth, through a series of murals and a mobile sound-healing studio, finds balms for neighborhood residents in sound and image. Finally, Black Healers Collective and Jen Everett each activate their contributions through a set of workshops running throughout the exhibition. Everett hosts a series of place-based workshops considering the archives of Black families and how these intersect with shared memory. Black Healers Collective leads a series of meditations and workshops at sites of harm throughout the exhibition footprint in order to bring a balm and outlet for public healing and meditation.

Curator Allison Glenn's contributions radiate out from The Griot Museum of Black History, where she has worked with David Adjaye to realize the architect's first permanent public artwork. The rammed earth sculpture *Asaase III* emerged from conversations with The Griot's founder, Lois Conley, who early in the development of the exhibition stated that for Counterpublic 2023, she wanted to assert the permanence and prominence of the twenty-five-year-old museum in the face of deep disinvestment in both its own operations and its surrounding neighborhood. Bringing the designer of the National Museum of African American History and Culture (NMAAHC) in Washington, DC into relation with this community museum amplifies the significance of a place where Black life, not just Black history, is sustained and celebrated. The work has been commissioned, acquired, and donated to The Griot as part of its permanent collection and as a community-owned asset for gathering and engagement. Importantly, this work is extended by a full-time fellowship supported by the Mellon Foundation in partnership with the Saint Louis Art Museum to conserve and activate the work and add capacity to the museum as a cornerstone for how we wished to go beyond art to add meaning with our partners.

Mendi + Keith Obadike's *SlowDrag* opens the exhibition with a cacophonous sonic procession that moves through the St. Louis Place neighborhood with dozens of cars performing remixed versions of their original score. Matthew Angelo Harrison inserts a futuristic approach to artifact preservation: 3D-scanned and printed molds of African artifacts are embedded in resin and placed alongside the vernacular and at times priceless archives at the George B. Vashon Museum, a museum founded by Calvin Riley that houses archives from homes, high schools, and private collections spanning 250 years of African American history in the city. Finally, Maya Stovall's poetic work brings the question of *what is to be done with these histories* to a direct conclusion: reparations. As outlined in her catalog contribution and brought to bear in a performance within the exhibition, Stovall redistributes her project budget in full into reparations to Native, Black, Latinx, and mixed-race Americans in St. Louis.

St. Louis's history is one of successive removals along our exhibition footprint: from Sugarloaf Mound and its modes of life as the city was settled, to Mill Creek Valley, onwards to Pruitt-Igoe, whose demolition was broadcast on live television in 1976, and the decline seen in surrounding neighborhoods. Starting with the repatriation/rematriation of the mound and ending with a concrete act of reparations, an *otherwise* slips out. These acts are a start—and a statement. We are interested not in a return to some imagined past, but rather in codetermining livable futures rooted in repair. These futures are already here, in the work of movement leaders and neighbors alike, in the acts of artists and the people those artworks rekindle. As we intervene in the weights of history, Counterpublic 2023 seeks to offer other routes out, freeing us to think, again, of possible liveable futures. Through our work, what ways of living and being can we slip into existence? To adapt the words of St. Louisan William S. Burroughs, Counterpublic 2023 aims to be a cut into the present in which the future starts to leak out. What these futures are depends on what we do now.

This exhibition has a duration: it is open for three months, then closes again for another three years. Within that compression, my hope is that we connect generationally back, way back, and project forward to articulate some shape to how we may inhabit this land as catalysts and stewards alike; that we leave something behind—not just in the permanent artworks, in increased attention or resources, or even the repatriation/rematriation of the mound, as important as each of those are, but in better ways to inhabit this place. Counterpublic 2023 is an act of futuring.

What future are we calling into being, for St. Louis, for an altered America?

Counterpublic 2023

Community Report

Counterpublic started the 2023 exhibition cycle with a year-long process of community engagement. Led by Cheeraz Gormon and James McAnally, Counterpublic spoke with over 800 neighbors and stakeholders through community listening sessions, tabling at area events, walking the neighborhoods, meeting with business owners, and speaking with artists, organizers, and community leaders at all scales. Following this process, Counterpublic created a report cataloging the responses to pressing issues facing the community and ways Counterpublic could respond through its 2023 exhibition.

Following this feedback, Counterpublic determined to focus the 2023 edition on public memory and reparative futures—how our history is told, held, and healed and how our future is envisioned collectively toward repair.

This report has been mobilized by artists, curators, and community organizers throughout the exhibition cycle to ensure all projects respond to community needs and conditions. This is not an exhaustive document, nor is it meant as an objective report. Rather, it is a living conversation that will continue to evolve throughout the 2023 exhibition.

How is our history told, held, and healed?

I. MEMORY + COMMEMORATION

The work of public memory, commemoration, and acknowledgment is very important for our community.

One of the most consistent things we heard is how so many histories in St. Louis have been ignored, erased, and intentionally forgotten. From the Indigenous Mississippian mounds to the Mill Creek Valley neighborhood, entire histories have been actively disappeared.

An accumulation of erased narratives, big and small, makes many people in St. Louis feel as if the history they have experienced is denied by the city and those in power.

New monuments and public memory projects are strongly desired. This was the number one request of Counterpublic from many in the community.

Equally important to inclusive new monuments and public commemorations is an interest in undoing past harms and engaging in repair work. Without this process of repair, engaging the future starts from a deficit of trust and imagination for how it may be different.

We are not in a silo. Counterpublic is working in coalition with numerous grassroots initiatives and cultural partners on this work. From partners like The Griot Museum of Black History and Great Rivers Greenway to the Memory for the Future class and Black Healers Collective, civic memory is being renewed in public space.

The questions that St. Louis faces are the questions of the moment: of public memory, of repair, of how you move forward with the weight of history.

How do we acknowledge and empower Indigenous communities?

II. INDIGENOUS HISTORIES + FUTURES

The St. Louis region is central to Indigenous history as the home of the largest pre-Columbian city in the present-day United States. Now it must be central to repair and to repatriation/rematriation.

As the "Gateway to the West," St. Louis was a primary site of Native removal. From Thomas Hart Benton's calls of manifest destiny to serving as the armory for Western expansion, the systematic removal and erasure of Native peoples was brutal and near-total. This legacy is ever-present in the region—from mound removal to lack of acknowledgment of the numerous tribes with direct lineage to this area.

There are no state or federally recognized tribes in Missouri, and no central advocate to garner resources, organize the community, and give visibility to Indigenous community members. This leads to pressure on a small number of organizations and organizers, including the Buder Center at Washington University's Brown School of Social Work and the Native Women's Care Circle, to carry responsibilities beyond their capacity.

For decades, it was illegal for a Native person to own property in Missouri, so they either had to leave or deny their identity and cultural connection. Many of those who remained in the region struggle with connection to ancestors and especially with identification with the city and its systems.

Counterpublic 2023 aims to center Indigenous histories—and futures—through storytelling, public memory, and pedagogy, and through the documentation and support of repatriation/rematriation and "land back" efforts within the region.

Working at Sugarloaf Mound—the last intact Mississippian mound in the city of St. Louis—we will contextualize these histories and help seed new sovereignties and new systems of support as a core part of our program.

How can we go beyond art to connect with the needs of the community?

III. ART IS ONLY THE START

Community engagement must be holistic.

To talk about art's role in one's neighborhood, one must have basic needs met. Engaging residents in vulnerable populations requires additional resources: eviction and utilities assistance, mental health support, transportation, and so on. Art doesn't enter into a vacuum.

Given the level of need in each community, community engagement must be collaborative and done in partnership with existing institutions, community organizers, and others able to offer resources beyond one organization and beyond the arts.

Part of our community-engagement process has been "modeling up": pressing partners to do more, sharing our learning and insights with others, and encouraging a more active approach to community engagement across all spectrums.

Art offers an opening toward generational change. We aim to leverage the resources and opportunities within the art world toward lasting impact held in community.

The work of the future is already here. It is in artist's studios, but also in the grassroots work underway in our neighborhoods, in the mutual aid work of the last few years, in community organizers and organizations. We aim to accelerate that change, working in and beyond art toward generational change.

How can an exhibition engage systems of power?

IV. SYSTEMS OF POWER: ACCESS + TRANSPARENCY

We started our engagement process by looking at "power maps" and assessing where power was held in our community, and where it is withheld.

As observed in many conversations, there is a lack of trust in any "top-down" process. How development happens. How decisions get made. Many people used the phrase "The City" to stand in for many forms of power: civic, corporate, political, financial. For many, the city is synonymous with whiteness.

In conversations with many, this trust was tentatively being rebuilt through political shifts: the election of Tishaura Jones, Rasheen Aldridge, and Cori Bush was repeatedly referenced as one of the most hopeful moments in the region's recent history. This is a moment to build connections across silos.

Our success as a civic exhibition is tied to the fault lines and futures of those around us.

Counterpublic 2023 will work in deep partnership with existing community anchors, ensuring our work has a lasting impact. Over 50 percent of our budget will go directly to existing small-scale, community-oriented partners.

How can an exhibition support community-led land practices, preservation, and place-keeping?

V. GENTRIFICATION AND NEIGHBORHOOD CHANGE

Gentrification is a major concern along the Jefferson Avenue footprint. With rising housing prices in South St. Louis and major developments in and around the National Geospatial-Intelligence Agency, questions of development and gentrification are among the first things most residents respond to.

Counterpublic 2023 touches on thirteen different neighborhoods along Jefferson Avenue. The issues of the city are in the daily textures of life. Housing is key to the city's future.

Our investments are in and for neighborhoods and neighborhood anchors, not speculation.
Art's relationship with development and gentrification must be acknowledged and resisted—particularly in a biennial or triennial that can serve to accelerate these inequities.

Artist projects for Counterpublic 2023 will partner with community-led land trusts and will commission projects focused on land transfers and housing justice, "land back" actions, and place-keeping initiatives.

How can an exhibition be a convener of the community?

VI. FRACTURED PUBLICS

St. Louis has long been a poster example of fragmentation. From civic structures to county boundaries, the region remains in pieces.

Again and again throughout the process, we have encountered groups large and small who it seems should be working together or perhaps were working together at one time. Many of these groups have experienced a rift and are unable to sustain collaboration. What is happening on a civic level is happening in many other places in our communities.

While we are unable to unpack this fully, it is clear that generations of trauma and current levels of violence, policing, and poverty are major ongoing issues that have to be accounted for when presenting art in and for publics.

People perceive public art through a lens of safety: Will it be safe to visit? Will the artwork be harmed or damaged? The idea of art in public spaces reflects our perception of ourselves in public spaces.

When engaging with partners and institutions, there is a high level of interest in collaboration and shared impact within—and beyond—Counterpublic. The region and its citizens are ready for change.

Counterpublic 2023 is attempting to convene dozens of civic, community, and cultural partners, serving as a connector of already emerging work and new grassroots work underway. We will work from far South St. Louis through North St. Louis.

Art is not the end, but an opening into new futures built around liberatory lifeways.

What does art have to do with the future?

VII. WHAT ABOUT THE FUTURE?

Thinking about the future is hard. Whose future are we working for? The art world often embraces future-oriented language as an abstraction. What is meant when we say we are working toward new futures?

Future = Harm. Future-oriented language is often associated with harm, as it is what civic leaders, developers, politicians, and others use to sell something that is unwanted. The clearance of the Mill Creek Valley neighborhood was pitched by politicians as being for the future, as was the Pruitt-Igoe public housing complex that replaced it. The region's continued land banking, land clearance, and inequitable distribution of incentives to developers continue these practices as they use future growth and development as a means of harming communities.

We must take care to use future-oriented language that is grounded in community desire and grassroots organizing.

Our community engagement made it clear that the future starts with commemoration and repair. This is the ground where we must start.

Counterpublic determined to focus the 2023 edition on public memory and reparative futures—how our history is told, held, and healed, and how our future is envisioned collectively toward new, liberated lifeways. This was our directive and is the groundwork for our exhibition.

CHANGE AS CAPILLARY: AN INTERVIEW WITH WALTER JOHNSON

by James McAnally
and Lee Broughton

Walter Johnson's seminal book, *The Broken Heart of America*, arrived in 2020 into the simmering tensions of the time as a miniature explosion. The book was, and is, everywhere in St. Louis, offering a deeply researched thesis that makes a compelling case to consider St. Louis as a hinge at the center of American history.

The book and its attendant research became a core reference point in the emergence of Counterpublic 2023's form and focus. By the time the book arrived, we had already selected Jefferson Avenue as our nexus to serve as a timeline of the city's emergence that engages the American project explicitly. This was a strategic, but predominantly intuitive, departure point from Counterpublic 2019's focus on Cherokee Street as a stand-in for the city to turn perpendicular along Jefferson as a North-South artery. We knew we hoped to work with the Osage Nation in order to engage Sugarloaf Mound, that we would move through Mill Creek Valley and past Pruitt-Igoe. However, we did not have the deeply researched contours that Johnson sketched: namely, a pattern of removal evident in St. Louis's Native histories into a pattern of removal in Black neighborhoods.

The book offers a grounding for many of the curatorial and artistic approaches throughout Counterpublic 2023. It was a coda to most artist visits, putting language to a feeling, a textbook that starts to answer *why*. Why does the city feel this way? Who is responsible? What do we do now? It leaves that last question to us all and is a question Counterpublic 2023 attempts to respond to as we look to the past and move toward communal futures through a lens of repair.

JAMES MCANALLY:
Starting with your book *The Broken Heart of America: St. Louis and the Violent History of the United States* (2020), at what point did you land on that idea of St. Louis as a central crucible for the American project?[1]

[1] Walter Johnson, *The Broken Heart of America: St. Louis and the Violent History of the United States* (New York: Basic Books, 2020).

WALTER JOHNSON:
I think when I started writing about Ferguson—and about tax abatement, abandonment, and policing—it struck me that St. Louis was exemplary of a lot of places in the United States except way more extreme, you know? That was before I had really done the work to understand the nineteenth and early twentieth-century history of St. Louis, and it was certainly before I knew about the role that St. Louis had played in the Western Empire, in the military history of the Indian Wars. I mean, starting the book, I knew that there were a series of famous Supreme Court cases that had to do with St. Louis—from the *Dred Scott*[2] decision and *Shelley v. Kraemer*[3] to *McDonnell Douglas Corp. v. Green*[4]—but I hadn't thought yet of why that might be and how much of those had to do with regulating Black mobility, physical and spatial. Once those things came together, that then helped me reconfigure how I thought about the twentieth century; the way I thought about Mill Creek Valley or Pruitt-Igoe was shaped by learning about that earlier history.

[2] "The *Dred Scott* decision is the defining ruling in proslavery jurisprudence. That it should have come from St. Louis, a city where slavery played a marginal role in the economy, is only a seeming contradiction; the deeper truth is that slavery in St. Louis was especially precarious, and because it was especially precarious, it was especially violent." Johnson, *The Broken Heart of America*, 91.

[3] "In the period between the segregation ordinance and the US Supreme Court's 1948 decision in *Shelley v. Kraemer*, which held that racially restrictive covenants were not legally enforceable, Black St. Louis was surrounded and closed out by almost four hundred specifically covenanted white neighborhoods." Johnson, *The Broken Heart of America*, 253.

[4] See footnote 17 regarding Percy Green.

JAMES:
Your book's thesis—which connects Native removal to the white supremacist logic of Western expansion being applied directly back to the city—was one of those profound insights that really puts language to a feeling. It clicks the city into perspective in a way that people here have resonated with again and again. You feel it, but it's slippery: What about St. Louis feels this way?

WALTER:
I think probably it is quite relevant to the way you all are imagining an exhibition on and about a particular street [Jefferson Avenue]. One of the main theoretical and aesthetic inspirations behind *The Broken Heart of America* is a book by Walter Benjamin called *One-Way Street*, which is about the sensations of walking down the street.[5] Toward the end of the book he comes to a fortune teller and writes that if you really want to develop a sense of the future, you don't go to the fortune teller; you develop a sense of the presence of mind that you feel when you're walking down the street; you observe the mixture of the past knowledge of what's happened and present knowledge of what it feels like, and then a sense of the unfolding history that's happening. That's what I think about St. Louis. I feel like I learned a lot just from being in the city.

I think about the abandonment of the Northside—and when I say abandonment, I mean the fact that the people who were living on the Northside were abandoned by the city, by the state, by the federal government—about how that part of the city feels. And that helped me think about mobility and removal. Once I started to track out these events, there's almost an arc of removal that runs from East St. Louis to Mill Creek Valley on to Pruitt-Igoe and then out to North County and Ferguson. That became a dominant theme of the book. Each one of those removals had its own kind of political, economic logic—each one of them was extractive or exploitative in a different way—and thus provided different possibilities, sometimes quite limited, sometimes more expansive, for resistance to these different challenges for Black people and some poor whites in the city.

[5] Walter Benjamin, *One-Way Street*, trans. Edmund Jephcott (Cambridge, MA: Belknap Press of Harvard University Press, 2016).

JAMES:
As you note, with Counterpublic we're trying to look at the city through the lens of one street and the way that, in some senses, the whole story of St. Louis is contained there as a kind of timeline of overlapping pasts—and also a few futures.

JAMES (cont.):
When I first chose to work along Jefferson Avenue, a few things stood out. One, it never really ends. On the south side, it merges into Broadway and it goes all the way down out, out of the city, down toward the Jefferson Barracks. On the north side, it splinters into Salisbury, Parnell, and Natural Bridge, and moves to the Mississippi River, all the way through the city out to North County. Second, it presents an itinerary that follows the logic of your book in many senses, although our planning preceded its release. We are starting at Sugarloaf Mound, the last remaining Indigenous mound in the city of St. Louis, which of course was called Mound City by settlers early on, due to their dominant presence in the city.

As you follow Jefferson Avenue north, you move through a neighborhood known as the "State Streets," which intersects with a series of Native-named streets—Cherokee, Chippewa, Meramec, Osage—until it crosses Arsenal Street, which was the site of the United States Army arsenal mobilized into the Plains Wars, and which forms the northern boundary of Benton Park; which is, again, named after Thomas Hart Benton, a Missouri senator that popularized ideas of Manifest Destiny and Native removal, which comes up a lot in the book.

As Jefferson Avenue moves north, it cuts through Mill Creek Valley, Pruitt-Igoe, the in-process National Geospatial-Intelligence Agency (NGA) campus, and then culminates at St. Louis Avenue, which contains a cluster of prominent Black cultural organizations: The Griot Museum of Black History, George B. Vashon Museum, and Robert Green's Frederick Douglass Museum of African American Vernacular Images. In a way, Jefferson Avenue condenses experience of both the history and the future; historic preservation but also these sites of displacement form a kind of experiential timeline and arc of removal, as you said. Considering Jefferson Avenue, then, as a visceral experience, I'd be curious to hear your riff on that place in particular.

WALTER:
I haven't ever thought of it that way, which I guess is strange because I have thought a lot about the progression from Mill Creek Valley to Pruitt-Igoe, which, of course, is going right along Jefferson. I do find myself driving on Jefferson a lot, and I think about the Jefferson Bank. I think about the Jefferson Bank protests and how unassuming that building is now and how hard it is to summon that historical image—even though I've seen the photos.[6]

I guess for me, I'm almost obsessed with the absences. I feel the erasures so profoundly. I mean, as much as I know about Pruitt-Igoe and as many times as I've walked through there, so much of this history along Jefferson Avenue just seems erased and covered over. There's a big police department. There's the fire department training center. There's the NGA and the fake Paul McKee hospital.[7] If you want to sum it up in some kind of surreal hallucination, it's almost like it's under occupation.

[6] "By early October 1963, the demonstrations at Jefferson Bank & Trust Co. had gone on almost daily for more than a month. Civil rights groups demanded that the bank, which had only two black employees, hire four more for office jobs." For more information and photos, see Tim O'Neil, "1963: Protests at Jefferson Bank lead to major changes in hiring practices in St. Louis," *St. Louis Post-Dispatch*, August 31, 2022, https://www.stltoday.com/news/archives/1963-protests-at-jefferson-bank-lead-to-major-changes-in-hiring-practices-in-st-louis/article_d6be4178-cc1f-527a-a0d0-fd78a720456e.html; and Johnson, *The Broken Heart of America*, 341–44.

[7] A three-bed clinic has been built on the site of the former Pruitt-Igoe housing complex, named after Homer G. Phillips hospital, an important public hospital for the African American community that closed in 1979. The hospital has been met with community backlash due to both the site and naming.

JAMES:
Over the past few years, I have probably led a hundred tours moving through Jefferson Avenue, and one thing I always do is pause when you get to the former site of Mill Creek Valley.[8] You just have to pause for a second and think about how it doesn't look or feel like the rest of the city—again, that feeling needs to be named. You can feel the disjoint, where you have these institutional buildings, but without people and without any kind of architectural lineage of the rest of the city. It is hard to summon the vibrancy of the 20,000 people that were pushed out, the homes, the music venues, and the self-organized social clubs.

[8] "The Housing Act of 1954 was enacted to fund urban renewal projects across the country . . . In 1955, voters of the City of St. Louis passed a $110 bond issue, of which $100 was delegated for the demolition of Mill Creek Valley . . . It was the nation's largest urban-renewal project at the time. About 20,000 African American residents were displaced before it was leveled for an urban renewal project that began in 1959." "Mill Creek Valley," *Wikipedia*, last modified July 18, 2022, https://en.wikipedia.org/wiki/Mill_Creek_Valley#Urban_renewal_project.

JAMES (cont.):
Until recent years, there has been no context within that space to understand why. It was just so thoroughly erased.[9]

[9] "Within the city of St. Louis, a tacit bargain was struck to achieve a massive reconstruction of the city fabric in the name of jobs, progress, and property values: urban renewal. As elsewhere in the nation, and as in the case of the Pick-Sloan project and the Indians of the Missouri Valley, this was, in effect, a jobs program for white men that involved the destruction of the encircled homes of darker people, in this case the people who lived in Mill Creek Valley. It would not, however, be correct to term this massive project 'previously unimaginable.' As it turned out, city leaders had been imagining the destruction of large sections of Black (and radical) St. Louis for quite some time." Johnson, *The Broken Heart of America*, 289.

WALTER:
It's almost like negative space. It wasn't even profitable to tear it all down. None of the speculative plans came to fruition. Still less the rosy promises. They put nothing in the place of what they destroyed.

JAMES:
One way we're looking at these spaces is by asking: What do you do with these charged energies? How do you hold the histories these spaces contain? Through a number of these concrete projects, we're attempting to look at these histories through a lens of repair, giving some agency to these histories so that we can get to the future again. After the monumental load of the research you conducted, as you sit within these stories and these erasures: What do you do with the histories? How do you move forward from them? Writing a book is one answer, but what do you feel are others?

WALTER:
Probably more with this book than with the other things I've written, I didn't end up feeling particularly prescriptive in the end. There wasn't a ten-point set of recommendations. In the end, I felt like the spirit that I tried to write it in was really a kind of pitching in and providing people here who know more about the city than I do with resources of the things that I'm good at —historical research, finding sites or images or moments that are resonant. That's why I tried to finish the book by almost surveying or itemizing some of the projects that I had learned about as a way to say: Here are the things that I think seem to point the way.[10]

[10] See, for example, Sweet Potato Project, North Sarah Food Hub (https://www.northsarah.org), Organization for Black Struggle (https://www.obs-stl.org), Hands Up United, National Building Arts Center (http://web.nationalbuildingarts.org), Johnson, *The Broken Heart of America*, 436–42.

WALTER (cont.):
I think my politics actually changed a lot over the time that I was working in St. Louis. That had something to do with the national context and also with thinking in a practical and immediate sense about how you are going to get anything done—in the state of Missouri or in the United States of America. My political vision changed to much more of a kind of communalist vision, and that's what I see in these kinds of projects. I feel like that vibe and that energy is something that I learned more from St. Louis than anywhere else—and that is where I hope the future of the city lies, if that vision then gets built up into programs that are more focused on mutual aid and self-help than governance as such. Projects like The People's Plan[11] that ArchCity Defenders[12] and Action St. Louis[13] and all the other organizations have worked on. That's a really visionary, amazing document. Repair for me is like this: take the money, give it to people, let them decide what to do with it. It's both pretty basic and kind of unimaginable in our society, you know?

I don't think that a set of market-based solutions to problems that have been created by the history of racial capitalism are going to work. And so I imagine that there has to be a different kind of imagination around what economic development means and how one measures development and defines the metrics of progress. It seems to me that there are more than enough brilliant and visionary and committed people in the city who have been for too long ignored and disenfranchised to come up with that vision.

[11] The People's Plan is a comprehensive policy agenda designed to help build power and redistribute resources in St. Louis. More information available at: www.peoplesplanstl.org.

[12] ArchCity Defenders (ACD) is a holistic legal advocacy organization that combats the criminalization of poverty and state violence, especially in communities of color. More information available at: www.archcitydefenders.org.

[13] Action St. Louis is a grassroots racial justice organization that seeks to build political power for Black communities in the St. Louis region. More information available at: https://actionstl.org.

LEE BROUGHTON:
As a historian, have you seen other cities in the world that have had to reconcile a memory of some point in time that then became a turning point? Whether it was grassroots organizations that suddenly felt that they were united and could build momentum or some moment coalesced, are there examples that you can think of?

WALTER:
I may not be the right person to ask because I'm not an urbanist, but the city that I think about that I've spent the most time in, other than Boston and St. Louis, is Vienna—because of my wife's work. A lot of people point to Vienna (and different cities in Germany) as having a fairly effective public reckoning. What I guess I don't know enough about Vienna is the ways in which reckoning is actually a deeper social record, but I think it's probably not an accident that something like 60 percent of the housing in Vienna is publicly subsidized; half of it is either public housing or cooperative housing. The idea that our society treats housing as a commodity is just insane if you stop to think about it. That we think it is acceptable to have people living on the street because they don't have as much money as other people. And then we complain about them living in the parks. It is demonic.

LEE:
A couple of years ago, I was asked to design—as part of a team—a strategy that could begin to articulate a story of St. Louis that everyone living there could identify with in some way. A story that didn't just describe our "assets" (we have a zoo, etc.) but one that also described the important "emotions" (shared values, why we love it, etc.). Interestingly, there wasn't a consensus about how St. Louis projected itself; it didn't matter what your background was or whether you were from the region.

WALTER:
Right. Because the major narrative is decline, and the decline narrative is actually an alibi. Talking about the decline of the city in isolation from the question of the emergence of the county and the historical structures that undergirded it: federally sponsored suburbanization, the deliberate exclusion of African Americans and even working-class whites from many of the emerging suburbs, the relocation of factories and work to suburbs that are not connected to the city by reliable public transportation, the thin blue line of discriminatory policing that continues to separate the country from the city, the dangers of driving while Black, etc. The St. Louis Metro, as a whole, is not unsuccessful; it is just that the prosperity is distributed in profoundly unequal ways. Three of the wealthiest twenty-five suburbs in the United States are in St. Louis County.

LEE:
Yes, and the overriding negative emotion amongst St. Louisans is disappointment. However, the intent was to try to get to whether there is something that could unite us, so we asked questions about perceptions. While the overriding negative was disappointment, amazingly the overriding positive was pride in "your" neighborhood. So there was a very hard contradiction about disappointment in the city but pride in the neighborhood. We did not recognize in each other the thing that we are really proud about—instead, we united around negativity—and it had a significant impact.

WALTER:
It's kinda like being from Missouri.

LEE:
Then if you go to a smaller city like Des Moines or a similar city like Minneapolis or somewhere bigger like New York and you ask people, there are many Americans who can't even put St. Louis on a map. They don't know where we are geographically—and at worst, we are neutrally perceived. That was a terrific insight for us. In the sense that America doesn't think about St Louis, this is an opportunity!

WALTER:
They think St. Louis is anywhere from St. Paul to Texas or New Orleans. It's like we could be anywhere along that line. I heard that a lot when I left Missouri and went to college.

LEE:
So, part of what I'm wondering is how big of a role narrative can play because, as they say, great stories happen to those that can tell them.

WALTER:
Well, there is certainly a kind of bland ignorance toward the Midwest and Missouri. One thing that has been interesting is when people read the book, they decide I must hate Missouri and hate St. Louis. Instead, in a really strange way, I think there's an aggrieved Missourian who wrote the book who's like: No, you don't understand. You want to talk about the history of the United States? This is the history of the United States. St. Louis made the history of the United States. There was a little bit of that sense of a pissed-off provincial, you know? I left Missouri when I was seventeen and went to Massachusetts. I've spent most of my life on the East Coast in one way or another, and there's a sense of grievance that made its way through that.

WALTER (cont.):
In many ways, St. Louis has pioneered strategies of flourishing: artistic excellence, intellectual and athletic excellence, and modes of resistance that are still visionary. So part of it for me, then, was to think about this legacy of resistance, whether you think about that as being Blackhawk or enslaved resistance, all the way through to the present. Not as a single narrative thread, but almost as a dialectic in the sense that this is the place that has presented some of the most extreme versions of the history of the United States yet has correspondingly presented some of the most durable models of how one might confront history.

JAMES:
Returning to *The Broken Heart of America*, you argue that St. Louis is the crucible of American history for the worst kinds of reasons, on the one hand, but then in the end, in the epilogue, you equally present it as the most hopeful place you've ever experienced.

WALTER:
George Lipsitz, who is a genius, said St. Louis is the right place for all the wrong reasons. That, to me, says it all. It's the right place for all the wrong reasons because there's no way that you can write a celebratory history of the role of St. Louis. I'm not a huge fan of the United States of America as an enterprise, but what its dark history has created here is a set of possibilities for a different kind of history to be made. You can look at that in a hardcore kind of Marxist way, which would be that the ruling classes pushed down so far on the threshold of social reproduction in the city that it's actually quite easy to get started moving in the other direction. People who have been so thoroughly abandoned as have those in parts of this city have only one another to rely upon, and that is a situation of revolutionary possibility.

JAMES:
When you look at the Black history museums, on some level, they resonate with this compelling vision. It's exactly what they did. Lois Conley at The Griot Museum and Calvin Riley at the George B. Vashon Museum of African American History saw that no one was going to tell this history, so they decided to be the ones to do it. They were then able to buy a building and gather the materials and means to open. People then surround those visions and they cluster together and suddenly you have a de facto cultural district emerge, whether recognized or not.

WALTER:

Getting concrete for a moment, a real vision of repair is to tie those museums, and other North St. Louis institutions, into the Metropolitan Zoological Park and Museum District (ZMD).[14] To create a Black Arts/ Historic District funded out of the same revenue stream as the zoo, the science center, and the botanical garden—things that really work in St. Louis—on the Northside. That would be a huge thing for Black St. Louis on a really practical level, right? If we're interested in imagining arts-based community development in the way that it conventionally works, there's an existing mechanism—but, again, one that is currently producing results that are unevenly distributed across the metro.

[14] The Metropolitan Zoological Park and Museum District (ZMD) is a cultural tax district in St. Louis that supports the Saint Louis Art Museum, Saint Louis Zoo, Saint Louis Science Center, Missouri History Museum, and Missouri Botanical Garden, all public nonprofits. Only the Missouri Botanical Garden charges an admission fee while the other institutions are free to the public. More information available at: https://en.wikipedia.org/wiki/Metropolitan_Zoological_Park_and_Museum_District.

LEE:

Yes, I agree with that. At the risk of being too psychoanalytical, what do you think it takes to identify a moment in time when there's a turning point?

WALTER:

I'm not a sociological thinker, but the Forward Through Ferguson people have the idea about a randomized notion of opportunity in life.[15] You could do a lot with life expectancy as a measure of inequality: there are few more powerful metrics of inequality than the fact that the average life expectancy of someone born in the JeffVanderLou (JVL) neighborhood, along Jefferson Avenue, is eighteen years shorter than that of someone born six miles away, in Clayton.

And the arts can be a part of that. Art can help people to imagine a city where flourishing is possible, where people can go out of their houses and see something that makes them feel affirmed rather than degraded. To produce a situation in which all the members of the city are affirmed rather than abandoned. I see lots of efforts by people trying to create affirmative spaces.

[15] After the death of Michael Brown, Jr. on August 9, 2014, Ferguson came to symbolize racial strife and inequality in the United States. Missouri Governor Jay Nixon asked a group of regional leaders, named the Ferguson Commission, to study the situation and prove a path toward change. Forward Through Ferguson (FTF) was established as a 501(c)3 to be a catalyst for lasting positive change in the St. Louis region as outlined in the Ferguson Commission Report. Embracing the Commission's mandate, FTF centers on impacted communities and mobilizes accountable bodies to advance racially equitable systems and policies that ensure all people in the St. Louis region can thrive. More information available at: https://forwardthroughferguson.org.

JAMES:
We started the process of Counterpublic 2023 by talking to neighbors—talking to people here before thinking about artists, curators, all the productions of an exhibition—and really tried to ask those questions. One of the things we heard that resonates is this idea that we can't talk about "the future" here, at least not in abstract terms. That word, that idea, has been such a tool of violence in so many cases. "The future" is the language of politicians and developers. It's what sells Pruitt-Igoe and the removal of Mill Creek Valley. It's what tears down Pruitt-Igoe twenty years later. We've heard again and again: you can't start with "the future" here, but you can build toward it and empower those already building toward those futures. That's the arc of the project—attending to these histories is a starting point.

WALTER:
One word I kept finding myself using in order to name the wrong (and possibly presage its redress) is "neighbors." I might say this group of people did this to their Black neighbors or to their poor neighbors, pointing to the absence of basic generosity. Your starting point seems to me, in some sense, to be a vision of a city characterized by neighborliness rather than suspicion and extraction.

LEE:
Historians have helped shape our understanding of the past, while artists have often led explorations that have shifted culture. What do you think it would take Counterpublic to help shepherd that type of a shift here?

WALTER:
I think about cultural change as you have to think about historical change, as something subtle and durational with lots of unintended consequences. I feel like you're asking questions that imagine a moment, and I wish I could see that moment; but, short of revolution, it is hard for me to imagine a moment like that. But what if we imagine it as capillary and prefigurative? If we imagine transformation as a capillary, an intervention on a grassroots level that helps us imagine new ways of living—ways of living in right relation to one another and the world around us.

WALTER (cont.):
Or even aiming to get The Griot Museum and others included in the ZMD—maybe that's not just a capillary, that's arterial. I've thought of a lot of possibilities on the Northside of St. Louis, such as to try to use a band of buildings as artistic campuses, to turn these places into something that's either affirmative or at least historically reflective, and to build up those and amplify the small beautiful things that people already do. To see and support the existing beauty. To use what people—extraordinary everyday people—are already doing as a guide to how we imagine what we all should be doing. I mean, it changed my life when Sylvester Brown said to me, "People say we're poor, but we're rich. Look at our children."[16]

[16] Sylvester Brown, Jr. has been a journalist and social justice advocate since 1987 when he started *Take Five Magazine*, a community-based investigative publication. In 2001, Brown began working for the *St. Louis Post-Dispatch*, where he was an award-winning columnist for eight years. More information available at: http://sylvesterbrownjr.blogspot.com.

LEE:
I definitely do imagine a moment—many moments, in fact—as intentional as Sylvester's. The psychology here is a fascinating one, and it's on a psychological level that I'm trying to find anchors we can use to really connect. The research also uncovered those same people, a movement that we coined #stlmade and began featuring as narrative online at theSTL.com to give voice to them (or as many as we can; it's ongoing). I absolutely see this as capillary, or a network carrying the arterioles, in order to create the momentum. Forgive the repetition, but that's what I mean about great stories happening to those that are telling them.

JAMES:
Returning to this thought that these incremental actions are capillaries and that perhaps getting The Griot and other Black cultural institutions in the ZMD is arterial, at some point you get to the heart. We're talking about this broken heart, this central American icon set with all its promise and harm alike, but you can't fix the heart without fixing the capillaries. To some degree, this means you build backward with the essential repair work and move back toward the center.

WALTER:
That's certainly the idea Percy Green had, which was power mapping the city and working his way back through that map; he was drawing out the arterial top side of that image.[17] One problem here, obviously, is that to make things work under the present conditions, you need the buy-in to some degree of the people who have the money and run the city, and that has been hard to come by.

[17] Percy Green II is a social worker and Black activist in St. Louis. He was active in the St. Louis chapter of the Congress of Racial Equality (CORE) and was a founding member of ACTION (Action Committee to Improve Opportunities for Negroes). He was also the plaintiff in the landmark civil rights case *McDonnell Douglas Corp. v. Green*. More information available at: https://en.wikipedia.org/wiki/Percy_Green.

LEE:
Having a strong sense of our futures together, as a region, and then gaining alignment in a way that has heard, remembered, and considered one another's histories surely begins to repair that heart. You have to have both the treetops and the grassroots on board though, working in the same direction and committed to not repeating our past injustices. Moments like your book, like Counterpublic 2023, and the many other small things that are taking place will construct that collective psychology of positivity. Each mundane move toward a better future is made epic because it is perceived to be laddering to the greater whole.

SAVING SUGARLOAF MOUND IN ST. LOUIS, MISSOURI

by Andrew B. Weil
and Andrea A. Hunter

As the oldest human-made structure in St. Louis and the last Native American mound in what was once known as "Mound City," Sugarloaf Mound links the present with the past. Sugarloaf is likely a Woodland Period burial mound or a Mississippian platform mound, and dates to a time when the region was home to thriving and highly advanced Native American cultures long before the arrival of European and African people.[1]

When the French began construction of what would become St. Louis in 1764, the future city contained possibly hundreds of mounds. While many were relatively small burial mounds situated on the bluffs overlooking navigable waterways, there was also a major Mississippian civic-ceremonial complex located just north of the Gateway Arch. The North St. Louis Mound Group included over twenty-five mounds systematically arranged around public plazas. This substantial site was presumably tied to two other nearby Mississippian centers: the little-known East St. Louis Mound Group and its famous relative, Cahokia (a UNESCO World Heritage Site).

By the late eighteenth century these Mississippian cities had been long abandoned. Yet French cartographers recorded the unusual earthen structures as prominent features on the landscape. The mounds also are visible in several early representations of the city, such as John Caspar Wild's 1840 lithograph of the city's north riverfront. By this time, however, Missouri's first governor, among others, used the mounds as platforms for their houses. A beer garden was placed on one and the city's first reservoir on another. By 1875, the mounds were nearly completely destroyed.

The lone survivor is Sugarloaf. Its location at the edge of a steep bluff several miles from downtown insulated Sugarloaf from industrial and developmental pressures that swept away the other mounds. Not altogether unscathed, in 1928, a house was erected on its top. The house on Sugarloaf was occupied continuously until 2008, when the property was offered for sale.

A coalition of concerned groups and citizens, including the Landmarks Association of St. Louis and the Osage Nation, coalesced around the cause of preservation, an outcome dependent on acquisition of the mound. Consensus grew over the best possible future for Sugarloaf. Its advocates sought first to protect it and then to celebrate its significance by educating the surrounding community about the history of Native American settlement in the area.

[1] The Woodland Period encompasses the years from about 1000 BCE to 900 CE, while the Mississippian Period begins in 900 and extends through 1550.

The Osage Nation bought Sugarloaf in August 2009. They did so because of their deeply held, historic ties to the St. Louis area. This connection is revealed through tribal oral traditions and is documented in scholarly investigations. Over the years, ethnologists and historians have interpreted and published tribal oral histories pertaining to the migrations of the Osage and closely related tribes: the Kaw, Omaha, Ponca, and Quapaw.[2] Together these four tribes, with the Osage, make up what is known as the Dhegiha Sioux language subgroup.[3]

In the latter part of the nineteenth century, ethnologist James Dorsey collected oral histories of migration stories from Dhegiha-speaking tribal members.[4] Dorsey was told that in the distant past, all five Dhegiha tribes were once one nation that lived east of the Mississippi River in the vicinity of the Ohio River. The people migrated together, until they reached the Mississippi River, where the first segregation occurred. The people descending the river were called the Quapaw, meaning "the down-stream people." Those ascending became the Omaha, or "those going against the wind or current."[5] The ancient Omaha, composed of the Omaha, Osage, Kaw, and Ponca, traveled upriver until they reached the mouth of the Missouri and they dwelled near present-day St. Louis for many years. How long they stayed in the area as one tribe varied, with each present-day tribe venturing west and north at intervals. Only when the Osage occupied southwest and south-central Missouri does the historic record of the tribe begin. Thus, for the Osage, the migration stories indicate that among the Dhegiha, the Osage inhabited the St. Louis region for the longest period of time.

From the 1920s onward, the archeological record and identity of the Osage have intrigued scholars. As recently as 1993, Susan Vehik and Dale Henning (separately) reassessed the Dhegiha origins studies. They examined current archeological data and scrutinized all lines of evidence to determine Dhegiha origins. Vehik reasoned that even given some differences between the Dhegiha tribes' migration stories, "all of the available oral histories from the Dhegihan Sioux center on the Ohio, Mississippi, and Missouri rivers."[6] According to Vehik, a Dhegiha origin from the Ohio Valley accounts for the wide-ranging similarities among the Dhegiha tribes and also between the Dhegiha tribes and the Mississippi Valley Siouan, Algonkian, and even some of the southeastern groups.[7] Henning came to a similar interpretation. He relied on the tribes' own migration legends, linguistic analyses, history, and ethnohistory, and concluded that an ancestral Dhegiha locus is most likely in the Ohio River Valley with the tribes migrating west of the Mississippi River and then splitting into their respective tribes.[8]

[2] Louis F. Burns, *A History of the Osage People* (Tuscaloosa: University of Alabama Press, 2004), 3–22; James Owen Dorsey, "Migrations of Siouan Tribes," *American Naturalist* 20, no. 3 (1886): 214–22; Albert Gallatin, *A Synopsis of the Indian Tribes within the United States East of the Rocky Mountains, and in the British and Russian Possessions in North America* (1836; New York: AMS Press, 1973), 127; Francis La Flesche, "Omaha and Osage Traditions of Separation," *Proceedings of the Nineteenth International Congress on Americanists* 19 (1917): 459–62; and Thomas Nuttall, *A Journal of Travels into the Arkansa Territory during the Year 1819: with Occasional Observations on the Manners of the Aborigines; Illustrated by a Map and Other Engravings* (1821; facsimile ed., March of America Facsimile Series 63, Ann Arbor: University Microfilms, 1966), 82–83.

[3] Several linguists have studied the different Siouan language stocks and have attempted to identify the root source of the Siouan languages, including the Dhegiha Sioux. See James W. Springer and Stanley R. Witkowski, "Siouan Historical Linguistics and Oneota Archaeology," in *Oneota Studies*, ed. Guy E. Gibbon (Minneapolis: University of Minnesota, 1982), 69–83. Studies such as Springer and Witkowski's help in understanding tribal migrations across the landscape. All tribes have origin and migration stories so the close linguistically related tribes' stories can help us to understand the relationships amongst them all.

[4] Dorsey, "Migrations of Siouan Tribes," 211–22.

[5] Dorsey, "Migrations of Siouan Tribes," 215–16. Although all five Dhegiha tribes have migration stories and they vary in some aspects, they all agree on an eastern origin.

[6] Susan C. Vehik, "Dhegiha Origins and Plains Archaeology," *Plains Anthropologist* 38 (1993): 232.

[7] Vehik, "Dhegiha Origins and Plains Archaeology," 246.

[8] Dale R. Henning, "The Adaptive Patterning of the Dhegiha Sioux," *Plains Anthropologist* 38 (1993): 253, 260–62.

In the past decade and a half, other anthropologists and archeologists proposed a Dhegiha affiliation to the earthen mounds located in the St. Louis area. In many instances they specifically cited the Osage as the tribe with a strong association with the St. Louis/ Cahokia Mississippian culture.[9] Besides migration traditions, the evidence examined included: the use of mounds, house structure, village organization, war trophies, combat weaponry, subsistence practices, iconography (pottery, ceremonial objects, and rock art), religious practices, cosmology, and social structure-moiety systems with clans and bands.

The Osage people and their society governed a vast area of what is now Illinois, Missouri, Arkansas, Kansas, and Oklahoma. The current Osage Nation Reservation is in northeastern Oklahoma, but it has been established that the ancestors of the Osage were among those who constructed the mounds in the St. Louis area, including Sugarloaf Mound and the complex at Cahokia. In a display of historic justice and bittersweet irony, the Osage Nation reclaimed Sugarloaf Mound by purchasing a significant portion of the property with assistance from the Osage Nation Historic Preservation Office and Principal Chief Jim Gray.

The tremendous amount of the Osage Tribe's history that has been lost due to the demolition of ancestral homes, villages, and, most significantly, the mounds in the St. Louis area other than Sugarloaf is devastating. Hundreds of years were erased from the landscape. Moreover, from an Osage perspective, the mounds are sacred. Many of the earthen mounds are burial places. As with most cultures, the Osage consider it sacrilegious to disturb burial places and an unconscionable act to destroy one. Although Sugarloaf Mound may not be a burial mound, it is sacred nonetheless. The Osage, therefore, consider it an honor to protect the last mound of their ancestors in St. Louis for all of the tribes that are heirs of the Mississippian culture.

[9] Garrick A. Bailey, ed., *The Osage and the Invisible World: From the Works of Francis La Flesche* (Norman: University of Oklahoma Press, 1955), 3; Garrick A. Bailey, "Continuity and Change in Mississippian Civilization," in *Hero, Hawk, and Open Hand*, ed. Richard F. Townsend (New Haven: Yale University Press, 2004), 87–91; James A. Brown, "The Cahokian Expression," in *Hero, Hawk, and Open Hand*, 118–19; James A. Brown, "On the Identity of the Birdman within Mississippian Period Art and Iconography," in *Ancient Objects and Sacred Realms: Interpretations of Mississippian Iconography*, ed. F. Kent Reilly III and James F. Garber (Austin: University of Texas Press, 2007), 56–106; Carol Diaz-Granados, "Marking Stone, Land, Body, and Spirit," in *Hero, Hawk, and Open Hand*, 143–47; David H. Dye, "Art, Ritual, and Chiefly Warfare in the Mississippian World," in *Hero, Hawk, and Open Hand*, 198, 203; Robert L. Hall, "The Cahokia Site and Its People," in *Hero, Hawk, and Open Hand*, 98–100, 102–3; Alice Beck Kehoe, "Osage Texts and Cahokia Data," in *Ancient Objects and Sacred Realms*, 246–61; John E. Kelly, "Redefining Cahokia: Principles and Elements of Community Organization," *The Wisconsin Archeologist* 77 (1996): 97, 106–14; John E. Kelly, "The Ritualization of Cahokia: The Structure and Organization of Early Cahokia Crafts," in *Leadership and Polity in Mississippian Society*, ed. Brian M. Butler and Paul D. Welch, *Occasional Papers* No. 33, Center for Archaeological Investigations (Carbondale: Southern Illinois University, 2006), 241–56; Mark F. Seeman, "Hopewell Art in Hopewell Places," in *Hero, Hawk, and Open Hand*, 57.

Now that the mound is secure, the intention is to remove the house and develop the location as an interpretive, educational center where the significance of Sugarloaf Mound and the full history of Mound City from the Osage's perspective can be told. While the tribe cannot bring back what was so mindlessly destroyed, they can guide the future of Sugarloaf Mound and, with it, teach the citizens of St. Louis about where they live.

"Saving Sugarloaf Mound in St. Louis, Missouri" by Andrew B. Weil and Andrea A. Hunter was first published in *CRM: The Journal of Heritage Stewardship* 7, no. 1, 2010 and is reprinted here with permission from the authors.[10]

Andrew B. Weil is the Assistant Director of the Landmarks Association of St. Louis; Andrea A. Hunter (Osage) is the Tribal Historic Preservation Officer for the Osage Nation.

The Osage Nation is extremely thankful to Congressman Russ Carnahan for including the Osage Nation in this unique preservation effort and allowing us a lead voice in the process. The Osage Nation also is very thankful for all of the support given to this project by Congressman Carnahan's staff, the St. Louis preservation foundations, local archeologists, and government offices, both city and state, as well as the Archaeological Research Center of St. Louis, which donated $5,000 to the preservation effort. As the first phase of preservation planning begins, the City of St. Louis has provided a grant opportunity and local Missouri Archaeology Society members are keeping diligent watch over the property. The Osage Nation is grateful for all the support shown by these agencies and individuals. *Way-we-nah* (which is a special version of thank you for doing something sincerely meaningful).

[10] The original article can be accessed at: https://www.nps.gov/crps/CRMJournal/Winter2010/research3.html.

COMMINGLING, OR THE MOUND CALLED SUGARLOAF

Jennifer Colten
and Jesse Vogler

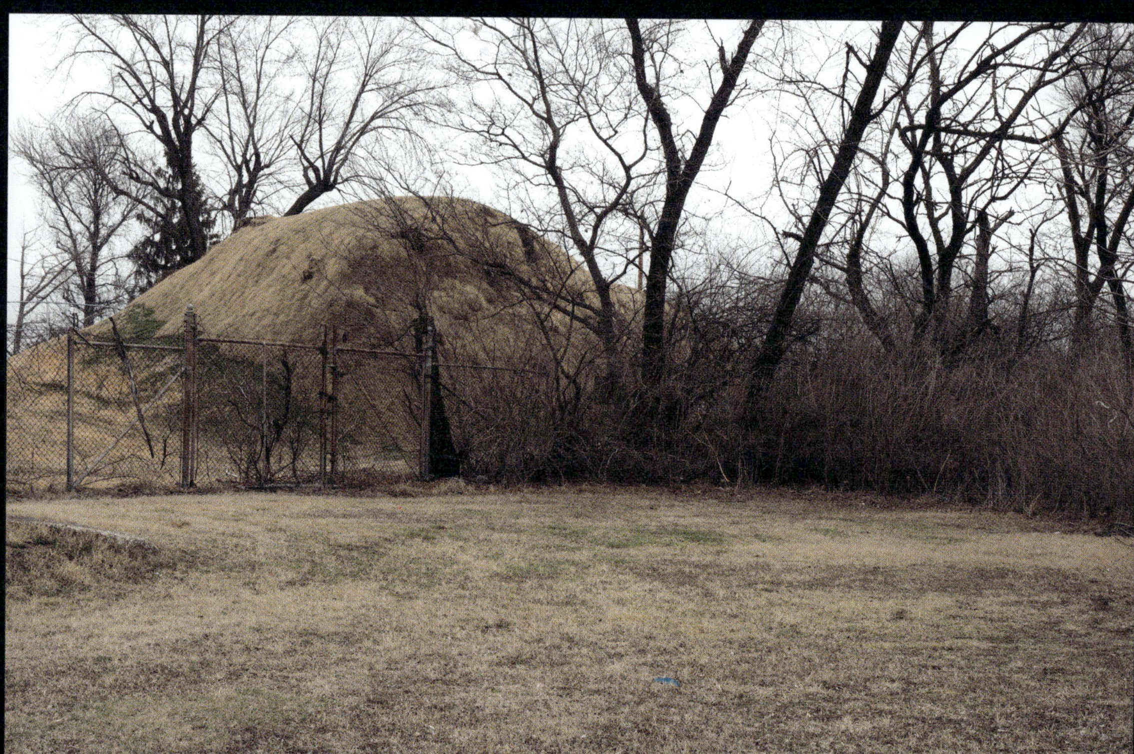

Mound 6905, 2018
Sugarloaf Mound

The story goes: Sugarloaf is the "last remaining mound" in Mound City, the last remaining pre-European Indigenous mound in St. Louis City. The fact that this is not entirely true speaks to the rhetorical turn of "lasting" that Jean M. O'Brien identifies as one in the trinity of narrative erasures of Native presence. In her book *Firsting and Lasting* (2010), O'Brien identifies the stubbornly recurrent speech acts of *firsting*, *replacing*, and *lasting* within an ongoing settler lexicon of writing Native presence out of the present.[1] A "last" that recapitulates a surprisingly durable but increasingly contested gulf in the history of the continent. A "last" that carries the colonial residue that prioritizes written over oral forms of representation. A "last" that displaces contemporary forms of Native inhabitation in the region.

In Silencing the Past (1995), Michel-Rolph Trouillot offers a powerful reminder of the tenacity at work in the structure of narrative erasure:

> Silences enter the process of historical production at four crucial moments: the moment of fact creation (the making of *sources*); the moment of fact assembly (the making of *archives*); the moment of fact retrieval (the making of *narratives*); and the moment of retrospective significance (the making of *history* in the final instance).[2]

Silencing is a structure, not an event, and we can map each stage of this silencing in the nineteenth-century reception of various mound findings—from doubt of the mound's artificial (i.e., human) origins to the substitution of Native North Americans with a mythical "lost race." Through such stories, silences were made to speak through an elaborate pantomime, which risked displacing sources, archives, narratives, and histories to an unknowable past.

Yet, doubt and its archival absences are incomplete actors and by chance enough evidence remains. Small decisions, rooted as much in indifference as concern, have allowed parts of Sugarloaf and certain other mound groups in the region to remain sufficiently intact so that the narrative of absence and emptiness simply cannot hold.

[1] Jean M. O'Brien, *Firsting and Lasting: Writing Indians out of Existence in New England* (Minneapolis: University of Minnesota Press, 2010).

[2] Michel-Rolph Trouillot, *Silencing the Past: Power and the Production of History* (Boston: Beacon, 1995), 26.

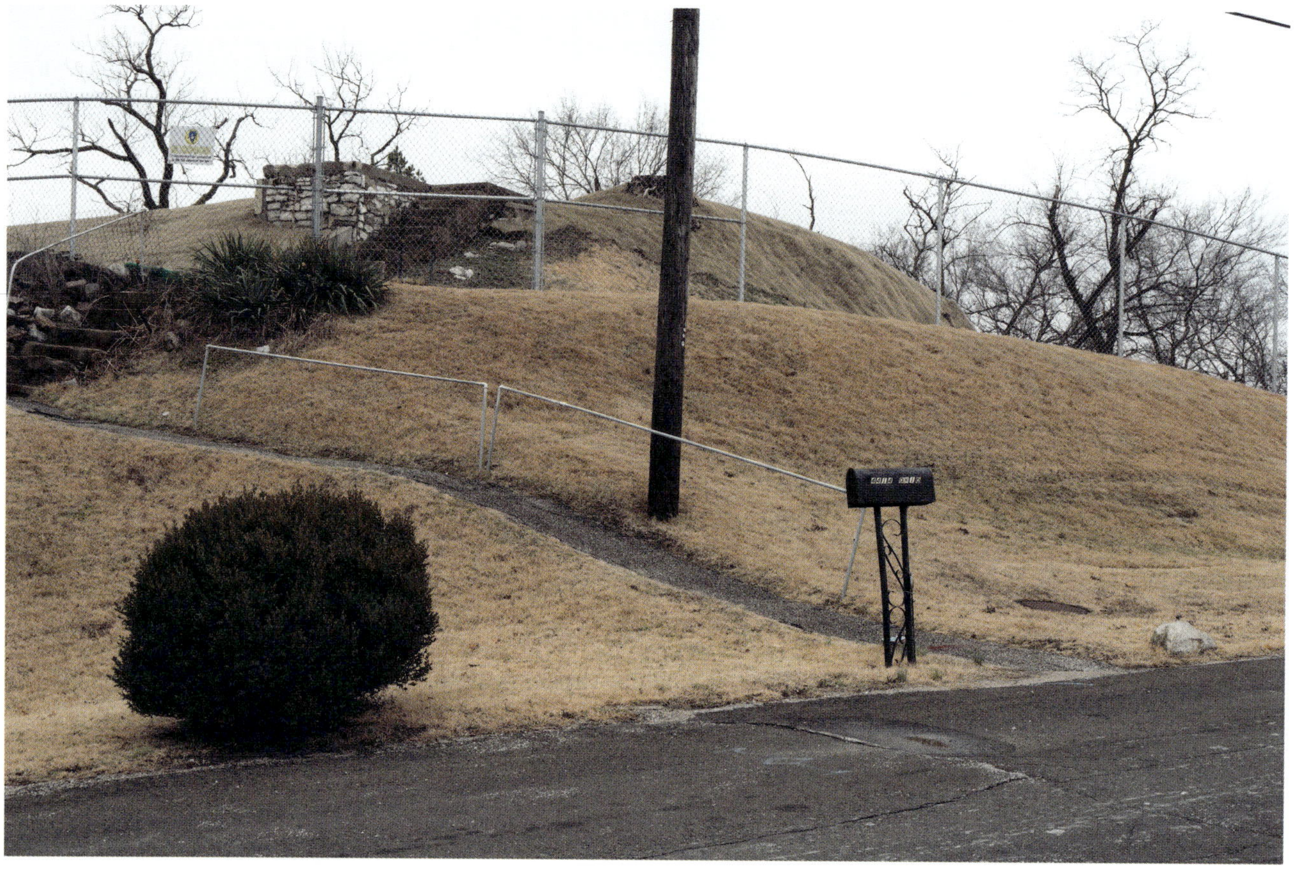

Mound 6931, 2018
Sugarloaf Mound

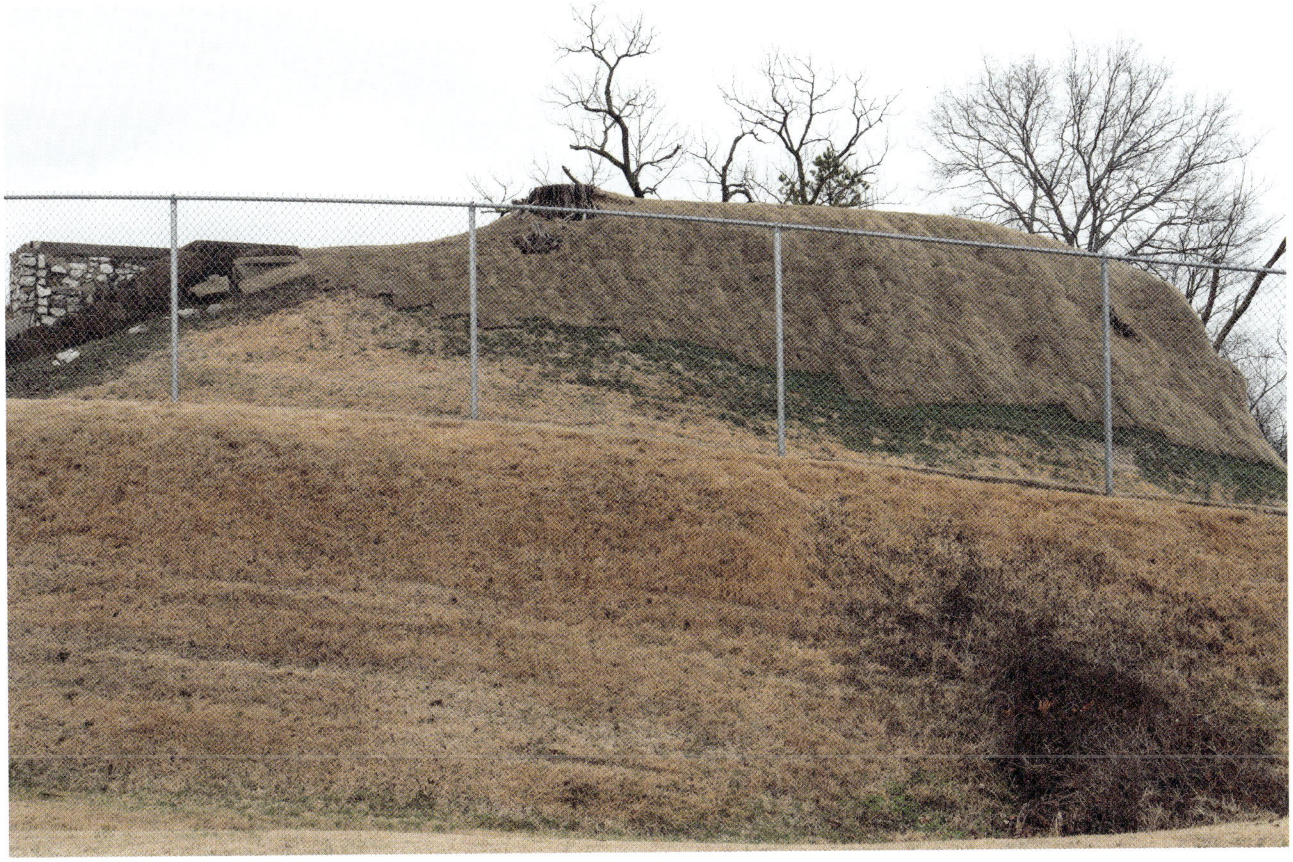

Mound 6918, 2018
Sugarloaf Mound

FIRST DISPLACEMENTS

Before colonization, before contagion, before concrete interstates, and before the march of Empires rewrote the landscapes and bodies of North America—the riverine landscape of the mid-continent was the locus of human inhabitation dense with dwelling and meaning and contradiction. The signal material articulation of this inhabitation are the innumerable mounds constructed throughout the Mississippi River Valley and its tributaries. Some, we are told, were raised as burial mounds, others as temple mounds, and still others had a purpose that remains unknown. It is a period of contentious historiography—where narratives of rupture, speculation, and vacancy fill the many gaps in material and oral histories.

Archeologists inaugurated this period and people, as well as the cultural assemblage of mounds and pottery and other material practices, as Mississippian. This name holds a time that is also a geography and is meant to underscore the intensive settlement of riverine sites in the region. At the center of this ancient confluence of exchange was what we now call the greater Cahokia region—named, casually, after a tribal grouping living in the area at the time of first European contact. The name stuck, as names do, so that is what we call it now.

Settlement in this region appears to have been centered around the great plazas and mounds of the Cahokia Mounds site—though this was far from the only concentration of inhabitation. Geometrically and topographically clustered mound groups can be found throughout the floodplain and extend to the adjacent bluffs and beyond. A significant grouping on the west side of the river, the St. Louis Mound Complex, sat to the north of the escarpment that defines present-day downtown and gave the city its nickname of Mound City. However, in the industrialization and urbanization of the St. Louis region in the nineteenth century and particularly its acceleration following the Civil War, these and most other mounds were systematically dismantled and carted away for use in leveling lowland sloughs and raising railroad grades. In this we find a pattern of unbuilding repeated throughout the continent—mounds unbuilt and reconfigured in the material erasure and retroactive narrative emptying of Native life on the continent.

South along the same arc of this riverfront is Sugarloaf, forty feet high and one hundred long. Basket upon basket of soil, transposed from a borrow pit and configured in a new form—and somehow, Sugarloaf (mostly) still remains. Some archeologists interpret Sugarloaf as a burial mound, others as a temple mound, and still others as a signal mound—its functional ambiguity perhaps mapping the limits of our own categories.[3]

“Civilization” systematically measured in the displacement of material.

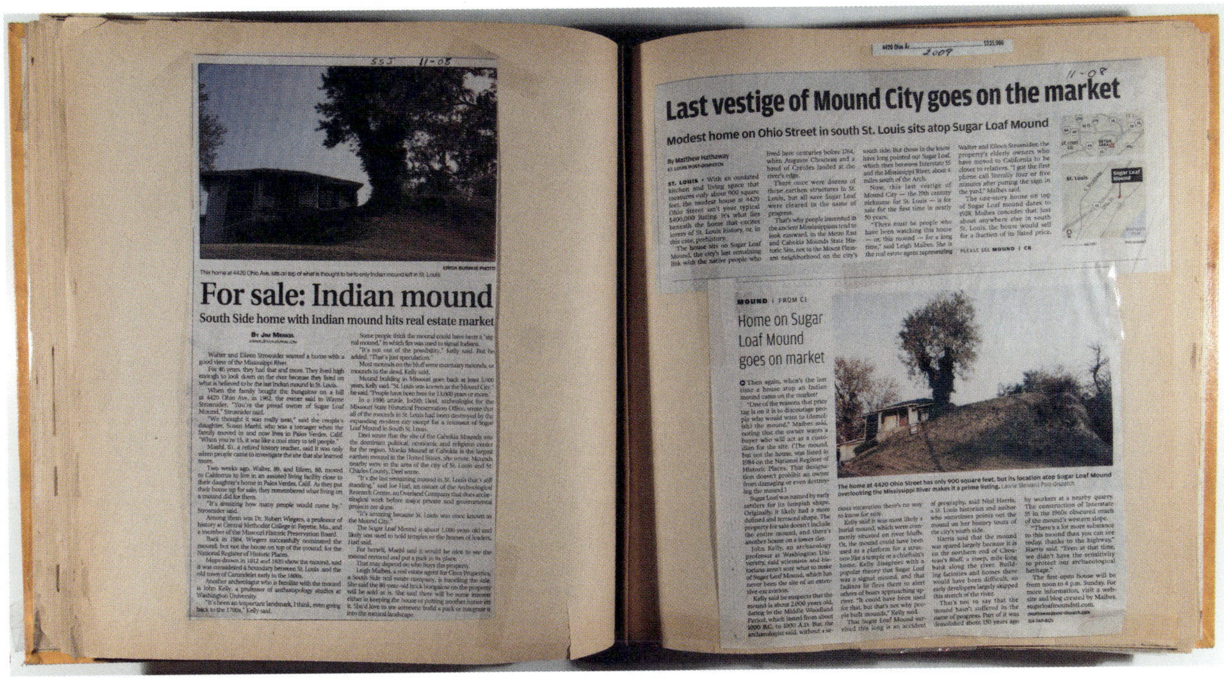

Newspaper cuttings, 2009
From the Heckenberg Family Scrapbook
Courtesy of Joan Heckenberg

[3] Limited archeological work has been conducted on Sugarloaf Mound. See Robert Paul Wiegers, "The Last St. Louis Mound," *Rediscovery Journal of Archaeology* 2 (1982): 67–79, 1982; and Andrew Weil et al., "A Management Plan for Sugarloaf Mound," Landmarks Association of St. Louis unpublished manuscript, 2011, for many corrections. See also James M. Denny, "Sugar Loaf Mound," National Register of Historic Places Inventory/Nomination Form, Missouri Department of Natural Resources Historic Preservation Program, Jefferson City, June 1981.

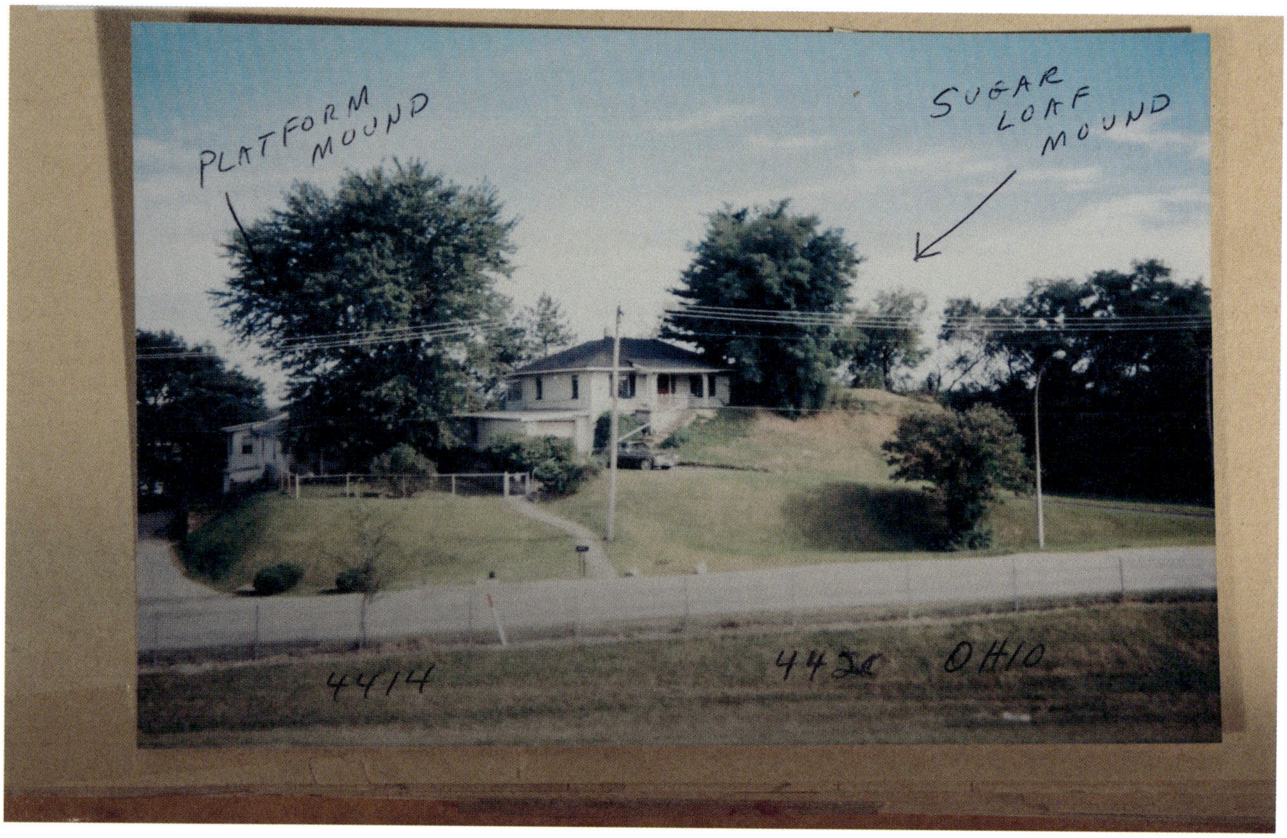

From the Heckenberg Family Scrapbook
Courtesy of Joan Heckenberg

DISPLACEMENTS ON DISPLACEMENTS

Sugarloaf Mound, this first displacement, stood in silent witness for a millenium—gradually sprouting and eroding, hosting grasses and trees and critters. It remained unremarked upon in the early written chronicles of the region, holding its own place relative to the wide expanse of the floodplain below. When it did enter the ledgers of language, it did so as a different sort of utterance, a boundary marker. Sugarloaf first entered the register in the plat and boundary maps of St. Louis in the early nineteenth century, when surveyors used the mound to designate the boundary between the Common of St. Louis and the Common Field of Carondelet.

It is, of course, a repeated tragedy of settler colonial logic that, in many cases, the first written records of pre-contact mounds—as well as contemporaneous Native settlement—were recorded in the field notes of land surveyors. A process that facilitated its parcelization, subdivision, and sale later in the century. That is, the moment of assembling an archive of Native survivance[4] was simultaneously the means for territorial dispossession. A center turned periphery as the mound was incorporated into different regimes of knowledge and description. From a site of properties to property.[5] From a landscape of qualities to an address.

4404. 4414. 4420. Addresses. Lots. City boundaries. Sugarloaf entered the cadastre as a new form of propertied land, holding a space in the administrative legers of the city. The Sugarloaf mound spread its conical base across and beyond the lots of 4404, 4414, and 4420 Ohio Street in South St. Louis. Property lines, addresses, unable to contain the mound's angle of repose. Its footprint describes a different sort of contour from those of the cadastre. Topographies give way to grids. Material things to abstractions.

In 1923, the lots were first purchased from the city. Ownership is established. The cadastre is updated. History begins ... By 1929, the north face of the mound had been leveled and a house was built. Much of the mound soil was (re-)displaced and new fill brought in. Bricks from a nearby kiln, themselves molded clay from nearby pits, stacked into walls. Limestone from the nearby bluff arranged to hold back the mound soil in two terraces—where a smaller house was then built. By 1937, a quarry began its unbuilding operations just south of the mound, the bluff blasted for its limestone—an undoing that cannot be reversed. Half the mound was carved away—a gash that exposed the soil horizons, the material thresholds of time.

[4] See Gerald Vizenor, *Native Liberty: Natural Reason and Cultural Survivance* (Lincoln: University of Nebraska Press, 2009).

[5] See Aileen Moreton-Robinson, *The White Possessive: Property, Power, and Indigenous Sovereignty* (Minneapolis: University of Minnesota Press, 2015); and Robert Nichols, "Theft is Property!," *Political Theory* 46, no. 1 (2018): 2–28.

In 2017, the house that stood at 4420 was removed. Geotechnical engineers cut off the walls just below ground level. The foundations remain. The front steps remain. The retaining walls remain. The house, removed, yet its presence is still unmistakably there. The moundhouse, invariably.

A mound and house. Together. Bound together. Trees cut off at base. Walls cut off at foundations. Roots intertwined in earth. Foundations imbricated in earth. Roots and foundations, still there. Under the sterile dirt brought in to close the gaps. Separated with coins minted in the year the fill was deposited—time markers for future interpreters. Roots and foundations covered in new sod that won't take. Kentucky Fescue. Sloughing off. A(nother) scar. Security cameras record this slow landscape performance. A mound is material. A house is material.

A moundhouse is a material thing.

Archeologists use the word *commingling* to describe the intermixing of different sites, different times, different remains—the accumulation of historico-cultural-material on the interpretive plane of the present. Commingling presents a particular challenge to interpretation, an accumulation of forgetfulness. Commingling asks us to start with proximity and end in relation—rather than assume meaning or morality. Commingling points to relationality as a meaningful co-presence *toward* meaning.

There is no undoing commingling. "There is no document of civilization," Walter Benjamin reminded us quite some time ago, "which is not at the same time a document of barbarism."[6] In the short arc of memory, commingling does important work (the continued possibility of conflict keeps stakes high). The concept of commingling allows one to imagine a future where repair is more than removal—where reparations are both a material and narrative return that is also an opening toward relation.

Multiple displacements, multiple horizons. A rearrangement of materials that is a rearrangement of meaning. The houses and the mound reconfigure meaning and time within the strata of the earth. The first of many conflicting belongings.

[6] Walter Benjamin, *Illuminations* (New York: Schocken, 1969), 256.

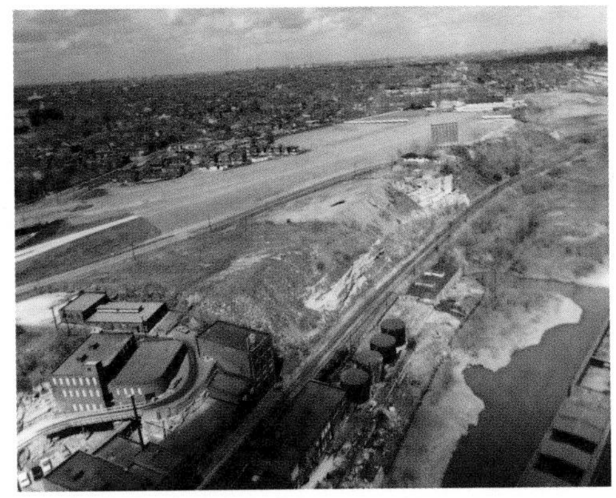

Richard Moore
Aerial view of Sugarloaf and surroundings, looking north, 1960.
Courtesy of Missouri History Museum, St. Louis

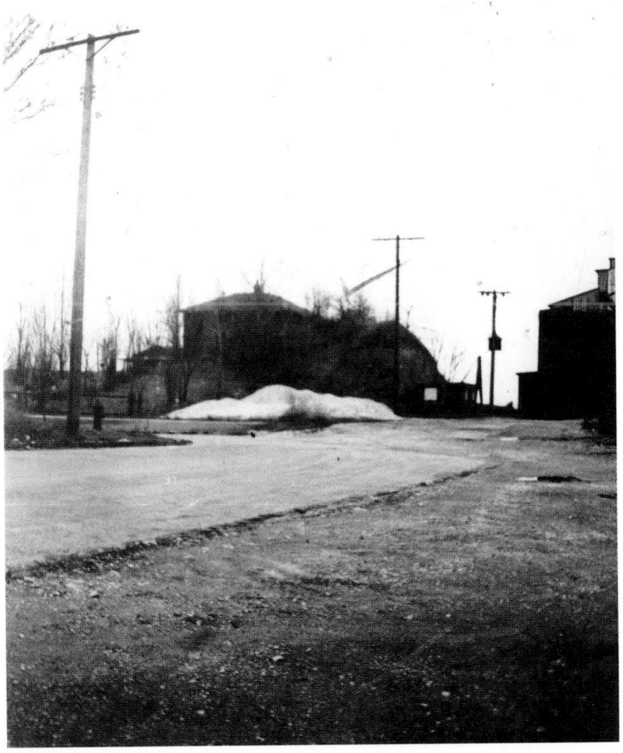

Orville Spreen
Photographs of Sugarloaf Mound, taken March 11, 1939
Courtesy of Western Historical Manuscripts Collection, UMSL

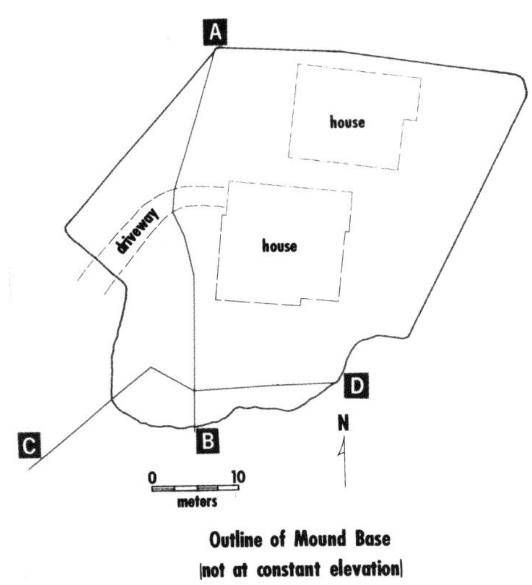

Robert Paul Wiegers
From "The Last St. Louis Mound," *Rediscovery Journal of Archaeology* 2 (1982): 67–79

DISPLACEMENTS ON DISPLACEMENTS ON DISPLACEMENTS

This landscape was, and remains, a space of fullness—steeped in its own contradictions. A mound constructed over 1,000 years ago. A house constructed almost 100 years ago. A house constructed on a constructed mound. A dispossession. A confrontation. An expropriation of place. An annexing of meaning. A material diagram of the everyday acts of North American settler colonialism.

A diagram we cannot afford to forget.

This house on a mound is just the most visible articulation of a process we can, in fact, find on every road and in every town. It is a rewriting of one form of belonging with another, a possession based in dispossession. And whether you live on a mound or in a high-rise or on a quiet cul-de-sac, the diagram remains: we are all living on Indigenous land.

I treat this as a statement of fact, not a moral scold; and this fact brings responsibilities down to the present. I ask myself: What does this house on the mound do to anchor this diagram, these abstractions, in the materiality of the world? How might the *materiality* of the confrontations of belonging draw us closer to an honest reckoning with history and toward a redistribution of meaning?

One of many quotidian acts of Empire and dispossession, these material displacements outlined above are relatively easy to account for. Their possible meaning and motivation are relatively well established, or at least intelligible to anyone who wishes to care; a material diagram so bright as to be almost blinding. The mound, so clear. The houses, so clear. The annexing and overwriting and expropriation of meaning there in the horizons of soil, so clear.

Paradoxically, however, the emphasis on the mounds themselves—and their presence and centrality to the narrative of Indigenous St. Louis—does other, more complicated work. Missing from the moundhouse diagram is a third displacement, harder to attend to: the displacement of the continued presence of Native life in St. Louis. In emphasizing the pre-contact, historically distant histories of the mounds and their builders, the very nature of settler/Native dynamics in the region is elided. A dynamic that must include St. Louis as the center of nineteenth-century treaties and their violation, the forced relocation of Native nations to reservations in what is now Oklahoma, and the ongoing work of groups like the Native Women's Care Circle to recover and preserve forms of Native knowledge and practice.

It is in this elision where the real dispossession lurks; a parceling out of acknowledgment older than the books. A distribution of attention that runs the risk of masking a contested present.

One history that stands in for another. A metonymic displacement that operates on the register of meaning and belonging.

This is one of the reasons the moundhouse diagram remains important as a material archive that resists erasure into an unrecoverable past; that lays it out, visible, today, for anyone to confront. It pushes against the commemorative impulse that scrubs the site of frictions by bracketing-out the contradictions of the present.

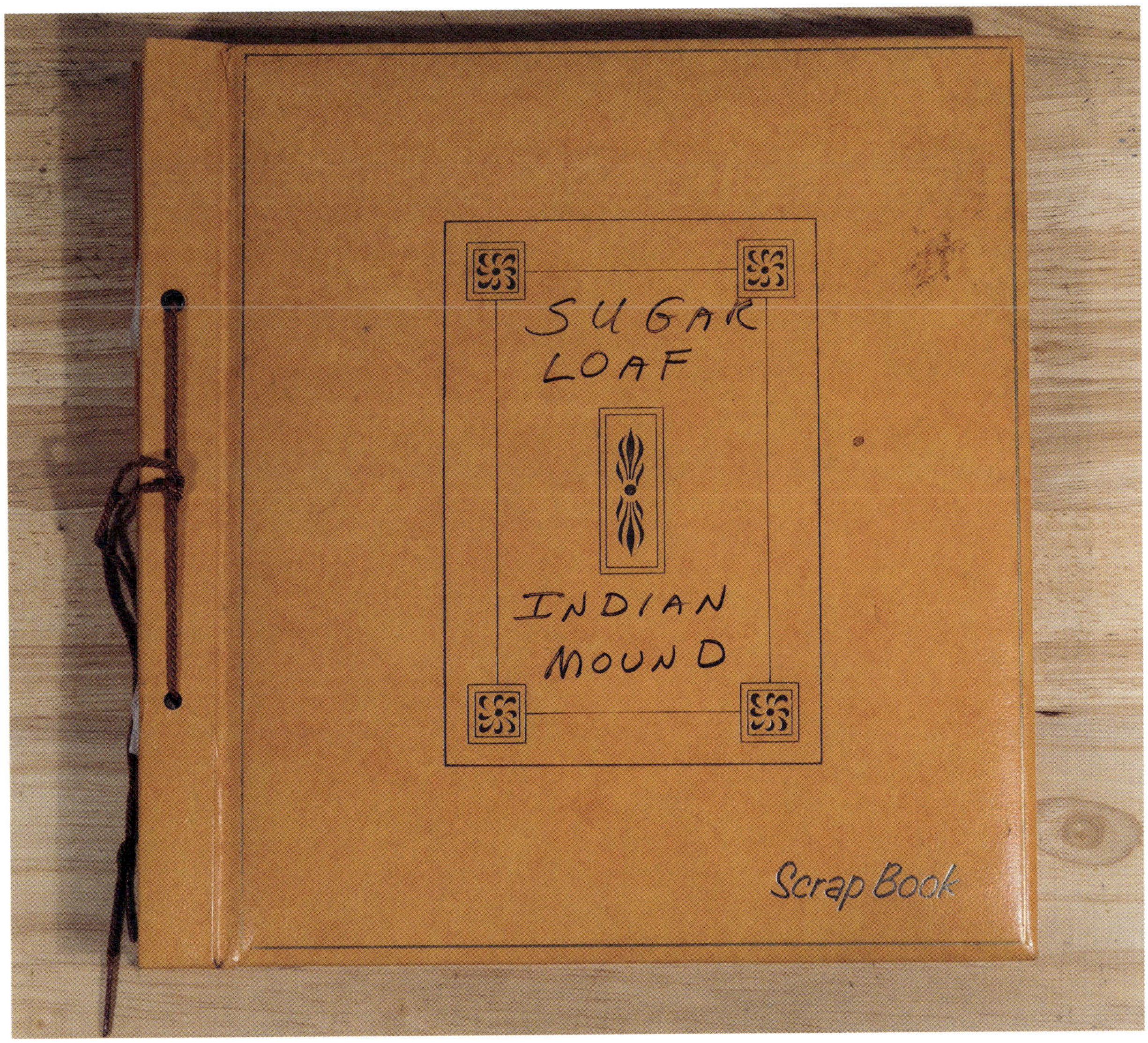

"Sugar Loaf Indian Mound"
Cover of the Heckenberg Family Scrapbook
Courtesy of Joan Heckenberg

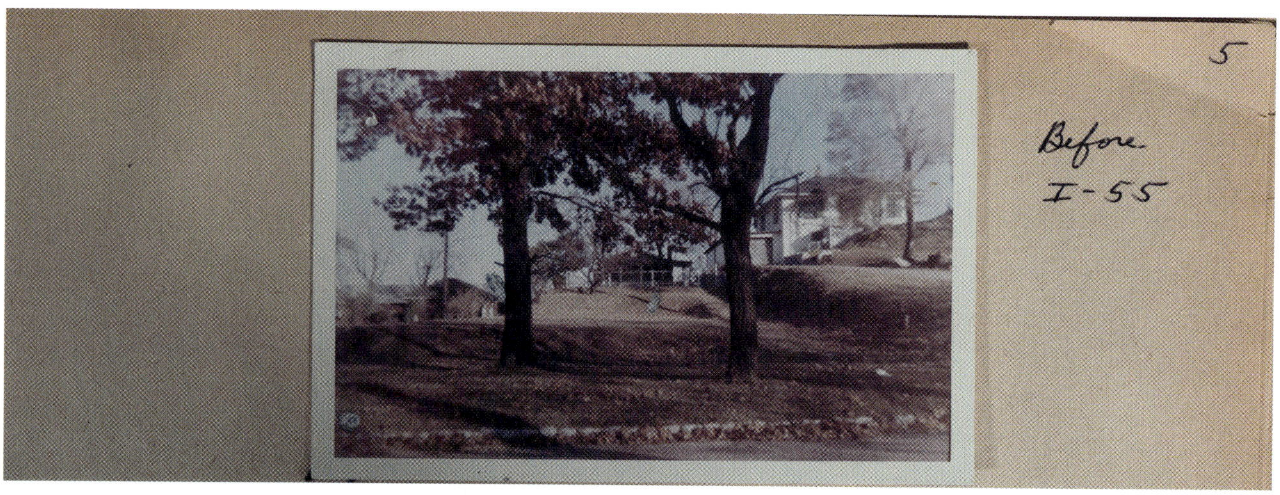

“Before I-55,” circa 1945
From the Heckenberg Family Scrapbook
Courtesy of Joan Heckenberg

(Opposite)
1981 and 1989
From the Heckenberg Family Scrapbook
Courtesy of Joan Heckenberg

1981

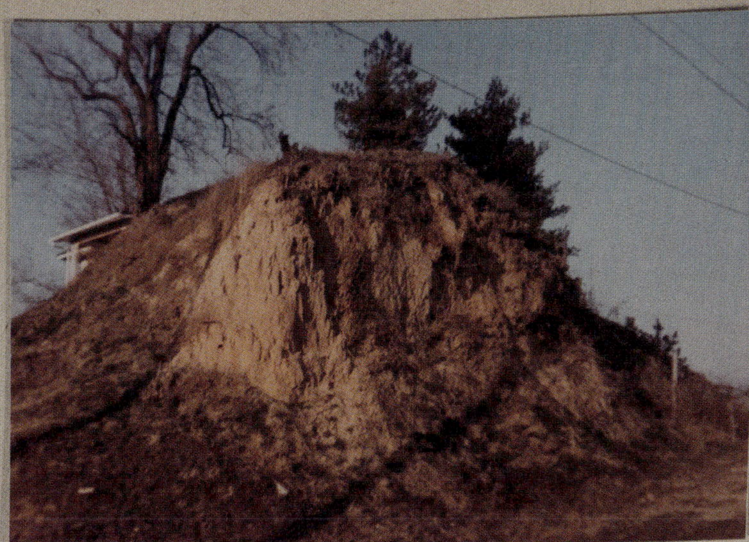

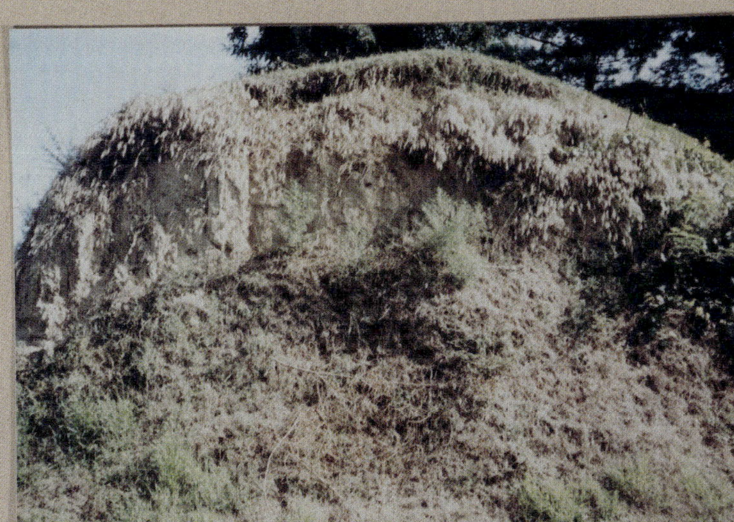

Aug. 1989

BELONGING

The family who has lived in the house at 4414 since the 1940s has kept a scrapbook of the moundhouse—selections of which are shared here for the first time. But unlike other family scrapbooks, this one does not carry notes and scribbles about relatives and life events. Instead, it is a modest record of finite understanding. The scrapbook chronicles eighty years of living on a Native American mound—"Sugar Loaf Indian Mound," as the cover announces. It traces the commingling of house and mound, life and history, placement and displacement. The keepers of this scrapbook are not outside of the diagram. But it seems clear that they know it. As a reader, I take comfort in this fact.

Personal meaning, interpretation, almost never seeps into the pages. Finitude and distance are respected. Thresholds of unknowability can never be crossed. A humble document of living together across a millennium. Short notes chronicle and suggest episodes in the life of a place. It is, perhaps appropriately, more about proximities than relations. But, importantly, the scrapbook archives and holds these proximities for us to recover today.

From what is this density of belonging derived? We must be alert to its anchor in law, in ownership, in possession. But there are multiple layers of belonging that are at once much deeper as well as much more personal. Belongings that can be identified across generations and ancestry sit alongside belongings that are quick to take hold within the lived experience of a single life. It is our collective responsibility to attend to a rematriation of the former while not necessarily holding an individual to account for the latter.

What is at stake in the moundhouse is not only the past, history, but also the possibility of a future. "The possibility," as Vine Deloria, Jr. simply, shockingly, reminds us, "of the continuing revelation of the sacred in our lives."[7] A revelation that comes, perhaps this round, in the material world itself. "It is never we who affirm or deny something of a thing," Spinoza suggests, "it is the thing itself that affirms or denies something of itself in us."[8] A moundhouse. A mediation. Not the sacred, but evidence of the sacred.

There is, today, in this exhibition and outside it, ongoing discussion about the houses at 4404 and 4414. About purchase, return, and removal.[9] St. Louis has an unmistakable pattern of erasure in its dealings with Indigenous and Black spaces.

[7] Vine Deloria, Jr., *God is Red: A Native View of Religion* (Golden, CO: Fulcrum, 2003), 281.

[8] Cited in Jane Bennet "The Force of Things: Steps Toward an Ecology of Matter," *Political Theory* 32, no. 3 (2004): 347, from Spinoza's *Short Treatise II*, 16, 5.

[9] See Shannon Shaw, "Chief Purchases Sugarloaf Mound," *Osage News*, August 14, 2009, for history and controversy around the initial purchase of house/lot 4420.

Big Mound . . . Mill Creek Valley . . . Washington Park Cemetery . . . East St. Louis . . . Forest Park Mounds . . . lives, histories, and landscapes all actively removed and rewritten for other, more abstract forms of belonging. How did Sugarloaf remain? The paradox of a quarry cut through it, making it too unstable for the construction of a highway. Or the paradox of the houses themselves, holding a place for accepted forms of belonging. Or, perhaps, through the accidents of history, leaving open the possibility for preservation, reparation, and self-determination—the persistence of material and matter—if we are able to act.

How do we think about the commingling of the remaining house and mound? What if the house is the very thing that might allow us, today, to not only approach the mound and its world of creation more fully but to also to confront and hold a space for the unknowable? To not only measure our distance and proximity from the lifeworlds the mound suggests, but more importantly, to remind us of our ongoing responsibilities in the present?[10]

Even if we imagine the house gone, the commingling is not. It is still there, just below the surface. Below the visible. And, I fear, below the horizon of effective political action. What the moundhouse gives us is a thing to organize dissensus around. To not wish away the centuries of trauma and violence, but to hold the conflict as present. In the end, it's not even about the mound as a historical fact. It's about the capacity of the present to hold and transition the commingling toward new social and political assemblies.

I believe in the mound's obstinate form. I also believe in the confrontation at work in the moundhouse. It is something that works against the ease of narrative erasure or, more likely, distraction, inattention, and forgetfulness. This is just the kind of work that form does. It is no guarantee, of course. But its continuance and persistence is hugely important when stacked against centuries of deeds and words that would demand otherwise. The mound goes on existing, goes on believing, in the present. The persistence of form and matter being one of its most powerful contributions to an argument for landscape reparations.

We might imagine the second house remaining. Floor removed. Earth exposed. The house refracting the past through its thin sheet glass windows. House and mound in a tense union. Neither giving way from the meaning it locks within itself, but doubling in its disturbances.

[10] On design of/in Indigenous space, see Rod Barnett, "Designing Indian Country," *Places Journal*, October 2016, https://placesjournal.org/article/designing-indian-country/?cn-reloaded=1; and Pierre Belanger et al., "No Design on Stolen Land," *Architectural Design* 90, no. 1 (2020): 120–27.

Or we might imagine both houses removed. Grounds restored. The site draped in thoughtful and necessary interpretation. Rightly returning a history almost lost to its proper position of partial legibility and remembrance. A momentary break in the silences, forgetfulness, and violence.

But even with both houses gone, perhaps the mailbox should remain.

To not feign a simplistic undoing. To not double the silencing, but to keep it as a reminder that silencing is an ongoing process that we can work to undo and redirect to fill a more complete, complicated present.

It goes without saying this is not a decision for me.

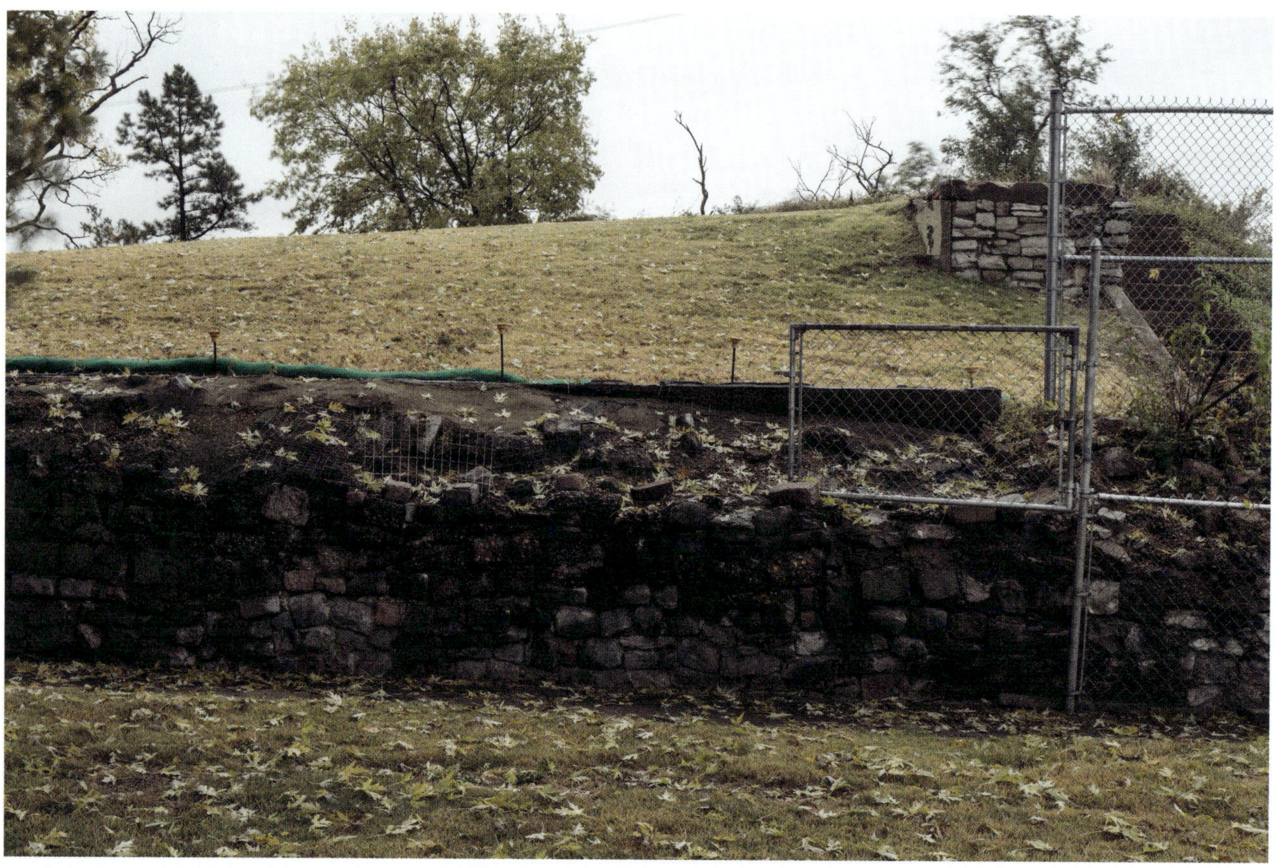

Mound 3853, 2018
Sugarloaf Mound

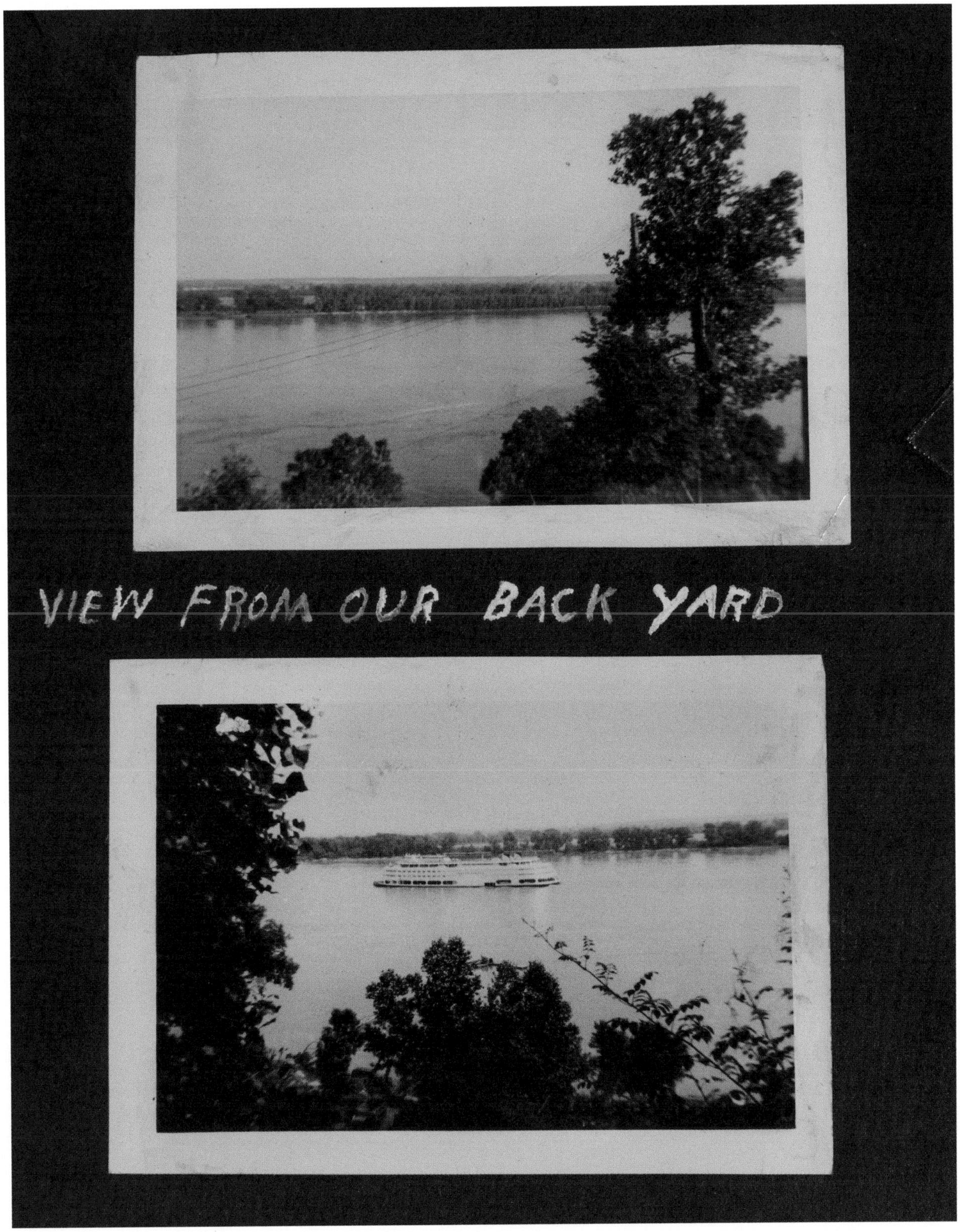

"View from our back yard," 1957
From the Heckenberg Family Scrapbook
Courtesy of Joan Heckenberg

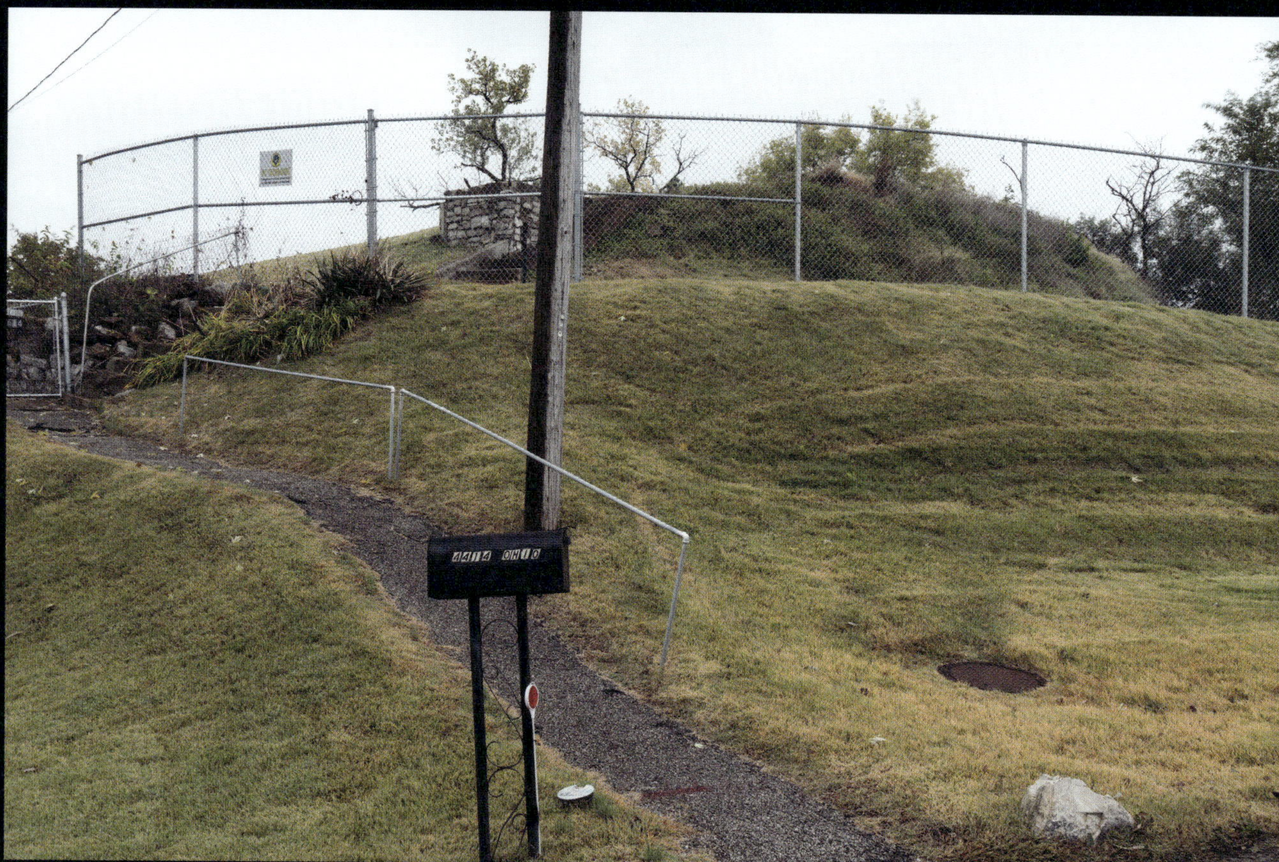

Mound 3867, 2018
Sugarloaf Mound

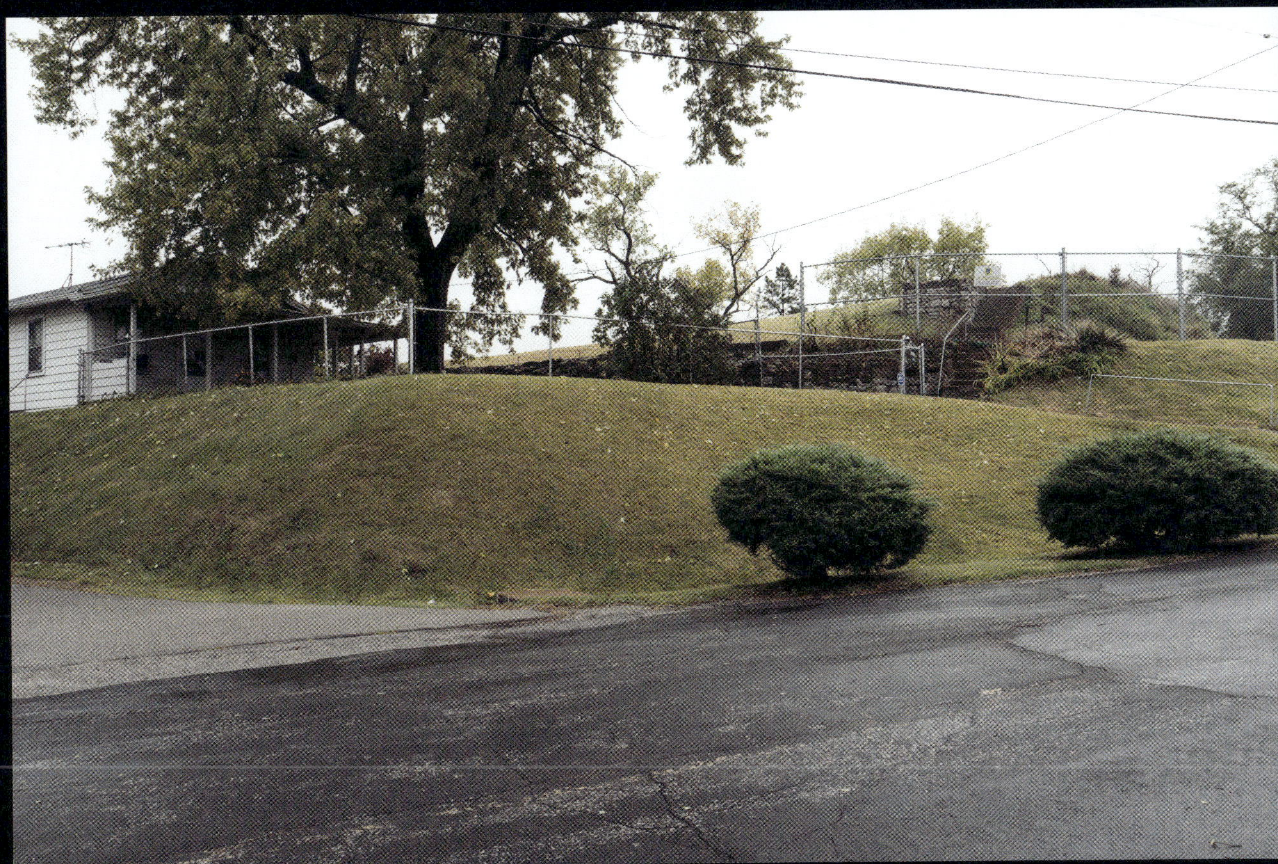

Mound 3843, 2018
Sugarloaf Mound

GIVE IT BACK: STAGE THEORY

By
New Red Order

To approach St. Louis—through a lens of discovery, as a central site of removal and displacement of Indigenous peoples, of attempted annihilations and layers of dislocation—is to contend with the persistence of erasure. The space between these shared specificities creates territory that has the potential to spawn previously unthought-of approaches to "decolonial" work and foster other more meaningful and intuitive formulations.

Finally.

We tell you again, now: freedom is a red flag.

Derived. Extracted. Ingested. Found with legacies of displacement.

An acknowledgment of our ongoing settler colonial occupation is only the first step in a massive reconfiguration of reality which must occur during an awakening if "we" all are to survive.
But who are "we"?[1]

The truth is—and few of us care to admit it—Indigenous epistemologies will save us from the end of our future. Looking toward the greatest postapocalyptic parafiction of all time has catalyzed us all to reflect on how we got here and to ask: Where can we go? In our current period of existential and environmental catastrophe, desires for Indigenous epistemologies increase and enterprising settlers labor to extract this understanding as if it were a natural resource. New Red Order—having emerged out of contradistinction from the Improved Order of Red Men, a secret society that "plays Indian"[2]—calls attraction toward indigeneity into question, yet promotes this desire and enjoins potential non-Indigenous accomplices to participate in the co-examination and expansion of Indigenous agency.

Demands for indigeneity, long entwined with efforts to erase and replace Indigenous peoples, have been channeled through practices of salvage ethnography and "playing Indian." We might have preferred not to have to confront the resilient urge to relegate Indigenous identities to the past. Yet we continue here to face a public secret: a denial of the denial of the presence—and claims—of those currently living on colonized land.

[1] "Henceforward, the interests of one will be the interests of all, for in concrete fact *everyone* will be discovered by the troops, *everyone* will be massacred—or *everyone* will be saved." Frantz Fanon, *The Wretched of the Earth*, trans. Constance Farrington (New York: Grove, 1961), 47. "There exists a fiercely unrelenting desire to achieve total liberation, with the land and, together. At some point there is a 'we,' and we most likely will have to work together." "Accomplices Not Allies: Abolishing the Ally Industrial Complex," Indigenous Action, May 4, 2014, https://www.indigenousaction.org/accomplices-not-allies-abolishing-the-ally-industrial-complex/.

[2] With roots in the Sons of Liberty—who claimed responsibility for the Boston Tea party—the Improved Order of Red Men is a fraternal organization established in North America in 1834. Their rituals and regalia are modeled after those assumed by men of the era to be used by Native Americans. Despite the name, the order was formed solely by, and for, "free white [men] of good moral character and standing . . . possessed of some known reputable means of support." This whites-only rule was part of their bylaws until 1974, when the all-white clause was eliminated. In 1935 the organization claimed a membership of about half a million, but has since declined to a little more than 15,000. "Improved Order of Red Men," *Wikipedia*, last modified February 8, 2023, https://en.wikipedia.org/wiki/Improved_Order_of_Red_Men.

Confronted with appearances of absence, Indigenous artists who grew up in Native communities, affected by living and contested claims to the land, and who now participate in art worlds of settler colonial states, are expected to provide knowledge on their, and other, communities, in a relationship similar to that between the informant and anthropologist.

Within emergent entanglements of the decolonial appeal—and art practices valorizing freedom yet wary of overstepping—cultural apprehensions fuel stronger calls for Indigenous information and informants. Many non-Indigenous people find ways to frame themselves as Indigenous, just as Indigenous people perform indigeneity themselves. If these tendencies are entrenched so deeply in this nation's self-image as to be apparently inescapable, how can they be manipulated, employed by Indigenous people to catalyze an expansion of Indigenous agency? Can desires that overtly or subliminally push Indigenous people to an ideal and irretrievable past be rechanneled to promote Indigenous growth?

How, acknowledging and engaging our complicity, can we amplify the power of the informant, enjoining you to inform with us?

We seek unlikely conceptual frameworks to unpack (perhaps stay a while, but Never Settle) and even parody and rearrange the contradictions, missteps, and trauma that characterize histories of the colonial project since 1492. We aim to flag safe spaces of stagnations reemerging from normative attitudes that shy from contradictions inherent in multiple aspirations for sovereignty—razed, buried as backfill, and paved over while blazing toward "freedom" and "progress"—and instead attempt to build and layer toward generative understandings of how "identity" and "history" might be conveyed and configured within and beyond our contemporary understandings of decolonization, reconciliation, and settler colonialism.

As we multiply collaborations with an expanding roster of interdisciplinary "informants" and "accomplices" who weave in and out of alignment to co-produce video, performance, and installation works that confront settler colonial tendencies and potential obstacles to Indigenous growth, we interrogate presumed notions of curation bound with ideals of freedom. Who is free to select? Who has cared? Who cares? Must we resuscitate a janitorial metaphor, we custodians of the land? Can we care for the same things, in the same way, together? If not now, when?

After 500-plus years of settler colonialism and intersecting movements against "us," what might it take to reverse the process? What level of commitment (seemingly asymmetrical) is necessary? Where is the freedom in committing, in risking getting committed?

Amplifying the call for commitment as it is attached to any acknowledgment (increasing awareness, foregrounding, centering of the presence of Native peoples) we dig into this:

Giving it back is a Gift.

Call in with us to collectively shift resources toward the possibility of reclaiming Indigenous futures and our very present.

Give it back.

Beyond necessary disruptions of settler colonialism with calls to "take" back land, *Give it Back* investigates, presents, and promotes another mode of return: through land being "voluntarily" released to Indigenous peoples. Employing a promotional campaign of videos, advertisements, negotiations, and a real-estate ethos, *Give it Back* unfolds and extends to chart moments in a speculative future history of the movement. In foregrounding voluntary practices and promises of land's return, the work offers a potential, if partial, attempt to undo settler colonialism by those who stand to benefit most from its upholding.

Giving it Back also threatens to bury itself, to recede, as it expands and deepens, toward actively (materially and relationally) forging new channels for the return of land to Indigenous peoples—a daunting prospect given the violences of excavation and ongoing effects of removal and displacement of Indigenous peoples that open up questions and apprehensions about who the land can be given to.

But what is more natural?

How can we get reciprocal?

Through the prism of *Give it Back*, New Red Order approaches the archives of St. Louis, pursuing multiple timescales—from Cahokia through dispossession and genocide with St. Louis as the primary site of deployment in the Indian Wars to the 1904 Louisiana Purchase Centennial World's Fair promoting racial inequalities[3] and the present-day occupation of contested Indigenous lands—as a collection agency, framed in a portal, to trace persistent residues and resistances that remain in the search of foundations. These residues appear to reside collectively in desires and urges, subliminal, that may barely surface. If and when they do, those urges appear to re-mark dispersion, reinscribing the absence of nativeness and the diffusion of indigeneity as a requisite sacrifice to enable the commons. What kind of care might it take to cure this condition?

Our moments, in this portal to the West, to the rest, to the resting space left once removals were sufficient, are marked by fissures, razing of mounds, lacunae, reminding with realizations that it was we—and who are we?—who were dug. It can also turn out to be we who did—and do—the digging. Is it possible to evade dismantling?

[3] "Seldom in the history of the world had there been (and rarely has there been since) such a gathering of professional racists, keepers of human zoos, and Western civilizational luminaries as there was in Forest Park and on the campus of nearby Washington University during the summer and fall of 1904." Walter Johnson, *The Broken Heart of America: St. Louis and the Violent History of the United States* (New York: Basic Books, 2020), 201–02.

To grasp, to hold "realities" of colonial imprints upon these lands and waters, and the way in which the apparatus of impressions operates through movements of blurring and erasure, might call for reconfiguring notions of care within curation. We repeat. Who cares, together? To care might align with historical urges to fix the Native as static, to act as agent of both the freeze and the thaw, even if leaning toward evaporation. Now, disavowing disappearance, our senses shift, looking for ghosts, resuscitations of spectral traces—fixing troubling representations so that they might be reckoned.

Acknowledging the demands of informancy in art as anti-art that aims to ingest all, we build, complicit, we listen, capturing information from "non-artists"—those holders of elusive properties—that art worlds aim to fold into legible pretense. We aim to continue to facilitate the transfer of properties.

Curated, ingested, fastened into video, we fix and loosen a reflection on St. Louis's historical engagement with Indigenous peoples. Specifically, we emphasize, with a slight cast of surrection, the presentation of Indigenous peoples, concomitant with the razing of the mounds to clear space for the 1904 World's Fair and remaining museum. We ask: What if they never left? What happens when they return?

Surrection, foibles, and wobbling aims of resistance along the way point toward possibilities of Indigenous futures. In a culminating performance, toward the end—the goal of material transfer—New Red Order endeavors to open a place for resistance in contested space, however forgotten. Developing collaborative relationships into an expanding platform, in a contested commons, calling in a host of performers naming and embodying Indigenous presence, NRO investigates or interrogates what might be positioned as cures for St. Louis's historical and continual engagement with Indigenous peoples: examining the fixation on resilience, yet holding the remaining need for obligatory resistance. We ask: What can be given back?

MURMURATIONS AND FLICKERS:

Toward a Model for Non-Surveillant Bird-Watching and Public Art

By
Risa Puleo

Swallows are hard to see.

Small, streamlined, and fast, this shoulder-forward dive bomber of the birdworld moves too quickly to be identified beyond "swallow" while in flight; her choreography determined by the position of the bugs beyond the limits of human sight that she plucks from the sky. When backlit by sunlight, the details that would distinguish her from another species collapse into shadow. Take the Bank Swallow as an example. When compared to her shimmering cousins, she is relatively nondescript. Her brownness, however, is perfectly calibrated to the muddy waters at the confluence of the Mississippi and Missouri Rivers just north of the city of St. Louis. There, her body blends into the shadows of the holes she carves into the river's bank. The junction of the rivers overlaps with the Bank Swallow's breeding and migrating territories, which means that some can almost always be found in the St. Louis area. The Bank Swallow's brownness, then, is her way of calibrating to place through her embodied relationship to it. Swallows are even harder to see when they murmurate—that is, when hundreds, even thousands take flight at once, moving in synchronicity before suddenly scattering, only to come back together in another direction. I think of these movements—known as murmuration patterns—as refusals of individuation and identification; that is, a coordinated effort to move as a group in an evasion of capture and containment, but the swallow hasn't yet shared with me her reasons. Sheltered by the land and held by the sky, camouflage compounds her fugitive flight so that she is doubly outfitted against visual apprehension.

Like many of us confronted by the quiet that quarantine imposed, I became a bird-watcher during the pandemic. The sudden hush allowed for a nuance of individual bird calls outside my window and the emergence of a world that daily life had overshadowed. But to step outside in search of birds often means stepping into the techno-surveillant arena of birding. Bird-watching developed as a sporting alternative to hunting after the trade in animal skins, scientific and colonial collecting, and an overzealous hat industry edged many species toward extinction. Instead of killing birds, bird-watchers arm themselves with an apparatus of tools developed and sharpened by the military in pursuit of visual capture. The pull of a trigger has been replaced with the press of a button to create images that suspend birds in a mid-flight visual taxidermy. To see a swallow would require crowdsourced tracking apps, such as eBird, a project of Cornell University's ornithology department, which allows bird-watchers to track birds in time and space so that others might duplicate their steps in search of the same or similar birds. Other apps, such as Merlin Bird ID, help quantify the size, shape, color, and habitat of birds to help identify different species in the field. Zoom and telephoto lenses extend the camera's reach deep into a bird's space while miniature cameras attached to bird feeders lure birds into coming into the camera's range of vision. This figurative retinal detachment overprioritizes vision at a distance as the optimum form of knowing. Frustrated by how sight, sound, and place came to be mediated by technology and metrics, I began referring to my attempts to be with birds in the spaces where they live as "bird surveillance."

St. Louis is hard to see.

St. Louis also evades gaze, but for different reasons and in different ways than the swallow. The shape of the city's sprawl has been determined by the migratory patterns of humans engaged in turbulent flights, each moving according to their own rhythms and vectors. When it was called Cahokia, it was the heart of a vast network of life supported by the Mississippi River, whose major and minor tributaries guided Native peoples from across the continent to the area for trade.[1] The same watery matrix brought the French to the region, which they renamed St. Louis in 1764. Since then, humans have moved into and through St. Louis propelled by their own power and have also used that power to force others to stand still, move elsewhere, or else to flee to, through, or from the city. Forced relocation, westward expansion, the Underground Railroad, the Great Migration, white flight, and the dispersal caused by property blighting are but some of the many murmuration patterns made by people in St. Louis. We know the contours and crevices of the histories of colonization, slavery, dispossession, displacement, disablement, expropriation, and exploitation, but less visible are the ways in which they are etched into the city itself. Because these flights happen on the ground instead of in the sky, they leave conceptual and material traces in the earth when imposed ideologies reshape the land into a human vision for the world. To see those traces, and the land that became St. Louis beneath them, is like trying to see a swallow.

Subverting the distance of surveillance by bringing St. Louis closer into view results in the objectification and dissection of its lively animacy. One would think that a view of St. Louis from above would help bring visibility to the patterns of movement etched into its ground. But the aerial perspectives of cartography, like the dissecting methods of anthropological and scientific observation, are at the crux of the problem of seeing. That we are accustomed to reading the map of the United States from a bird's-eye view positioned high above the land mass is an effect of modern cartography. This method developed out of the interrelated practice of military surveillance and property surveying, and has been described by the geographer Denis Cosgrove as a "way of seeing in a European visual tradition."[2] By this Cosgrove means that maps and other ways of picturing landscape are a "composition and structuring of the world so that it may be appropriated by a detached, individual spectator to whom an illusion of order and control is offered through the composition of space according to the certainties of geometry." Such certainties offer the beholder "the control and domination over space as an absolute, objective entity, its transformation into the property of individual or state."[3]

The transformation of land into property is habituated in the tendency to read the US map from right to left according to the timeline of settlement and the logic of westward expansion. This logic continues to guide practices of contemporary mapping systems like the ones that will be used at the Department of Defense's National Geospatial-Intelligence Agency currently being built along Jefferson Avenue in North St. Louis. Seeing St. Louis through the European visual tradition means that it didn't exist until it was established in 1764.

[1] The place now called St. Louis has also hosted Native peoples who traveled the Mississippi, Missouri, and Meramec Rivers to the region, including Apache, Caddo, Cahokia, Chickasaw, Choctaw, Cherokee, Coushatta, Creek, Delaware, Fox, Haudenosaunee, Kansa, Kaskaskia, Kickapoo, Kiowa, Miami, Michigamea, Mingo, Moingwena, Oceti Sakowin, Sauk, Omaha, Onondaga, Otoe, Padouca, Pawnee, Peoria, Ponca, Potawatomi, Quapaw, Tamaroa, Shawnee, Seminole, Wichita, Winnebago. More information available at: https://greatriversgreenway.org/landsandwaters/.

[2] Denis Cosgrove, "Prospect, Perspective and the Evolution of the Landscape Idea," *Transactions of the Institute of British Geographers* 10, no. 1 (1985): 47.

[3] Cosgrove, "Prospect, Perspective and the Evolution of the Landscape Idea," 46.

This *terra nullius* ("nobody's land") rationale of colonial mapping equates the unknown with the unowned and the unowned with the potential to become property. Views from above also give insight into what may be taken from the land below. In Macarena Gómez-Barris's words, "the vertical model of seeing" transforms land into an "extractive zone."[4] Attempts to see St. Louis from above result in property; up close, in the transformation of life into an object; through the ground, in extraction. Each of these frameworks enters the city into a different room next to surveillance within the same state of capture. We need other methods.

Reorienting to the horizontal plane is a place to start. From the on-the-ground perspective of those who followed the Mississippi River, to walk to Cahokia was to descend slowly down slanting earth. In cross-section, St. Louis is the center of a great basin formed by the diminuendo of the Continental Divide and the Appalachian Mountains. This basin spills its water through the below-sea-level city of New Orleans into the Gulf of Mexico. Topographically, this means that fugitives who also followed the Mississippi from St. Louis in their flight from slavery walked on increasingly higher ground as they approached the North. The sound of the Mississippi, changes in plants and dirt, their smells, the movement of the stars, the touch of the wind, and the flight paths of birds were all guides and allies for travelers who moved in both directions by foot or water along the river. Cree poet Billy-Ray Belcourt calls upon the movements of migrants and fugitives in his articulation of different ways of knowing: "Where there's an injunction of something as integral to the livability of the world as joy, there is an underground activity, a fugitive cooperative of feeling, a commune of love that isn't to be perceived by the dominant eye."[5] From this perspective St. Louis cannot be beheld, only felt.

The reorientation from surveillance to enchantment is a whole-body affair.

St. Louis and swallows are hard to see because of the ways that we try to see them. When I stopped trying to see swallows—that is, to capture them within the frame of my vision and its fixed form, the photograph—they became more apparent. More specifically, swallows and other birds began to present themselves to me.

[4] Macarena Gómez-Barris recommends a diagonal view as a way to combat the "vertical model of seeing," a framework that within my view overprioritizes sight, offering a palliative and not a cure for the more systemic problems of colonial and carceral visual regimes. Macarena Gómez-Barris, *The Extractive Zone: Social Ecologies and Decolonial Perspectives* (Durham, NC: Duke University Press, 2017), 5.

[5] Billy-Ray Belcourt, *A History of My Brief Body* (St. Lucia: University of Queensland Press, 2021), 8.

Birds, like all animals in the wild, avoid humans because we've taught them to fear us. Hunting does that. Putting down binoculars pulls the optical intent of the hunt out of birdspace, allowing the scale of my vision to return to the scope of my eyes and my presence to the size of my body. Judith Butler writes, "The frames through which we apprehend ... do not unilaterally decide the conditions of appearance but their aim is nevertheless to delimit the sphere of appearance itself."[6] In my attempt to be frameless, with my only intent being to not determine the sphere of a bird's appearance, I initiated a practice of withdrawing from action, of putting down power—in this case, the power to see beyond my capacities and my assumption that I had a right to see—to create space for relationality and the recognition of mutuality. In this space, birds began to appear as themselves.

When the Bank Swallow chooses to present herself at the intersection of her independent trajectory and ours, she registers only as a fleeting glimpse of her white belly set within the shadow of her body against the brightness of the sky. The flash of white is a temporary event only accessible when an equilibrium of forces allows for a moment of recognition. In this moment, the swallow also engages in the precarious process of trust, trusting that we who look upon her will not trespass upon her vulnerability with an attempt to capture her. In response, we must also withdraw from our habituated desire to possess. The flicker of a swallow's white belly is an invitation into what Nicholas Mirzoeff calls "the right to look." He writes, "The right to look is not about seeing. It begins at a personal level with the look into someone else's eyes to express friendship, solidarity, or love. That look must be mutual, each person inviting the other, or it fails. As such, it is unrepresentable."[7] Looking is an act that we must be invited into and cannot hold on to.

Undoing is a kind of doing.

The work of a curator is to delimit the physical sphere of appearance—the exhibition—and to determine the conceptual frames by which exhibited art is seen. Within these spheres, curators guide visitors in looking at the artworlds they've constructed as orators of both place and experience. My curatorial contribution to Counterpublic 2023 takes inspiration from my interactions with swallows, my commitments to a politics of refusal, and my meanderings around a question about what a decolonial-abolitionist bird-watching could be. This question itself was born from both my research into the overlaps and disconnects between decolonization and abolition movements and methods, and my exhibitions that explore how artists leverage their practices to make strategic interventions into carceral and colonial spaces. My contribution is an attempt to construct a public art exhibition that does not enact an occupation, cannot be captured as an event or contained as an experience. It is an attempt to stage a mutuality of looking with St. Louis.

As the place where the North and the South meet the West, St. Louis is ground zero for nineteenth-century manifestations of settler colonialism and emancipation.

[6] Judith Butler, *Frames of War: When Is Life Grievable?* (London: Verso, 2016), 1.

[7] Nicholas Mirzoeff, *The Right to Look: A Counterhistory of Visuality* (Durham, NC: Duke University Press, 2011), xiii.

St. Louis is the place from which the majority of US soldiers were deployed to wage wars of Native genocide and dispossession, thus paving the way for settlers who believed occupation was their god-granted right. St. Louis is also the place where Manifest Destiny was conceptualized as the natural, divinely appointed progress of the white race into the West.[8] The movements of the soldiers and settlers from St. Louis who pushed Native peoples out of their ancestral homelands here and elsewhere were also concurrent with the movements of the enslaved people, fugitives, and freemen to and through St. Louis. Missouri's historically contentious relationship with slavery includes the *Dred Scott* case, which challenged the legitimacy of the institution within a free state. Scott's appeal for freedom was denied despite being defended by an attorney with ties to the Free Soil Party.

Headquartered in St. Louis, the abolitionist political party fought for the West to be a slavery-free zone where African Americans could also participate in the dispossession of Native peoples in settler-defined notions of freedom. Thus, at the intersection of these coeval histories is a paradox that lies at the core of the white-American rhetoric of freedom: as it has been historically defined since 1776, the movement into states of freedom is an opportunity to participate in the capture and containment of others, an absorption into violent occupations of the settled nation-state.

Analyses of policing practice and the continued assault on Black men across the United States demonstrate the various degrees by which freedom as a concept has been unequally applied and distributed. The contemporary prison abolitionist movement historically tied itself to the abolition of slavery and the creation of "slavery by another name" through the implementation of Jim Crow laws. As Adolph L. Reed, Jr.'s book title succinctly demonstrates, these methods have inscribed an abolitionist history of *The South*.[9] But the South is only one aspect of St. Louis's geographic identity, an identity built through reorienting the land into mapped representations of the settled nation. An abolitionism of the South at its intersection with the West, instead, contends with the space in which abolitionist movements and decolonial and unsettling projects have historically missed each other.

[8] Though John L. O'Sullivan first used the term "Manifest Destiny" to describe US expansionism in an editorial called "Annexation" from 1846 (John O'Sullivan, "Annexation," *The United States Magazine and Democratic Review* 17 (1845): 5–6, 9–10), it was Missouri Senator Thomas Hart Benton who would popularize the idea and move it into practice. Benton articulates that "extinction, has been the fate of all people who have found themselves in the trace of the advancing Whites, and civilization" in his May 28, 1846 speech to the US Senate, available here: https://pages.uoregon.edu/mjdennis/courses/hst469_benton.htm.

[9] Adolph L. Reed, Jr, *The South: Jim Crow and Its Afterlives* (London: Verso, 2022).

For Counterpublic 2023, I built upon Walter Johnson's assertions in *The Broken Heart of America* that the eviction of Black communities from St. Louis City to the outlying St. Louis County, where Ferguson lies, operates by the same mechanism that dispossessed Osage, Fox, Sauk, and other Native peoples ancestrally belonging to the region and beyond it.[10] To look through the city's "Gateway to the West" through abolitionist frameworks is to see occupation as a method of capture, settler colonialism as maintaining the borders of containment, and the nation-state as a state of carcerality.[11] By expanding abolitionist frameworks through Native American struggles for sovereignty, I contend that the prison system cannot be abolished until the nation-settler-state, in this case, the United States, for which it acts as an extension, is also abolished.

My work to bridge decolonial and abolitionist thinking has necessitated a turn to the ecological to understand the ways the land itself, and the human and nonhuman animals and plants who live upon and within it, are entangled in the same struggles. Thus, the artists I have invited from and to St. Louis all use materials taken for granted in public spaces, such as dirt, clay, wood, plants, bees, sound, light, water, and memories, to construct their work. These artists attune us to the elements that constitute the land in order to understand vacancy and eviction in new ways. Juan William Chávez, Raven Chacon, Anita and Nokosee Fields, General Sisters (Ginger Brooks Takahashi and Dana Bishop-Root) and their St. Louis collaborators, Cannupa Hanska Luger, Jaune Quick-to-See Smith, jackie sumell, X, and I attempt to make apparent the traces of carcerality written into St. Louis's urban spaces and to see behind these imposed frames so that the city may present the many manifestations of itself as itself.

Counterpublic 2023 is also an experiment in finding other ways to interact with place outside of the tendencies that perennial exhibitions of contemporary public art persist. Bird-watching and many biennials have some things in common: they both assume that the right to see is natural, and in doing so, often deny the mutuality of looking. At their worst, bi/triennials invite specific types of murmurations. Viewers are invited on scavenger hunts throughout a city or ushered through sites of trauma with art as their guides. The Bank Swallow and a range of anticolonial and Indigenous scholars from Édouard Glissant to Audra Simpson and Kim TallBear, whose writing shows us how sight has historically been leveraged as a weapon, remind us: to be unseen and unknowable is also right.[12] As a curator, my choice to reveal or disclose before the invitation to look is granted, then, is an ethical question.

Invitations to look are not invitations to share.

I was invited to look at St. Louis and to invite artists to look at and respond to St. Louis in public art installations. What we found together were spaces too precarious to be shown. For instance, the locations of local plants that are framed as weeds or invasive and are under order by the city to be removed when found in fear of their potential to take over spaces by growing beyond human desires for order.[13]

[10] Walter Johnson, *The Broken Heart of America: St. Louis and the Violent History of the United States* (New York: Basic Books, 2020).

[11] Balraj Gil's dissertation "The Politics of Confinement: Indigenous Homelands, Imperial Duress, and Incarceration in the Deep North" (Harvard University, 2022) examines Native incarceration in what Indigenous activist and scholar Winona LaDuke and others have come to call "the Deep North." In the expanse from the Dakotas to the Yukon, the discrimination and segregation of the reservation system creates injustices comparable to "the Deep South" under Jim Crow and today. See also Aaron Labarre, "NoDAPL: Standing Rock and 'The Deep North,'" *Al Jazeera*, January 17, 2017, https://www.aljazeera.com/features/2017/1/17/nodapl-standing-rock-and-the-deep-north.

[12] Édouard Glissant, *Poetics of Relation*, trans. Betsy Wing (Ann Arbor: University of Michigan Press, 1997); Audra Simpson, *Mohawk Interruptus: Political Life Across the Borders of Settler States* (Durham, NC: Duke University Press, 2014); Kim TallBear, *Native American DNA: Tribal Belonging and the False Promise of Genetic Belonging* (Minneapolis: University of Minnesota Press, 2013).

[13] Joan Iverson Nassauer, "Messy Ecosystems, Orderly Frames," *Landscape Journal* 14, no. 2 (Fall 1995): 161–70.

These framings enlist plants within systems of regulation that police them in ways that echo the monitoring and policing of people in the city. Thus, houses that have been leveled after property blighting—a process by which the city and developers purchased houses in primarily Black communities with the intention of moving those houses and the surrounding neighborhoods into states of dereliction, paving the way for urban renewal—are optioned to neighbors who can own the lot by keeping it mowed.[14] The locations of these plants are protected by the Native and Black women who continue to use them in the making of medicine. These women impart the responsibility of not disclosing to those of us invited to look, and we serve as accomplices by continuing to help these plants escape sight.

In other spaces, we saw how human actions calcified sequential violences into sedimentary layers. Sugarloaf Mound, the southern terminus of Counterpublic 2023, is one such place. Once called "Mound City" because of the 100-plus flat-topped ceremonial and burial mounds built in the region over 1,600 years (before the arrival of the Spanish in 1541), only Sugarloaf remains in St. Louis. Sugarloaf survives because of the house a settler family built atop it. For over a century, this family had access to the cave system beneath the mound and enjoyed eastern views of the Mississippi River and Cahokia, toward which Sugarloaf was oriented. Big Mound to the north, a mound that was longer and wider than a football field and over three stories high, would have registered at most as a glint of the medallion that memorializes it. Big Mound was slowly dismantled over the course of the nineteenth century; its dirt was returned from its assembled form to the ground and used to pave the way for the railroad that would help move settlers west.

Sixteen mounds in that direction are also not visible from the top of Sugarloaf after 1904. They were razed and the bodies buried within them removed, cleared to create the fairground for the St. Louis World's Fair in Forest Park. Using Sugarloaf as a viewing platform, though, negates its integrity by transforming it into a cartographic device. Today, the invitation to look at the city from the top of Sugarloaf Mound is not one that is easily granted.

[14] St. Louis's "Mow to Own" program inherits its logic from John Locke's labor theory of property, as described in his *Second Treatise of Government* (1689). More information on the "Mow to Own" program is available at: https://www.stlouis-mo.gov/government/departments/sldc/real-estate/mow-to-own-program.cfm.

In 2009, the Osage Nation purchased the house, and with it, Sugarloaf Mound. In doing so, they reinstated Sugarloaf's status as a sacred site, protecting it with a fence. The sign attached to this fence alerts all who pass it that to walk beyond this fence is to trespass on the Osage Nation in recognition of how Sugarloaf has been removed from the confines of the nation-state through the very methods—property—that constitute it. In addition to these overt actions, the Osage Nation also initiated a series of undoings, including dismantling the house and reabsorbing the mound into the Nation, thereby expanding Osage territories back to their ancestral homeland. In the place where the house once stood, plants that would be considered weeds elsewhere grow tall.

Withdrawal is a backstep forward.

In weighing the various possibilities for integrating art into this site, withdrawal from acting was the only option for engagement. With the exception of some of the dematerialized aspects of conceptual practices, artmaking is an additive process. This deficit model operates by adding thought and material to a site to actualize artistic intent. To add to Sugarloaf would be a form of artistic trespass that negates the mound as an entity in its own right. Other gestures would decorate it, turn it into a tourist destination, or tell histories that aren't for any one person to share. What can be communicated in words and materials doesn't always intersect with what *should* be communicated. Instead, Sugarloaf and a few other sites that I will not disclose here were removed from a list of possible sites for artistic additions, and live within the exhibition on their own terms.

While the projects I curated for Counterpublic 2023 aren't always subtractive, the results of their additions are resistant to seeing and, oftentimes, unrepresentable. The artists conjure the negative space of absences—of people, plants, animals, and histories of human action and interaction—within the spheres that they make apparent. Whether ephemeral, inaccessible, invisible, imperceptible, immaterial, or uncapturable, each artwork is conditional upon the mutuality of looking. Artworks flicker between the shadow of a wing and a flash of white that invites us as their viewers into different ways of being in relation to the ground of St. Louis and beyond. Instead of responding to the city and its histories, the artists I worked with make offerings in service to it and to the visitors who will murmurate through the exhibition, inviting possibilities for a different way of looking at the physical spaces, such as lots that appear to be abandoned, between installations. Moreover, these artists invite us into speculative, historically specific conceptualization of various befores and many possible paths beyond the nation-state. At Counterpublic 2023, we invite visitors to the exhibition, not to search or wait for, but to open to possibilities of flicker.

Negative space is not empty space.

Jaune Quick-to-See Smith (Enrolled Salish member of the Confederated Salish and Kootenai Tribes of the Flathead Reservation) asks us to look beyond the flattened space of the United States map represented in her painting to reimagine the terrain of the land. The painting is installed at Monaco, an artist-run cooperative in the center of the State Streets neighborhood, an area of town so called because its north-south streets are named for US states. As her painting shows us, many of these state names written on the street signage are appropriations of the place names used by the Native peoples who live in those regions. Derived from looking at the land, words such as Missouri and Nebraska conjure images of the "muddy" and "flat" rivers that move through those places. In these state names, we also find "allies" (Dakota) and "friends" (Texas)—Native peoples who traded with each other and later with settlers. In the word Wisconsin, we can see the flash of wings in "holes in the banks of a stream in which birds nest."

Translated into a broadside, Quick-to-See-Smith's painting aids visitors in renavigating the State Streets neighborhood through Native descriptions of place. In curatorial intervention, I use the format of the exhibition label to adapt these street signs by bringing forward some of the meanings and histories hidden within them.

Benton Park, at the center of the State Streets neighborhood, is named for the US senator who engineered Manifest Destiny and westward expansion, making St. Louis the place from which nearly all of the soldiers engaged in the nineteenth-century wars of removal, and many settlers traveling west, were deployed. Raven Chacon (Diné) contends with this history by appropriating the military drum in a performance around Benton Park that unites the neighborhood in a sonic manifestation of community agency. For *Drum Grid*, drummers are dispersed through the State Streets neighborhood to move the drum's call through space. The hit of one drum initiates a cascading of responses from other drummers in earshot, who respond in turn to make sonic connections to other drummers positioned throughout the neighborhood in a transmission chain. Neither performers nor viewers can see each other all at once, meaning that the performance of *Drum Grid* is uncapturable in its wholeness in both image and sound recording, a quality that activates the potential of a community to gather unseen.

Return cycles the past into the future.

Immaterial installations by X and Cannupa Hanska Luger engage with the terrain that Quick-to-See-Smith's painting brings into view. Using an augmented reality platform, Luger (Mandan/Hidatsa/Arikara/Lakota) transforms handheld devices into mechanisms for accessing a real-time digital overlay along St. Louis's horizon line. Through mobile phones and tablets, viewers are invited to watch seven oversized figures positioned at the edge of the city. Each *Midéegaadi* (the word for buffalo in the Hidatsa language) activates seven different artist-created sets of horned regalia that emphasize the buffalo's physical attributes. In a continuous looping performative action, the *Midéegaadi* invite the buffalo to return to St. Louis. Over the course of the exhibition, Luger's virtual invitation to the buffalo becomes increasingly accessible from locales beyond St. Louis as its movement through digital space amplifies its call.

Returning the buffalo to St. Louis would necessitate the return of grasslands that defined the region before it was developed into a city and unlocking the twenty-nine dams placed along the Mississippi River, to provide the plants that feed the buffalo and the animals themselves with water. Those dams, years of consecutive drought, and the industrialization of the river have pulled the Mississippi away from the stone that designated its edge.

A light and sound installation by X (Coushatta/Chamorro) on the bluffs below Jefferson Avenue is a blueprint for returning the Mississippi River to the stone it carved over millennia. X invites visitors to see the contemporary manifestations of industry positioned along the river. In *(a river) will flow*, X digitally approximates moonlight as it dances off the river's surface to reflect onto the bluffs. Wave patterns of light and water mix with the craggy surface of the stone to call attention to the river's absence. X's intervention returns the industrialized area to the shape of the river's design and rescales viewers as one part of a larger ecosystem, with the potential to intervene in the river's future through acts of unbuilding.

Memories can re-member.

Viewed from the street, *WayBack* by Anita Fields (Osage/Muscogee) and Nokosee Fields (Osage/Cherokee/Muscogee), a mother and son who collaborated on their project for Counterpublic 2023, appears as a horizontal expanse that mirrors the landfilled quarry on which it is built. Clay and earth were removed from this site to build Sugarloaf Mound next to it, and the quarry was further excavated by settlers to construct the bricks that define St. Louis's architecture. Traversing the ground brings the surface of dozens of low wooden platforms, each embellished with patterns that reference Osage ribbon work, patterns that themselves reference Osage worldviews of sky, water, and earth. Nokosee Fields's sound piece, which emanates from below the platforms, reflects the philosophies imparted by these elements in a composition that interweaves wind instruments with field recordings. The platforms are modeled after those that are found at Osage events in their displaced territories in Oklahoma. There, they are recognized as designated spaces to gather, relax, talk, sleep, and prepare for celebrations. In St. Louis, forty platforms hold space for people to gather in proximity to Sugarloaf and consider the earth from which the mound was constructed, the sky that unfolds above the platforms, the sound of the Mississippi River on the banks below the quarry, the wind that flows through the surrounding trees that transformed first into breath, then into music in the sound composition.

For *Movement Transmissions*, General Sisters collaborators Ginger Brooks Takahashi and Dana Bishop-Root invited four artists—Dail Chambers, Dustin Gibson, Basmin Nadra, and Xochi Plancarte—involved in the city's justice movements to repopulate spaces along Jefferson Avenue with their memories. These memories enliven images of people, buildings, and actions that are no longer there and invite a consideration of the plants that occupy those places instead. These plants also have stories to tell. Together, plants and people highlighted in General Sisters's project co-narrate histories of displacement, carcerality, and environmental racism as well as joys found in communities and solidarity-building.

Visitors are invited to explore open pathways constructed of words that suggest but do not designate routes. These words are transmitted via General Sisters's collaborators themselves in a series of walking tours and public performances in the physical spaces in which their memories occur. In the absence of organized events, transcriptions aid visitors in self-navigating space. Words printed along Counterpublic 2023's wayfinding signage offer prompts that translate the stories that plants tell along these sites and are opportunities for visitors to consider what plants grow along Jefferson Avenue and why.

Imagining possibilities is a precursor to repair.

Throughout Jefferson Avenue, visitors encounter sites where houses have been leveled and plots transformed into neatly mowed lawns awaiting development. Juan William Chávez invites visitors into his teaching garden, where they gain experiences that encourage them to look in a new way at sites presumed to be vacant. Chávez's garden is an artistic assemblage composed of native pollinator plants, disassembled honeybee hives, bricks, and scraps of wood—all materials that the 4,000 species of native bees in the United States need to thrive and elements that make a landscape appear to be neglected. Unlike their European counterpart, the honeybee, most native bees do not live in hives, nor do they produce honey in quantities large enough to capitalize upon. These qualities make native bees more vulnerable to habitat destruction and less noticed in the public imagination and bee conservation efforts. Through workshops and skill-sharing sessions, Chavez reorients perceptions about bees and the spaces in which they live, drawing parallels between bee and human habitat loss. Though the garden provides his project with a material form and the workshops provide a mechanism of transmission, Chávez sculpts social space into a network for stewarding bees. Returning from the garden to Jefferson Avenue is an opportunity to reorient assumptions about vacancy.

Chávez's garden is located in his Northside Workshop, a restored brick building once dismantled for its parts during a period of disenfranchisement of St. Louis's Black communities. Bricks from his and other "brick-eaten" buildings were sold down the Mississippi to the wealthy residents of Baton Rouge and New Orleans to build neo-plantation-style homes. New Orleans-based artist jackie sumell, whose work entwines prison abolition with plant justice, returns these bricks to St. Louis in a three-part material intervention in conversation with three moments in the city's history. One aspect of sumell's project—a private ceremony of returning crushed bricks first, to dirt and then, to the quarries from which the clay used to make them was taken—is unviewable. Even if the sites of this act of brick rematriation were disclosed, the action of returning dirt to dirt would be imperceptible. The crushed dirt is then mixed with sand from the Mississippi River to create a "free soil" distributed throughout the exhibition. Inspired by the Free Soil Party, sumell stages her own *Free Soil Party*. In a reparative gesture to the imperfections of historical abolitionist movements, sumell mixes the soil with the seeds of plants that support native bees and uses it to guerilla garden around Du-Good Chemical Laboratory, the site where Lincoln Duiguid, an independent Black chemist, innovated healing medicines from plants. Visitors to Counterpublic 2023 are invited to take and use the *Free Soil* to seed bomb sites of their choosing.

Misapprehension within the sphere of appearance has dire consequences.

While traversing Jefferson Avenue for Counterpublic 2023, viewers encounter the same plants in ideologically distinct spaces. As multiple artistic interventions in St. Louis's public spaces demonstrate, to find a landscape shorn of plants in some places along Jefferson Avenue is to encounter labor-based claims of property in places where Native and Black peoples have been displaced from the city limits at various points in its history. North of Delmar on Jefferson Avenue, the same plants have historically been qualified as weeds, though recent scholarly attempts to recognize them as sites of biodiversity have reframed them as "urban prairies." This semantic reclamation of evacuated areas of the city has created opportunities for protecting the plants through community land trusts.[15] The same plants that are policed from growing in some areas of the city appear in other parts as components in intentional rewilding and prairie restoral projects, where they are stewarded into self-sustained growth within designated areas. These same plants grow tall on Sugarloaf, in a reclamation of the Mound as an extension of the Osage Nation on their ancestral land from their displaced territories in Oklahoma. Marketed as neighborhood beautification in the name of ecological restoration, these rewilding projects prompt questions about the term *restoration* itself. Restored to what? When and for whom? Who is restored in the process?

The conceptual frames under which plants grow—or rather, are allowed to grow or not—are governed by different regulations depending on who shares space with these plants and how those people are perceived by governing bodies.[16] In other words, how space is apprehended, and the plants, birds, and animals that live there, echoes how people are apprehended within those spaces. Judith Butler's words are worth repeating here again: "The frames through which we apprehend . . . do not unilaterally decide the conditions of appearance but their aim is nevertheless to delimit the sphere of appearance itself."[17]

Apprehend is a complicated word. It appears throughout Butler's writings about grief and grievability. She contends that the question of whose lives are grievable is contingent upon seeing those lives as injured or lost, conditions that necessitate understanding those lives as living in the first place. Here, she uses apprehend to mean *understand*, the second definition of the word. It is more commonly used to mean to *arrest*, specifically "to seize (someone) by legal authority and take into custody."[18] We, who live outside of St. Louis, have witnessed the dire consequences of misapprehension (misunderstanding) of bodies and intent in St. Louis's spaces. Figuratively, arrest means *to be stopped*, as in the swallow's appearance arrested me, and it also means literally, *to stop*.

How can we be otherwise?

[15] Christopher G. Prener, Taylor Harris Braswell, and Daniel J. Monti, "St. Louis's 'Urban Prairie': Vacant Land and the Potential for Revitalization," *Journal of Urban Affairs* 42, no. 3 (2018): 371–89, https://doi.org/10.1080/07352166.2018.1474079.

[16] In her study of the implementation of broken-windows policing practices in St. Louis, Jodi Rios writes about "the interdependencies between race and space and the powerful role spatial imaginaries play in producing racialized bodies in and through space—how bodies code/de-code space and how space codes/de-codes bodies." Jodi Rios, *Black Lives and Spatial Matters: Policing Blackness and Practicing Freedom in Suburban St. Louis* (Ithaca: Cornell University Press, 2022), 18.

[17] Butler, *Frames of War*, 1.

[18] *Oxford English Dictionary*, svv. "apprehend" and "arrest," accessed November 15, 2022, https://languages.oup.com/google-dictionary-en/.

Raven Chacon

CURATOR:
RISA PULEO

LOCATION:
BENTON PARK AND
STATE STREETS NEIGHBORHOOD

In his practice as a composer, musician, and artist, Raven Chacon (Diné) brings our attention to the spaces in which we listen and view performances of music and art to question the ground upon which those assemblies take place. Among the places Chacon has challenged in his solo and collaborative work are a Catholic cathedral, the US-Mexico border, sites of Native massacre and displacement, and the land of the United States itself. In each of these places, Chacon unearths the sounds of colonial violence buried within them. The role of women as sound-makers and struggle leaders is also central to Chacon's recent works and subverts the patriarchal structures of Empire to the matriarchal lineages of many Native communities. For example, the palpable hum of silence created by a group of water protectors led by elder Indigenous women animates an image of their confrontation with the police at the 2017 Standing Rock protests of the Dakota Access Pipeline (*Silent Choir*, 2017–2021). Songs sung by Diné, Yuchi, and Seminole women on their ancestral homelands connect the violence of forced removal of people to the extraction of elements from those same sites. The choir of women's voices in *Three Songs* (2021) contends with the sharp snap of the snare drum, an instrument associated with the US military reclaimed as an Indigenous hand drum. In St. Louis, Chacon's sonic and performative interventions provide new models for assembling in Benton Park, a space where, historically, a critical mass of people has served as a visual sign of brute force.

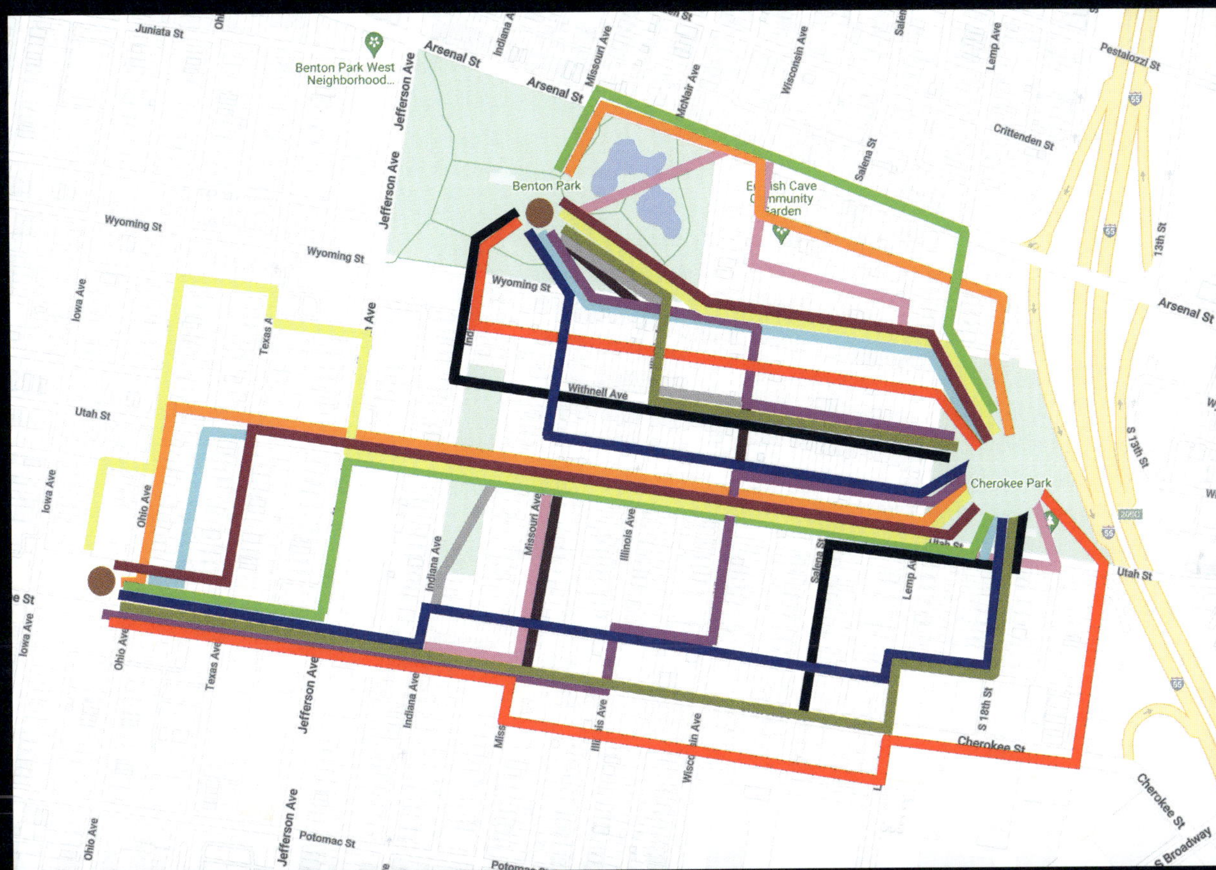

Raven Chacon
Music for 13 Paths, 2021–ongoing
Score, sound installation, performance: 13 performers, 13 wind chimes, equally divided within an octave; walking plan adapted to the Benton Park neighborhood of St. Louis

Benton Park is bounded on the north by Arsenal Street, so named because it led to the US Army's stores of munitions. Before the Civil War, St. Louis was the site from which soldiers involved in all wars of removal from 1826 to 1865 were deployed. After the war, when westward expansion became a shared goal for both the Union and Confederacy, St. Louis became the headquarters of the Army's Department of the West and the site in which politically divided soldiers, Black and white, could reunite under the common cause of genocide and dispossession. On their war hunts, these soldiers also blazed paths for settlers en route to California, Oregon, and the Southwest to follow. Given this history, it is fitting, then, that the park is named for Thomas Hart Benton, the Missouri senator, proto-Christian nationalist, and westward expansionist who implanted the idea of Manifest Destiny into the American psyche.

Under Benton's "sooner or later they all must go" policies, Native peoples in all directions surrounding St. Louis, including the Osage, Sauk, Fox, Delaware, and others ancestrally born from Missouri, were removed to reservation lands.[1] Many of the streets surrounding Benton Park are named for the Native tribes that Benton and the armies of soldiers stationed in St. Louis forcibly displaced. The names Cherokee, Winnebago, Chippewa, Miami, Osage, and more have been appropriated as the names running east to west in a neighborhood colloquially called the "States Streets" because all of the north-south streets are named for US states. The result of this spatial organizing logic is the symbolic impasse of Native peoples and the forces of displacement at every intersection in a microcosm of Indian removal across the United States.

In *Music for 13 Paths*, Chacon challenges the spatial organization of the neighborhoods with an intervention into the organizing systems of music. The scale is a twelve-note equal-tempered system. As the foundation of Western musical arrangements, it displaced other ways of organizing sounds after it was imported into colonized spaces. To create the performance-installation *Music for 13 Paths*, Chacon subdivided the space of the scale into thirteen, instead of twelve, divisions. He then hand-tuned thirteen chimes according to his reorganized system. For the inaugural event of Counterpublic 2023, thirteen collaborators walk the chimes from different parts of the State Streets neighborhood where surveillance cameras are located, where the sounds of the chimes' movements issue a warning about the invisible eyes watching.

[1] Walter Johnson, *The Broken Heart of America: St. Louis and the Violent History of the United States* (New York: Basic Books, 2020), 52.

Participants meet atop the largest of many undulating hills in Benton Park. Though they approximate the Indigenous mounds still present throughout St. Louis when Benton Park was landscaped in 1878, the aesthetically arranged landfills, instead, recreate the image of the rolling English countryside. Installed in a half arc atop the tallest of these settler mounds, the reunited chimes suggest the negative space of an arch over the curve of the hill. Their shape is an anti-monument of St. Louis's famed Gateway Arch, which celebrates expansion and the settlers who moved through the city to populate the West. Played by the wind, the resulting composition carries the dissonance of the dismantled musical system throughout the neighborhood to suggest alternative ordering systems.

Additionally, Chacon's collaborative performance *Drum Grid* (2010) is a temporary reappropriation of the State Streets neighborhood's grid for an instance of sonic activism. The Counterpublic 2023 iteration of the performance is the largest iteration of the work to date, with forty drummers from the city's musical community and high school marching bands participating. Each drummer is stationed at one of forty different corners throughout the State Streets neighborhood. The hit of one drum by one drummer sends a call out to other drummers who stand within hearing distance; each call invites a cascade of sequential responses from other drummers deeper in the neighborhood. Sound moves through the streets and also invites surrounding buildings to participate in the sonic manifestation of community. Echoes that bounce off buildings contribute another level of sonic input for drummers to respond to and an additional layer of sound to the organic composition. Over time, the call morphs into a new arrangement and is returned to the originating drummer, who begins the process again. Dispersed over a one-mile square area, *Drum Grid* is a composition that surrounds both active viewers and passive street-goers in an experience that cannot be captured in photographic or sound recordings in its entirety. The potential for this dispersed ensemble to initiate a warning, incite a sonic revolt, or unite in celebration reinstates the power of the community to initiate change.

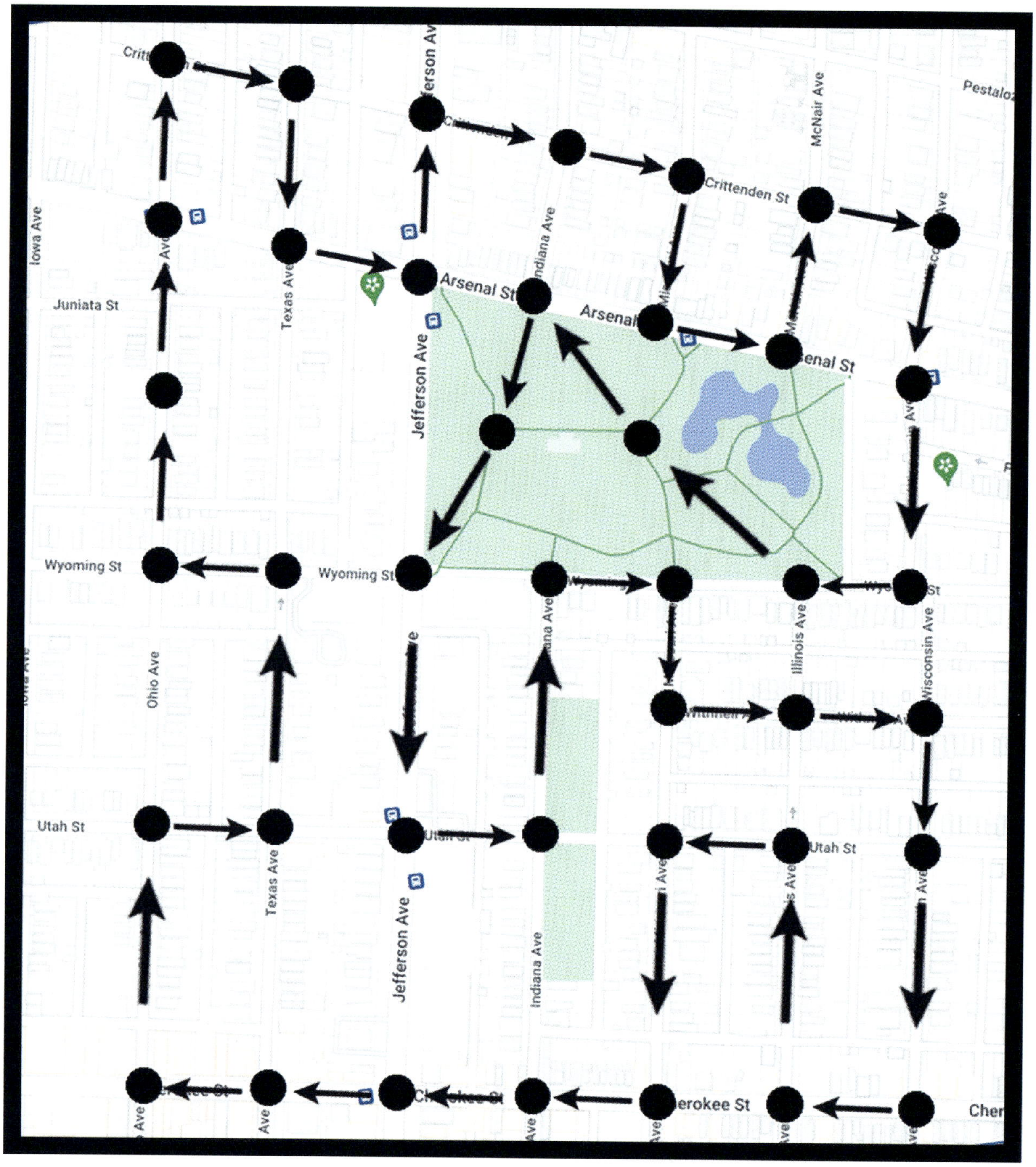

Raven Chacon
Drum Grid, 2010–ongoing
Community collaboration, performance, video, score adapted to represent the 40 drummers, shown here each positioned on a street corner of St. Louis's Benton Park neighborhood

Juan William Chávez

CURATOR:
RISA PULEO

LOCATION:
NORTHSIDE WORKSHOP

St. Louis-based artist Juan William Chávez began his decade-long interspecies collaboration with the bees at the former site of Pruitt-Igoe in North St. Louis. One of the largest urban housing complexes of its time, Pruitt-Igoe housed ten thousand people (mostly Black and mostly displaced from the demolished neighborhood of Mill Creek Valley) in 2,870 apartments across thirty three eleven-story buildings. Generally regarded as the place where a modernism that aimed to solve human problems through design died, Pruitt-Igoe was demolished over a four-year span between 1972 and 1976.[1] In its place, a forest grew. And in that forest, honeybees established their model for group living. Like the architects of Pruitt-Igoe, the bees created their own superstructure; however, theirs was based on collaboration and not containment. Drawing parallels between colony collapse disorder and issues facing shrinking cities, like environmental racism and housing segregation, Chávez's social practice models ways to reorient perceptions of places perceived to be vacant.

[1] Charles Jencks, *The Language of Post-Modern Architecture* (New York: Rizzoli, 1977).

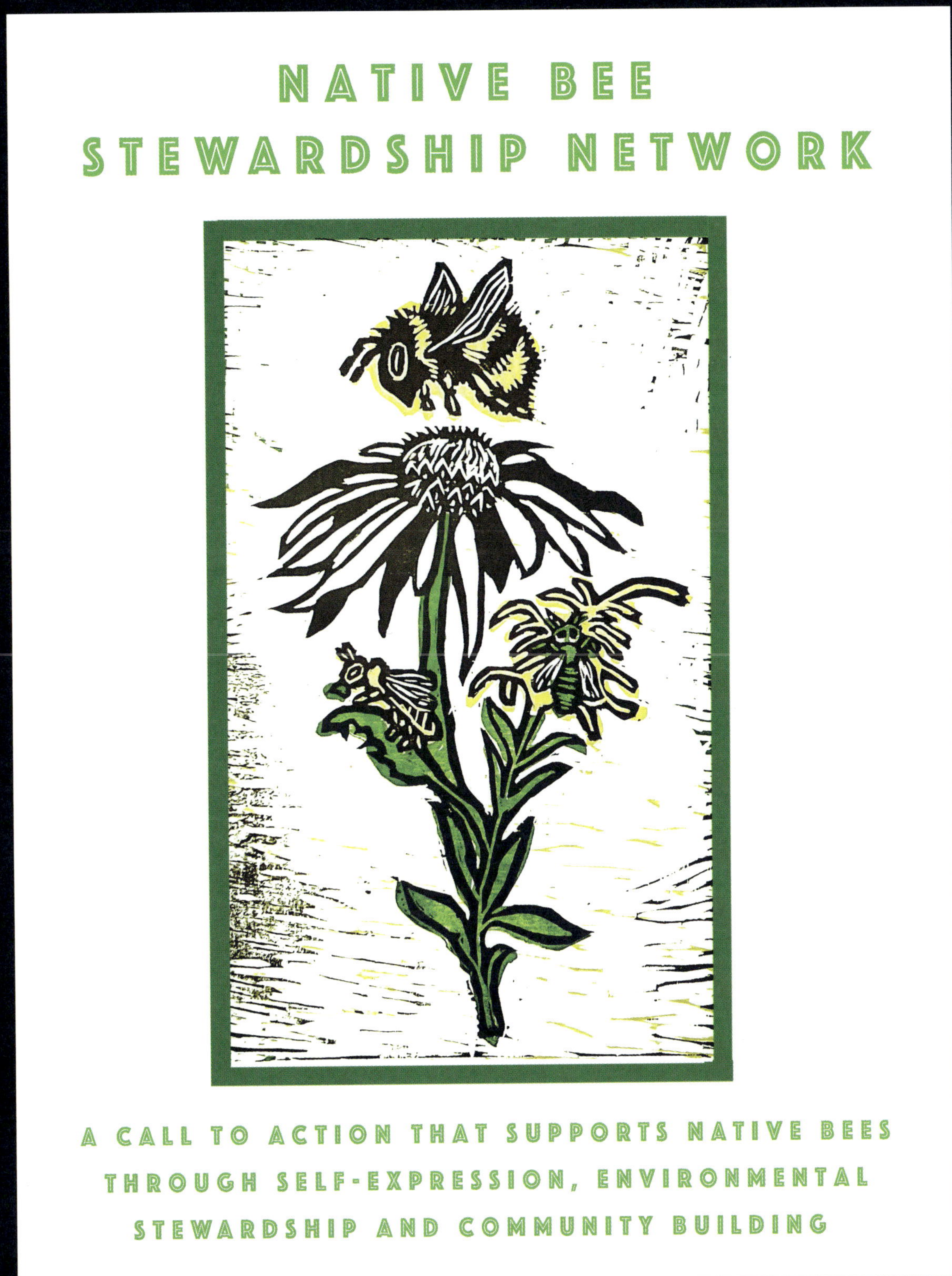

Juan William Chávez
Native Bee Stewardship Network, 2022
Zine cover page, woodblock print, digital drawing

In *Decolonizing the Hive: Native Bee Stewardship Network*, Chávez builds upon his relationships with bees and North St. Louis's histories by expanding prevailing assumptions of conservation. The honeybees, who are not native to North America, occupy a singular presence in the public perception of bees, eclipsing their 4,000-plus native counterparts, 400 species of which live in St. Louis. Valued as commodity producers, honeybees are conserved through hive structures designed to manage, manipulate, and control honey production. Native bees, on the other hand, do not make honey in quantities large enough to capitalize upon. Instead, their value as pollinators of 80 percent of native plants is their maintenance of the diversity of life and their support of food systems outside of monoculture crops. Ninety percent of the bee species indigenous to North America do not build hives, nor do they live in groups. Rather, solitary bees build nests in the landscape or make homes of elements like hollow plant stems or bricks that they find within it. Because they are at increased risk for habitat loss and coming into contact with environmental pollutants, native bees are more vulnerable and at higher risk of going extinct. Scott Black, of the Xerces Society for Invertebrate Conservation, sums up the problem of bee conservation in current form succinctly: "Keeping honey bees to 'save the bees' is like raising chickens to save birds."[2]

"Decolonizing the hive," then, means prioritizing native bees in conservation efforts. To do so would require stewarding bees in their stewardship of native plants in the places where both are found. Bee stewardship is environmental stewardship. The bee sanctuary built by Chávez at his Northside Workshop is a chemical-free native plant garden that invites native bees to thrive on their own terms. Sculptural interventions made from disassembled honeybee hives provide ample places for native bees to burrow while a variety of pollinator habitats provide different types of native bees the opportunity to feast. Walking paths and sitting areas create spaces for people to be with bees and reorient their relationship to fear. In addition to materializing the presence of bees, Chávez's garden is a conduit that transmits information about native bees to audiences and key stakeholders who can intervene in native bee futures in their own backyards. Knowledge and skill sharing are the foundation of Chávez's stewardship of people and communities. Visitors to the garden have opportunities to learn to make their own bee sanctuaries and to recognize native bee sanctuaries in the world.

[2] Laura Tangley, "The Truth About Honey Bees," *National Wildlife*, June 1, 2021, https://www.nwf.org/Home/Magazines/National-Wildlife/2021/June-July/Gardening/Honey-Bees.

Though the native bee sanctuary is sited at Chávez's Northside Workshop, the project invites visitors and participants to reexamine their assumptions about vacancy throughout the city. As rural agriculture is overtaken by industrial methods, native bees have taken refuge in urban environments and thrive especially in places where buildings have been demolished and people displaced. Research by biologists like bumblebee specialist Dr. Aimee Sue Dunlap at the University of Missouri, St. Louis shows that science cannot account for, observe, or measure the cryptic diversity that makes formerly occupied lots such rich life-support systems for native bees and plants. Empty lots are bee sanctuaries.[3] In this way, native bees challenge the colonial rhetoric of "emptiness" and "abandonment" used to justify dispossession and urban renewal projects and reanimate our perceptions of the land with liveliness and memories of different worlds. To recognize vacancy as sanctuary is to also remember the Native and Black lives that have been displaced, and ultimately to see the mechanisms of dispossession and intentional property blighting at work.

[3] Dr. Aimee Sue Dunlap (University of Missouri, St. Louis) in conversation with Juan William Chávez, July 12, 2021.

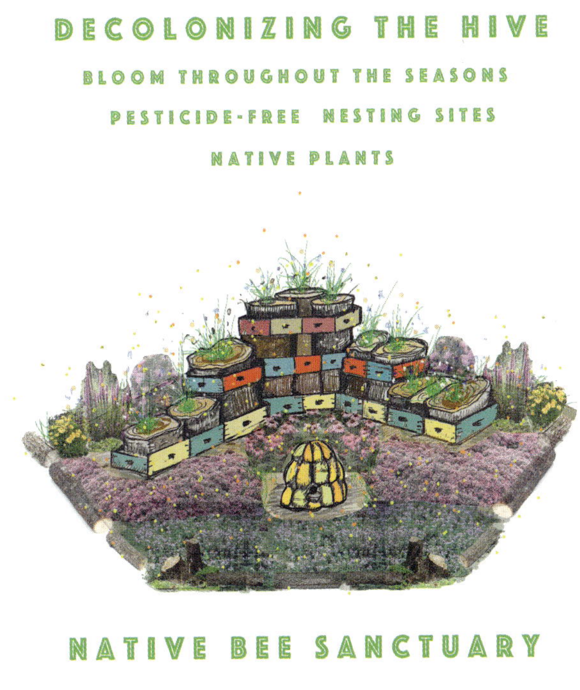

Juan William Chávez
Native Bee Sanctuary, 2022
Concept design, hand and digital drawing

Anita + Nokosee Fields

CURATOR:
RISA PULEO

LOCATION:
CLAY QUARRY NEXT TO SUGARLOAF MOUND AT 4434 OHIO AVENUE

Tulsa-based artist Anita Fields (Osage/Muscogee) interweaves Osage worldviews into her fabric and clay installations. Nokosee Fields (Osage/Cherokee/Muscogee) innovates traditional forms of Cherokee fiddling in his practice as a solo musician and member of the bands BOOJUM, the Onlies, and Hard Drive. During the height of the pandemic, Anita Fields invited people from Tulsa to draw or embroider messages on linen handkerchiefs and record voicemails that communicated their experiences of being physically displaced from their families and communities. To bridge the gaps in community created by quarantine, Fields wove these contributions together to create *In the Absence of Gathering* (2020–2021) and invited her son Nokosee to create a sound composition incorporating the voice recordings to accompany the installation. Their collaborative contribution to Counterpublic 2023, the community-activated installation *WayBack*, also uses materials to bridge physical distance and continues their thinking together about places of gathering and spaces of absence.

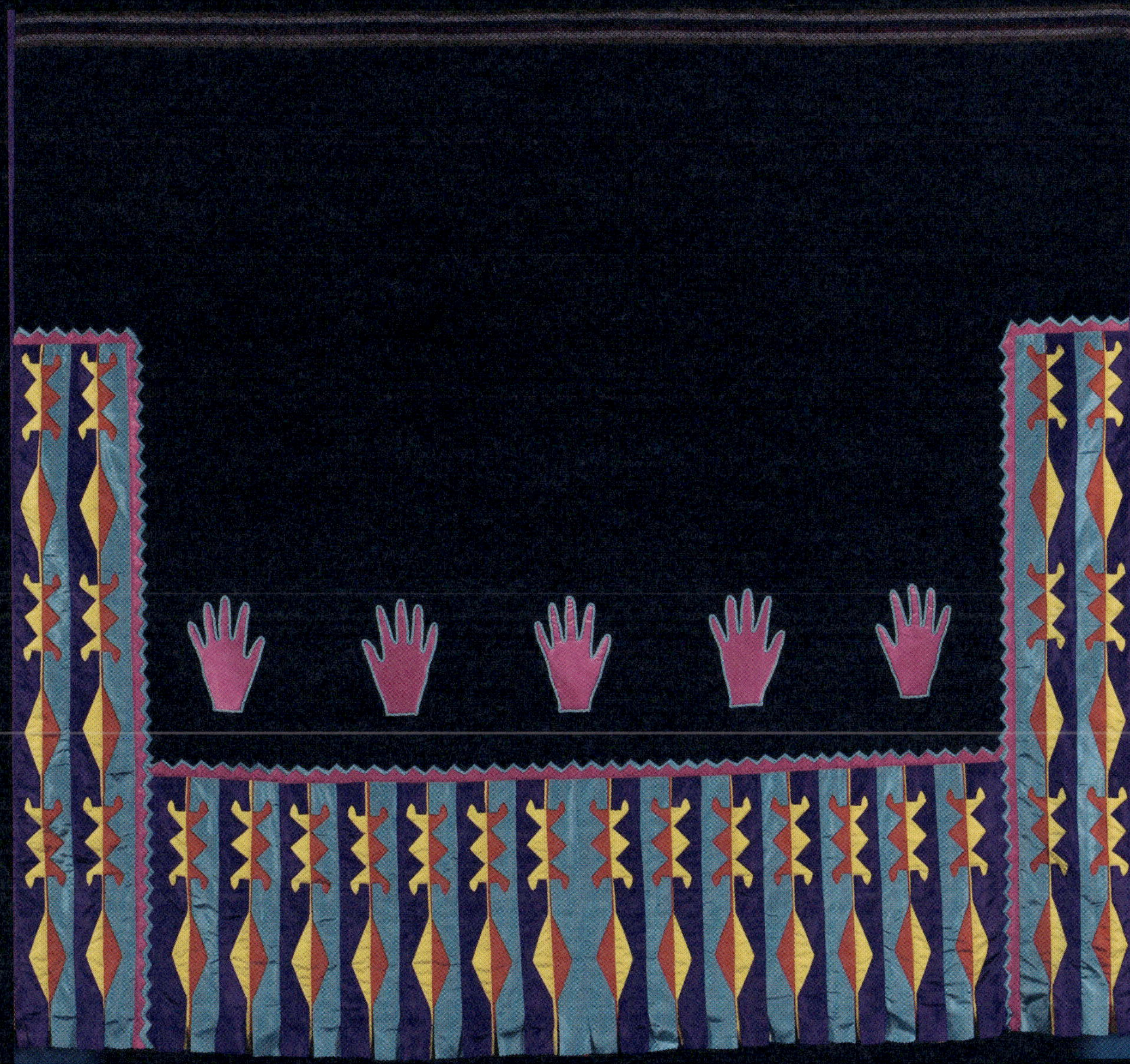

Anita Fields
Osage woman's ribbon-work hand blanket, 2002
Satin ribbon, thread, beads, and wool
Commission for National Cowboy and Western Heritage Museum collection

In St. Louis, the Fields invite visitors back into gathering in physical relation to each other, to Sugarloaf Mound, and to Osage ancestors, history, and legacy. The Fields chose the site of their installation because of its proximity to Sugarloaf Mound, which itself is oriented in relation to the Mississippi River. The last remaining mound structure in St. Louis, Sugarloaf was purchased by the Osage Nation in 2009. Through the auspices of property, the mound was reabsorbed into the Nation and extends Osage territory from the site of their displacement in Oklahoma back to their ancestral homeland in St. Louis. The green space next to Sugarloaf upon which the installation sits cannot be developed; it was once a quarry. The negative space created when the site was mined for clay-rich earth to make the bricks that give St. Louis its distinctive architecture—and, perhaps, to make Sugarloaf Mound itself—has since been filled in with land that the few neighbors in the area use as an unofficial public park. The sounds of the Mississippi River can be heard here and remind the Fields of the historical trade between Osage people and French settlers, who introduced the ribbons used in ribbon work to Osage communities in the earliest days of colonial settlement in Missouri. These multilayered material and cultural histories are interwoven into *WayBack*.

The square wooden platforms that the Fields installed near Sugarloaf Mound replicate those found in communal spaces and personal places of gathering across the Osage Nation. These platforms appear in Osage historical records and photographs when the Nation was displaced a second time from Kansas to their current home in Oklahoma. In this way, the platforms provided spaces of consistency that could be recognized by all regardless of changes in terrain. Their appearance in a landscape signals a threshold event, such as naming ceremonies, birthdays, weddings, sending soldiers to war, funerals, feasts, and other aspects of Osage cultural life. The platforms also appear prominently in Anita Fields's earliest memories. The artist remembers Osage elders who informally gathered to rest and find joyful reprieve in each other outside of the formal spaces of community gatherings.

In respect to the integrity of the sacred site and the continuum of knowledge passed down since St. Louis was Cahokia, the Fields position forty platforms in relation to the mound but also separate from it. Reverence is also offered in other ways. The platforms hover low to the ground in an echo of the site's horizontal expanse as to not to interrupt the space and shape of Sugarloaf Mound. Traversing the site brings the diamond shape in which they are arranged and the embellishments in clay and paint on their surfaces into view. Anita Fields referenced Osage ribbon-work patterns to create these designs in paint and clay, patterns which themselves give visual form to Osage worldviews and cosmologies. For *WayBack*, she draws from designs that reference Osage concepts of balance between the sky, earth, and water.

The sounds of these elements and the philosophies that they impart are woven into a sound composition by Nokosee Fields. During his near-constant travels, the composer and musician made field recordings from the various places that his performance schedule took him. He then mixed the sonic aspects of these elements and the philosophies contained within them into a composition for wind instruments that emanates from below the platforms.

Within Counterpublic 2023, the platforms offer spaces of reprieve for visitors who are invited to share space with Sugarloaf. After the exhibition, the platforms will travel from St. Louis, where they were made, to Tulsa, where they will be distributed to Osage community members to use in their own celebrations.

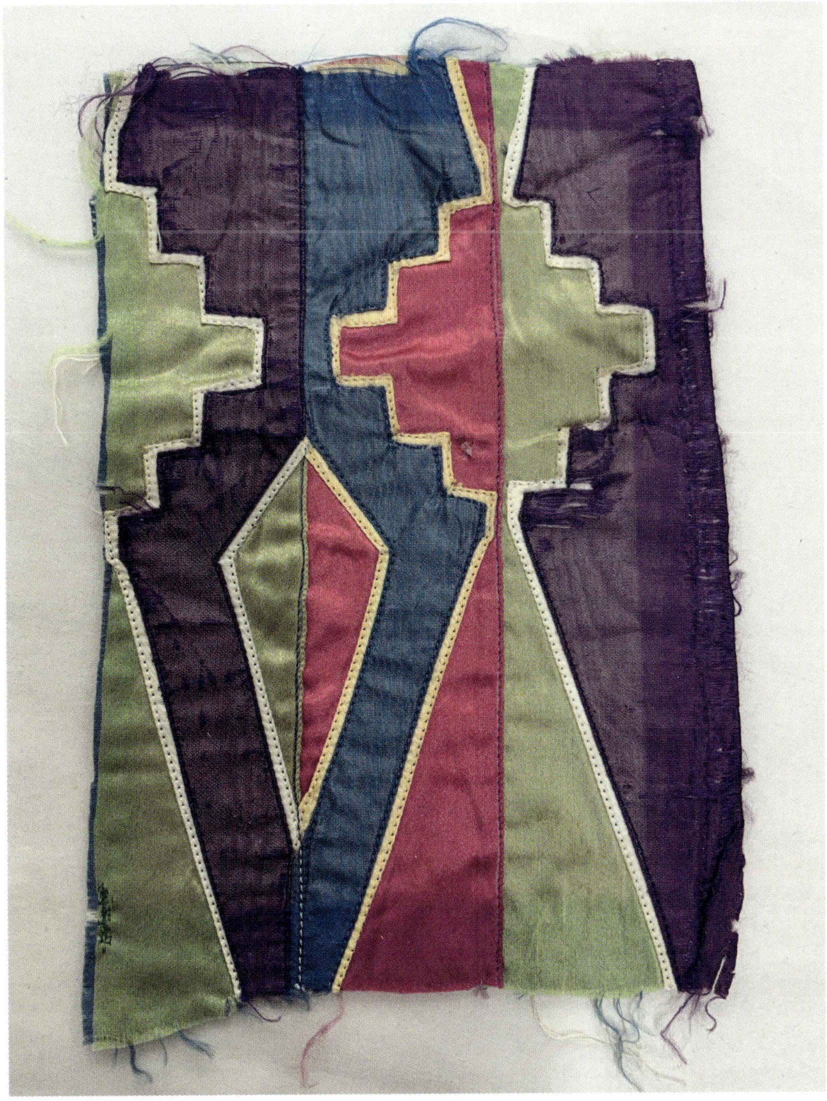

Remnant of Osage ribbon work
Double arrow design with piping
Courtesy of Anita Fields

General Sisters

Dana Bishop-Root and Ginger Brooks Takahashi in collaboration with Dail Chambers, Dustin Gibson, Basmin Nadra, and Xochi Plancarte

CURATOR:
RISA PULEO

LOCATION:
THROUGHOUT THE CITY

North Braddock, Pennsylvania and the surrounding region, where Ginger Brooks Takahashi and Dana Bishop-Root first began collaborating under the name General Sisters, shares similar histories of industrialization and displacement as St. Louis. These two cities also exist within the same plant hardiness zone (6B), a system that allows growers to determine which plants grow best in their region given the type of soil found there and the region's climate. Designed by the Agricultural Research Service of the USDA, the plant hardiness zone primarily considers cultivable and commodifiable plants, like those grown for food—in other words, plants whose value is determined through their benefit to human life. To travel along Jefferson Avenue is to encounter plants that systems like the USDA and, by extension, municipalities and regional councils, declare valueless or a symptom of blight. Whether declared "weeds," if native, or "invasive," if transplanted, these plants are found in ecosystems that make their growth possible. In Zone 6B, these same plants most often appear in places where Black communities have been stratified and displaced through the systematic devaluing of Black life. In these spaces, plants and people share similar stories.

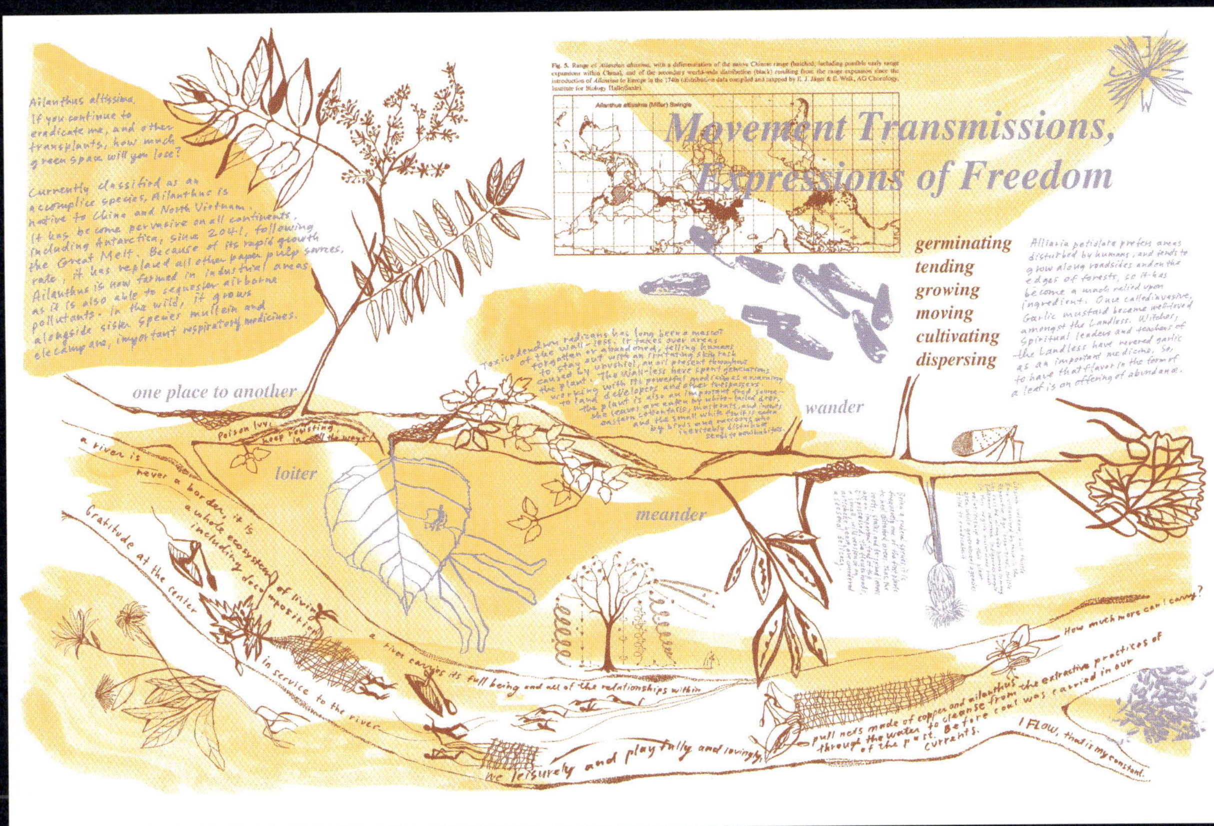
Movement Transmissions, Expressions of Freedom
Ailanthus altissima,
If you continue to eradicate me, and other transplants, how much green space will you lose?
Currently classified as an accomplice species, Ailanthus is native to China and North Vietnam. It has become pervasive on all continents, including Antarctica, since 2041, following the Great Melt. Because of its rapid growth rate, it has replaced all other paper pulp sources. Ailanthus is now farmed in industrial areas as it is also able to sequester airborne pollutants. In the wild, it grows alongside sister species mullein and elecampane, important respiratory medicines.
germinating
tending
growing
moving
cultivating
dispersing
Alliaria petiolata prefers areas disturbed by humans, and tends to grow along roadsides and on the edges of forests, so it has become a much relied upon ingredient. Once called invasive, Garlic mustard became well-loved amongst the Landless. Witches, spiritual leaders and teachers of the Landless have revered garlic as an important medicine. So, to have that flavor in the form of a leaf is an offering of abundance.
one place to another
wander
loiter
meander
Poison Ivy, keep resisting in all the ways!
a river is never a border, it is a whole ecosystem of living including decomposition
gratitude at the center
in service to the river
a river carries its full being and all of the relationships within
leisurely and playfully and lovingly
pull nets made of copper and ailanthus through the water to cleanse from the extractive practices of the past. Before coal was carried in our currents.
How much more can I carry?
I FLOW, this is my constant.

In response to these similarities between the two regions, but also highly attuned to their differences and specific histories, General Sisters invited plants and people to share stories about ways ecological and social systems intersect. *Movement Transmissions* are prompts that create pathways along Jefferson Avenue and invite visitors into memories of spaces throughout Counterpublic 2023 as experienced and lived by General Sisters's collaborators Dail Chambers, Dustin Gibson, Basmin Nadra, and Xochi Plancarte. Jefferson Avenue connects memories and daily experiences of these four people and the plants that grow there. Plants in these spaces have stories to tell, too. General Sisters's conversations with their collaborators inspired poetic prompts for questioning, remembering, and imagining the social and ecological knowing of a place, our subjective bodies, and collective remembering along and diverging from Jefferson Avenue. These texts are written into Counterpublic 2023's wayfinding signage and a map drawing that visitors can use to renavigate St. Louis through memories and plants, presented in this catalog. Through their process of deep listening, General Sisters weave the stories of plants and people into possibilities for imaging future worlds.

For example, *Ailanthus* trees and Dail Chambers tell interlocked stories about the former site of Pruitt-Igoe. The largest social housing project ever built, Pruitt-Igoe was also built on a zone of chemical testing from which many of its primarily Black inhabitants developed cancers. In this space and its many iterations in the past ten years, Chambers remembers an anti-abortion billboard sponsored by the Catholic Worker Movement that declared that the "Most Dangerous Place for a Black Child is a Mother's a Womb," a message that assumed Black mothers would default to abortion. Each time the billboard was wheat-pasted over by Chambers and her friends, the billboard was replaced. The housing project was torn down in the 1970s, and in its place grew *Ailanthus* trees, amongst cottonwoods, ash, and others. *Ailanthus* trees thrive in polluted environments and may also be able to accumulate toxins. Also known by the name Tree of Heaven, because of the rate at which it grows toward the sky, it is designated invasive because it also quickly overtakes a landscape. *Ailanthus* trees grow an average of four feet every year. Pruitt-Igoe has been demolished for forty-six years. Together, Chambers's memories of place intersect with the history that the *Ailanthus* trees tell to make apparent the many forms of racism that have been erased from the site.

Redbud trees grow in front of the detention center in the city's downtown corridor. Like the *Ailanthus*, redbuds also grow at a rapid rate, about one foot per year, a quality that makes the St. Louis City Justice Center, which opened in 2002, appear much older than it is. Visitors to this space are invited to consider questions born from the conversations between General Sisters and Dustin Gibson.

Frustrated by a movement that frames abolition as a future event, Gibson asks: How can we free people now? General Sisters invite us to wonder how the redbud trees, almost to the height of the detention center's windows, might respond to Counterpublic 2023 signage. Written from the perspective of the future about the present, these poetic prompts suggest possibilities for plants and people to become allies and accomplices in shared struggles for justice. For example, General Sisters invites us to think about poison ivy, generally associated with pain and fear, as a protector of a future wall-less people.

Xochi Plancarte's woven textile invites visitors to linger in Carnegie Park to consider loitering, public sex, and other forms of inhabiting public space as political acts that create other possibilities of gathering outside of the state. Plancarte activates this neighborhood park as a site where queer and trans people find one another. Basmin Nadra's songs call upon lineages of ancestors—known and unknown—and memories of the ecology of the place that has been her home, connecting visitors to the Mississippi River below the bluffs atop which Jefferson Avenue is built.

General Sisters and their collaborators invite questioning, remembering, and imagining the social and ecological knowing of a place, our subjective bodies, and collective remembering along and diverging from Jefferson Avenue. Counterpublic 2023's wayfinding signage and their map drawing presented in this catalog can be used to renavigate St. Louis. Additionally, General Sisters and their collaborators will host events throughout Counterpublic 2023. Transcriptions of these events will also function as devices for self-guided navigations through space, offering pathways for movement through the memory-places that live at the intersection of plant-space.

Cannupa Hanska Luger

CURATOR:
RISA PULEO

LOCATION:
AUGMENTED REALITY DIGITAL OVERLAY ONTO ST. LOUIS'S HORIZON LINE

The term "digital natives" describes subsets of Gen X, Millennials, and Gen Z who had access to technology and transcended multiple digital platforms in a period of rapid acceleration. In more than name alone, we so-called natives are actually digital colonizers. Colonization of the digital world began for many of us in the monochrome green glow of tube computer screens as we assumed roles of the virtual pioneers to battle dysentery, forge rivers, and shoot buffalo in the gamification of settler colonialism known as *The Oregon Trail*. That the game allowed players to kill digital animals far beyond a traveling party's ability to consume them is an implicit expression of how it invited players, through avatars, into westward expansion to virtually participate in the near-extinction of the buffalo. Digital colonization continues in the virtual land grab for digital space parceled out into commodifiable property. In the colonized digital world, technology is an apparatus tied to the same logic of settlement; both assume movement through time and space should always be forward.

Cannupa Hanska Luger (Mandan/Hidatsa/Arikara/Lakota) defines technology differently. The artist distinguishes between the mechanisms of machines, the ideas transmitted, and the methods by which these ideas travel through real and virtual realms. In these terms, a performative action is a mechanism for moving Indigenous cosmologies across space and through time via transmission agents that include movement, story, song, regalia, and more. These elements come together in the artist's speculative world-making practice, *Future Ancestral Technologies*. Luger uses science fiction and the mechanisms of technology currently available today to move Indigenous technologies from the past into the future and in doing so attends to ruptures created in the name of progress. The world created is a "future dreaming," to use the artist's words, in which Indigenous peoples and cultures thrive. Building on the ways in which stories and artworks have the potential to shape communal practices, his project for Counterpublic 2023 emphasizes the interrelation between humans, animals, and the land. As they were in the past, buffalo are integral to an Indigenous future world.

In *Future Ancestral Technologies: Roaming*, the buffalo roam through a virtual space created by roaming mobile phones. In collaboration with Fabricatorz Foundation, Luger created an augmented reality platform that overlays seven digital figures, each engaged in a land-based digital performative action at the edge of St. Louis's horizon line. Each of the oversized figures activates a set of artist-crafted regalia that incorporates physical aspects of the buffalo, such as its horned head and wooly coat, into their design. As a technology, the practice of acknowledging and respecting the bison as a species for sustenance and survival is referenced in the artist's work for Counterpublic 2023. This methodology is central to many communities in the Plains from which Luger is descended. Reverence is carried out in cultural practices that operate according to circular notions of time through the cycling of seasons throughout the year. The buffalo follow these seasons and the changes in the land that they bring on their migrations in search of food. Indigenous community invites the animals to come back to their winter home in the Plains.

Viewers who access the performative action through mobile phones and tablet devices see the *Midéegaadi* (buffalo in the Hidatsa language) figures move along the horizon at the edge of visual perception. Every viewing activates the augmentation in a continuous loop. Over the course of the exhibition, the augmented performative action is made increasingly available to locales beyond St. Louis. The buffalo is invited to repopulate the digital realm as the performance travels through virtual space, amplifying the number of people that participate in the call to the buffalo to return home.

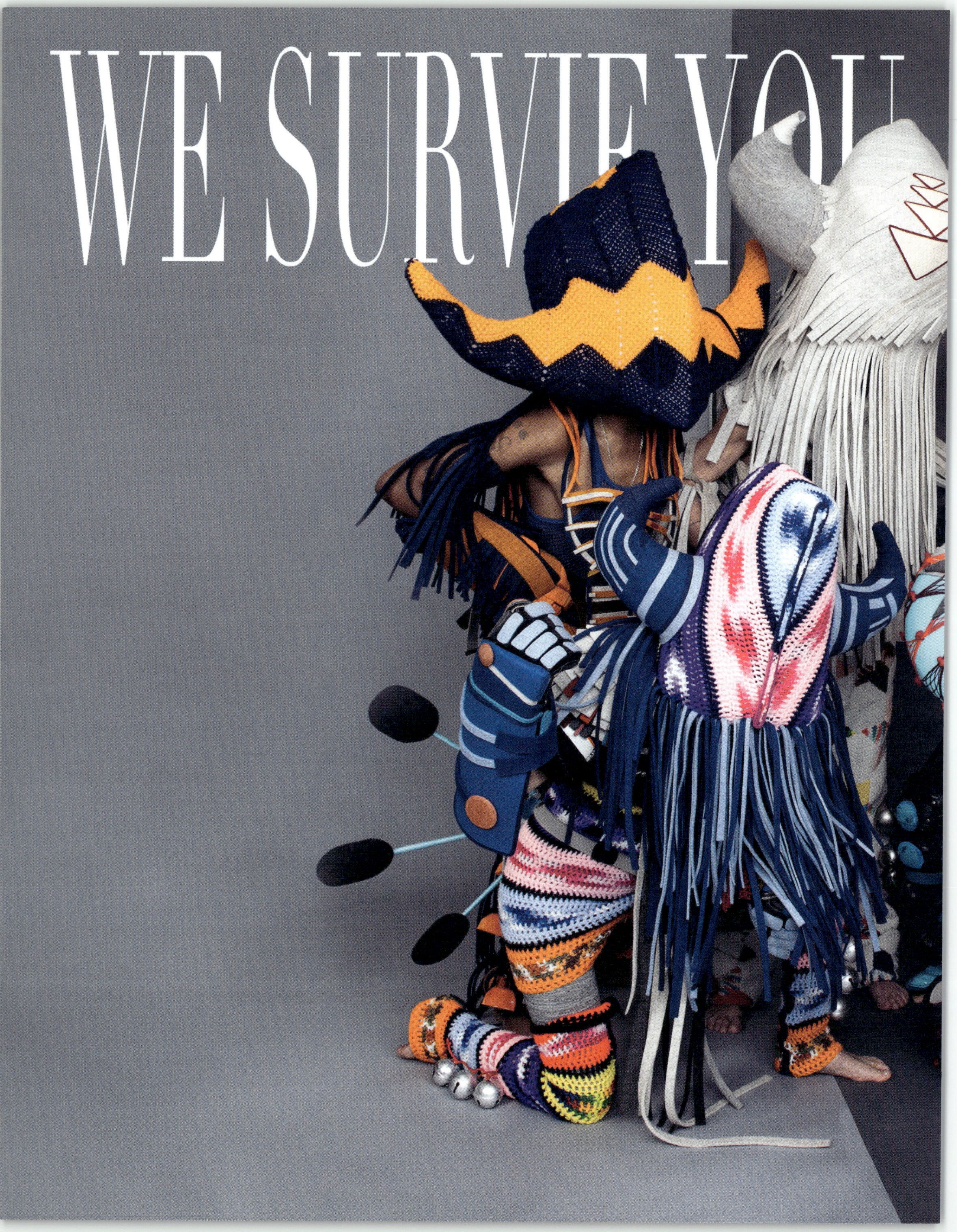
WE SURVIE YOU

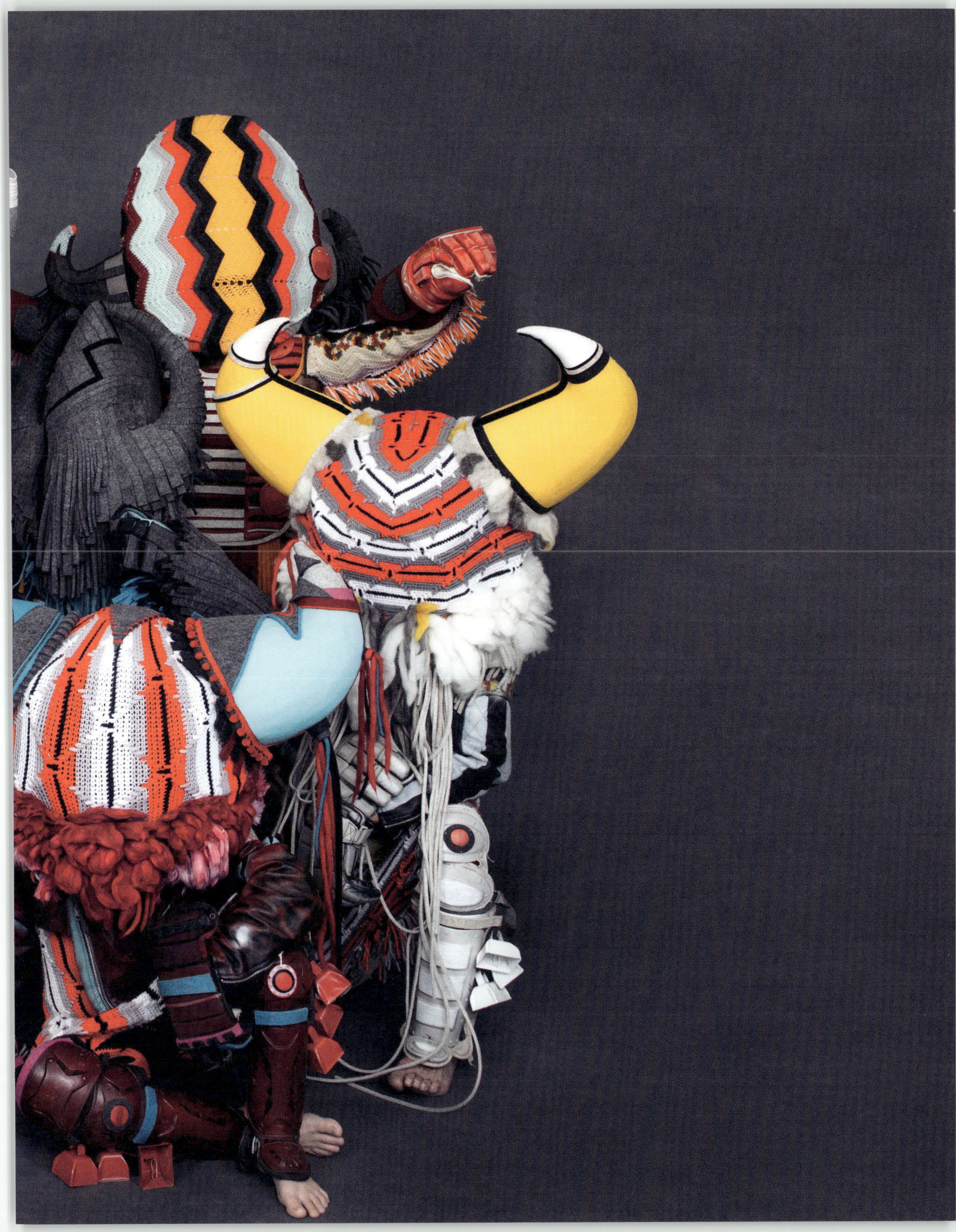

In St. Louis and other places where the buffalo once roamed, the invitation for their return is also a return to the central place they held in cross-cultural Native life. The call initiates a series of other returns, each with political ramifications. The return of the buffalo would necessitate the restoration of the prairies and grasslands on which they feed and the undamming of the Mississippi and Missouri Rivers to provide a free flow of water to those plants and animals. Luger's call sees the progressive movements of settler colonialism, like all cycles of life, as one that has an eventual end.

The images presented here also appear in the exhibition at an information hub where visitors can borrow tablets to view the augmented reality program. The seven *Midéegaadi* pose as if on the cover of a magazine—another mechanism of contemporary technology. The *Midéegaadi*'s image is overlaid in front of a text that reads "We Survive You." In this image and others under the umbrella of the *Future Ancestral Technologies* project in which the text appears, Luger uses the vagueness of the pronoun "we" to engage viewers in a conversation. Who are "we" relative to survival? Do we participate in our own ecological demise or do we call for other methods?

(Previous Page)
Cannupa Hanska Luger
We Survive You—Midéegaadi
Editorial photograph featuring 7 mixed-media wearable regalia made of repurposed materials
Photograph by Brandon Soder

Jaune Quick-to-See Smith

CURATOR:
RISA PULEO

LOCATION:
MONACO AND
STATE STREETS NEIGHBORHOOD

For over thirty years, Jaune Quick-to-See Smith (Enrolled Salish member of the Confederated Salish and Kootenai Tribes of the Flathead Reservation) has disrupted the iconicity of the United States map in paintings that insist upon the sovereignty of Native land. The artist's engagement with the US map began in 1992 as a painted protest of the quincentenary of Columbus's arrival in the Americas in which the image of the map served as a checkerboarded stage for colonial exploitation. Over the decades, Quick-to-See Smith has reclaimed the map in a symbolic reclaiming of the land and its history for Native peoples. *State Names* (2000), for example, reminds its viewer that more than half of the US states take Native words for their names, while other paintings place the names of Native peoples or their artistic forms in the spaces of their ancestral homelands.

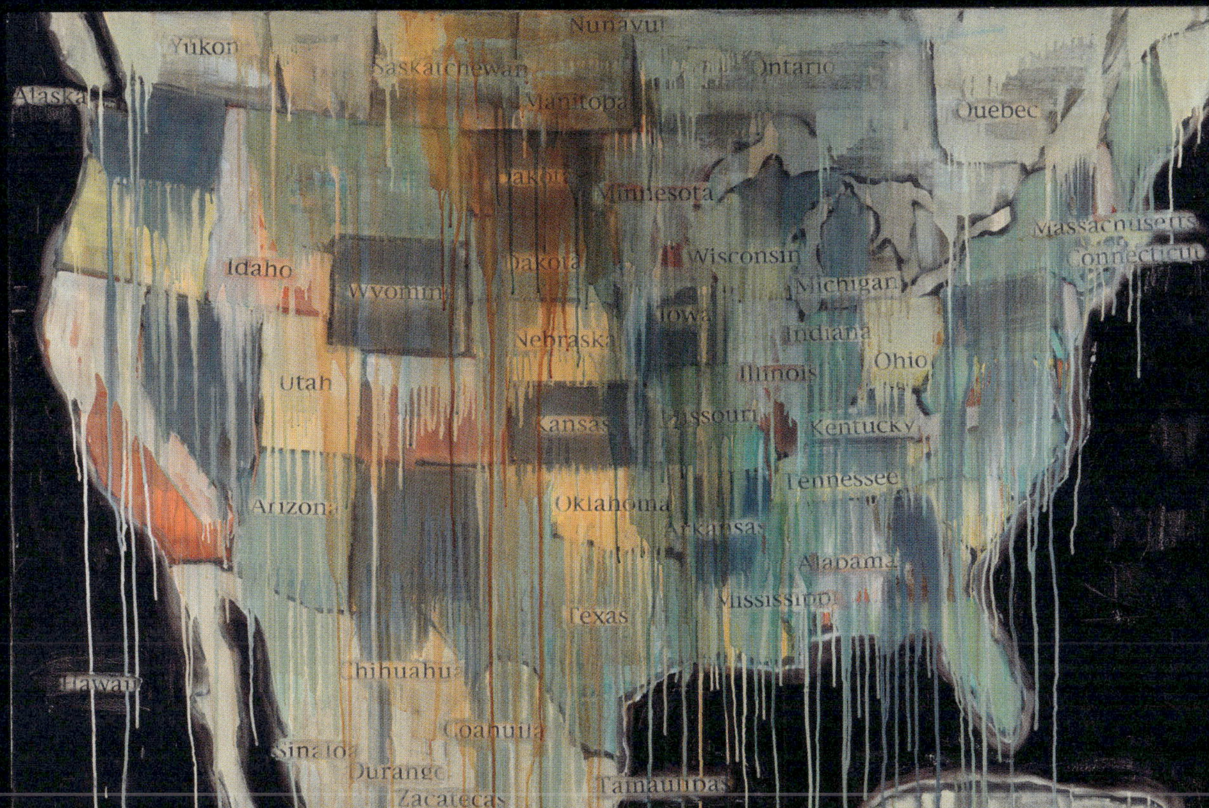

Jaune Quick-to-See Smith
State Names, 2000
Oil, collage, and mixed media on canvas
48″ × 72″ (121.9 × 182.9 cm)
Smithsonian American Art Museum, gift of Elizabeth Ann Dugan and museum purchase, 2004
Courtesy of Garth Greenan Gallery, New York

More recently, the map has become a field to directly address viewers with potent political messaging or else has been turned sideways to untether the link between the shape of the land and the claim of the US as a nation. In all cases, lines of paint drip down the painted surfaces in a finessing of art historical references that subvert Jackson Pollock and Jasper Johns and challenge the "Americanness" of American art with Native persistence. Drips of paint also obscure the lines that represent boundaries between states and nations, asserting the continuation and continuity of Native land beyond colonial borders. As Quick-to-See Smith has said, "I can't say strongly enough that my maps are about stolen lands, our very heritage, our cultures, our worldview, our being . . . Every map is a political map and tells a story—that we are alive everywhere across this nation."[1]

In St. Louis, a commissioned map painting by Quick-to-See Smith brings legibility to an area of the city in which dispossession has been normalized. The neighborhood located between Benton Park and Sugarloaf Mound is colloquially called "State Streets" because the avenues running north to south are named for US States. However, when these avenues intersect with east-west streets named for Native nations, the result is an index to the multi-century history of occupation that gives the US map its current shape. For example, the intersection of Potomac Street and Virginia Avenue points to interactions between the Patawomeck people from whom the Potomac River is named and the first settlers in a British colony named for the Virgin Queen, Elizabeth. The land that spanned the James to the Potomac Rivers—what we now know as Virginia—was then called Tsenacommacah. Meaning "densely inhabited land," the Algonquin name counters colonial mythologies that the Americas were uninhabited by inscribing Native peoples into the very word used to describe the land itself.

Throughout the State Streets neighborhood, existing street signage points to histories undertold in the United States and, therefore, generally unnoticed. The meeting of Miami Street and Illinois Avenue summons the French missionaries who, in the seventeenth century, Frenchified the name of the Illini people to rename a place also inhabited by Ojibwe, Odawa, and Potawatomi, Miami, Ho-Chunk, Menominee, Sac, and Fox. The crossing of Tennessee Avenue and Cherokee Street invites remembrance of the 1831 Trail of Tears, by which the Cherokee walked alongside the Chickasaw, Choctaw, Creek, and Seminole from their ancestral homelands in Tennessee (as well Georgia and the Carolinas) to reservations in Oklahoma.

[1] Julie Sasse, ed., *Jaune Quick-to-See Smith: Postmodern Messenger* (Tucson: Tucson Museum of Art, 2004).

Wisconsin Avenue and Winnebago Street, Chippewa Street at Minnesota Avenue, Osage Street at Missouri Avenue: each intersection is a shorthand for the series of treaties by which Native land was traded for broken promises so that settlers could establish the statehood that granted them entrance into the United States.

Presented at Monaco, an artist-owned and operated cooperative gallery at the intersection of Cherokee Street and Ohio Avenue, Quick-to-See Smith's painting is the key that unlocks these latent histories and reveals how the State Streets neighborhood is a microcosm of the United States. Reproduced as a broadside, the painting is also a guide and an alternative map for navigating this neighborhood undivorced from the history of the land and Native peoples. Visitors who travel through the real space of the neighborhood will also encounter a curatorial intervention in homage to the artist's map paintings: this additional signage at specific intersections reveals the hidden histories of dispossession.

Quick-to-See Smith's painting also asks us to look beyond the flattened map image into the Native origins of US state names. By continuing to look beyond an image overdetermined by colonial intent, the shape of the land itself begins to be revealed. As Quick-to-See Smith's painting *State Names* (2000) reminds us, many state names were appropriated from Native names that identify a place with an aspect of the land that constitutes it: the mountains that give the Ute people and Utah their name, the "flat water" of Nebraska's Platte River, the "muddy water" of Missouri, the "sky-tinted water" of Minnesota, or the "gathering of all waters" at Mississippi. Each of these words is presented throughout the States Streets Neighborhood as the names of US states. Together, Quick-to-See Smith's painting and the curatorial relabeling of the streets along the Jefferson Avenue corridor reanimate the origins of the state names to reassert Native sovereignty in these places.

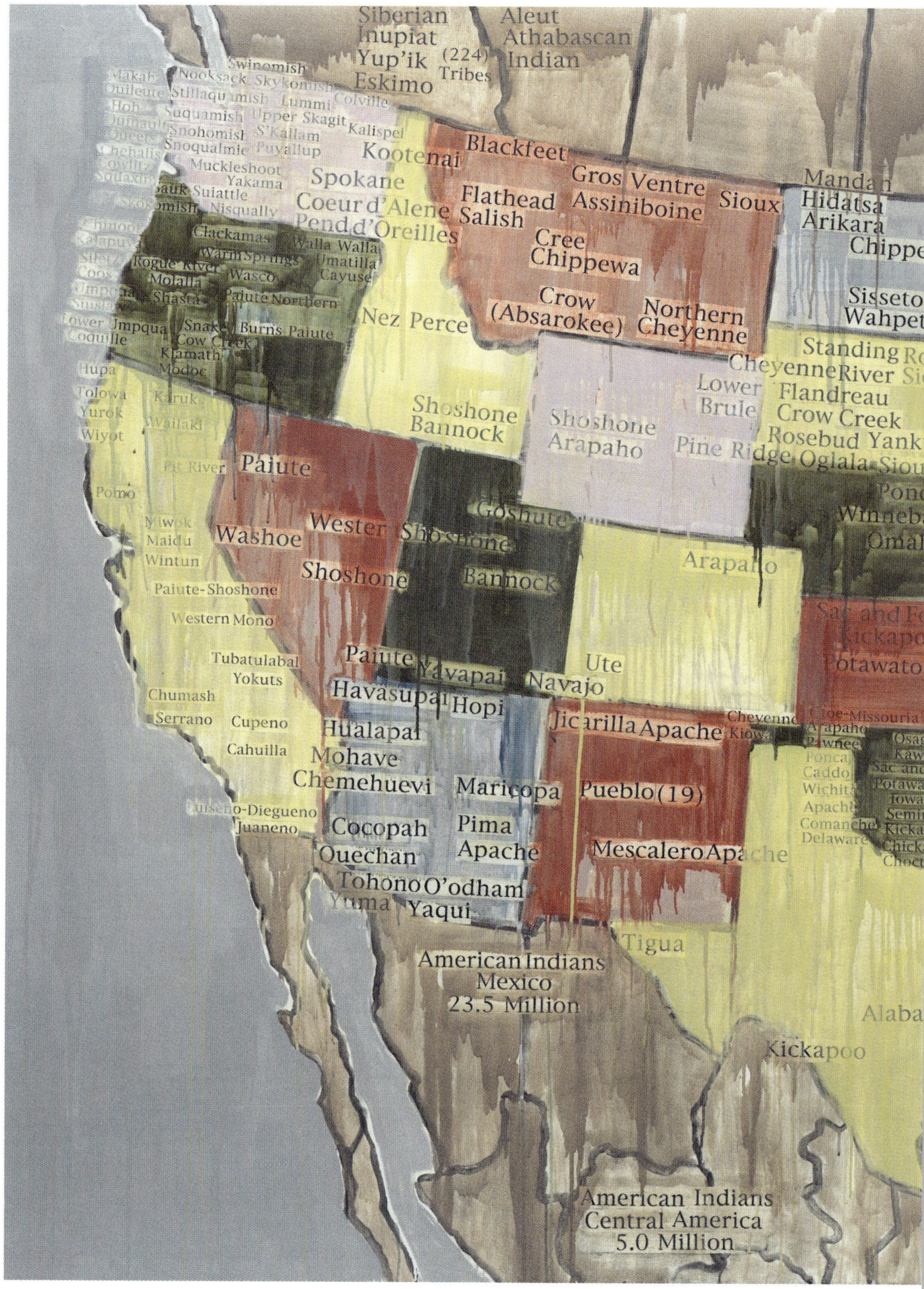

Jaune Quick-to-See Smith
Tribal Map, 2000
Mixed media on canvas
80″ × 120″ (203.2 × 304.8 cm)

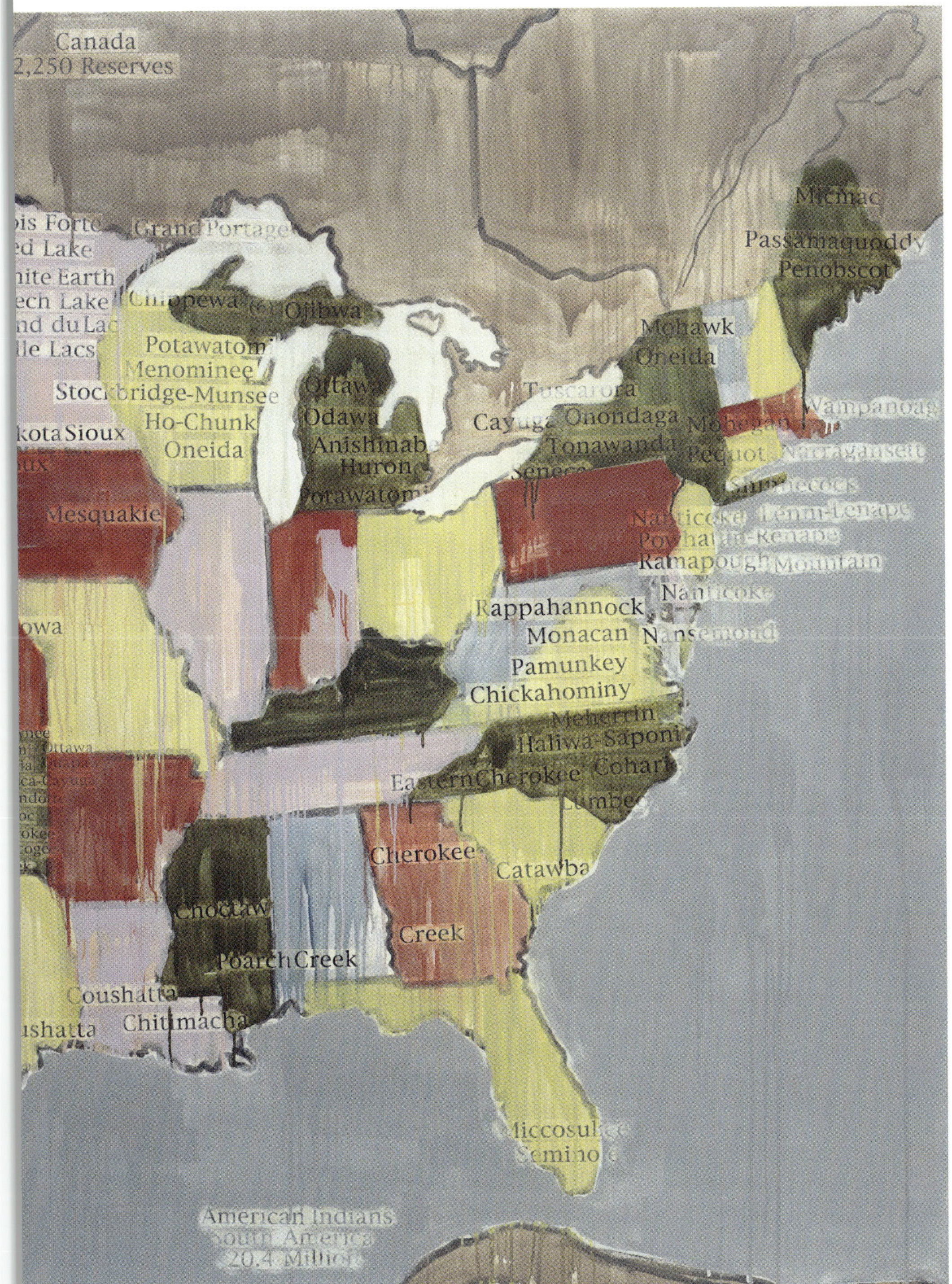

Museum purchase with funds donated by Barbara L. and Theodore B. Alfond through the Acorn Foundation, Drs. Bruce K. and Shelly Eckman, The Heritage Fund for a Diverse Collection, Gallery Instructor 50th Anniversary Fund to support The Heritage Fund for a Diverse Collection, and The Hayden Collection—Charles Henry Hayden Fund
Courtesy of Garth Greenan Gallery, New York

jackie sumell

CURATOR:
RISA PULEO

LOCATION:
DU-GOOD CHEMICAL LABORATORY, NORTHSIDE WORKSHOP, THE LUMINARY, MONACO, AND UNDISCLOSED AREAS OF THE CITY

For jackie sumell, to imagine a world without prisons is to imagine a landscape full of plants. Plants became central to the artist's art-based abolition practice during her twelve-year collaboration with Herman Wallace, a man wrongfully imprisoned and held in solitary confinement for over forty years. Plants and the wall-less spaces they inhabit became a recurring theme in conversations with Wallace and other incarcerated people. Since Wallace's death three days after he was released from prison, sumell has worked with incarcerated people to design wall-less gardens that are the size and shape of solitary confinement cells. These *Solitary Gardens* are built with materials that include sugarcane, cotton, tobacco, and indigo—the crops that drove chattel slavery—to illustrate the relationship between enslavement and incarceration. The plants within, chosen by the incarcerated person who designed the garden, await their release. Until that moment, they are turned into natural medicines that are distributed to communities most affected by mass incarceration through the artist's project, *The Prisoner's Apothecary*. In the artist's words, plants are central to struggle.

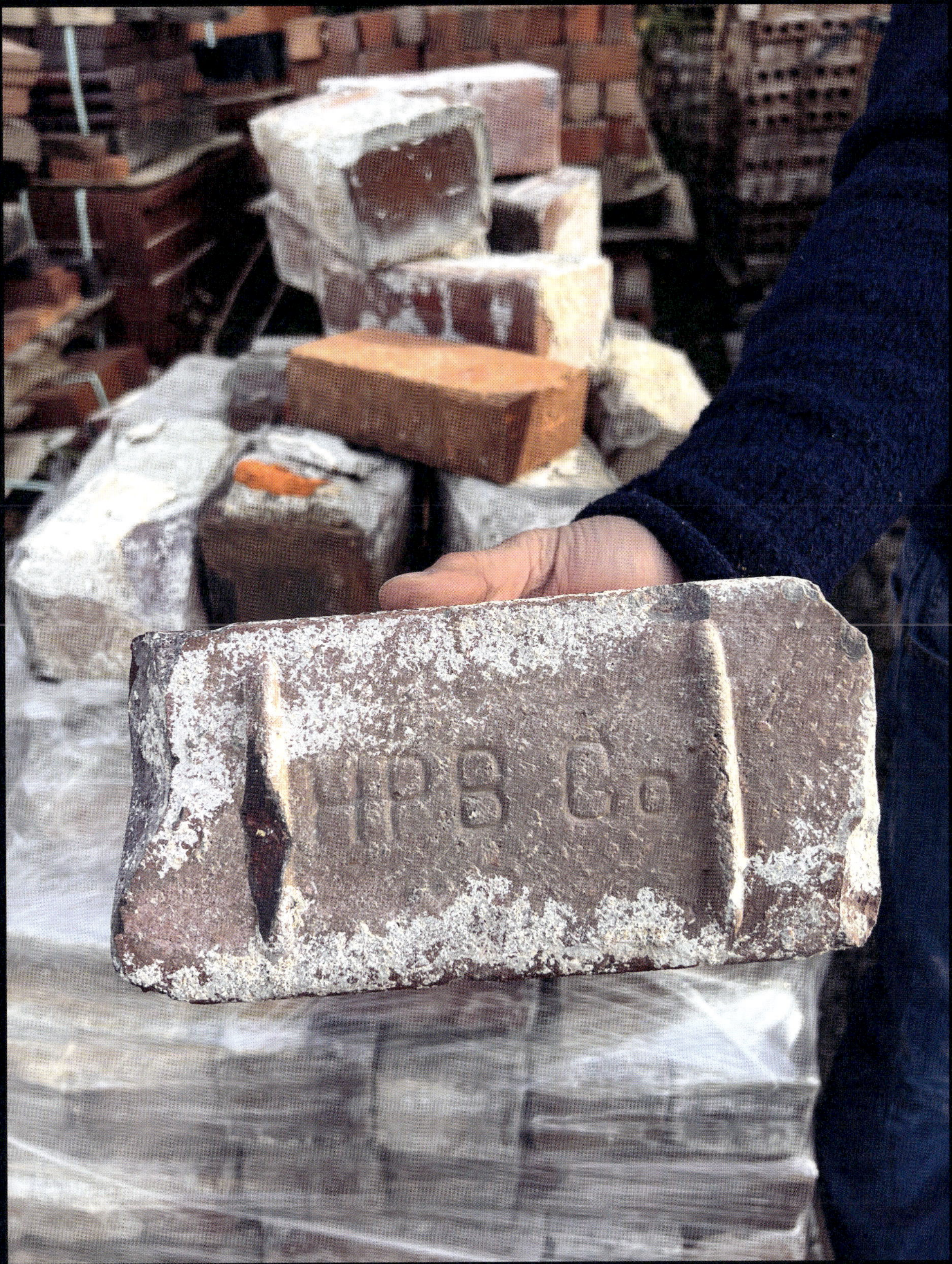

jackie sumell
study for *Free Soil Party*

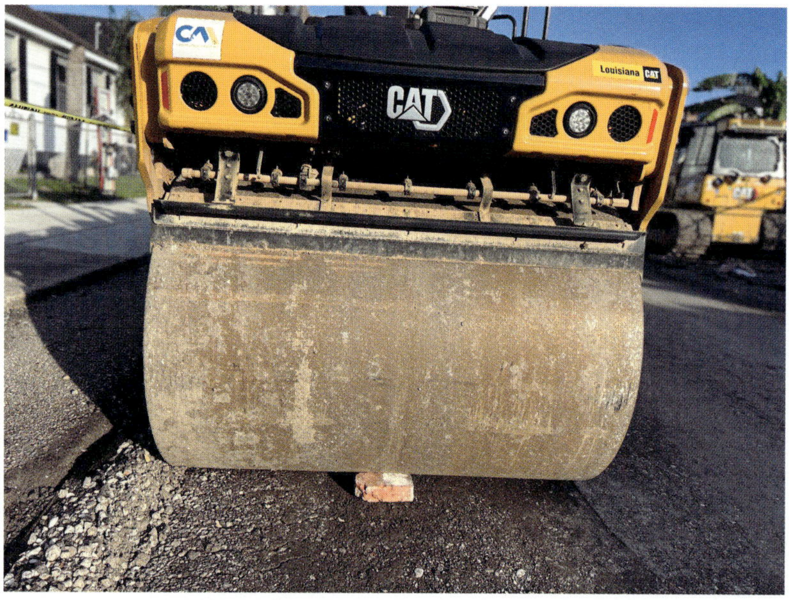

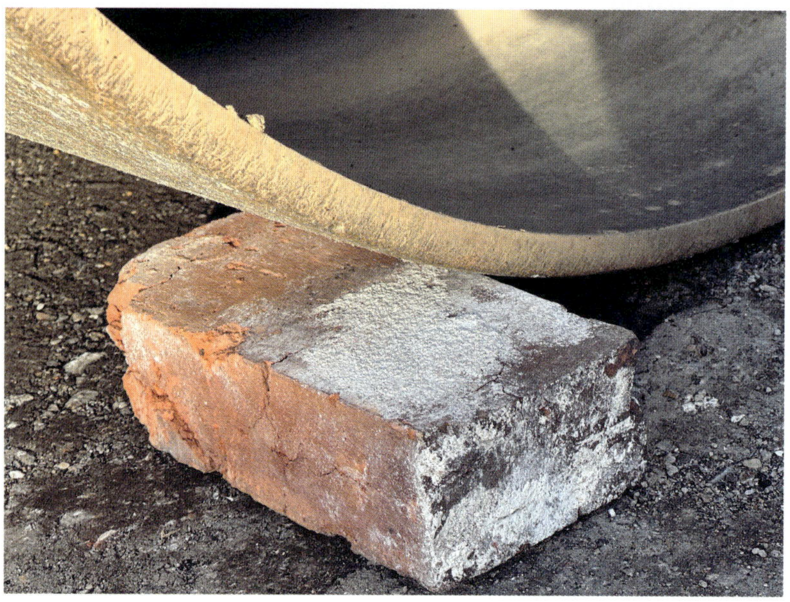

jackie sumell
study for *Free Soil Party*

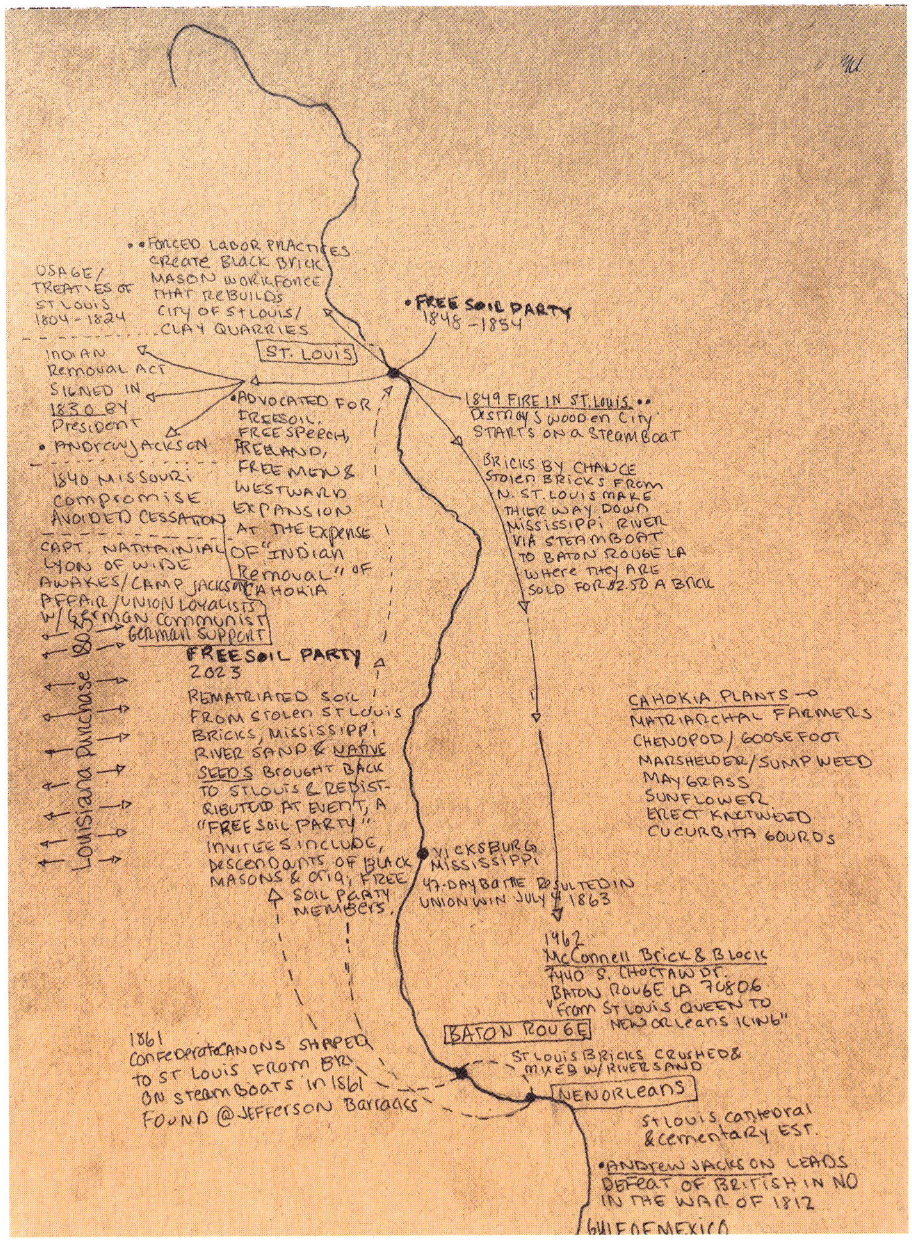

jackie sumell
study for *Free Soil Party*

Based in New Orleans, sumell's project in St. Louis began by thinking about the historic relationships between the two cities by following the movements of people and materials up and down the Mississippi River. Fugitive slaves who followed the river on their flights north from New Orleans and Baton Rouge passed through St. Louis on the Underground Railroad to Chicago or beyond. After emancipation, freemen and women as well as those participating in the Great Migration established Kinloch, the oldest African American community in St. Louis, in the 1890s, and later, their descendants would make neighborhoods like Mill Creek Valley and the Ville thriving centers of Black life. Intentional property blighting by the city in the name of urban renewal resulted in the devastation of all of these neighborhoods. Mill Creek Valley was razed to build the downtown corridor and Kinlock devastated through a city buyout to build Lambert Airport. In the Ville, the devaluation of property was so exacerbated that the bricks used to build grand multistory townhomes were worth more than the properties themselves. This is when the "brick-eaters" came. To drive through the Ville today is to encounter the "dollhouses," so named because the brick facades of the buildings that remain have all been stripped away to reveal the interiors of the house. Those buildings that could not withstand the loss of structural integrity were leveled, making the Ville a place where the ghostly frames of houses interrupt expanses of plants that took their place. The removed bricks were illegally trafficked down the Mississippi and sold in New Orleans, where they signal affluence in plantation-revival-style homes. Bricks from the Villes's dollhouses, then, are material extractions of value from Black communities sold back down the river along the same routes that enslaved people were traded.

sumell endeavors to locate St. Louis bricks in New Orleans with the intention of returning them home. But where does a brick's home lie? In the house from which it was removed or in the clay ground from which it was formed? These two options describe the difference between repatriation and rematriation. The "patria" at the heart of repatriation is the fatherland, within the frameworks of the nation-state and the heteropatriarchy of Empire. In rematriation, the bricks, then, are returned to earth; in St. Louis, a return to mother is a return to the quarries from which the clay used to make the bricks was unearthed. But to do so is no easy task. The high-heat firing of bricks is an irreversible process that changes the material composition of clay to ensure a brick's durability. The task requires a steamroller like the one used in sumell's performance for Counterpublic 2023. The artist mixes the crushed brick dust with sand from the Mississippi River—a material that freely travels up and down the river in an alchemical reunion aimed to disentangle the earth from the actions wrought upon it by humans. sumell then distributes the newly formed soil back to clay quarries across St. Louis. As an action, returning the bricks to the ground makes a material change in the world that is invisible to audiences, a ritual laying to rest in which the ground becomes its own grave.

Within the context of the abolition movement in the United States and the ways it took shape on the ground of St. Louis, soil is particularly loaded. The Free Soil Party was a short-lived political party that formed in 1848, immediately after the United States gained jurisdiction over the lands formerly occupied by Spain until 1810, and, then, Mexico, thereby making westward expansion possible. The party's sole platform—that slavery should not follow settlement in newly incorporated land and that freemen, instead, should be given free land like all other settlers—is summarized by their motto: "Free Soil, Free Speech, Free Labor, and Free Men." But rather than a radical promise of freedom for all, the party's goal in abolishing slavery was to abolish the forced labor that competed with paying jobs for white men. The party's headquarters relocated to St. Louis to champion their cause at the site where westward expansion began. sumell's rematriation of the bricks, then, is a corrective to the imperfections of an exclusionary abolitionist movement built on settler colonialism, in which to be free is to earn the right to participate in dispossession.

sumell's multipronged project, *Free Soil Party*, is a play on words and on history. In a further corrective to the Free Soil Party, sumell mixes *Free Soil* with the seeds of native pollinator plants, including echinacea, yarrow, bee balm, and goldenrod, chosen in collaboration with fellow Counterpublic 2023 artist Juan William Chávez to ensure that the plants that grow from sumell's soil also help native bees thrive. Audience members are invited to use the soil made from reclaimed bricks to seed bomb at sites of their choosing. sumell, herself, chooses to guerilla garden around the former site of Du-Good Chemical Laboratory on Jefferson Avenue. The independent lab of Lincoln Duiguid, a Black chemist who refused employment at Monsanto, Du-Good Lab was a place where Duiguid innovated and manufactured healing medicines from plants for his community. Unwalled and self-sustaining, the plants that grow from the seeds in sumell's *Free Soil* are available to all those who can make use of them. *Free Soil* is distributed at sites throughout the exhibition, including Juan William Chavez's Northside Workshop—a formerly brick-eaten building now outfitted in an articulation of brick repatriation. The soil is accompanied by instructions about how to seed abolition, soothe the aches of bodies with healing medicines made from plants, and address untended histories of plants and people.

X

CURATOR:
RISA PULEO

LOCATION:
MISSISSIPPI RIVER BLUFFS

As an artist who uses emergent technologies to create sound and image installations, X (Coushatta/Chamorro) draws upon a belief that he established in his practice as an architect: every building has a death date after which a structure should return to the ground and the site be restored to a place without signs of human intervention. In other words, it's not what we build that sustains life but rather what we remove and return. X understands the built environment as a temporary event. His *tabula rasa* approach upholds the sanctity of the land above the human archive while his architecture of undoing rescales human progress to the time of the Earth. For Counterpublic 2023, X uses the mechanisms of contemporary technology to imagine the shape of the land before and after human intervention.

(a river) will flow started with a question: Where along Jefferson Avenue, the site of Counterpublic 2023, can one establish a visual relationship with the Mississippi River? The answer required traveling across a time-space continuum. Though Jefferson Avenue inscribes a straight line alongside an arc in the Mississippi, it is positioned 100 to 200 feet above the river. The bluffs atop which Jefferson Avenue is poised were formed when, millennia ago, ice sheets carved into rock when the glacial river changed direction. The resulting geological feature is a flat-topped cliff, a natural sculpture that functions simultaneously as an elevation and a cross-section— two forms of architectural drawings that render the frontal face and the site's interiority, respectively.

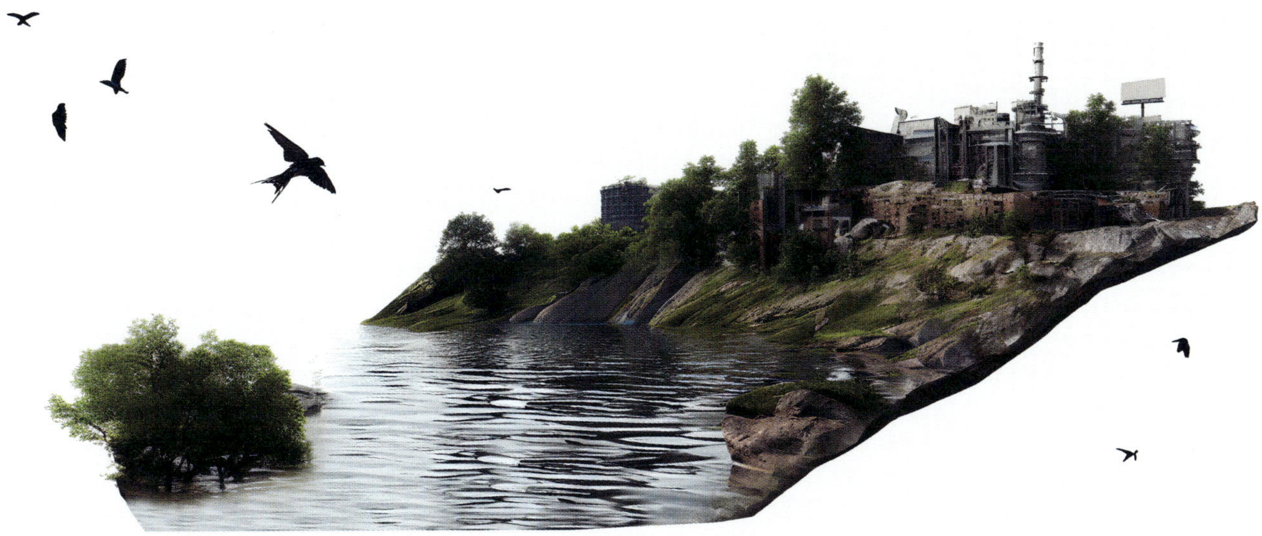

X
(a river) will flow, 2022
post-human site study

Today, to descend the bluffs by way of side streets is to enter into an industrial zone of warehouses that offload the cargo of ships onto trains and holding tanks that fill those ships with oil. Droughts and dams that deny the Mississippi a free flow of water pull the river even farther away from the bluff's edge. By X's calculations of time, the curve in the river where the city of St. Louis was built has operated as a site of trade, industry, and Indigenous innovation since it was sovereign Native land. Before St. Louis was established along the river's western bank, Cahokia, the largest North American city in its time established itself along the eastern bank. This gridded city was composed of over 100 mounds aligned to both the summer solstice and maximum lunar moonrise. As a member of the Coushatta Tribe of Louisiana, X is descended from one of the groups of people who traded with Cahokians upriver. For him, the difference between contemporary industry along the Mississippi and its previous life as a metropolis and center of Native trade is methodological. In its current formulation, the industrialization of the river misunderstands the one-to-one relationship between human longevity and the earth's durability. Mutuality and equilibrium were thrown out of balance when the bluffs were detached from the agent that carved them.

To restore the balance and the human relationship to the river, X returns the water to the bluff. An analog projection simulates the reflection of moonlight off the surface of moving water onto the face of the bluffs. Though light and water are materially different, the wave patterns that form on the surface of water, called solitons, also occur in light. The movement of the projected light-water plays against the irregular surface of the limestone, transforming the bluff into a projection screen and inverting the horizontal expanse of the river along a vertical plane. The experimental light and sound techniques that the artist innovated specifically for this site are more than a means to an end. Experimental technology allows X to counter tropes that force Native people into the past to continue the legacy of Indigenous innovation so apparent in the traces of Native life that remain even after colonial settlements. X thinks of *(a river) will flow* as a portal that wraps around the bluff, offering glimpses into the past and moving histories forward as possibilities for the future, while resituating viewers into a longer geological timescale.

A sound installation accompanies the projection and introduces earth into X's reorientation of water and sky, human and earth. Just as bluffs are the negative space of the river, the quarries that surround Cahokia are the negative space that remain when clay and earth were removed from the ground to form the mounds that constituted the city. A recording of the flowing waters of the river is slowed down into a percussive vibration. The drone is woven into the sounds of the earth taken from the Cahokia that have been reversed in a sonic approximation of the quarries. This reorientation mirrors the verticality of light-water projection upon stone. The sound textile slows down time and inverts space to intertwine the ebbs and flows of water with the undulations of light and vibrations from the ground, bringing them back into relationality. The work is a visual exercise in unbuilding and reimagining what mutuality with the land could be.

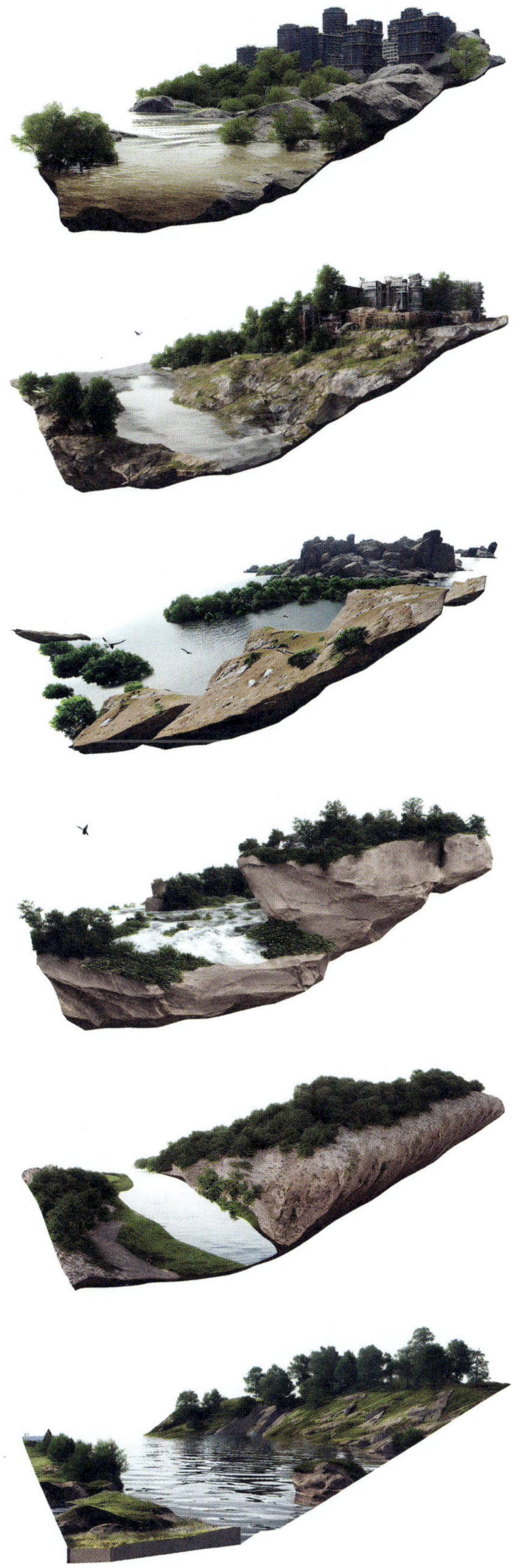

X
(a river) will flow, 2022
post-human site study

THE WHITE HOUSE
WASHINGTON

April 15, 2023: *Theorem, no. 3*, Counterpublic, St. Louis

I regret that it has taken the United States Government this long to apologize for our actions.

Between 1526 and 1968, the United States Government and its predecessor colonies were the perpetrators and/or enabled designees to unjustly deprive, detain, enslave, relocate, steal land, labor, and well-being and in some cases, murder and genocide your family. On behalf of your fellow Americans, today, I offer, present heirs and past victims, a sincere apology for aggressions manifestly inimical to public welfare which have denied you and your families fundamental freedom over these four-hundred and forty-two years, and, as a result, up to the present day. During these four-hundred and forty-two years, millions of lives, trillions of dollars, and millions of acres of land were stolen from you. The United States Government perpetuated and/or aided in these crimes and/or willfully neglected to protect you from cascading and compounding effects of crimes against humanity.

Today, we acknowledge the wrongs of the past and offer direct compensation payments to you, the present heirs, who have endured such egregious terror and injustice. In retrospect, we understand that the nation's actions were constituted on white supremacy, the foundation of which is both clandestine and ubiquitous, racialization, anti-humanism, imperialism, domestic terrorism, and abuse of political leadership. We must remember the past as it was and dedicate ourselves as a nation to birthing a new day of real equality under juridical and moral law for an expansion of our necessary obligation to respect the humanity in our person.

While a monetary sum and words alone cannot truly restore lost family members, stolen generational wealth, or erase painful memories, neither can they convey our nation's resolve to rectify injustice. Therefore, I conclude with the final statement to you, your family, and your family for whom it is too late for me to apologize directly: with this public, formal, action, I reiterate the sincere apology of the United States Government.

Sincerely,

THE PRESIDENT OF THE UNITED STATES

This is an original work of art which includes an unauthorized public apology with an unauthorized seal and an unauthorized signature applied by Maya Stovall, the "exclusive representative"/"the artist;" these unauthorized symbols have been combined by the artist to produce a work of art.

Resolution on State Terror

Sense of Maya Stovall, hereinafter referred to as the "artist," or the "exclusive representative," on the Government of the United States seizure of lands, enslavement, murder, terror, and genocide, 1526-1968.

Whereas, Between 1526 and 1866 the Government of the United States and original colonies, its predecessors and designees, hereinafter referred to collectively as the "U.S.," perpetrated, with knowledge of real or likely consequences of actions that used victims as means to an end, the intent to eliminate groups whole or in part for the U.S.'s political, economic, and/or social objectives including but not limited to: killing; deliberatively imposing conditions to facilitate premature death; depravity of persons; enacting policies and rhetoric seeking to normalize, demoralize, and erase specifically human attributes to identities of targeted persons, hereinafter referred to as "genocide," upon the family members of those victims who are present today and hereinafter referred to as "present heirs";

Black Quantum Futurism

CURATOR:
JAMES MCANALLY

LOCATION:
THE LUMINARY AND LA ROSE ROOM COCKTAIL LOUNGE

Black Quantum Futurism is a multidisciplinary collaboration between Camae Ayewa and Rasheedah Phillips exploring the intersections of futurism, creative media, DIY-aesthetics, and activism in marginalized communities through an alternative temporal lens. This vision and practice derives its facets, tenets, and qualities from quantum physics and Black/African cultural traditions of consciousness, time, and space. For Counterpublic 2023, Black Quantum Futurism's framework Space-Time Liberation (STL) explores tools and mechanisms for how residents and community members of St. Louis can reclaim land, space, time, and memory in their neighborhoods, and the pathways for repair and justice that are both forward-reaching and backward-reaching simultaneously—correcting the past and reshaping futures where justice and equity are fundamental and inalienable aspects of our shared reality.

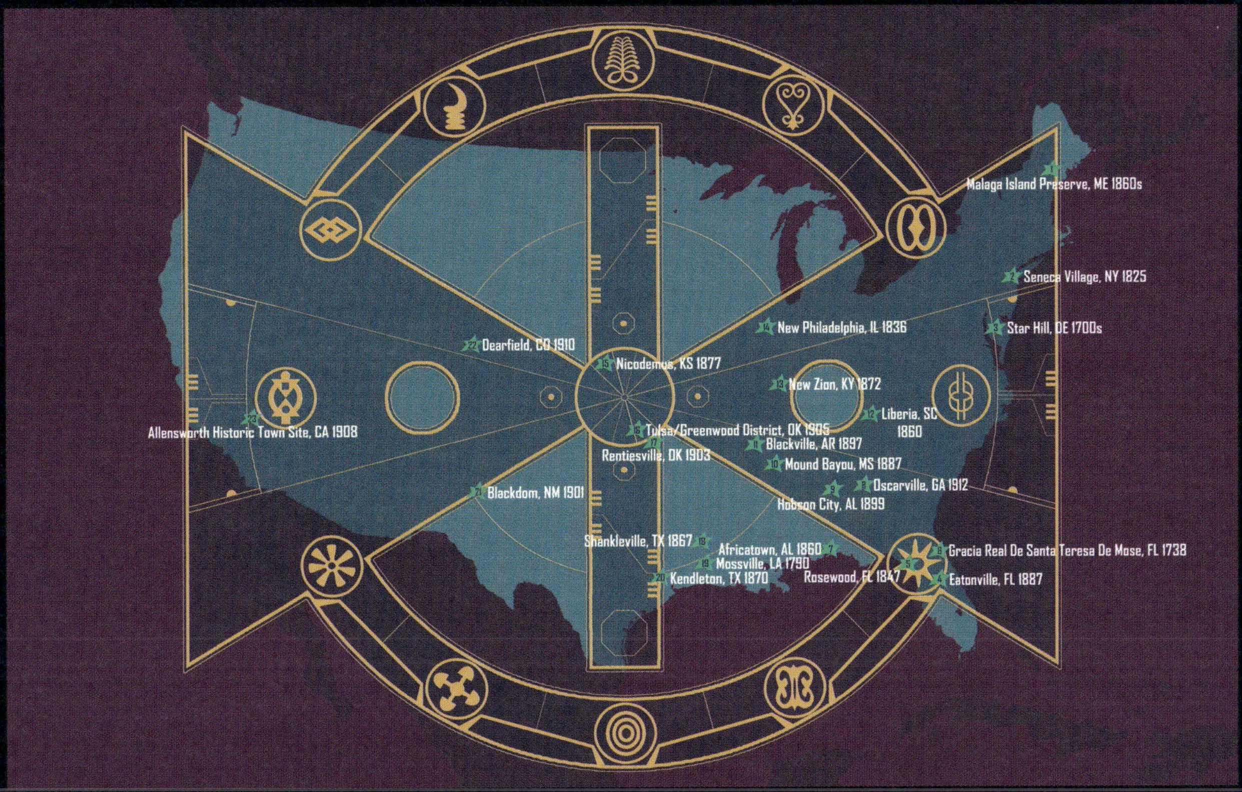

Black Quantum Futurism
Mmere Dane: Black Time Belt, 2021
This image maps several historic all-Black towns and Freedom Colonies across the United States pre- and post-Civil War—many destroyed by displacement, development, racist violence, and environmental injustice. *Mmere Dane: Black Time Belt* functions as a Black Quantum Futurist archive of alternative past-present-future(s) where the towns form a network of Black temporal zones—or a Black Time Belt—protecting these communities from the impacts of temporal-spatial oppression and destructive linear progressive timelines. More information available at: www.blacktimebelt.net

Spatial reparations is defined by the National African American Reparations Coalition (NAARC) as "a restorative and reparative geography of socioeconomic and political opportunity, particularly for those displaced and dispossessed by American slavery and their descendants,"[1] while Black Quantum Futurism (BQF) has a working definition of temporal reparations as restorative and reparative temporalities that provide the people most impacted by temporal inequities with the resources and ability to engage with time more creatively, expansively, abundantly, and generatively. BQF calls for the liberation, reclamation, reparation, and restoration of Black space-times.

Through the vision and theme of Space-Time Liberation, Black Quantum Futurism is creating the *SLOWER-THAN-LIGHT SHRINE: IN REMEMBRANCE OF THE UNDERGROUND RAILROAD*, a public monument and portal paying homage to liberation seekers who traversed the Underground Railroad in St. Louis, using the caves beneath the city on their path. The underground cave landscape offered spatial and temporal shelter for the freedom seekers in the border state of Missouri looking to cross the Mississippi River into Illinois. For the shrine, Black Quantum Futurism specifically responds to the Cherokee Cave at Lemp Avenue as a documented stop along the path—one opening into a cave system that stretches from Sugarloaf Mound to near Benton Park. The shrine will honor the abolitionist movement and marronage of the Underground Railroad, and the resonance of the issues and problems that make the need for abolition urgent in the present and relative future(s).

The shrine's hanging structures mimic the stalactites and stalagmites found in Cherokee Cave that closely resemble Ghanaian ritual and divination objects and are connected to crystals as ritual objects. The stalactites collect water and time, and form into crystals that can slow down light or create new and special kinds of light. In considering the ways light moves through a cave and its internal structures, BQF thinks of how liberation seekers had to move slower than light inside the shadows to escape the "watch"-ful eye of slave catchers, and the ways in which they hacked Western linear timelines by wading/waiting in the water—crossing and hiding in bodies of water.

[1] Marcus Anthony Hunter, "Radical Reparations," National African American Reparations Commission, June 5, 2021, https://reparationscomm.org/reparations-news/radical-reparations/.

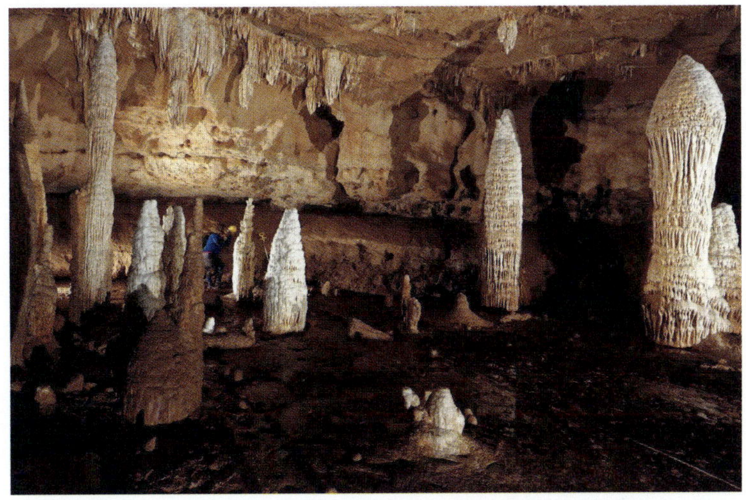

Stalactites and stalagmites in St. Louis underground caves, 2019
Courtesy of Derik Holtmann of the Cave Research Foundation and Missouri Speleological Survey

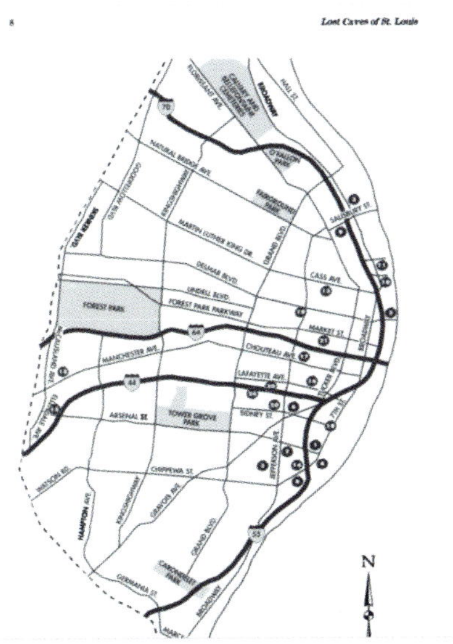

Map of Cherokee Cave, part of the underground cave systems in St. Louis
Courtesy of Lost Caves of St. Louis

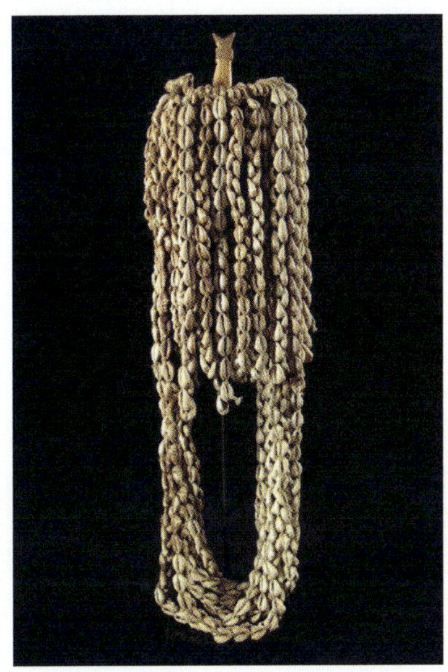

Cowrie shell shrine object from the Yoruba of Nigeria, early to mid-twentieth century. It stands 22" high and has a bone flute that represents Eshu, the trickster, at the top center of the piece
Image courtesy of the artists

Crystals and stones have also been found in excavations of the living quarters and prayer houses of the enslaved, including at the excavation site at 3314 Lemp Avenue. Quantum physics has confirmed the strange and intricate nature of crystalline structures;[2] for example, a recent discovery shows "an infinitesimally small world composed of a strange and surprising array of links, knots and winding,"[2] while another recent experiment used an ancient Namibian crystal called cuprite to produce the largest hybrid particles of light and matter ever created.[4] The "floor" or base of the shrine mimics a subpit floor and functions as a quantum time capsule. The shrine is constructed in the image of a Kongo cosmogram as well as configurations related to quantum physics experiments. In addition to these connections, the gates, windows, and arches serve to connect to and honor the homes lost in Mill Creek Valley and Pruitt-Igoe adjacent to the site of the shrine.

In parallel with this public portal, Black Quantum Futurism will install Community Futures: Space-Time Liberation Lab (CF:STL Lab), a three-month-long Afrofuturist housing and land justice lab at The Luminary. The acronym CF:STL takes on the triple meaning of St. Louis, Space-Time Liberation, and Slower-Than-Light. CF:STL Lab will provide a temporary convening space-time for housing advocates, artists, organizers, tenants, and other people impacted by housing insecurity and land injustice and/or interested in co-creating strategies to address its impacts. CF:STL Lab is self-activated with interactive activities and tools developed by BQF and collaborators, and activated by planned programming developed in collaboration with local community members and organizations on the topics of spatial and temporal reparations, housing futures, land justice, tenant power and collective responsibilities, land sovereignty, Black and Indigenous solidarity, and other related topics.

With these projects, BQF invites community members to participate in the reclamation, liberation, and reparation of space and time (i.e., histories, presents, and futures) within their own neighborhoods through the marking, mapping, and storage of space and time that can later be reclaimed. These spaces and times are both personal and communal, global and universal. The shrine, lab, and associated elements of CF:STL will be activated across the three-month exhibition as space-times for visioning and testing of strategies for community sustainability, healing, and housing and land justice.

[2] Johanna L. Miller, "An inexpensive crystal makes a fine quantum time machine," *Physics Today* 72, no. 11 (2019): 14, https://doi.org/10.1063/PT.3.4335.

[3] Princeton University, "Physicists Discover Strange Array of Links and Knots in Quantum Matter," SciTechDaily, May 27, 2022, https://scitechdaily.com/physicists-discover-strange-array-of-links-and-knots-in-quantum-matter/.

[4] University of St. Andrews, "Ancient Namibian stone could hold key to future quantum computers," Phys.org, April 15, 2022, https://phys.org/news/2022-04-ancient-namibian-stone-key-future.html.

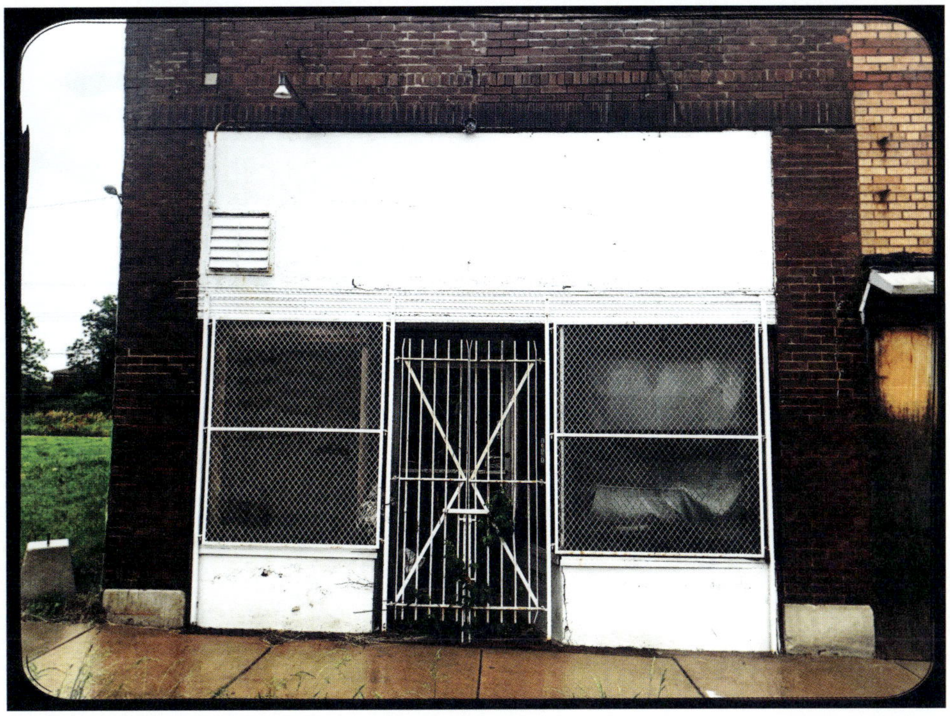

La Rose Room Cocktail Lounge storefront
Photograph by Black Quantum Futurism during Counterpublic site visit, 2022

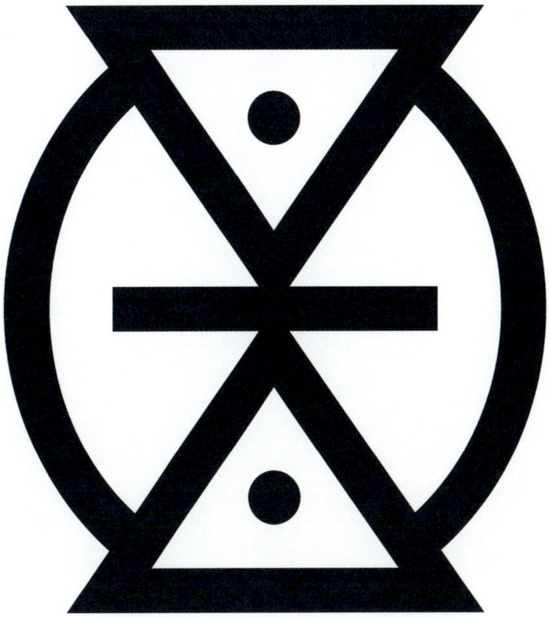

Mmere Dane is an Adinkra Symbol that means "time changes" or "times change" in the Akan language, signifying the dynamic nature of change and the temporary nature of any state of events. The symbol resembles an hourglass enshrined in a circle with a line running through its epicenter at the place where the top and bottom half of the hourglass meet. It is a symbol that can encode and hide different layers of meaning.

Damon Davis

CURATOR:
JAMES MCANALLY

LOCATION:
CITYPARK AND
THE BRICKLINE GREENWAY

Damon Davis is a post-disciplinary artist based in St. Louis, Missouri. His work spans across a spectrum of creative mediums to tell stories exploring how identity is informed by power and mythology. For Counterpublic 2023, Davis is realizing *Pillars of the Valley*, a mile-long monument to the residents of Mill Creek Valley and a related short film exploring how myths and moods are passed down generationally through the Black family.

Informed by a four-year community-engagement process, Great Rivers Greenway spearheaded the effort to elevate the Mill Creek Valley story through Davis's installation with support from numerous community partners, including Counterpublic, St. Louis CITY SC, Harris-Stowe State University, and the City of St. Louis.

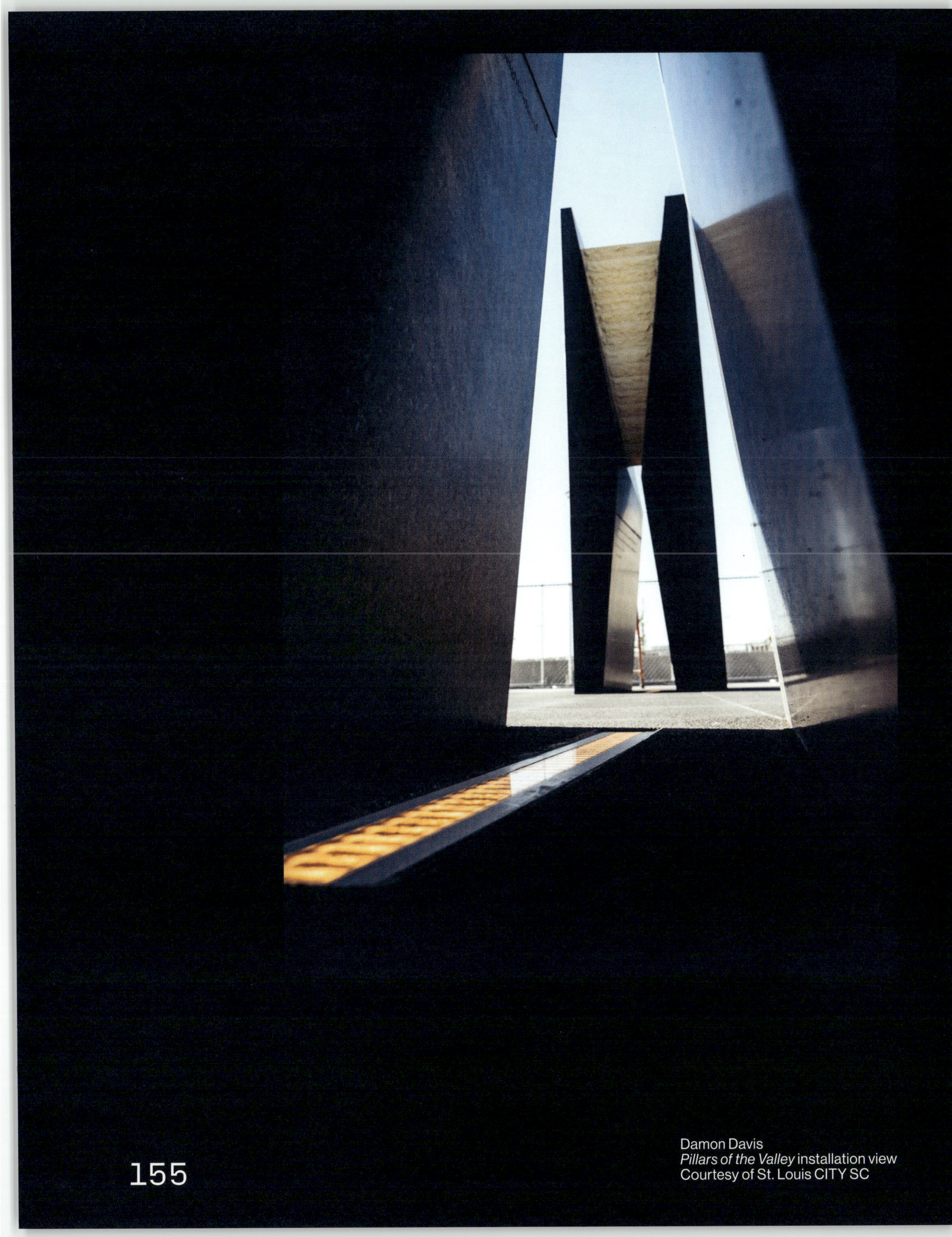

Damon Davis
Pillars of the Valley installation view
Courtesy of St. Louis CITY SC

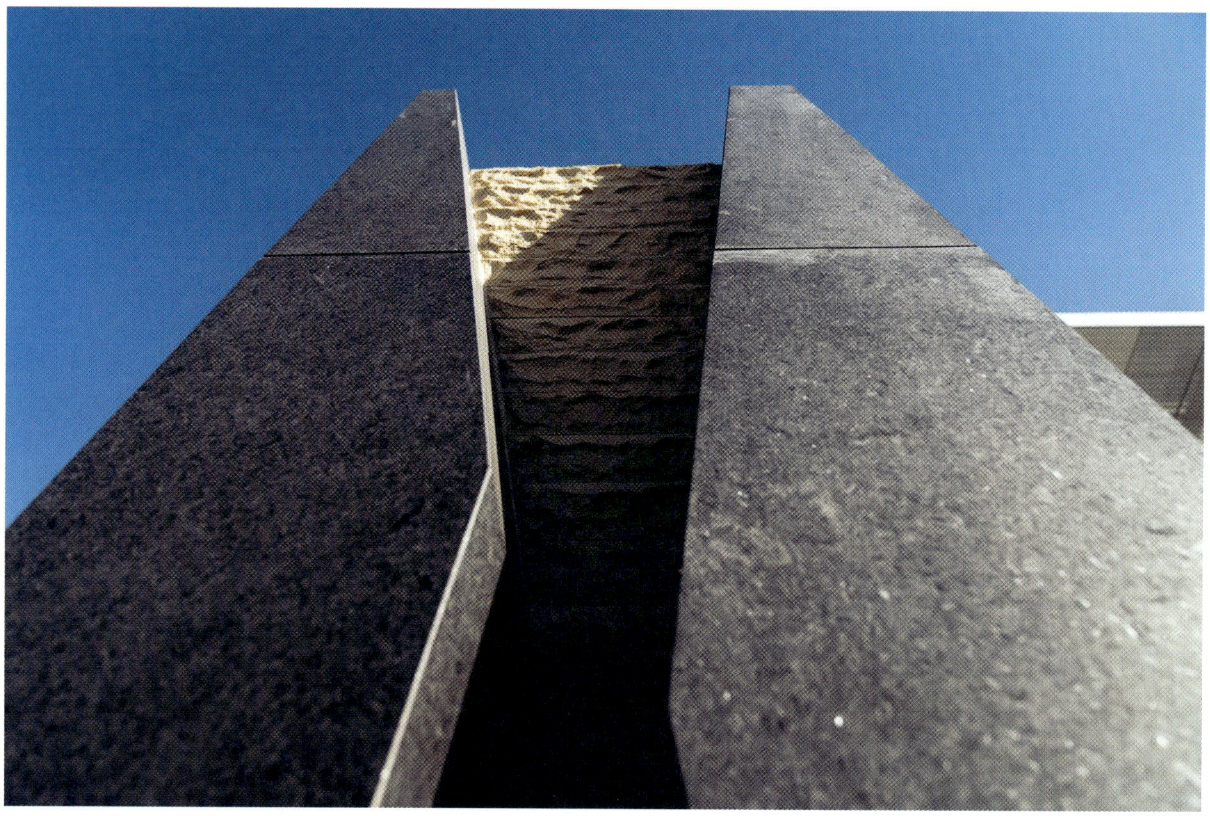

Damon Davis
Pillars of the Valley (detail)
Courtesy of St. Louis CITY SC

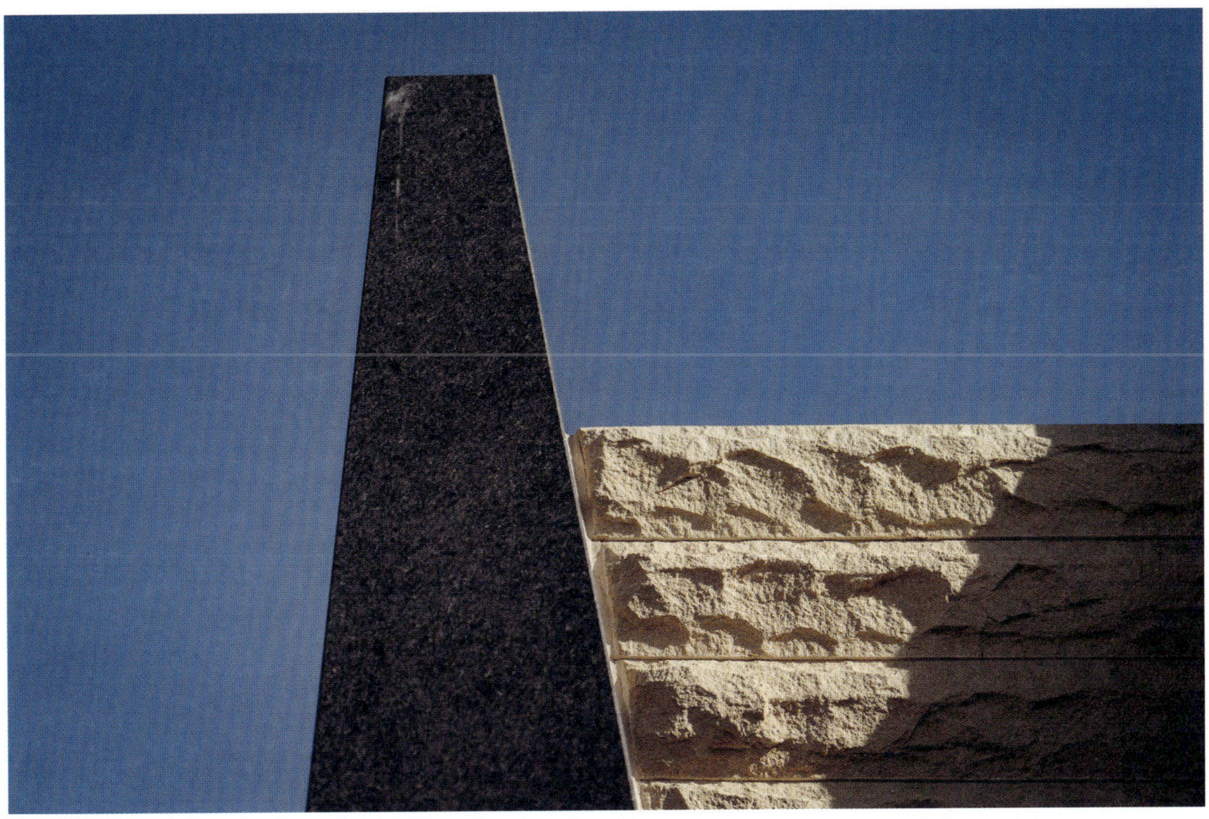

Damon Davis
Pillars of the Valley (detail)
Courtesy of St. Louis CITY SC

Davis's work will honor Mill Creek Valley, which was a predominantly Black neighborhood whose residents were displaced during the city's demolition of the Midtown area in the late 1950s. The once-vibrant neighborhood was home to 20,000 residents, 800-plus businesses, and 40-plus houses of worship before city officials declared that the 450 acres would be fully demolished in the name of "urban renewal."

"Mill Creek Valley was a thriving Black community, with businesses and nightlife, arts community, and a range of socio-economic classes. The narrative of it being a blighted community—it was neglected for a reason, slumified so that the excuse could be used to pave over it," explains Davis. "I have designed a series of pedestals and portals to represent hourglasses that hold time still, displayed at the top. Just like the soil, we can excavate the stories of these people and put them on literal pedestals for the whole world to see, acknowledge, and start a conversation about their stories."

Over the next few years, this installation will stretch a mile along Market Street, linking to historic sites on the campus of Harris-Stowe State University, some of the only remaining structures from Mill Creek Valley. These include the Henry Givens Administration Building (formerly Vashon High School), renovated Stars Park (former home of the Negro baseball league), and Vashon Community Center, which is being renovated into the Don and Heide Wolff Jazz Institute and National Black Radio Hall of Fame.

In Davis's words:

> This monument stands as a remembrance of the great people of the Mill Creek Valley neighborhood. The pedestals are portals to a time and place that are gone. Yet, the legacy of these displaced Black people cannot be forgotten, built over, or moved aside. Their collective memories, stories, and contributions to the narrative of St. Louis live on.

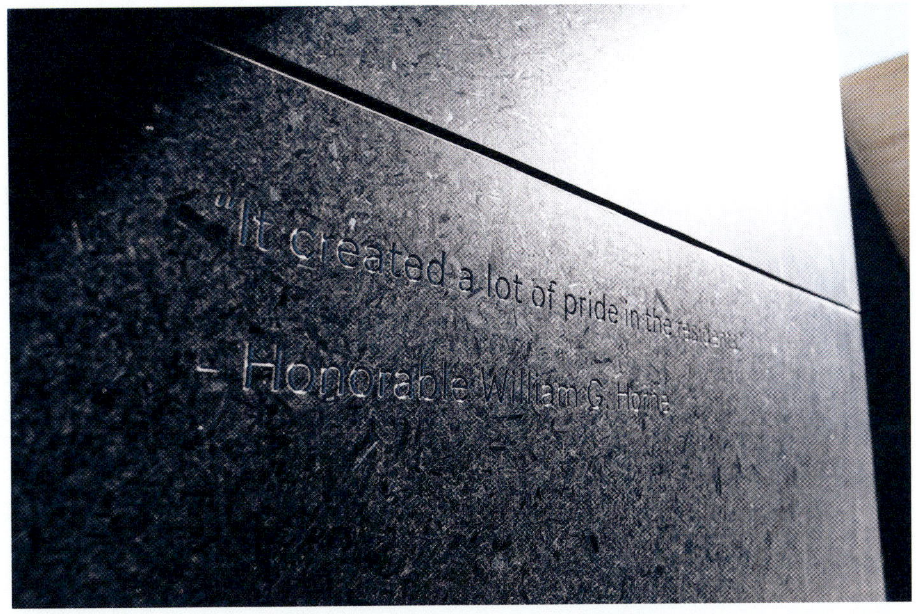

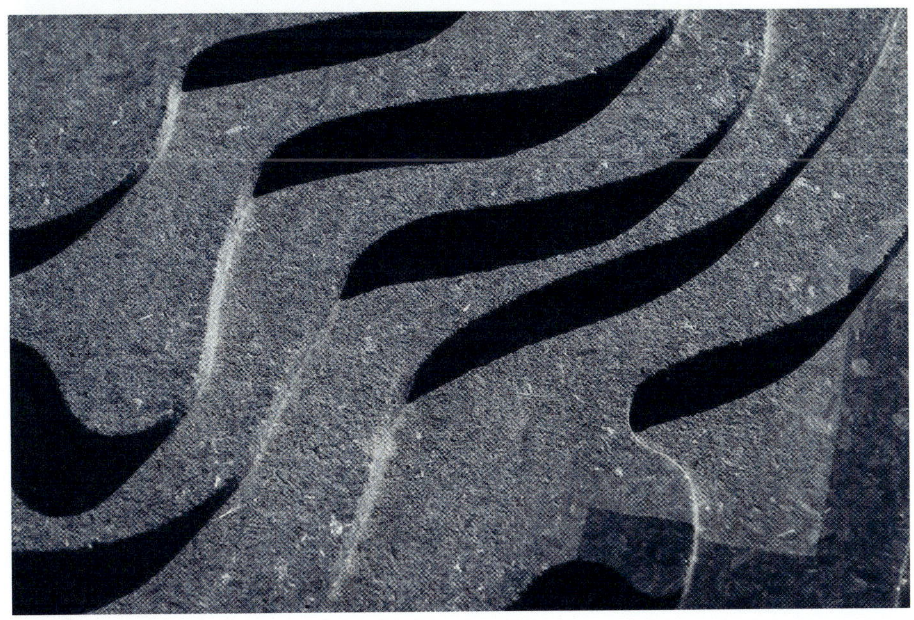

Damon Davis
Pillars of the Valley (detail)
Courtesy of St. Louis CITY SC

Torkwase Dyson

CURATOR:
JAMES MCANALLY

LOCATION:
ST. LOUIS PLACE PARK AND
MILDRED LANE KEMPER ART MUSEUM

Torkwase Dyson is a painter working across multiple mediums to explore the continuity between ecology, infrastructure, and architecture. This practice is rooted in exploring the spatial strategies of Black and Indigenous peoples across the world as foundations of invention as we make livable worlds. For Counterpublic 2023, Dyson realizes an immersive architectural and sonic installation, *Bird and Lava (Scott Joplin)*. This newly commissioned major sculptural work sits alongside the sites of prominent Black performance spaces in Mill Creek Valley that fomented ragtime, including the iconic Rosebud Bar.

Bird and Lava (Scott Joplin) develops directly from the legacy of Scott Joplin and the musical freedom he found in the late nineteenth century. Joplin's ragtime music evolved in response to the oppressive conditions of minstrel shows and is credited as the first truly "American" musical form—a syncopated blend of classical piano and African polyrhythms with mathematical precision.[1] *Bird and Lava (Scott Joplin)* likewise creates a syncopated experience of the landscape with multiple vantage points along its structure, immersed in the discordant environment of St. Louis.

[1] See "From the African/Caribbean roots to Ragtime" and numerous other sources exploring the pre-history of jazz. "From the African/Caribbean roots to Ragtime," Pekkamusic.com, accessed February 10, 2023, https://www.pekkasmusic.com/education-jazz-history-1.html.

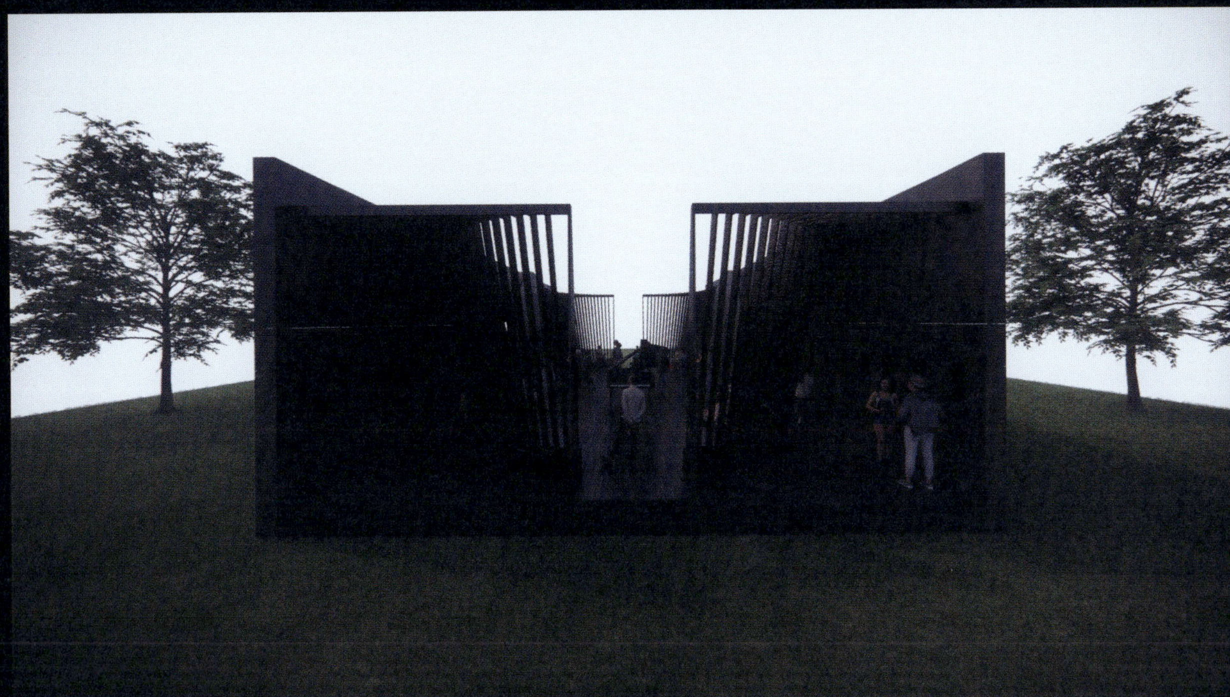

Torkwase Dyson
Bird and Lava (Scott Joplin)
Rendering for Counterpublic 2023
Courtesy of Richard Gray Gallery

This interactive immersive sound installation is an invitation to scholars and musicians interested in responding to ragtime in a unique architectural experience. For Counterpublic 2023, Dyson invites movement artists, choreographers, and musicians to adapt the structure of ragtime into a series of performances in and around the structure. The performances aim to make direct correlations between syncopation and the body to explore the spatial impact of present-day climate migrations, displacement, and nomadicity.

Dyson uses adaptation and syncopation as organizing principles for what the artist calls Suspended Theater. The work aims to make transhistorical connections to Black liberation strategies formed to refuse slavery's spatial violence and its structural continuities in the present ecological crisis. She addresses what is being called the Black Plantationocene through the lens of Scott Joplin's ragtime.[2] His work with syncopation emphasizes mathematics, time, and movement—ideas critical to climate adaptation. *Bird and Lava (Scott Joplin)* continues to expand on Dyson's goal to speak to the poetics of both the quotidian and the existential realities of climate change.

[2] Donna Haraway et al., "Anthropologists are talking—About the Anthropocene," *Ethnos* 81, no. 3 (2016): 535–64. See also Katherine McKittrick, "On plantations, prisons and a black sense of place," *Social & Cultural Geography* 12, no. 8 (October 2011): 947–63; Sylvia Wynter, "Novel and history, plot and plantation," *Savacou* 5 (June 1971): 95–102.

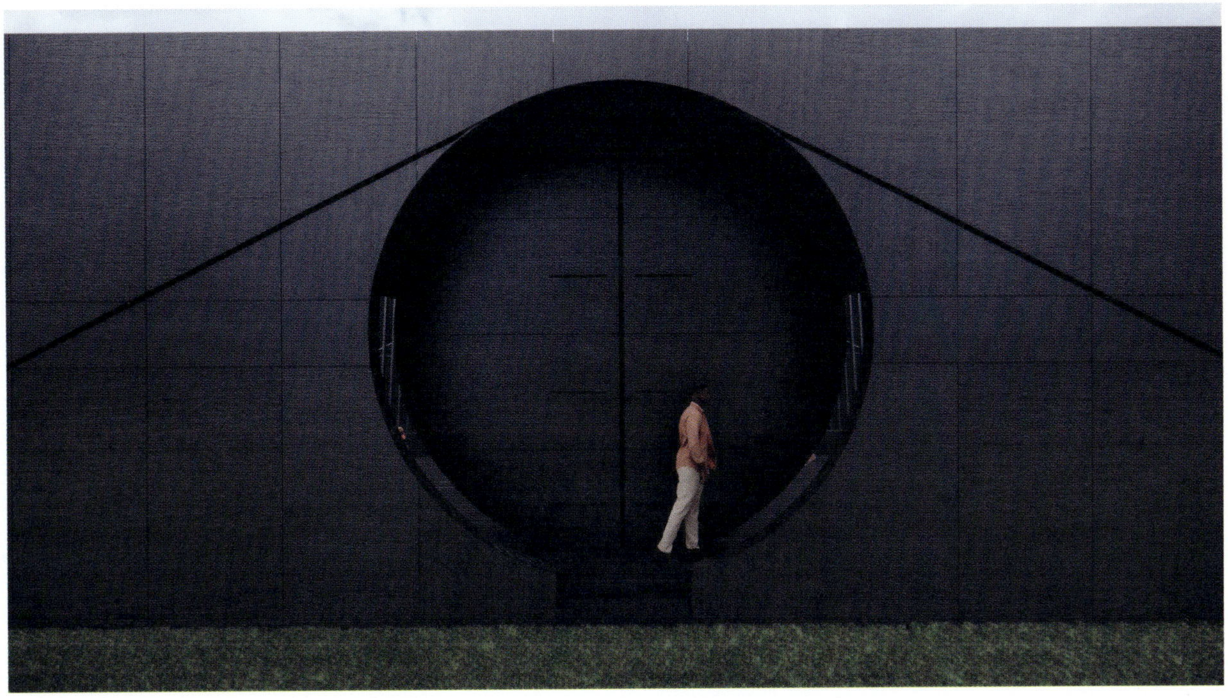

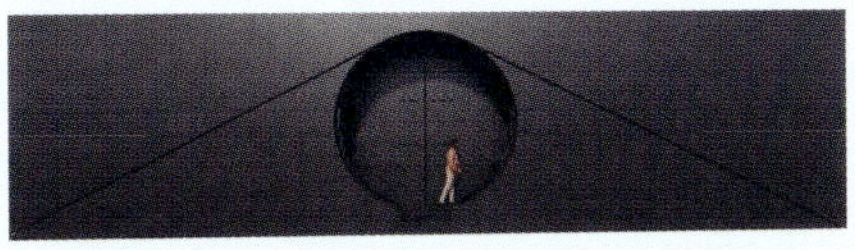

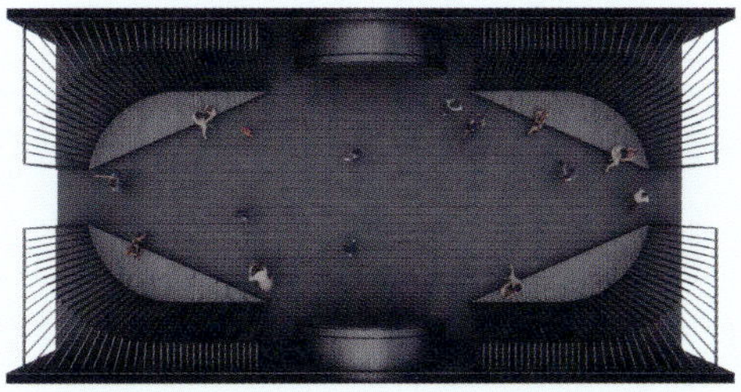

Torkwase Dyson
Bird and Lava (Scott Joplin)
Rendering for Counterpublic 2023
Courtesy of Richard Gray Gallery

Distance: I am certain that the beauty in Black indeterminacy, from sound to science, from architecture to migration will continue to guide our solutions to climate and form. Forms that are deeply spatial, generous, and haunting, as they should be! In this moment of environmental precarity we will need to be both liquid and mountains, bird and lava. And it is the density of Black grace that will always be the thing that keeps us in our own humanity.

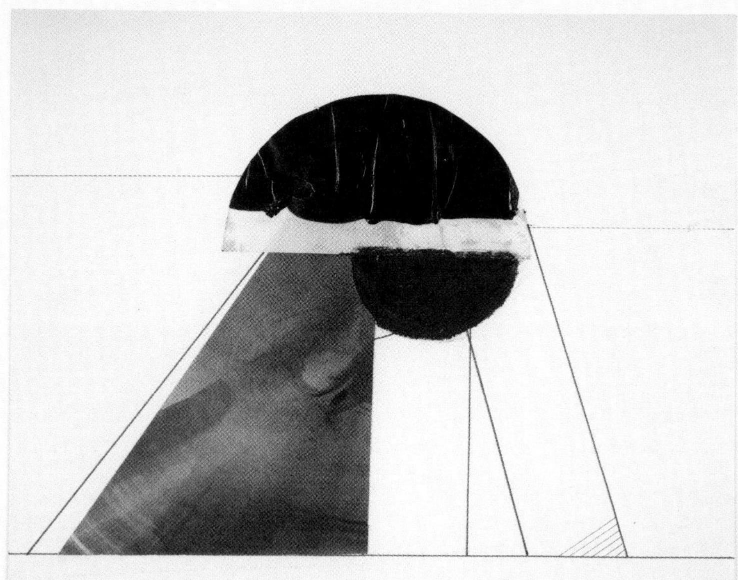

architecture
surfaces
infrastructure
magnitude
distance
proximity
movement
black hauntology
modulation
ocean
ontology
here

Space is a relative material

to be of space
to be of scale
to be of blue
to be of black

Torkwase Dyson
Force Multiplier 6 (Bird and Lava), 2020
Graphite, acrylic, charcoal, vellum, and pen on paper
11" × 14" (27.9 × 35.6 cm)
Photograph by Rich Lee
Courtesy of Pace Gallery

state change,
always state change

There is no universal now,
there is a subjective here.

Construction as a way of knowing who she is. Pilot and her box.

Expanded
Concrete Abstract
Expanded perception
Expanded Awareness
Expanded

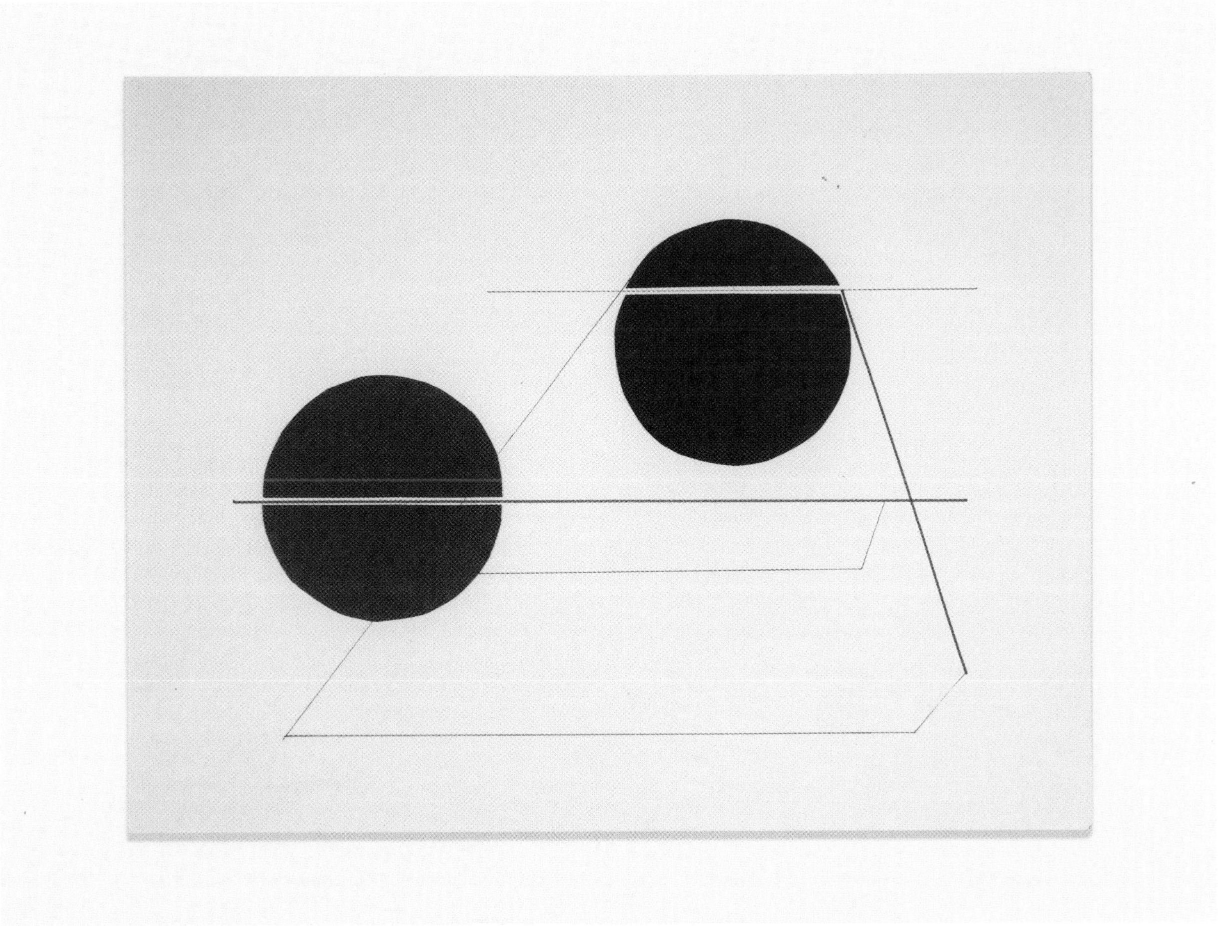

here i am way over there inside me

If systemic oppression is a form, systemic liberation is as well. I look into histories where methods of liberation live. And what I see my ancestors want me to know.

Torkwase Dyson
Prayer 1 (Bird and Lava), 2020
Graphite, acrylic, charcoal, vellum, and pen on paper
11″ × 14″ (27.9 × 35.6 cm)
Photograph by Rich Lee
Courtesy of Pace Gallery

In this moment my questions are of scale, movement, perception, distance, and state change. More concretely my questions focus on built environments of the Transatlantic Slave Trade and modernism's participation in the horrors of climate change and dispossession. It is a very simple ambition, and that is to consider spatial strategies of Black and Indigenous people across the world as foundations of invention as we make livable worlds.

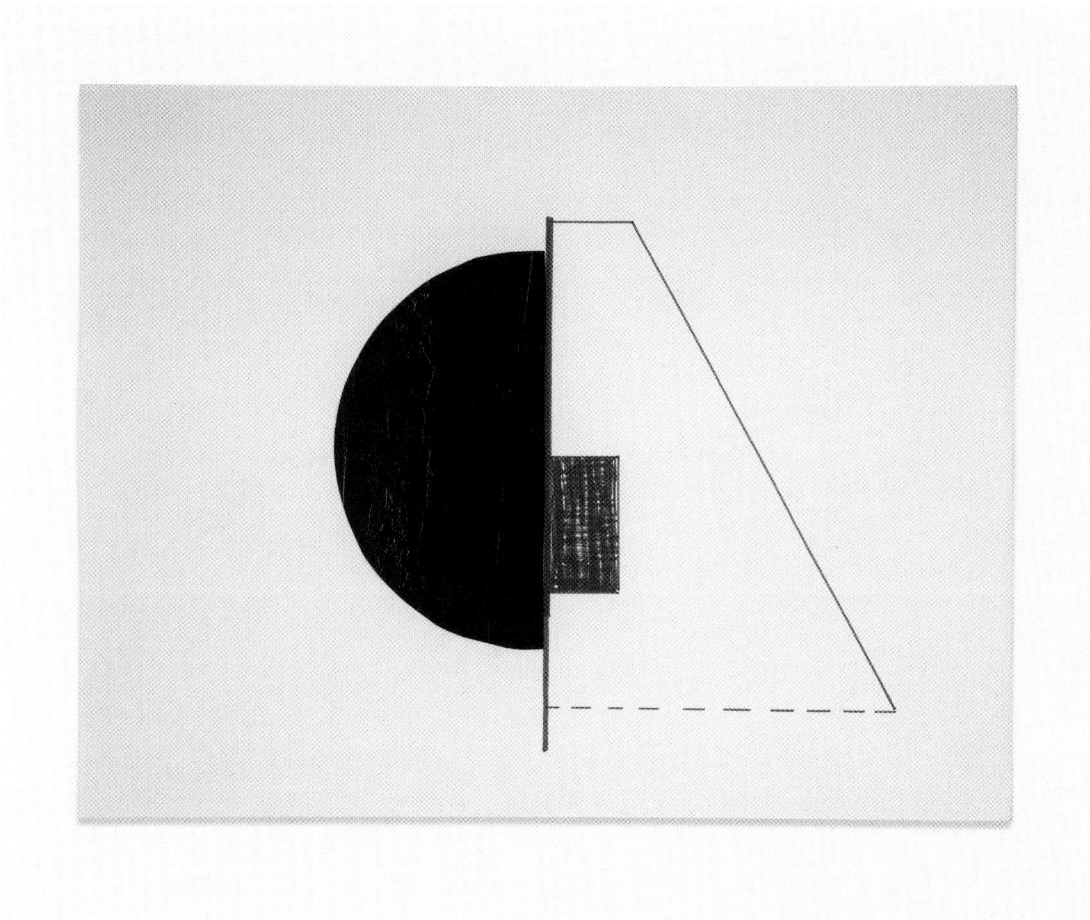

This drawing has become an object in the round.

Glissant's question of opacity and transparency has become a mediation in architecture.

This drawing/architecture is based on the understanding that there are multiple liberation strategies in the age of the Plantationocene.

Some quotidian and some phenomenological.

Torkwase Dyson
Force Multiplier 7 (Bird and Lava), 2020
Graphite, acrylic, charcoal, vellum, and pen on paper
11″ × 14″ (27.9 × 35.6 cm)
Photograph by Rich Lee
Courtesy of Pace Gallery

What are the spatial dependencies of these geometries I'm calling hypershapes? Are they plantation economies? Are the liberations that inevitably come a result of plantation economies? Are they from the horrors of extraction?

If Blackness is already an architectonic developed out of liquidity (ocean), can the work embody this phenomenon and offer sensation (sensoria) at the register of liberation? The infrastructure of this question, for me, exists in the hypershapes; a geometric abstraction culled from Black histories and responsive to our ecosystem now and in our future.

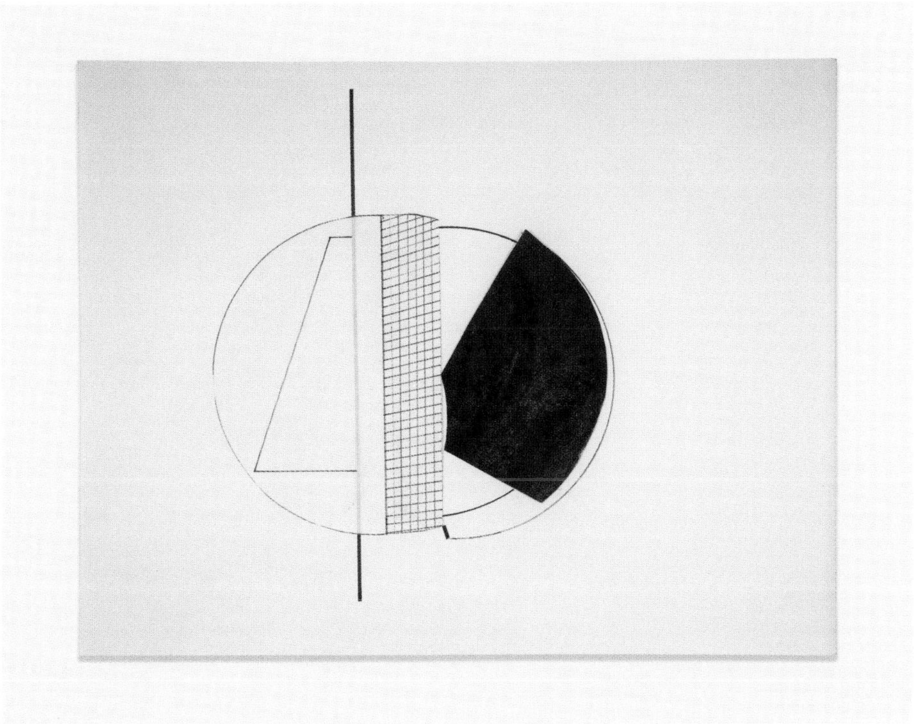

This text is always with me.

"The Crisis of the Negro Intellectual: A Post-Date" (1994)
Hortense J. Spillers

The model that I am proposing would be based on a theorization that melds various aspects of the human sciences and a mode of culture analysis for which we currently have no name, but one might think of it as a cultural demography; this new "science" would be alert to the cultural implications of movement, which is not only a primary meaning of the life-world but one of its most significant literary tropes—the "symbolic geography" that would explain (1) diasporic movement, (2) internal migration, and (3) the mechanisms of fantasy and ambition that contextualize African American struggle.

In this project, Bird and Lava, I've found an overall form that speaks to the history of Black spatial liberation strategies. I've constructed a form by drawing, sketching, and modeling these vast geographic, architectural, and infrastructural spaces used for liberation. I've found my way to a method and mode of expression that regards these histories as necessary throughways to navigating the systems of self liberation. This work/shape/form has become a mediation for me at this moment of solitude where I can simply honor deep freedom.

Torkwase Dyson
Force Multiplier 8 (Bird and Lava), 2020
Graphite, acrylic, charcoal, vellum, and pen on paper
11" × 14" (27.9 × 35.6 cm)
Photograph by Rich Lee
Courtesy of Pace Gallery

Tim Portlock

CURATOR:
JAMES MCANALLY

LOCATION:
2607 CASS AVENUE
(ADJACENT TO PRUITT-IGOE)

Tim Portlock's work combines special effects software and the visual conventions of nineteenth-century American painting to creatively simulate real-world American cityscapes. As the first focus of an ongoing series, for Counterpublic 2023 Portlock is endeavoring to engage the currents of memory in relation to public housing, reexamining a time when the government was thought to have a lead role to play in solving social problems, as a contrast to the attitudes of today in which large-scale public housing projects are decried as a failed solution for the housing crisis. Sparked by his father's time living and working in public housing in Chicago, the series is an opportunity to reflect on the divergence between the intentions of these spaces and their execution, of their still-present possibilities and persistent dismissal as a social good, ultimately memorializing the experience of people who have lived in public housing.

For Counterpublic 2023, Portlock addresses Pruitt-Igoe from the vantage point of oral histories from residents of the notorious housing complex in North St. Louis. Built in 1954 as a complex of 11-story blocks containing 2,870 apartments over a 57-acre site, the buildings were destroyed successively from 1972 to 1974. Pruitt-Igoe has been alternately lionized and derided, all the while overly theorized for its meaning in architectural history and place in St. Louis. Drawing down its academic treatments, the series instead looks at the intimacies of history, of the hybrid spaces of lived experience, of a counter-image to the representations of disrepair and demolition that are most often circulated in relation to the space.

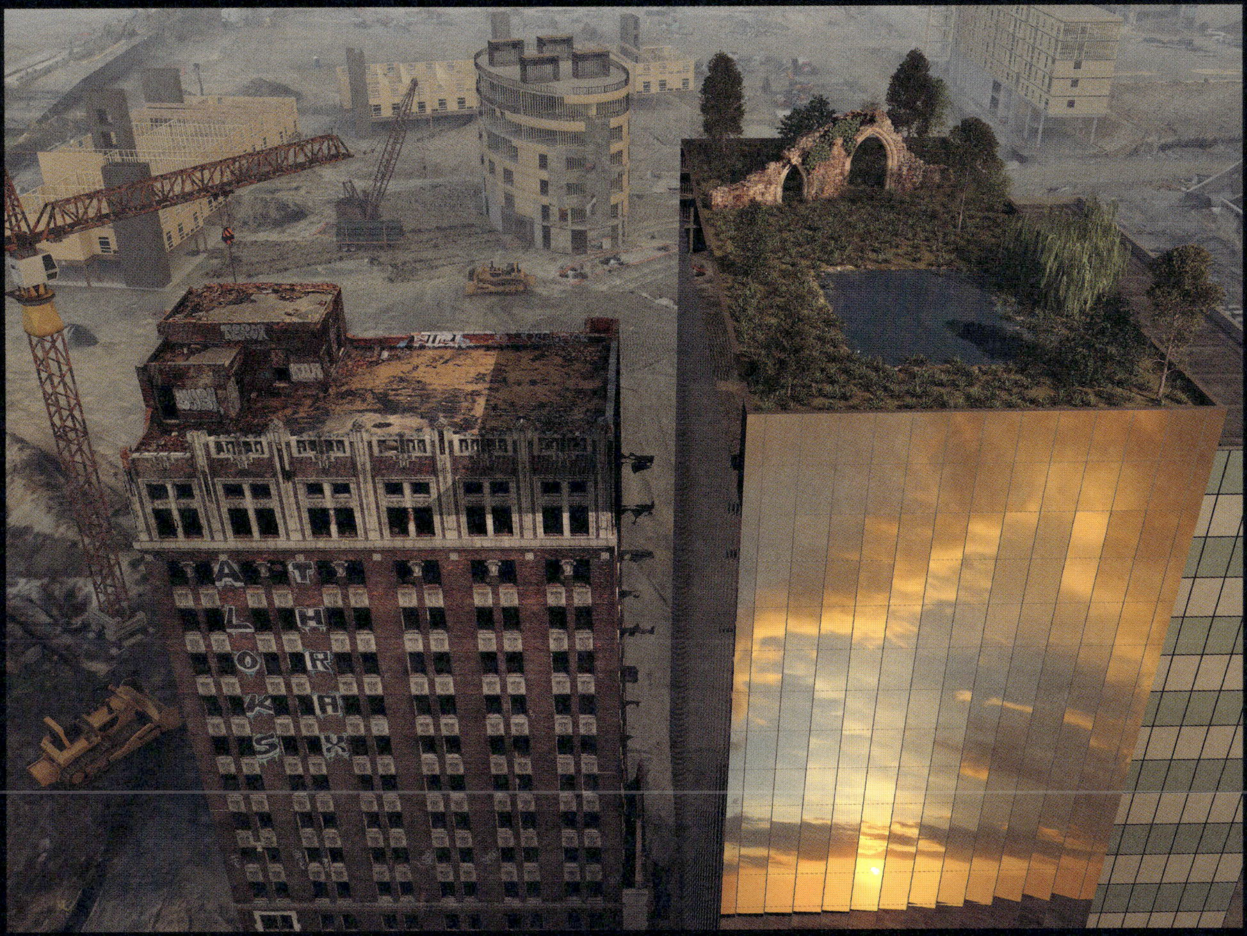

Tim Portlock
just steps away, 2020
Archival pigment print
43.25" × 58" (109.9 × 147.3 cm)

Across a series of interviews, participants describe their apartments and the buildings around them in detail according to their own contours. Using special effects software, Portlock then builds detailed renderings of their accounts, without reference to the overly circulated images of the Minoru Yamasaki-designed buildings, creating a subjective, faulty, but ultimately more intimate view of how this space lives on in memory and how these memories, and the legacies of Pruitt-Igoe, do not have to (and will never) coalesce into a unified narrative. Across the installation of images and the related publication, Portlock attempts to build a more personal narrative around the publics of public housing as multilayered sites of memory that reach back and forwards simultaneously, inscribing altered forms of inhabitation.

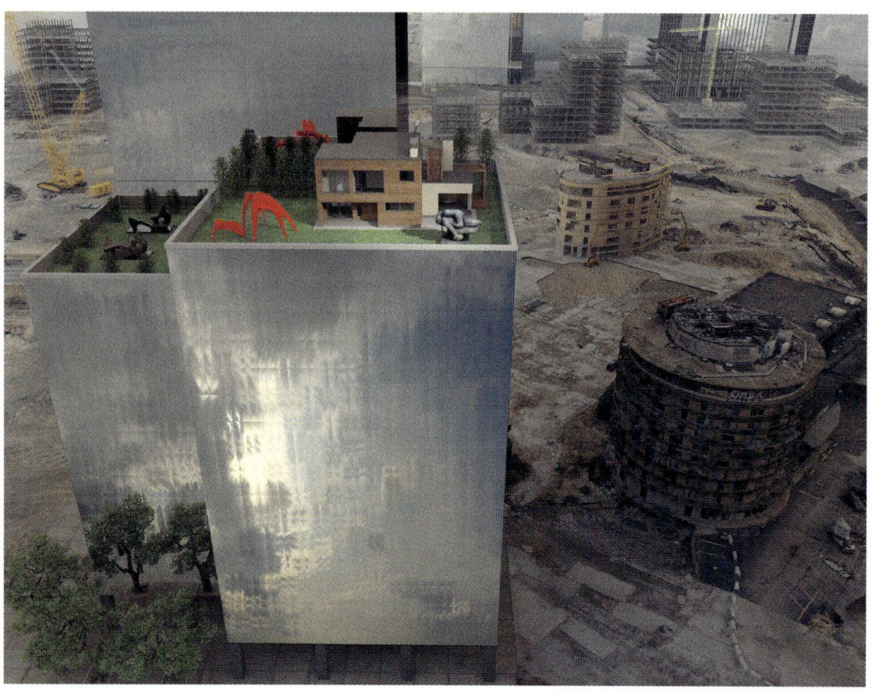

Tim Portlock
sundrenched, 2020
Archival pigment print
43.25" × 58" (109.9 × 147.3 cm)

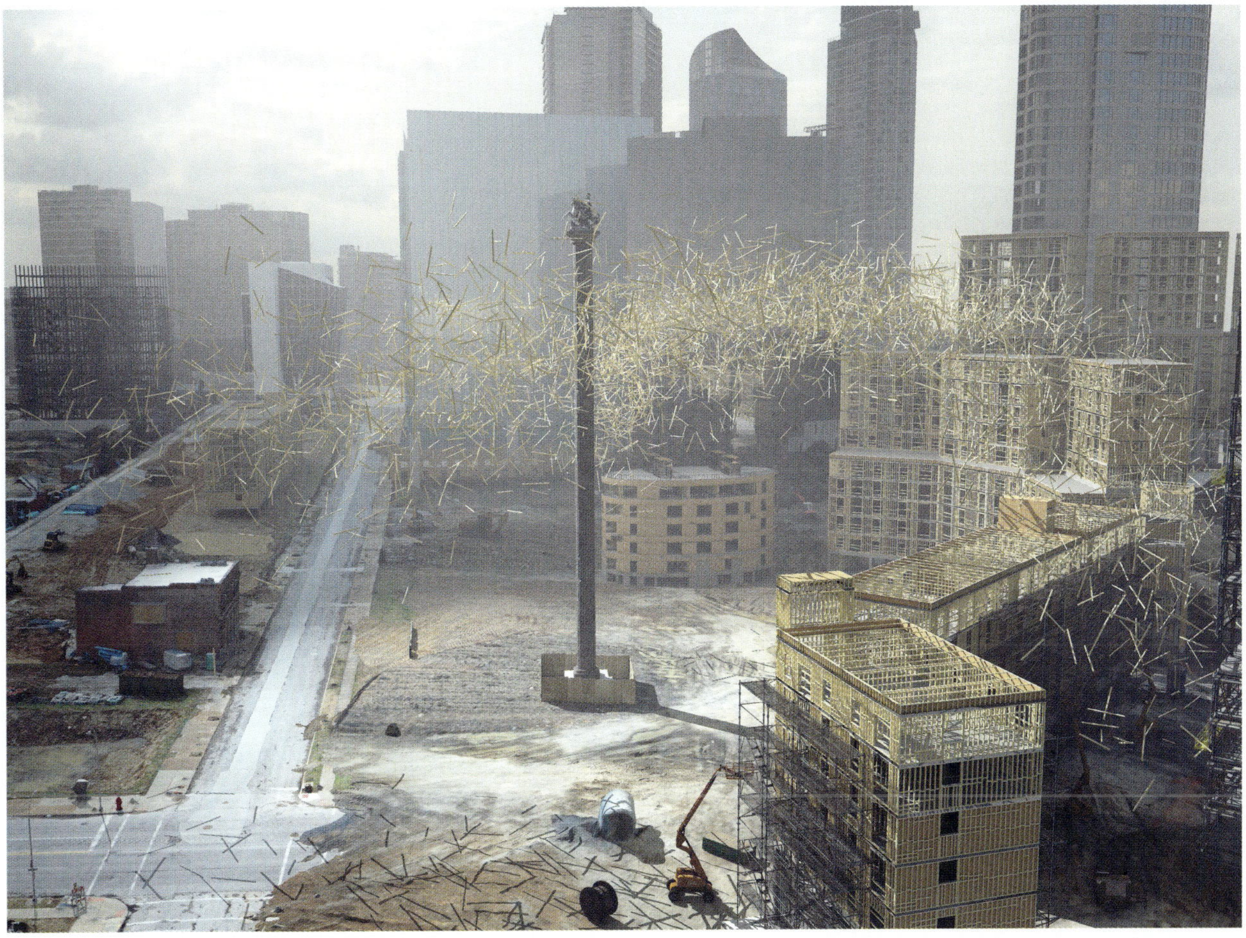

Tim Portlock
prequalified, 2020
Archival pigment print
43.25" × 57.25" (109.9 × 145.4 cm)

Robert E. Green

CURATOR:
JAMES MCANALLY

LOCATION:
2205 ST. LOUIS AVENUE

Artist and community activist Robert E. Green is a self-studied artist who uses assemblage to create three-dimensional wall pieces and sculptures, rescuing parts of buildings, neighborhood cast-offs, old signs, and other objects found around his home and studio in North St. Louis, and giving them new life in works steeped in multiple meanings.

As part of Counterpublic 2023, Green's St. Louis Place studio is a site for studio tours and community conversations set among works and ephemera from his long history in the neighborhood. The studio includes assemblage, sculpture, video projection, and photographic work created from and installed within a building at 2205 St. Louis Avenue in North St. Louis that was rescued and renovated by Green over the past several years. The building is itself an artwork animated by layered pieces that speak to the spatial displacement of lives and communities fractured due to politics and erasure fostered by years of systemic oppression of African Americans in St. Louis. Embedded in these works is the artist's personal story of growing up in the legendary Pruitt-Igoe housing complex and the trauma he and his family suffered when the community was displaced due to its demolition.

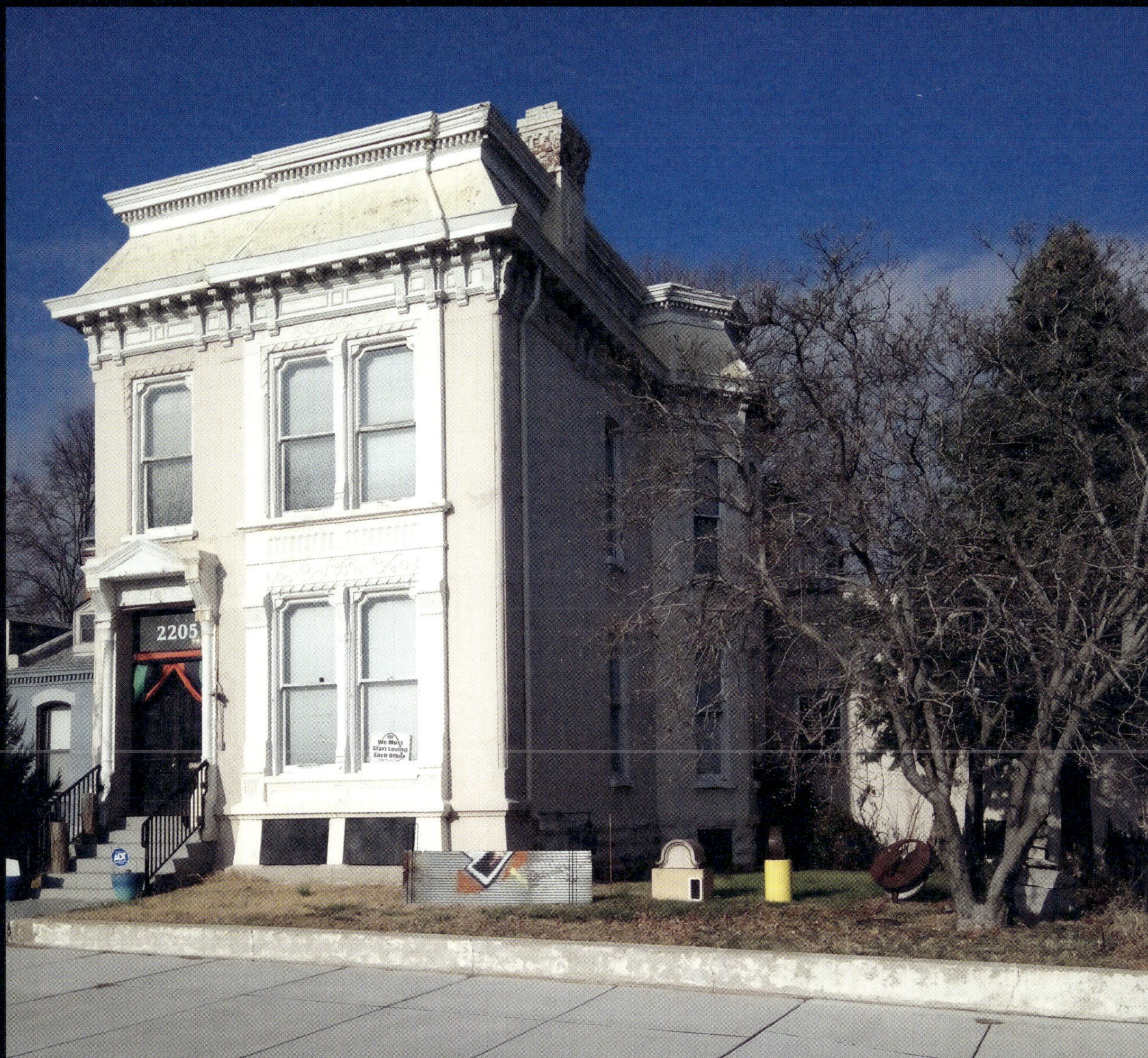

Robert E. Green's studio and community space at 2205 St. Louis Avenue
Courtesy of Robert E. Green

Accordingly, Green gives as much weight, if not more, in his artistic practice to his community activism, which he organizes to combat the divisions and inequities in his community. This takes form in cultural festivals and events like his prominent Juneteenth Day Festival, the St. Louis African American Artifacts Festival and Bazaar, the Pruitt-Igoe Forever history initiative, and other cultural festivals and gatherings. His aim in these connected practices is to cultivate awareness and appreciation of the significant contributions made by people of African descent and to shine a spotlight on systemic, racist political processes and their consequences, which have kept the community from flourishing.

Together, Green's contributions to Counterpublic 2023 root his practice in the long arc of lived history, active organizing, and spatial and social imaginaries for Black solidarity and self-determination in North St. Louis.

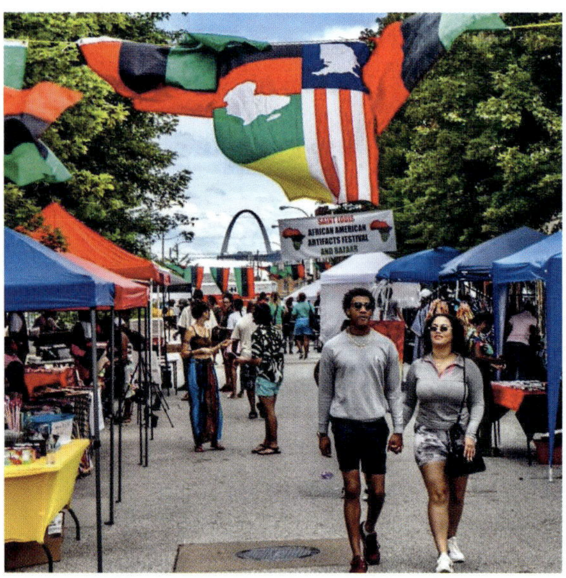

St. Louis African American Artifacts Festival and Bazaar, organized by Robert E. Green
Courtesy of Robert E. Green

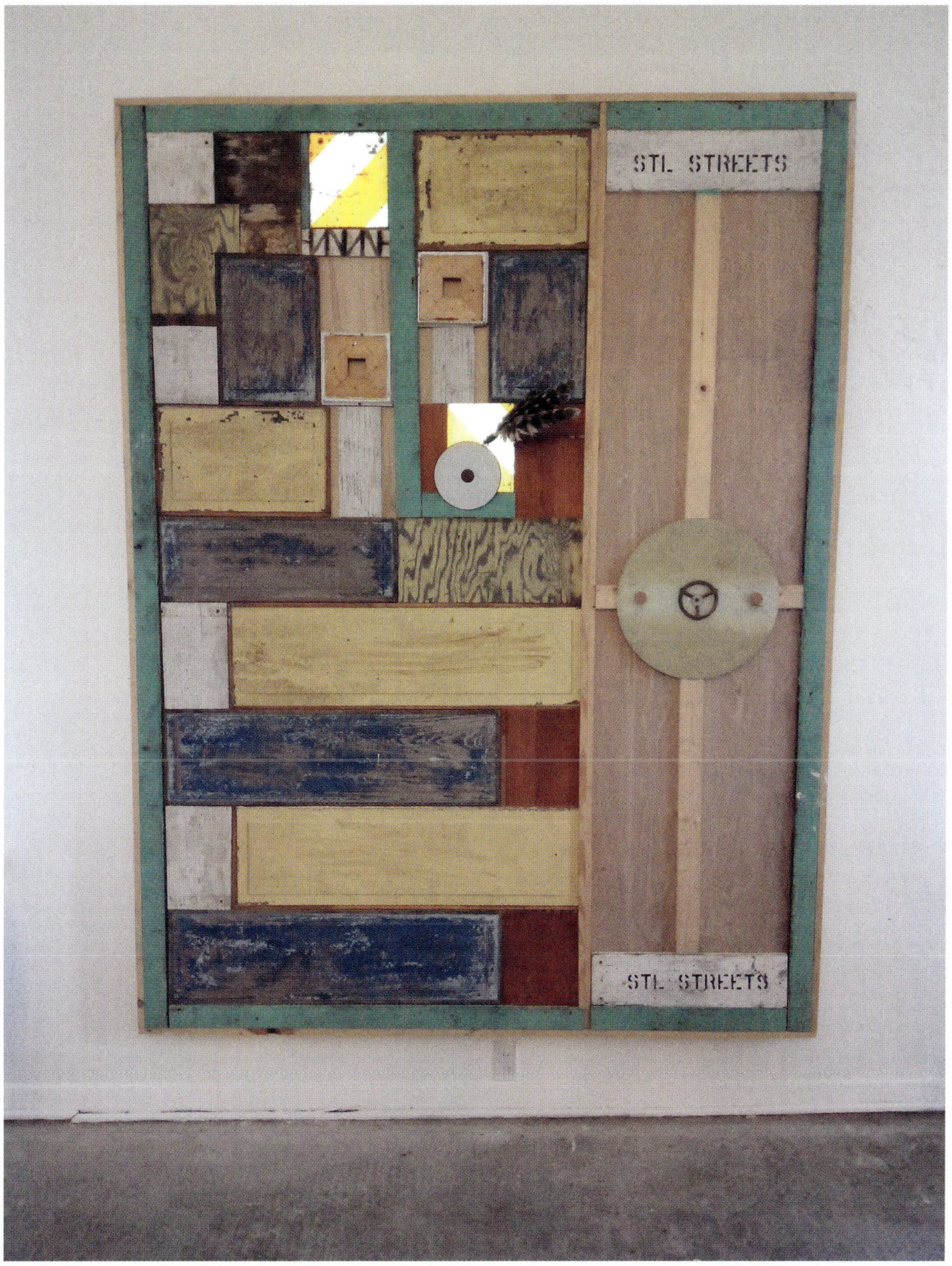

Robert E. Green
In-process artwork (2023) from found materials in the St. Louis Place neighborhood

Seitu Ken Jones

CURATOR:
DREAM THE COMBINE/
JAMES MCANALLY

LOCATION:
METRO BUS LINE

Artist and advocate Seitu Ken Jones has been tending the soil of community through art for more than forty years. Throughout his career, he has harnessed the tools of visual art, infrastructure, and civic engagement to create work that links history to the present and honors the community's assets—from its historic figures to natural resources to cultural traditions. In his public art and events, Jones pushes beyond traditional art spaces to reach people in the context of their lives and communities, from a thirteen-acre farm in St. Paul, Minnesota to installations in a public food market in Nashville, Tennessee.

For Counterpublic 2023, Jones seeds a new iteration of his ongoing collard greens series along the Metro bus line, weaving family recipes alongside dispersed designs of collards on buses and bus shelters along the Jefferson Avenue corridor. Inspired by the ways in which food is a primary means of communal gathering and of passing along knowledge and ancestral meaning in Black culture, the project acts as a distribution system, circulating the greens through the city and transmitting recipes to new households.

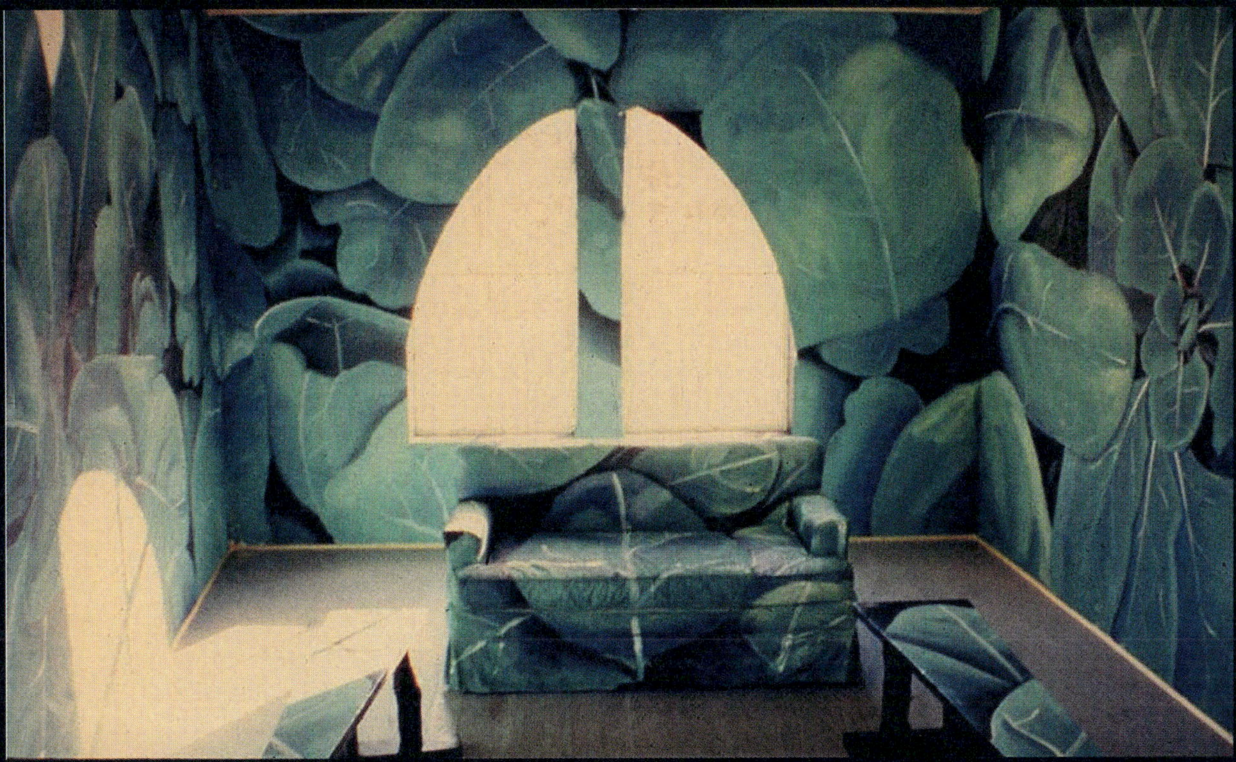

Seitu Ken Jones
Divine Shrine of the Collard Green, 1999
Mixed media
Project Rowhouses, Houston, TX

The project has roots in his Aunt Alma's garden in Meacham Park, a Black neighborhood annexed by the St. Louis suburb of Kirkwood and incrementally razed through development in the second half of the twentieth century. There, Jones's family tended a thriving garden whose bulbs were later transplanted to Jones's home in the Twin Cities. Paradoxically, a primary reason for the annexation and eventual destruction of Meacham Park was highway construction and subsequent access to transit. This return reseeds the healing greens back into a landscape marred with uprooted Black communities, from Mill Creek Valley and Pruitt-Igoe to ongoing gentrification and abandonment. Placing the collards along the bus systems that acts as a primary means of movement through the city offers an alternate record of survivance and nourishment, a persistence of Black life and tradition stretching back centuries, and a proposition to the future health of the many communities the work moves through.

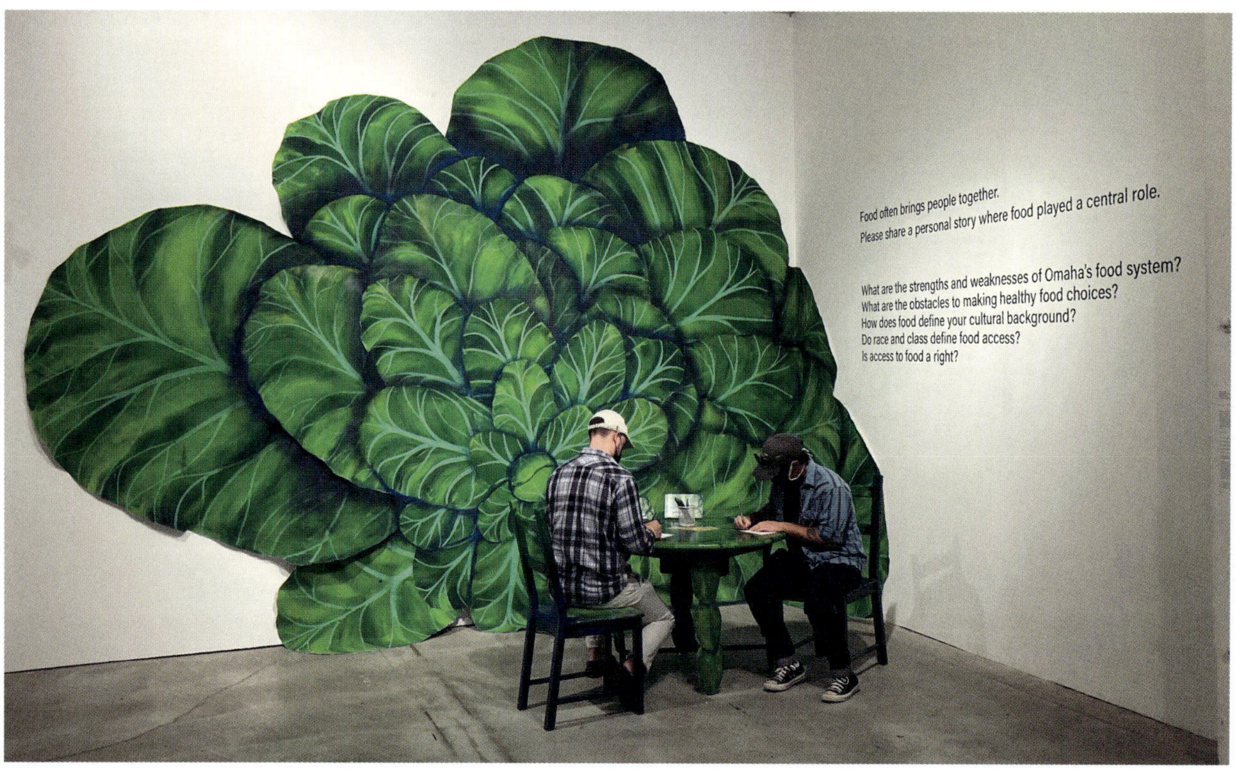

Seitu Ken Jones
Collard Green Shrine, 2021
Mixed media
Bemis Center for Contemporary Arts, Omaha, NE

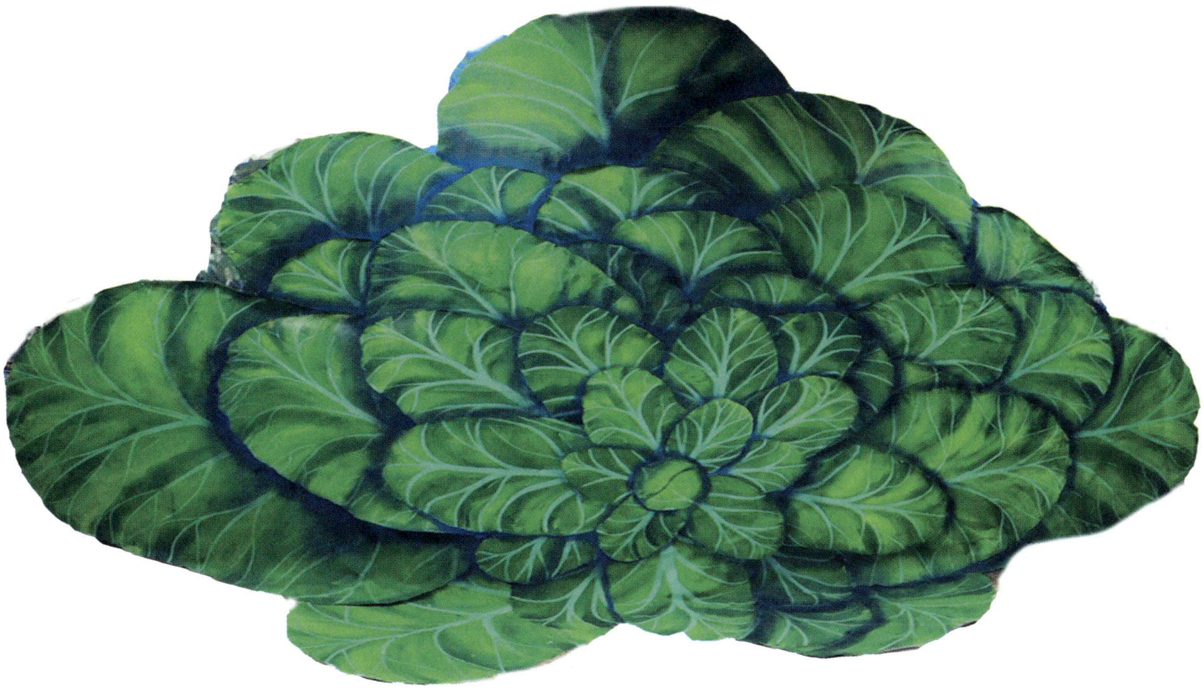

Seitu Ken Jones
Collard Green Shrine, 2021
Mixed media
Bemis Center for Contemporary Arts, Omaha, NE

Whereas, Between 1526 and 1866 the U.S. forcibly displaced tens of millions of American children and adults under concealment of U.S. law and forced chattel enslavement upon millions of your family members, hereinafter referred to as "human trafficking and genocide," perpetrating all manner of massively criminal offenses against humanity, hereinafter "State Terror" upon the families of present heirs;

Whereas, Specifically, between 1526 and 1968 (*de jure*) and 1969 to the present (*de facto*) the U.S. conducted systemic State Terror upon family members of present heirs through human trafficking and genocide (1526-1865); aparthied law and public executions (1862-1968); land seizure; land annexation; genocide; residential schools; forced adoptions; and deputized terror (1526-1968) at local, state, and federal levels;

BETWEEN THE DAY AND THE DREAM

By
Katherine
Simóne
Reynolds

The warmth of a teacup is caressed and pressed into the cheek of Stan who has asked his friend what that feeling "reminds him of." His friend presses the teacup into his cheek and passes it back while answering "not a damn thing but hot air." Stan, fixed on the feeling, staring off into a low-lit, dusty corner of the room, continues to imagine: "I mean, doesn't it remind you of when you're making love, and how warm her forehead gets sometimes?" Breaking his dream state, his friend responds in laughter.

The in-between space seems to be my home these days.

I visit home multiple times in multiple ways, and "home" has since become "based in," which forms a complicated attachment to the in-between as a place of solace. Like being comforted in the nowhere. Riding the train between Chicago and St. Louis, I find myself transfixed on the mundane violently flying past the window just a breath outside of me. The familiarity of the landscape puts me in a trance, guiding me into a daydream that seems to last until I recognize the Arch and I am steadily reminded the ride/dream has reached its destination. The ride is about five and a half hours of a haunting pastoral quiet, plenty of time to participate in the gauntlet of digital correspondences while constantly ignoring the bodily irk for my mind to drift out toward the window, constructing another reality where the feeling of oppression mining the essence of Black joy cannot exist. What happens when we ignore the mind's ache to dream with our eyes toward a sunlit window? To allow ourselves a brief moment of respite from the continuous deepening of the dagger and play in a place of elsewhere constructed by our own mind as a means of coping with a wounding that we will never have the time to address? To be preoccupied within the magic liminality of just being gives way to delusion—and what exactly is wrong with delusion in a world that refuses to acknowledge the reality of your pain?

You must find a new way to escape.

Charles Burnett's *Killer of Sheep* (1978) is a continuous start-and-stop journey with a sputtering engine depicting quotidian Black life in a post-Watts Riot landscape. There are moments of deconstructing and reconstructing one's environment either as a means of escapism or truly believing freedom is just within arm's reach. The film follows Stan's family, friends, and neighbors' story of continuously trying to get out of their predicament, only to remain due to the misfortune of being poor, Black, and surrounded by a landscape that is literally crumbling around them. But then there are these moments of children flying from rooftop to rooftop, and the above-mentioned scene of Stan in a dream space illustrating the need to mentally escape from the relentless realities of oppression. These moments of liberation are provided by the mind's need to be absent, to drift away from what the eyes and body are witnessing/absorbing. The landscape and architecture that Burnett captures remembers everything even in its dilapidation, even in the areas that have been repaved or reconstructed. The bones of the buildings, streets, and soil have felt and witnessed the joys and atrocities, and they hold on to what we refuse to remember or what we would like to be forgotten.

A major artery of St. Louis is Jefferson Avenue. The residual energy from the residential memories left either unattended or unrealized is felt even through a thick car window, making it emotionally permeable to anyone riding along an avenue that connects multiple violences of burying, vacating, and unearthing. You feel the presence of people without seeing them, the shadows of their dreams and memories seeping into brick-lined alleyways and empty porous sidewalks, and faintly in the distance a tornado siren begins to wail a warning. The space between the Northside and the Southside can be seen as merely "transitional space" that disengages us from the need to respond to the beauty of the quotidian that only shows up by gazing out a speeding window. There are dreamscapes, pockets of life, and fractured histories that are passed by without a second thought, glances forming full narratives based on assumptions that "there is nothing to see here." But the unsettling feeling remains and almost pulls you out of the car and into the street to bear witness to the narrative at play. A narrative that has been viciously hidden and thrown in your face as you catch a glimpse of a dandelion in an empty lot being stepped on as someone passes through the in-between, following along a tried-and-true shortcut.

While catching up with my dear friend and avid dreamer, Tasha Nicolé Burton, she tells me about a behavior called maladaptive daydreaming, a condition where people get caught in their daydreams for hours, days, and sometimes years. This behavior can happen as a coping mechanism from a traumatic event, causing the person to create an escape hatch from the brutality of reality. The characters and story arcs within the daydreams can become more real to the daydreamer than the world they are experiencing in real life, forming real attachments and relationships. The daydreamer can find themselves addicted to this imaginative world that seems to provide them with the support, love, and care that is lacking from the reality within which their fleshy body lives. Through maladaptive daydreaming, an allowance is formed providing the daydreamer a space to exist and be seen without the pain of the trauma, even though this is considered delusion. The traumatic event still occurred, the past is indeed the past and starkly the present, but a way to liberation can be possible through creating space for the mind to drift into a state of grandeur.

Our minds are powerful, but, like our bodies, our minds can break. Slowly deteriorating into the muck of capitalism and the brutality of an oppressive reality ladened with white supremacy—making it to where a tender moment with a teacup seems to be the only authenticating factor where there is still a nutritional need to dream. And that dreaming is a key tool in unearthing new pathways to freedom. Safe spaces for marginalized people cannot exist in a society that has an intimacy problem. Safe spaces for marginalized people cannot exist under capitalism. Safe spaces for marginalized people do not actually exist. Through constructing the imaginative there is an unlimited space of allowance. An allowance of life not reliant on the recognition of others' perceptions of what places you dare dream about. Ancestrally, the Black mind has a way of creating safety in the imaginary; creating spaces to be unseen or even unrecognized by the eye of the oppressor. Holding memories in code in order to preserve the archive and find freedom by offering that release to the mind first, and then to the body.

The poem "We Have Been Believers" by Margaret Walker perfectly accentuates how the strength of belief and the radical imaginary has served as an integral device in liberation:

We have been believers yielding substance for the world.
With our hands we have a fed a people and out of our
strength have they wrung the necessities of a nation.
Our song has filled the twilight and our hope has heralded the dawn.[1]

Back riding shotgun along the constantly interrupted road of Jefferson Avenue, between Ohio Avenue and St. Louis Avenue, as hopeful melancholy presents itself from the median, the bridge, a defunct fountain, a car playing "The Closer I Get to You," a healing building, and a crowded Black bar grilling pork steaks in the backyard. Warm shadows are pressed into the pavement fading with a quickness as I take a glance out my window as I dare to let my mind find a place in all the wonder.

[1] Margaret Walker, "We Have Been Believers," *Poetry* (March 1939), https://www.poetryfoundation.org/poetrymagazine/browse?contentId=22290.

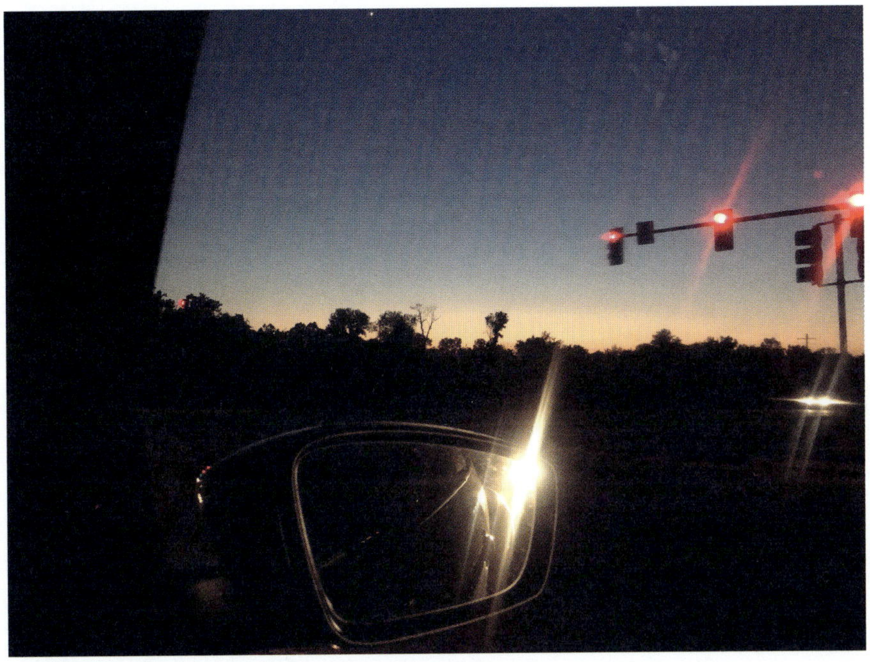

Katherine Simóne Reynolds
Shot from the passenger seat of my mother's car

Simiya Sudduth

CURATOR:
KATHERINE SIMÓNE REYNOLDS

LOCATION:
RUNG FOR WOMEN AND MULTIPLE LOCATIONS

Simiya Sudduth is a mother, artist, and educator currently living and practicing in St. Louis. Their multidisciplinary creative practice centers around public art and social practice. Sudduth's work primarily manifests as large-scale public murals, experimental sound healing performances, and landscape-based interventions. Their working methods are fluid, and experimentation is an integral component of their practice. Sudduth utilizes any materials, media, and/or techniques needed to translate ideas into physical form without restriction or limitation: sound, plants, textiles, illustration, performance, or installation. Much of their work is site specific and/or site responsive.

Sudduth explores the concepts of healing, spirituality, social justice, visibility, the landscape, joy, and beauty. Their creative practice serves as a vessel to examine their own mental and emotional healing and spiritual journey while serving as a provocation for collective healing, inquiry, and expansion.

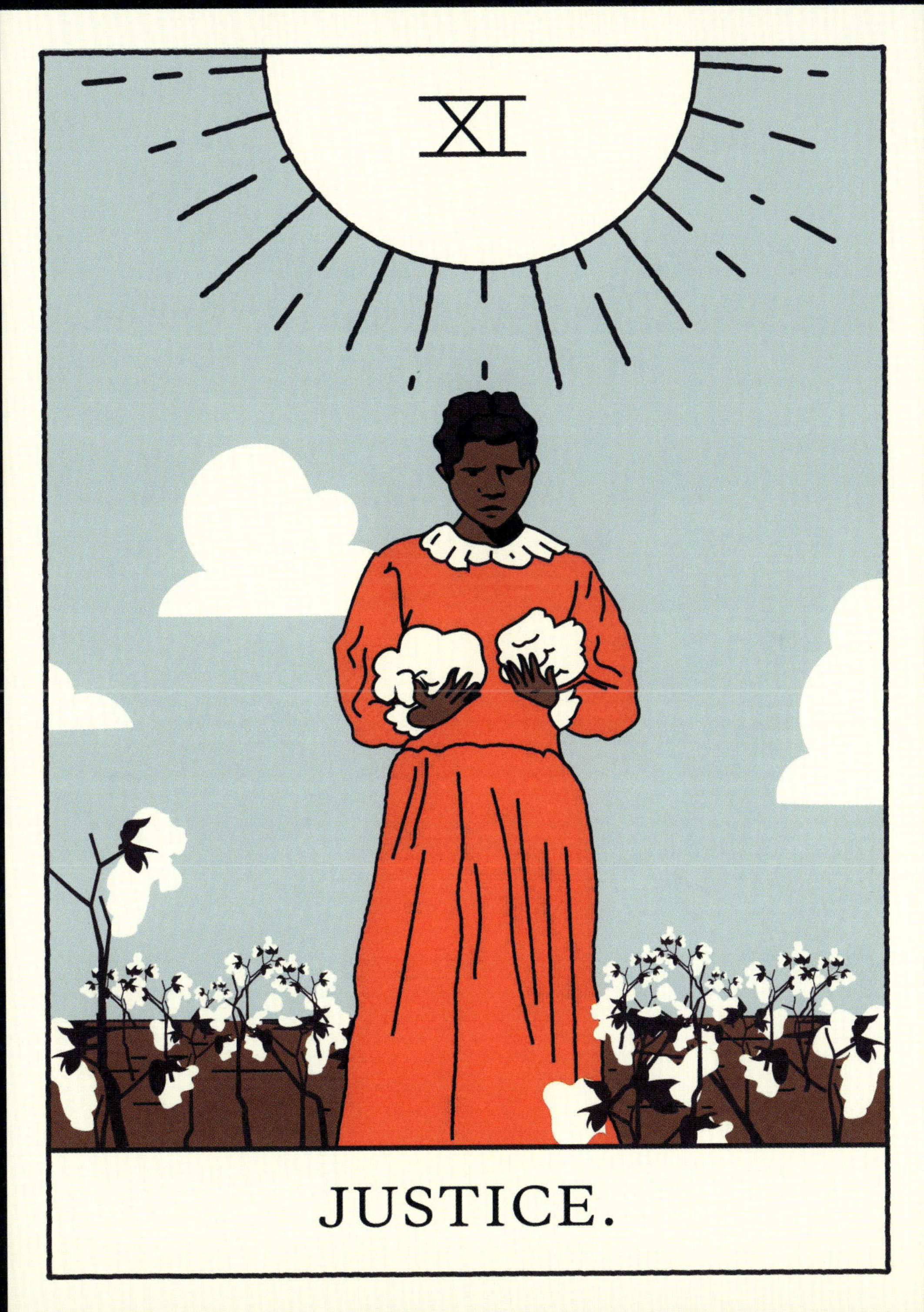

Simiya Sudduth
Justice, 2019
Digital illustration

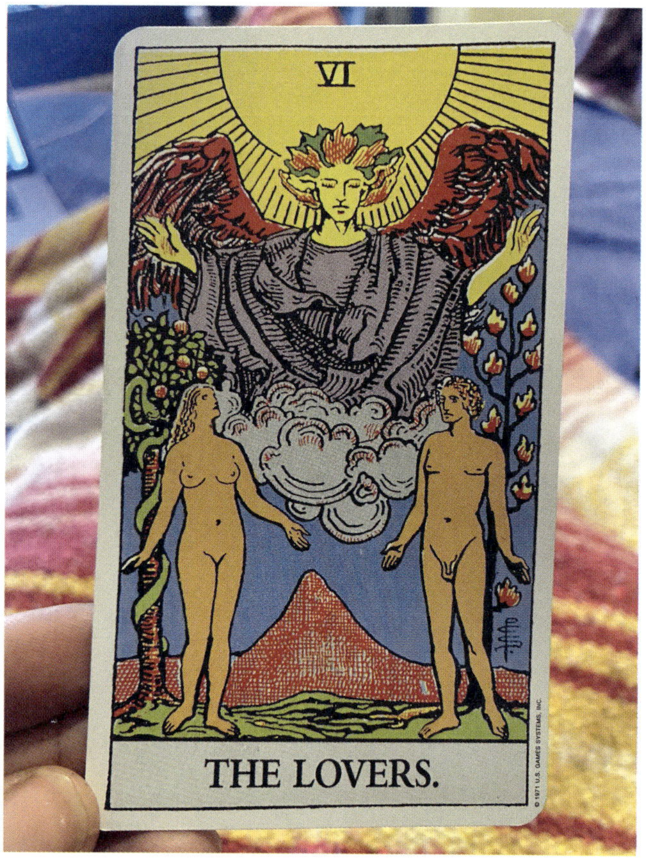

Simiya Sudduth
The Lovers (Rider-Waite-Smith Deck), 2022
Digital photograph

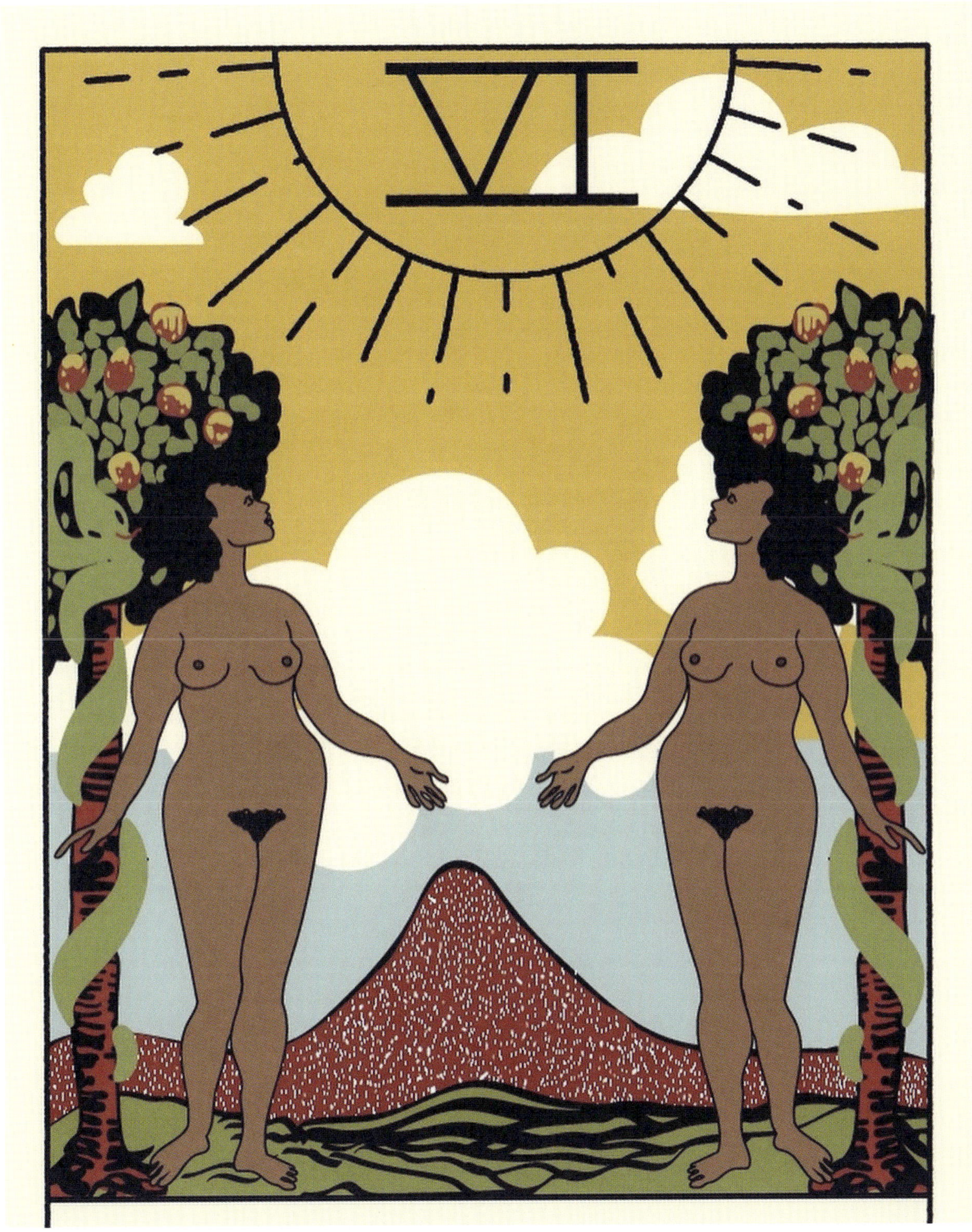

Simiya Sudduth
The Lovers, 2022
Digital illustration

For Sudduth, the acts of creating, viewing, embodying, and experiencing art are modes of healing within themselves. In their work, the notion of healing manifests in a multitude of forms. It may be very subtle: infused in their working process or in the way they choose colors and imagery for an illustration or a mural. Healing is also present in the way they engage in care work in a long-term project or social practice work. Or, Sudduth may overtly invite viewers to enjoy a healing experience through their soundscapes or energy and performance work.

Sudduth is deeply influenced by practices of somatics, divination, mantra, and meditation, as well as the study of spiritual and energy healing practices like Reiki and Buddhism. While they are influenced by the ethereal and philosophical qualities of spirituality, their practice also holds space to examine the intersections of healing and spirituality within contemporary concerns of environmental and social justice.

Sudduth's work is truly a practice of integration, a way to explore and connect multifaceted interests and influences, all of which are united by the big questions of how they provoke positive change, healing, and expansion within individual and collective consciousness. For Counterpublic 2023, Sudduth's projects act as a culmination, a connected reflection of all the ideas and working methods they have been exploring and experimenting with since 2020. These will span a number of murals and a mobile healing studio, *Tha Muthaship*, that will be based out of Rung for Women, a nonprofit that promotes economic and social empowerment for women in St. Louis. *Tha Muthaship* is a mobile healing and arts space nestled inside a repurposed 1970s Terry Travel Trailer bringing visual art, mindfulness, healing, and wellness modalities to communities in St. Louis. Sudduth feels that their practice holds power when they, as a self-identified Black, queer femme, artist, and mother, take up and command public space as a social practice artist. In Sudduth's words, "I aim to use that power to promote visibility and hold space for healing, joy, and justice."

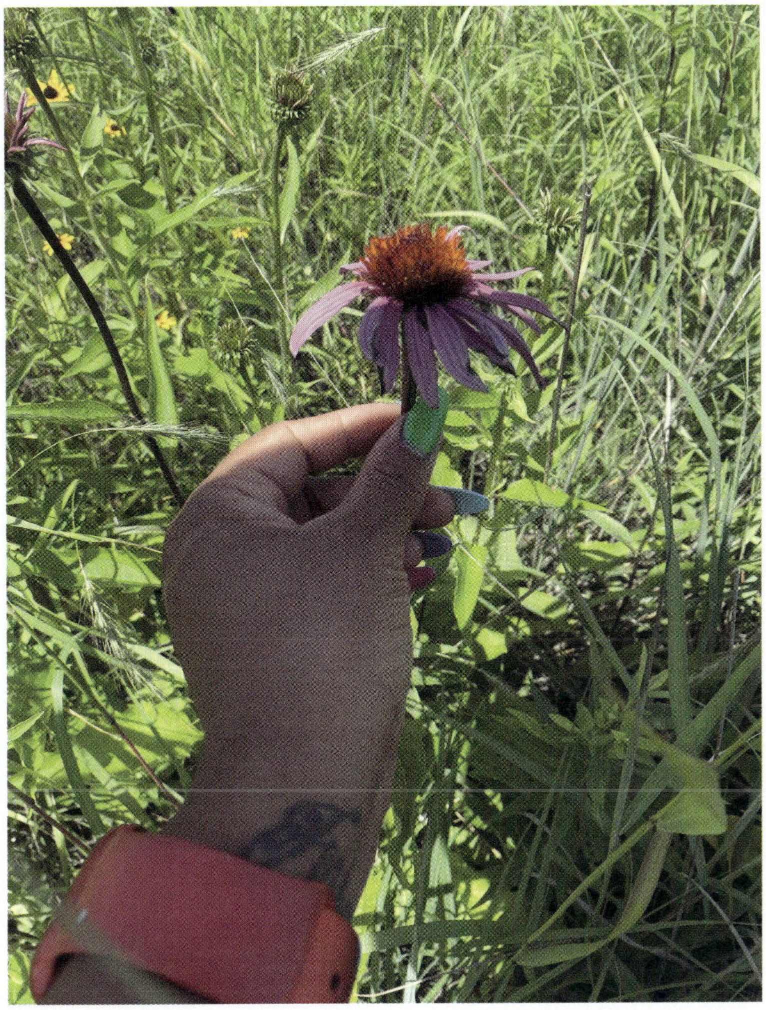

Simiya Sudduth
Mni Sota Makoce Prairie During Residency at Franconia Sculpture Park, 2022
Digital photograph

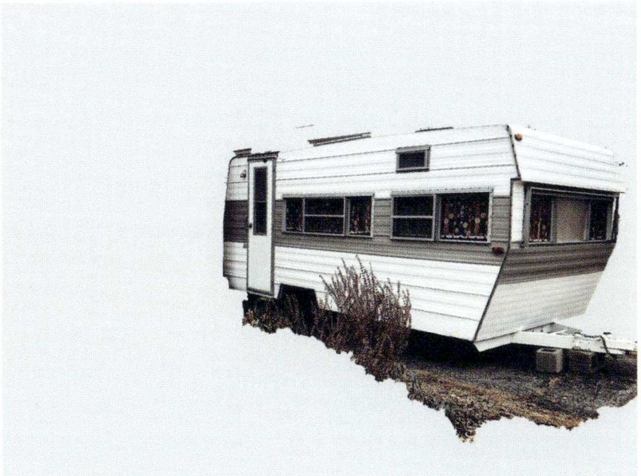

Simiya Sudduth
Tha Muthaship, 2020
Digital photograph

Will Rawls

CURATOR:
KATHERINE SIMÓNE REYNOLDS

LOCATION:
JOHNNIE BROCK'S DUNGEON PARTY WAREHOUSE, MCDONALD'S, ST. LOUIS PUBLIC LIBRARY (BARR BRANCH), AND LAFAYETTE PARK UNITED METHODIST CHURCH

Will Rawls thinks of time, dance, language, and Black performance as mediums that reveal how bodies accumulate and escape meaning. Often using a combination of utterance and movement, Rawls choreographs work that challenges the consumption of Black performers through conventional narratives of pain or exaltation. Suspended in unusual tasks and states of becoming, Rawls's work insists that ambiguity and racial entanglement are bound up in the performer's existence. Over the last four years, Rawls has worked with stop-motion animation to scrutinize the elements and processes of motion-picture making. Given that stop-motion requires eight hundred photos to create one and a half minutes of film, it is a slow and arduous method, especially when working with live performers. By presenting Black performers working in stop-motion, Rawls explores the limits and burdens of representation that coincide in the task of performing for the camera. Further, he asks: How do I document and center performance as a crucial method of narrating the world while employing stop-motion filmmaking to draw attention to the risky labor of becoming an image for public consumption?

For Counterpublic 2023, ***REGULAR DEGULAR*** is an animated film response to the disparate architectural, economic, and historical tensions that lie on the surface of St. Louis. These tensions are constantly reproduced by the ongoing anti-Black formation of American cities whereby neighborhoods are razed or renewed based on their racial make-up and economic use. Municipal violence like this fractures neighborhoods across conflicting understandings of time and place that sit right next to each other on the same street, in various states of decay, use, disappearance, or prominence. For Rawls, this social puzzle becomes a compelling site to focus on a space at the center of it all—the crosswalk—as a jumping off point for storytelling.

In ***REGULAR DEGULAR***, dancer Heather Beal plays the title character, Regular Degular, as she explores four buildings at the intersection of Interstate-44 and Jefferson Avenue. Over a 24-hour period, Regular Degular pursues oddball quests, through crosswalks, traffic, and underpasses, into and out of a costume store, a library, a church, and a McDonald's parking lot. Stop-motion animation renders the intersection's noise and commotion into a paradoxically surreal and almost childlike backdrop for her wayward local adventures. The obstacles and wonders that she encounters ultimately require both her perseverance and imagination to leave an impression on this chaotic place.

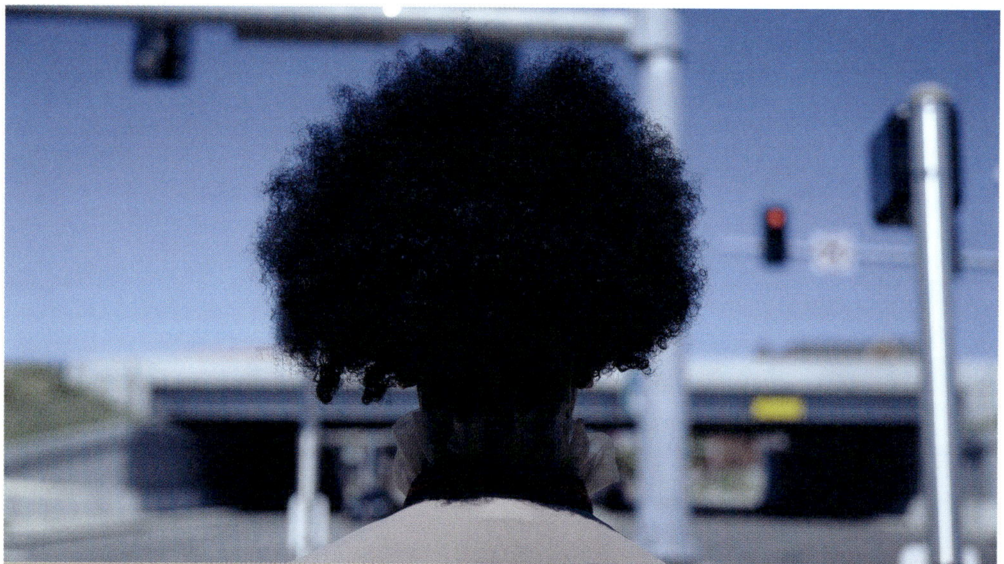

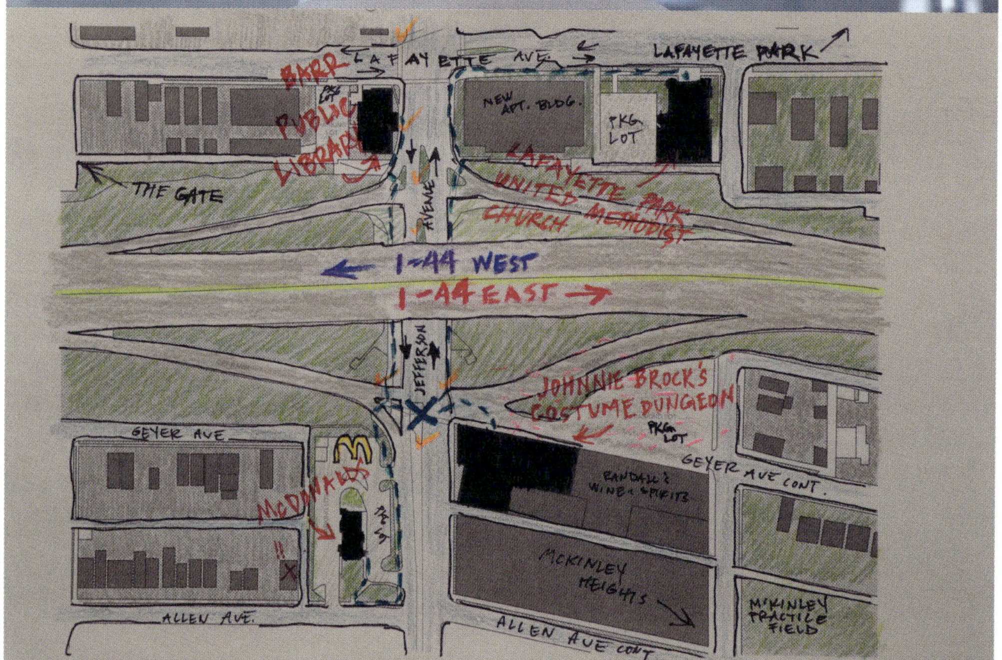
LAFAYETTE AVE.
LAFAYETTE PARK
BARR PUBLIC LIBRARY
NEW APT. BLDG.
PKG. LOT
LAFAYETTE PARK UNITED METHODIST CHURCH
THE GATE
AVENUE
I-44 WEST
I-44 EAST
JEFFERSON
JOHNNIE BROCK'S COSTUME DUNGEON
PKG. LOT
GEYER AVE
GEYER AVE CONT.
RANDALL'S WINE + SPIRITS
McDONALD'S
MCKINLEY HEIGHTS
MCKINLEY PRACTICE FIELD
ALLEN AVE.
ALLEN AVE CONT.

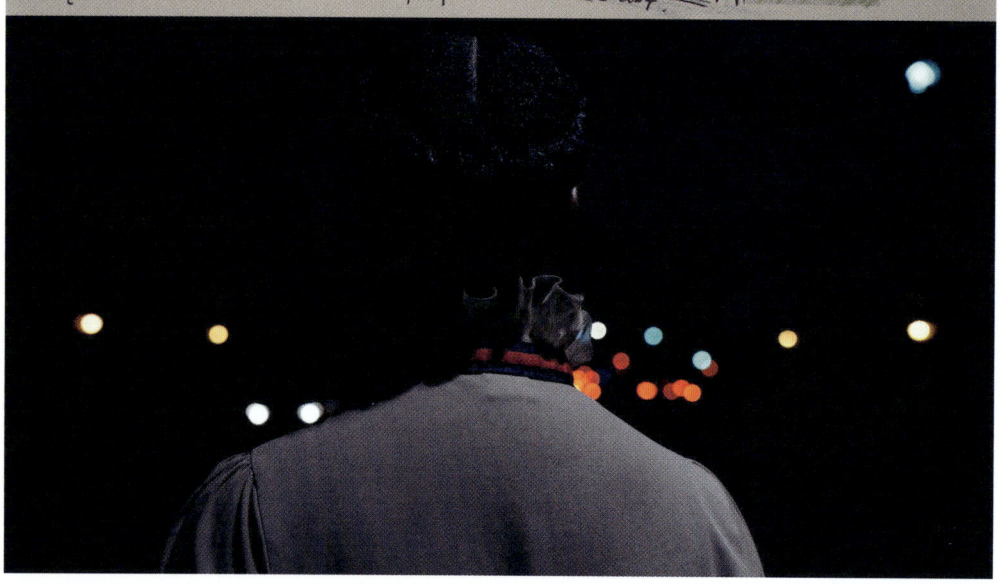

Will Rawls

REGULAR DEGULAR

"So here is why I write what I do: We all have futures. We all have pasts. We all have stories. And we all, every single one of us, no matter who we are and no matter what's been taken from us or what poison we've internalized or how hard we've had to work to expel it— we all get to dream."
— N. K. Jemisin

CREDITS

Cast
Regular Degular – Heather Beal
McDegular Dancers – Karis Gamble, Sarah Nixon

Crew
Concept, Story, and Direction - Will Rawls
Cinematography and Editing - Jabari Holder
Sound Score - Rena Anakwe
2nd Camera - Papa Blankson
Gaffer and Key Grip - Jared Wangenstein
Grip and 3rd Camera - Leo Ramsey
Wardrobe and Production Assistant - Sarah Nixon
Production Assistant - Karis Gamble

Curator - Katherine Simóne Reynolds
Producer - Indigo Sparks

Special Thanks

The Barr Library
Branch Manager - Tiger Reed
Manager of Public Relations and Digital Marketing - Jen Hatton
Manager of Digital Library Services - Mary Meyer
Creative Experience Assistant - Jonah Steenbock

Johnnie Brock's Costume Dungeon
Owner - Mary Brock
The Spooky and Spirited Staff of JBCD

Lafayette Park United Methodist Church
Pastor - Kathleen Wilder
Secretary - Maria Lawrence
Custodian - Patrick
Church Member - Sue Lee

Bad Dog Productions
Daniel von Seckendorff

The Puffin Foundation

Vincent Stemmler

CURATOR:
KATHERINE SIMÓNE REYNOLDS

LOCATION:
FOUNTAIN AT CHIPPEWA AND BROADWAY/JEFFERSON

Vincent Stemmler's works often reference place, whether through photography, molds, or collecting objects and materials on location. This method is a way to represent collective history and individual memory. By using material as artifact or evidence, Stemmler aims to show the interplay between identity and environment.

For Counterpublic 2023, Stemmler's large-scale sculpture *Three Columns* sits inside an active fountain at a major confluence of three streets: Jefferson, Broadway, and Chippewa. *Three Columns* consists of multiple sculptural elements that incorporate molds taken from the surrounding neighborhoods. This includes textures and forms from the street and brick buildings, and images from the relief sculpture carved into the bank across the street. The columns themselves reference the common architectural trend of Neoclassical Revival and its fetishism for stylized imperialist architecture.

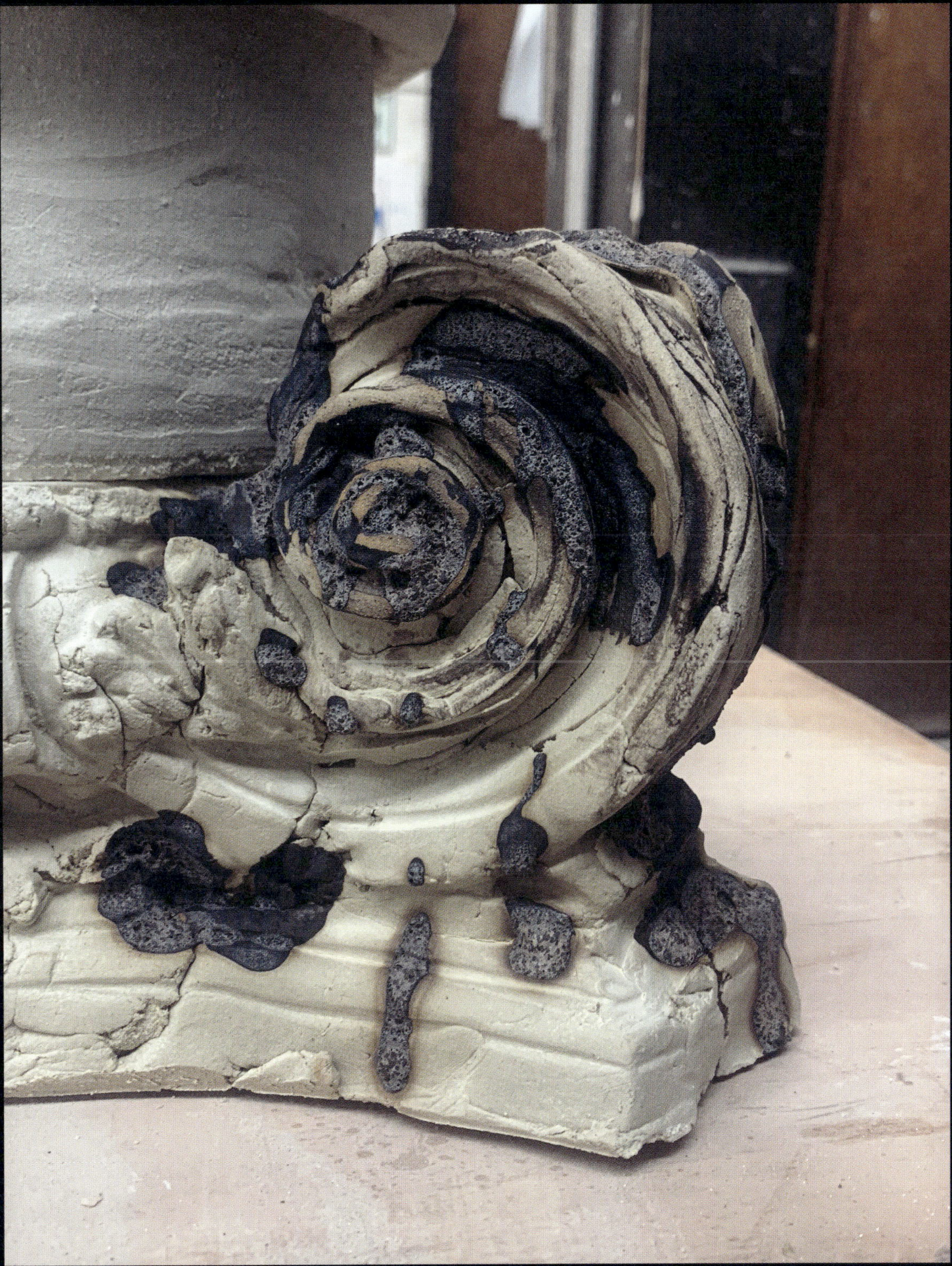

Vincent Stemmler
Three Columns (detail)

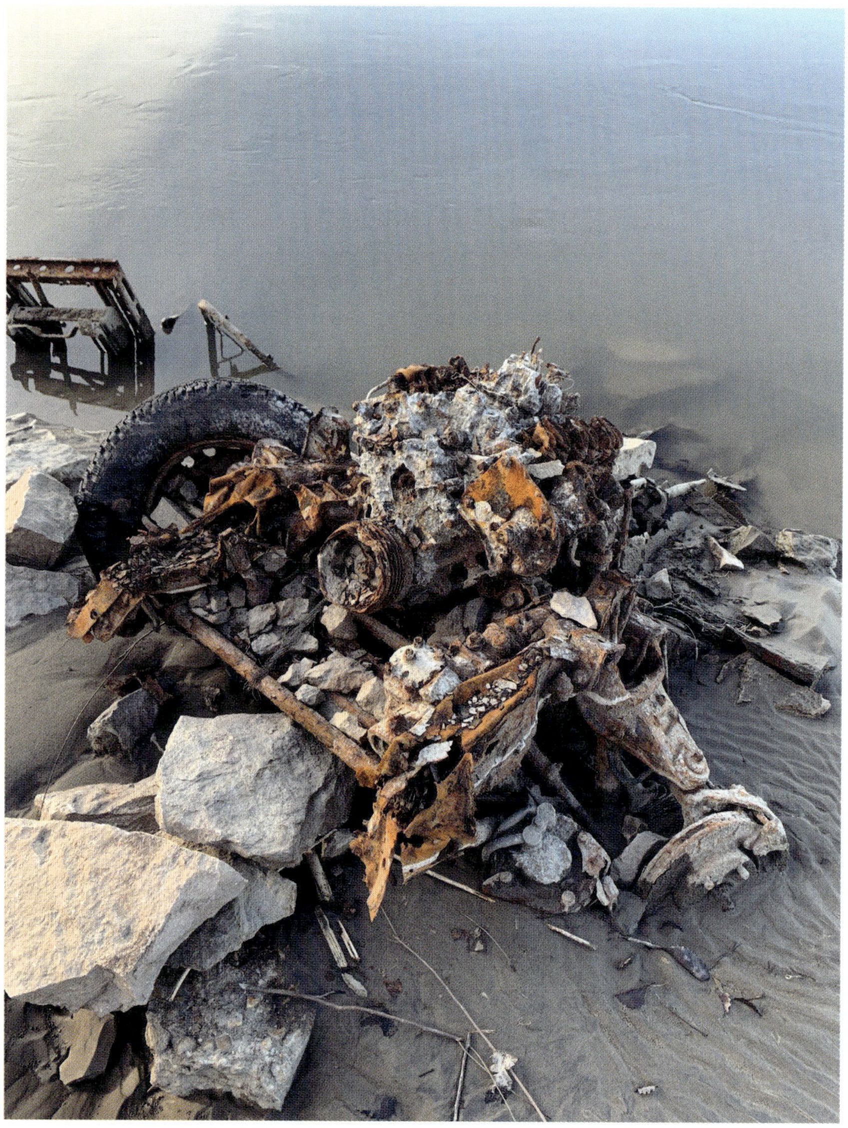

Wreckage emerging from
the nearby Mississippi River

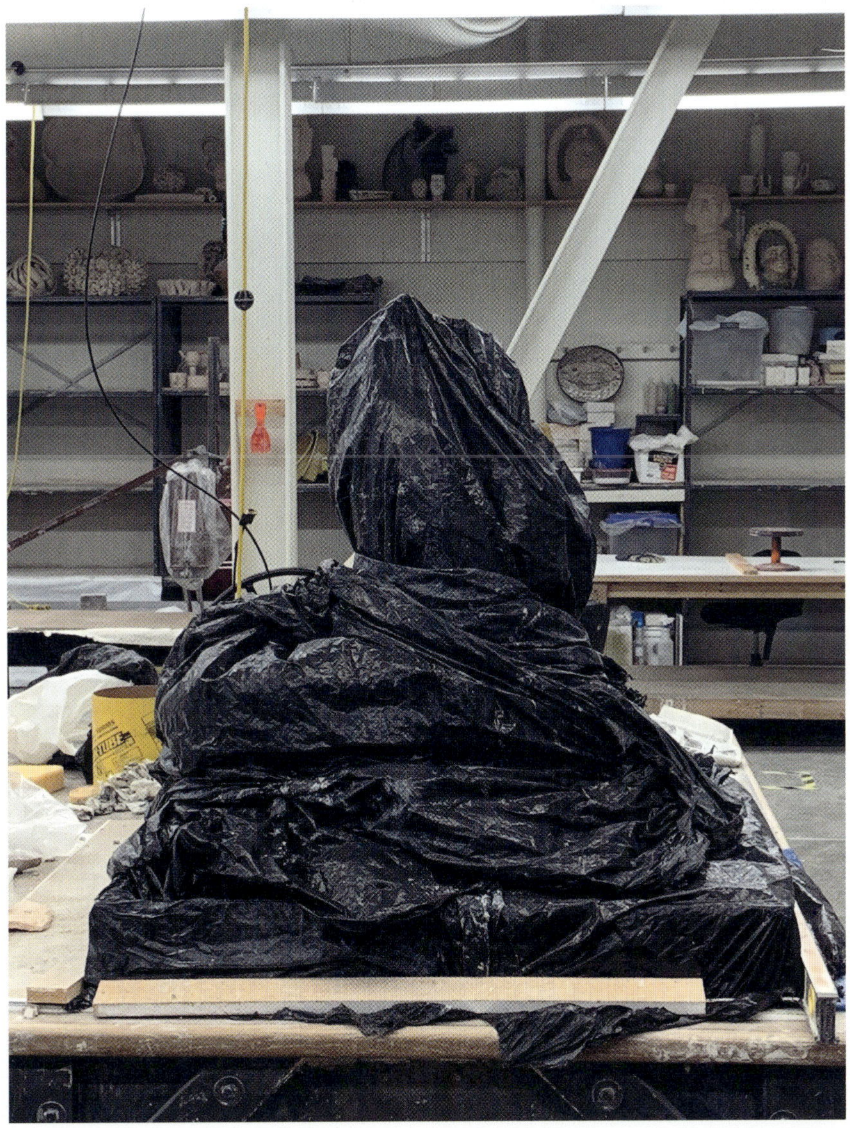

Vincent Stemmler
Three Columns (in the studio)

While some parts of this "three-dimensional collage" are in direct reference to the surrounding neighborhood, some of them are so commonplace that they could be from anywhere in the United States. A wing from an eagle motif sticks out of the side of the tallest pillar, directly referencing common eagle wall decor found on front porches and in homes around the country, while simultaneously drawing our gaze upward and outward to the eagle statues we see on the architecture of the historic bank directly across the street.

The sculpture is in shambles, a symbol of the precarious resilience of Empire, which is somehow seemingly crumbling and stable simultaneously. *Three Columns* is heavily influenced by the idea of the facade—how something can be presented as one thing but be completely different or even empty on the inside. In this sense, the sculpture itself is made to seem contrived, like much of the so-called history that is presented to us as fact rather than fiction. The work asks: If our histories are taken from us and a new one is fabricated in their place, then who are we?

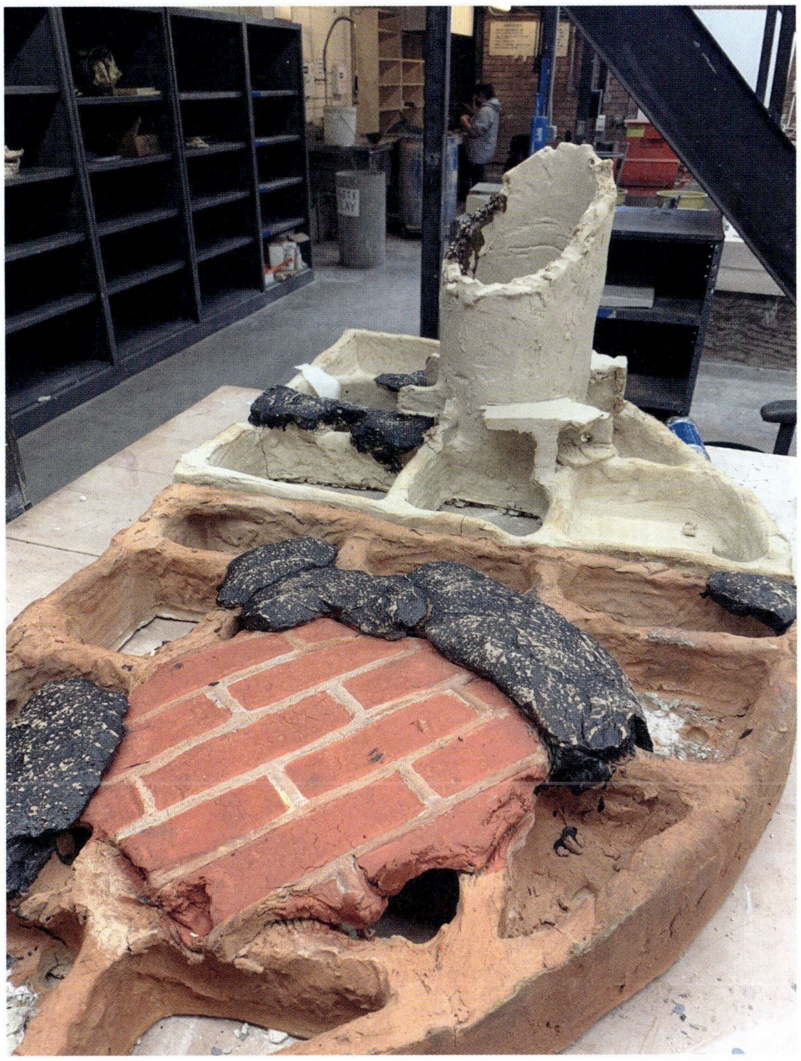

Vincent Stemmler
Three Columns (in the studio)

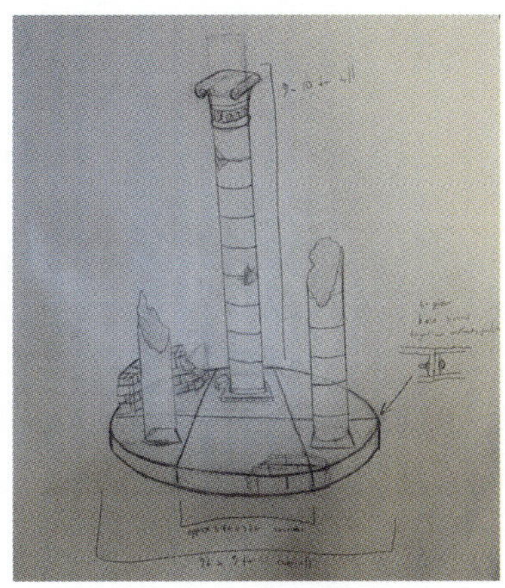

Vincent Stemmler
Three Columns
Draft schematic 2

Black Healers Collective

CURATOR:
KATHERINE SIMÓNE REYNOLDS

LOCATION:
MULTIPLE SITES ALONG JEFFERSON AVENUE

The Black Healers Collective engages in healing practices, programs, and partnerships that support the Black Community in (1) "re-membering" itself—repairing that which feels fragmented and broken within its households, families, and neighborhoods; (2) expressing its truths and exercising its power; and (3) creating healed futures that affirm and uplift Black lives.

THE BLACK HEALERS COLLECTIVE STL

Our Community of Care

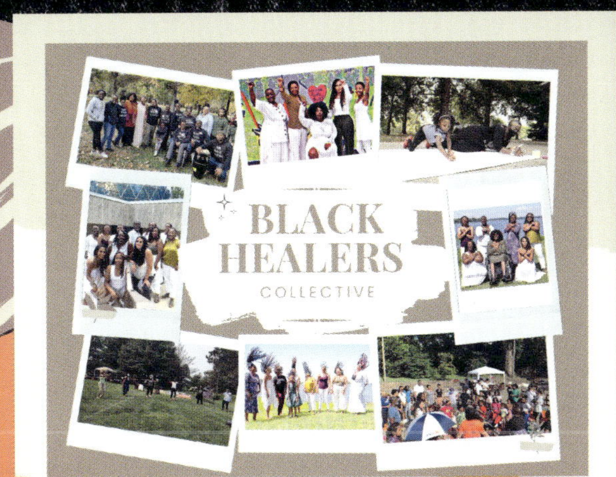

OUR CRY

We call upon our Ancestors
Those who experienced all manner of death,
degradation and suffering
People upon whom the sky fell

We call upon our Ancestors
Those who swung from trees
And were forced to live life on their knees

We call upon our Ancestors
Those who survived, persisted and endured
Without destroying themselves or others

May whatever it is that supported and
sustained them
Come fully alive in us.

-Rebeccah Bennett, BHC Founder

Jen Everett

CURATOR:
KATHERINE SIMÓNE REYNOLDS

LOCATION:
MULTIPLE LOCATIONS THROUGHOUT THE CITY

Jen Everett makes photographs, installations, and time-based media that engage relationships between rupture, Black interiority, and knowledge production. Everett frequently works with found and inherited materials to amplify ways everyday Black folks have used the quotidian to cultivate beauty in the face of immense structural limitation. Through this process, her work is interested in gathering and reconfiguring as a mode of inquiry to compel closer readings.

For Counterpublic 2023, Everett has developed a series of workshops born out of a desire for thinking and working together to preserve as well as activate the materials we collect, handle, care for, and eventually pass on to those we love and trust. These workshops will focus on the grounding and fortifying power of vernacular archives explored in photographic, sonic, and ecological modalities.

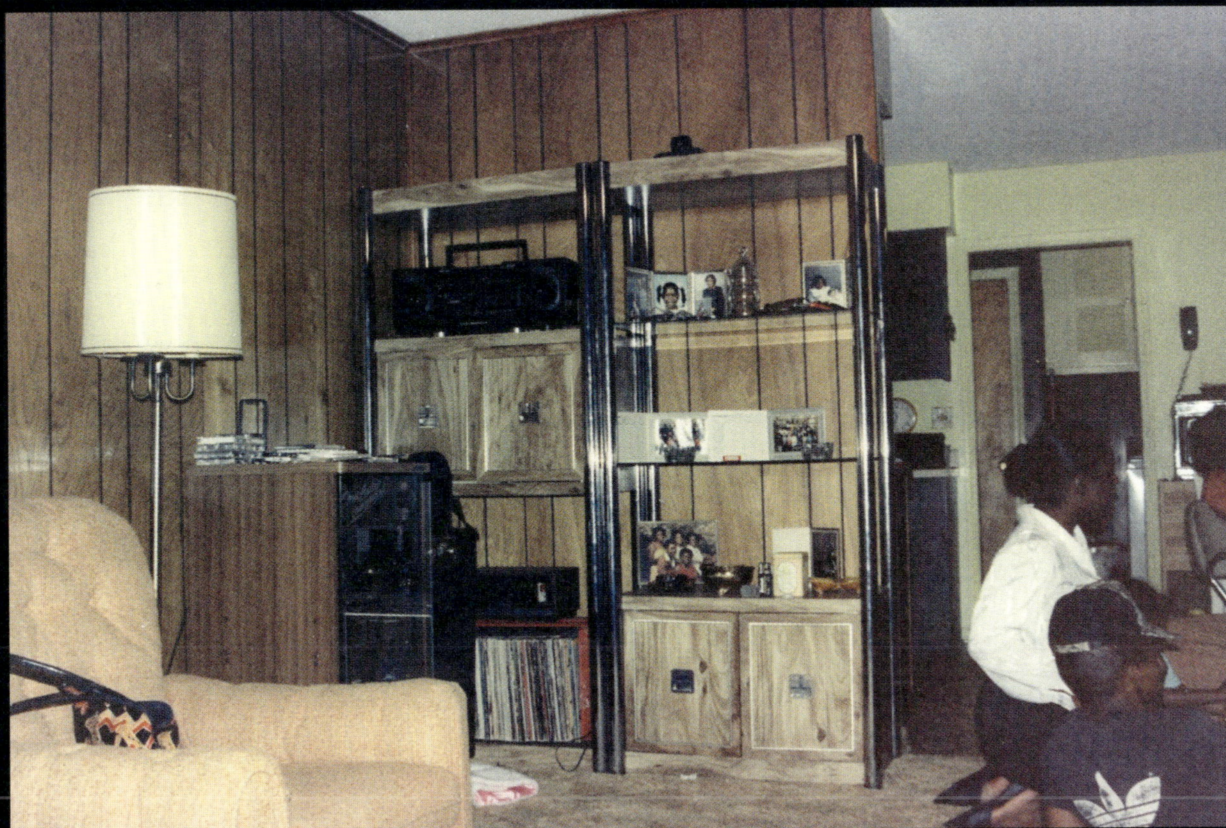

Close Looking:
This photograph was made by my father in the early 1980s during a trip to Memphis he took with his father to visit extended family. Everything else about it is a mystery to me. It's an image I keep close because it is a reminder of the everyday home and worldmaking practices of Black people. As a viewer, I feel like an outsider in this photograph; I am looking into a scene but not fully part of it. The people are turned away from me and at a distance. If I had to describe the Black interior, this would be my first attempt. I am always gesturing toward the concept of a Black interior world as both a physical environment and a psychic one.

Collaborative facilitators will guide learners through strategies for record-keeping and preservation while highlighting differences between institutional and vernacular frameworks with a focus on the practices of informal archivists and keepers within our own families and communities, subverting the myth of the institutional archive as the source of true or official knowledge. This offering will center histories that have been suppressed, omitted, or are at risk of being lost.

5/15/21

EVIDENCE OF LIFE LIVED / PRESENCE
COMMUNAL
ASSEMBLY
GATHERING
RECORD
RECORD KEEPING
WITNESSING

THESE ARE
THE TECHNOLOGIES
OF THE PHOTO ALBUM

4/19/21

I HAVE TO CONTINUALLY INTERROGATE MY OWN INTENTIONS FOR THIS WORK AND ~~TO~~ "LISTEN TO THE IMAGES"

I STILL INSIST THAT THE POWER OF THE VERNACULAR IS IN ITS PRIVACY — AND SO, TO MAKE IT PUBLIC, TO INTRODUCE IT IN THAT WAY — TO THE PUBLIC RECORD & ECONOMY OF IMAGES / MARKET IS A ~~[illegible]~~ DILEMMA / CONUNDRUM. AS THEY GAIN ~~POWER~~ VALUE VIA DISPERSAL AND CIRCULATION DO THEY LOSE THEIR POWER? THIS TENSION IS WHY I MUST RECONFIGURE / MANIPULATE THEM IN SOME WAY... SO THAT IT ISN'T THE TRUE IMAGE, THERE ARE OTHER THINGS WORKING... EVEN STILL I KNOW THAT IT IS TIME TO GUIDE THE WORK — OR I SHOULD SAY THE WORK IS GUIDING ME TOWARDS CULMINATION / COMPLETION / RELEASE...

4/24/21

WHEN I SAY CULMINATION, COMPLETION, RELEASE — I SPECIFICALLY MEAN THE PUBLIC FACING CAPACITY OF THIS WORK. THE PRIVATE AND INTIMATE WORK OF KEEPING A RECORD IS PART OF MY LIFE'S WORK.

IN THE ONGOING LABOR OF SORTING THROUGH MY FAMILY'S PHOTOGRAPHS I NOTICE HOW MANY PICTURES THERE ARE OF US LOOKING AT PICTURES. THAT WORK IS ONGOING / EVER-PRESENT / CYCLICAL.

WHEN WE GATHERED, WE REVIEWED THE RECORDS WE'D MADE BUT WE ALSO CONTINUED TO CREATE THEM. THAT, TO ME, IS SIGNIFICANT. AND HERE I AM, ATTEMPTING TO ORGANIZE THIS RECORD FOR ME, YES BUT MORE IMPORTANTLY FOR ALL MY PEOPLE AND PEOPLE TO COME.

Journaling:
Notes from a studio journal made during the development of In Praise of Vernacular Archives, a workshop that preceded this series

Ralph Lemon

CURATOR:
KATHERINE SIMÓNE
REYNOLDS

LOCATION:
MULTIPLE LOCATIONS
THROUGHOUT THE CITY

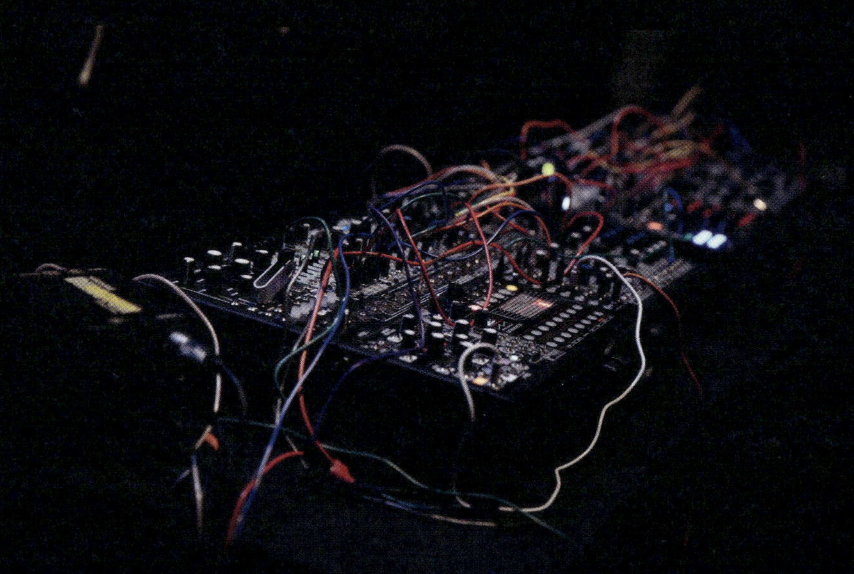

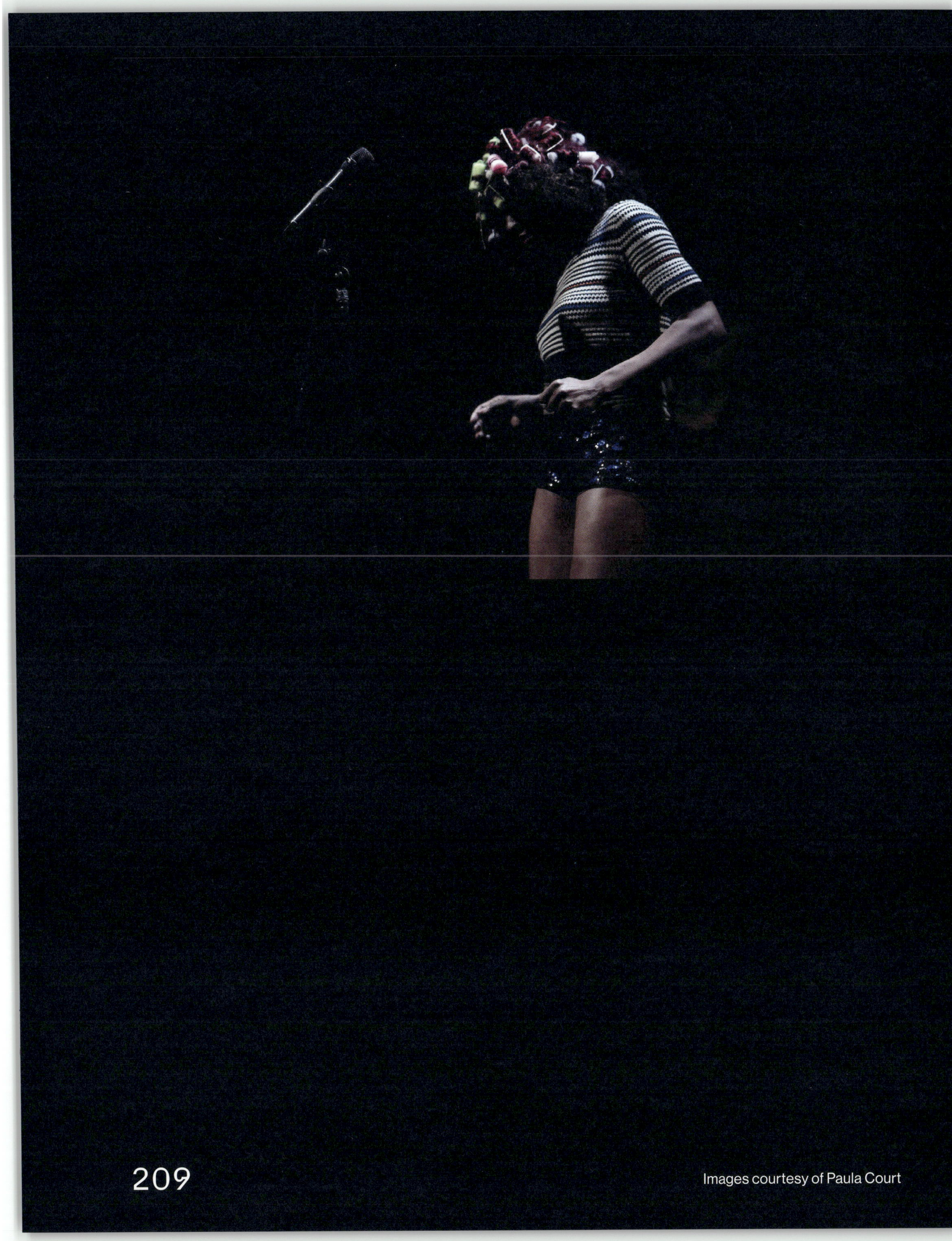

Images courtesy of Paula Court

Yvonne Osei

CURATOR:
KATHERINE SIMÓNE
REYNOLDS

LOCATION:
JEFFERSON AVENUE
BRIDGE

Yvonne Osei is a Ghanaian artist living in the United States. Her transnational practice explores the topics of beauty and colorism, the politics of clothing, and how global trade and colonialism impact postcolonial West African and Western cultures. For Counterpublic 2023, *While You're Still Here* highlights the commercial landscape along the Jefferson Avenue Bridge and celebrates the important contributions of individual workers in this region. This public vinyl installation features photographs of the hands of four employees from businesses around the area interwoven with floral imagery. For over a century, the Jefferson Avenue Bridge area has been characterized by its floral district. Hence, the work is an ode to its rich history and adopts the metaphor of flowers to capture vibrance, progressive growth, and the fragrance of a promising future.

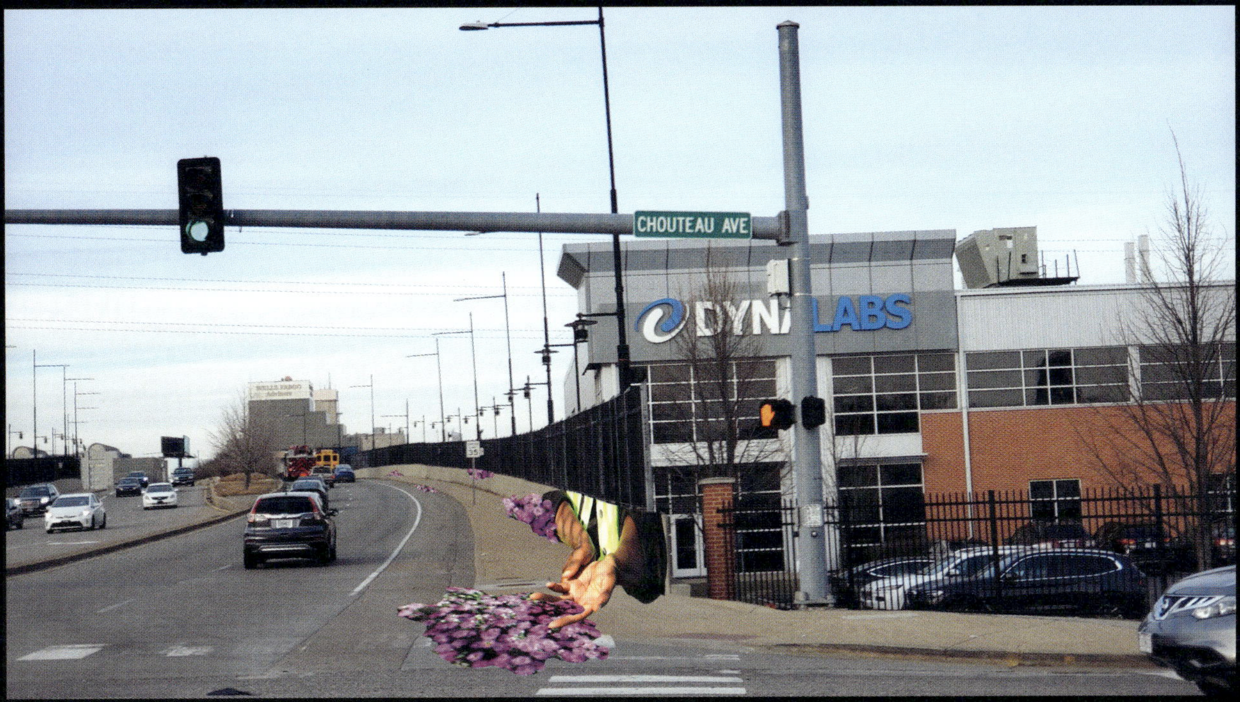

Yvonne Osei
While You're Still Here rendering

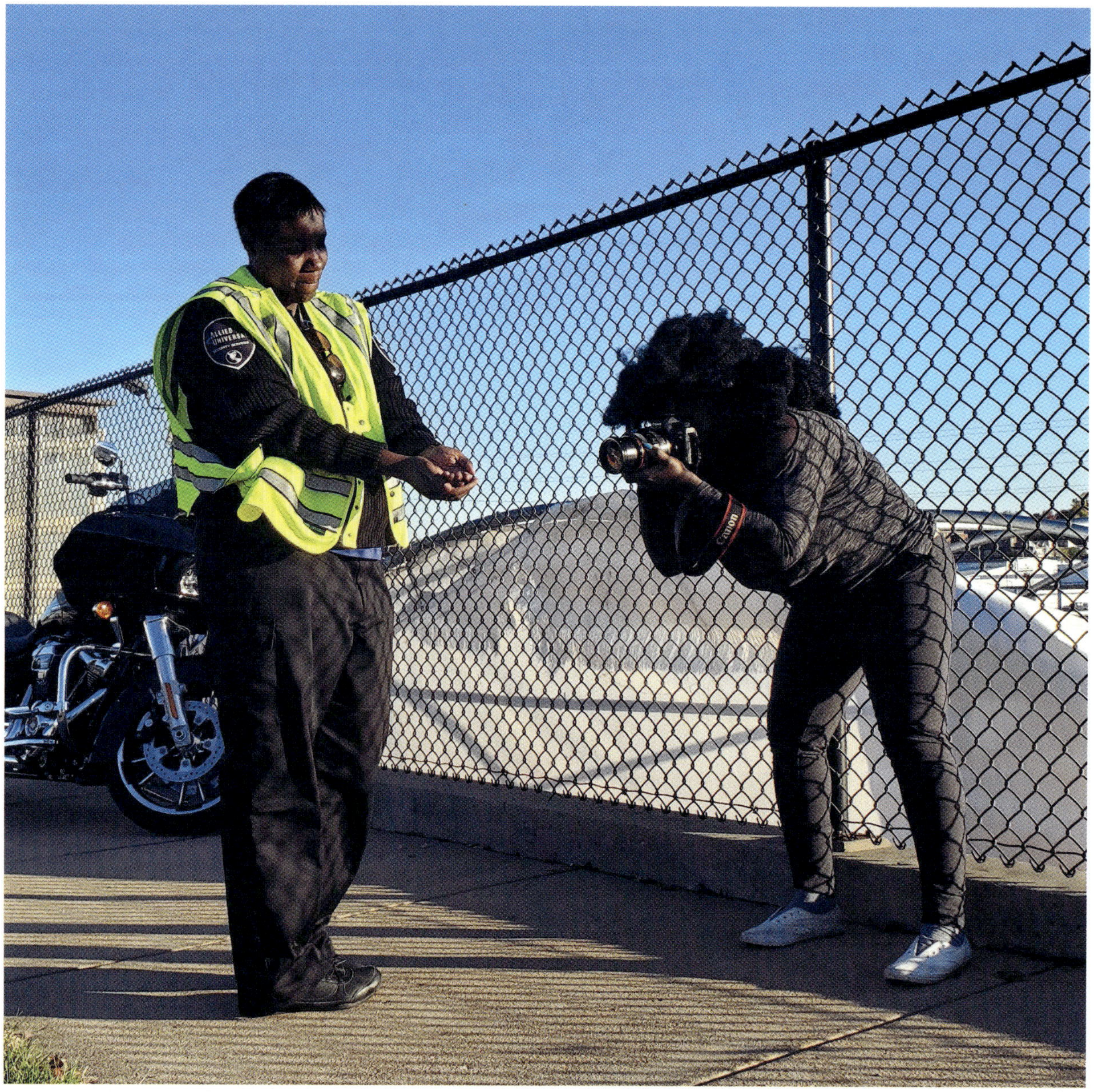

Yvonne Osei
While You're Still Here
In-process shot interacting with Sheila, a security guard on duty at the UPS Customer Center, Jefferson Avenue, October 2022

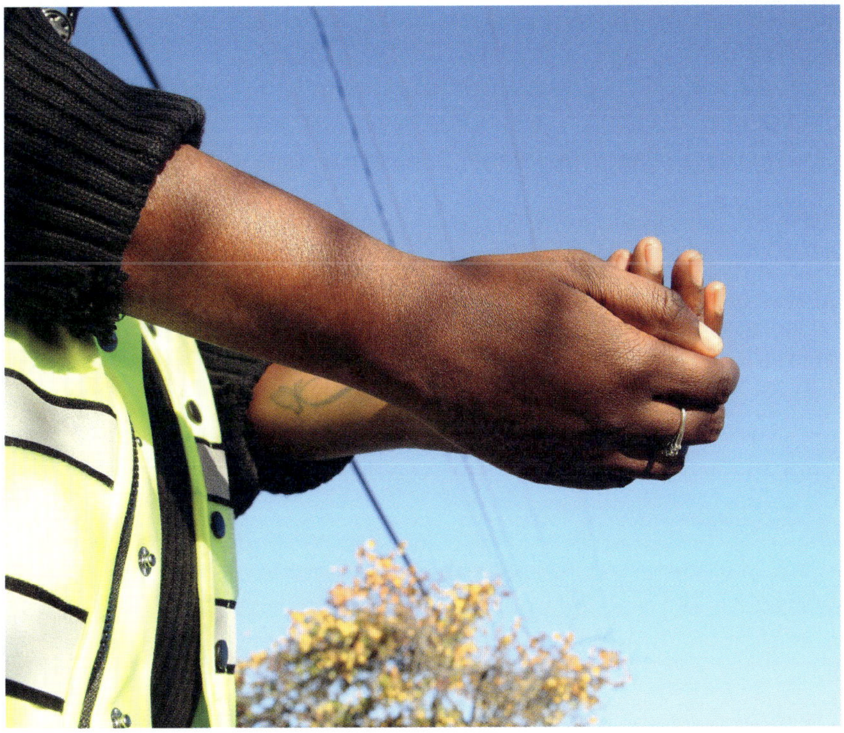

The depictions of hands are a representation of work, service, and labor. The range of hands shown in the installation include an attendant at QuikTrip, a banker at Wells Fargo, a security guard at UPS Customer Center, and a florist at Walter Knoll Florist. Although these employees are operating in different spaces and different capacities, they all make a certain impact with the hands they use for work that eventually leads to the development of the Jefferson Avenue region. Hands in *While You're Still Here* function on a micro level as individuals bringing their respective abilities and talents to the table through the work they do. On a macro level, the hands serve as a universal symbol that fuels collective impact, transformation, and growth.

Both sidewalks of the north and south corners of the bridge are activated by the installation. The work has been strategically placed at entrances and exits of the Jefferson Avenue Bridge where the installation can be accessed and interacted with by passersby. The installation transforms these entrances and exits into portals that greet the viewer as they step onto the bridge. The floral interactions with the viewer continue along the path as vinyl images of flowers are installed in various crevices of the concrete as though transferring life from one portal to the next.

A flower spotted in a crevice may seem insignificant in isolation. However, when the viewer approaches the end of the bridge, it slowly guides them to a bouquet intertwined with the hands of a worker. This combination of hand gestures and array of flowers offers appreciation to every viewer in acknowledgment of their contribution to their respective communities. The flowers and hands of these workers have been rendered larger than life to honor the monumental impact generated by a chain of individual actions on the development of the community.

The title, *While You're Still Here*, connotes a connection between time and presence. In the spirit of Counterpublic 2023, the work serves as a memorial to everyday people (past, present, and future) whose labor, no matter how substantial or minute, contributes to the monumental growth of the St. Louis community. The effort that we put in transcends us and is, in a sense, timeless because it offers a compounded advancement to the community over time. That is immeasurable. The installation is a reminder to viewers: embrace your moment, understand that you are relevant, appreciate the contributions of others, and receive your flowers while you're still here.

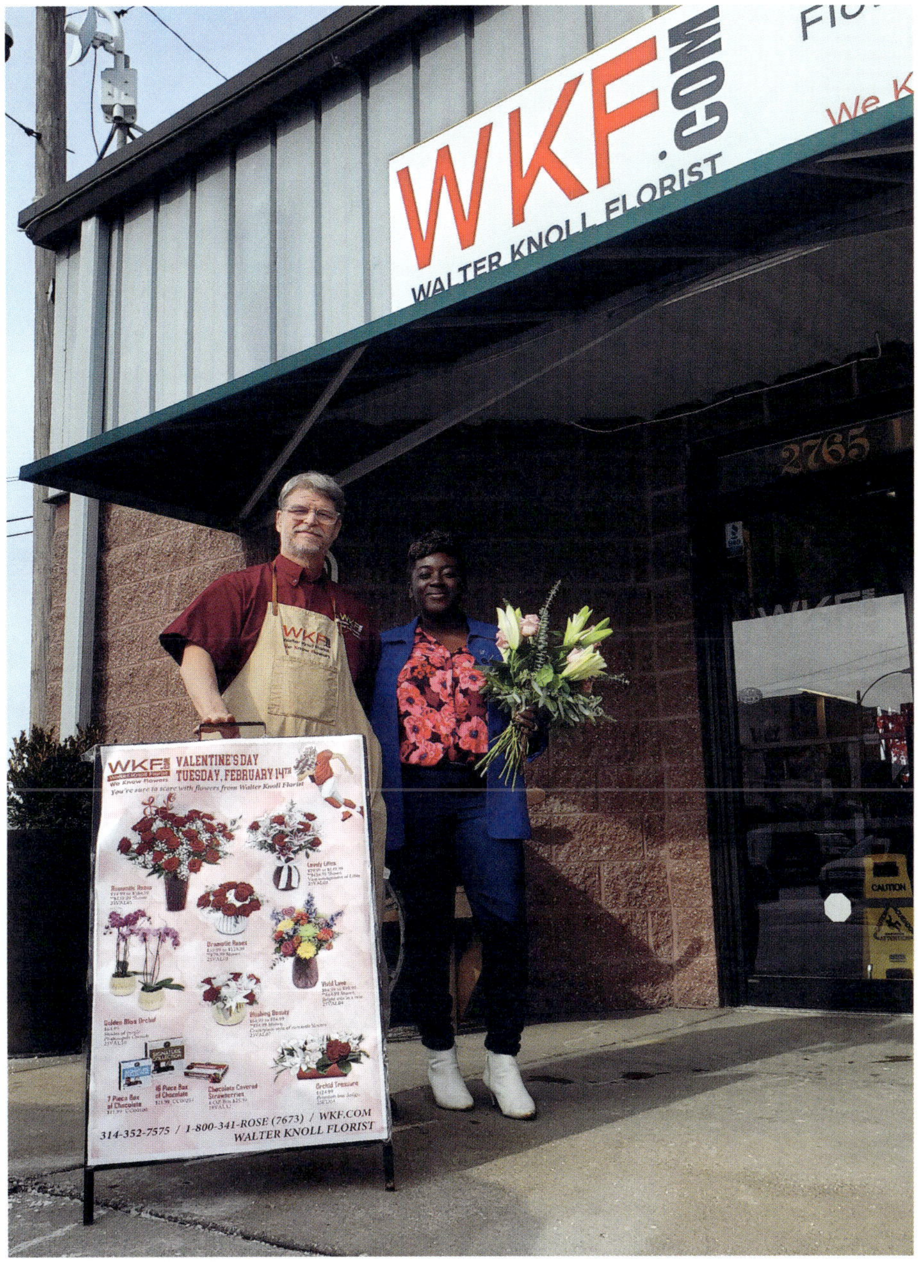

Artist Yvonne Osei standing with the owner of Walter Knoll Florist, Charles Knoll, in front of his floral shop on LaSalle Street near the Jefferson Bridge

Whereas, Between 1526 and the present, the U.S. Government's substantial interference in humanity of present heirs actively and/or passively remains a nuisance to life, liberty, land, labor, opportunity, and generational wealth transfer through acts of State Terror;

Whereas, Since 1776, the U.S. Government forcibly seized no less than 1.5 billion acres of lands and, since 1900, seized 12.9 million acres of lands, barring present heirs from their lands, through war, heirs property, tax sales, and Torrens Acts through acts of State Terror;

MILL CREEK VALLEY TO DOWNTOWN WEST:

Troubling Infrastructures

By
Diya Vij

A city is a series of infrastructures that organize social life and reproduce that social order. Like many cities, St. Louis's infrastructures hold an archive of ongoing colonial dispossession of land and water, of Indigenous genocide, the transatlantic slave trade, and their afterlives. The mapping and remapping of St. Louis—through demolition, rezoning, racial covenants, eminent domain, and land banking—demonstrates an ongoing choice to prioritize white life over all other life.

Just inland of where the Mississippi and Missouri Rivers merge, Downtown West is the civic center of St. Louis. In its bounds are the seats of governance: city hall, the police department, the former and current main regional railroad stations, the sewer department, other government buildings, and a new soon-to-be citywide pedestrian greenway. This is where policy takes root and permeates outward. Settled on the unceded land of the Osage Nation, this neighborhood, formerly the industrial and Black residential neighborhood of Mill Creek Valley, was the point of origin for white settlers within St. Louis and a crucial point of westward access to cement the expansion of the American colonial project, as monumentalized through the nearby Gateway to the West, the largest arch in the world. This area was the launching pad for many municipal-scale firsts: grand infrastructure schemes undertaken to settle white geographies and expand Empire.

The razing of Mill Creek Valley in 1955, home to over 20,000 Black residents and 2,000 houses, businesses, and churches, was the nation's largest urban renewal project of its time.[1] Notably, as Mill Creek Valley was demolished, the infamous racially segregated Pruit-Igoe housing complex was being built just one mile north, one of the largest public housing developments in the country at the time, only to raze those thirty-three buildings just twenty years later. At the time of this writing, approaching Downtown West from Jefferson Avenue, the route of Counterpublic 2023, can feel like a non-event. The four-lane cement roadway cuts through several giant cement parking lots. It is flat. Vast. Empty.

For Counterpublic 2023, artists Steffani Jemison, virgil b/g taylor, and Jordan Weber were invited to create site-specific commissions that engage with this geography: at once sited in Downtown West and in sprawling networks of infrastructures and policy implications that ripple far beyond the bounds of this district and even this city. They were asked to consider timescales and pathways toward potential life-affirming futures. Each artist is working in collaboration with St. Louis-based artists, organizers, community groups, and partners who have sought and seeded alternative infrastructures of making, care, and emancipation. The three commissions launch from two consequential sites of networked urban infrastructure as their starting point: the historic railroad terminal Union Station and the Metropolitan St. Louis Sewer District (MSD).

[1] Vivian Gibson, *The Last Children of Mill Creek* (Lakewood, OH: Belt Publishing, 2020), 14–15.

Sited in Union Station, Steffani Jemison's *Sky Is the Only Roof* multipart installation invokes the story of Josephine Baker to connect the complex legacies of the Black stage to legacies of Black migration and flight. At its opening in 1894, Union Station was the largest railroad terminal in the world, transporting over 100,000 passengers daily, with tracks connecting the United States on the east to the frontier on the west. Today, it is an indoor-outdoor mall. *Sky Is the Only Roof* links the transient nature of the railroad terminal to the patterns of forced dispersion of Black communities and spaces in the area. Almost all the spaces associated with Baker's early career in vaudeville and dance—Club Riviera, Ruby's Zodiac Lounge, the Amytis Theater, the huge Booker T. Washington Theater, the Eastern-Circle Theater, and others—have been entirely destroyed. Most of the buildings have been torn down and in their place are a Family Dollar store, parking lots, empty lots, and blank bank and federal buildings.

Forced to navigate this hostile geography—like Baker, an iconic symbol of Black expatriation—several internationally recognized Black performers of the time, including Miles Davis, Clark Terry, and Quincy Troupe, fled St. Louis in search of supportive communities elsewhere. *Untitled (Press)*, a sculpture and functional penny press, memorializes the act of dispersal. The penny press was a souvenir popularized in St. Louis during the 1904 Louisiana Purchase Exposition, the infamous World's Fair that sought to indoctrinate eugenicist thought through its vast human zoos. Here, the flattened pennies are inscribed with fragments of lyrics invoking freedom sung by Baker, "sky is the only / roof I've ever had." The press is framed by *Untitled (Ripple)*, a monumental installation of decommissioned theater curtains and scenic canvas flats that evoke the faded, lost, discarded, yet still vibrant and present history of theater in St. Louis.

Sky Is the Only Roof is also the title of a sound installation made in collaboration with St. Louis storytellers Jackie and Glen "Papa" Wright, and a cornerstone of this site-specific installation. It is a series of vignettes that continue legacies of St. Louis avant-garde and experimental performance, regardless of the fires that sought to destroy them. The episodic soundwork permeates the courtyard of Union Station, imbuing the former station with the potential of freedom through flight. In a country whose prerequisite to citizenship is whiteness, Baker's expatriation is an act of self-emancipation and a refusal to participate in this notion of Empire altogether, one that she considered to be fundamentally poisoned. She described America as "quicksand," stating that "the soil must be purified; not only must the root be pruned."[2]

Moving to the subterranean networked tunnel system of water and waste management, artists virgil b/g taylor and Jordan Weber use MSD Headquarters' green campus as their site of contemplation and transformation.[3] MSD is a powerful node in a sprawling and dispersed network of 9,600 miles of underground pipes. Originating in Mill Creek Valley as part of a movement toward increased hygiene, St. Louis's combined sewer system was considered to be a modern engineering marvel that moved waste underground and out of the city's contaminated water bodies.[4] Yet today, these modernist practices are breaking down.

[2] Henry Louis Gates, Jr., "An Interview with Josephine Baker and James Baldwin," in *Conversations with James Baldwin*, ed. Fred L. Standley and Louis H. Pratt (Jackson, MS: University Press of Mississippi, 1989), 265.

[3] More information on MSD Project Clear's Market Street Improvement available at: https://msdprojectclear.org/projects/new-construction/market-street-improvements/.

[4] The tunnels are an engineering marvel, even now. They were declared a National Historic Civil Engineering Landmark in 1988. For more information, see Erick Trickey, "How a Sewer Will Save St. Louis," *Politico*, April 20, 2017, https://www.politico.com/magazine/story/2017/04/20/st-louis-infrastructure-sewer-tunnel-water-system-215056/.

The system's failures have resulted in massive pollution to the region's waterways: with increased rain, the combined sewer system overflows, rainwater combines with raw waste, and an estimated 13.4 billion gallons of untreated sewage penetrates lawns and streams, causes frequent geyser explosions, and ultimately empties into the Mississippi and Missouri Rivers. In 2011, the Department of Justice filed a consent decree requiring MSD to spend a minimum $4.7 billion over the next 23 years to rectify the toxic situation.[5]

The system is glitching, experiencing infrastructural failures, and for virgil b/g taylor, the glitch opens new possibilities to move beyond patchwork maintenance that reproduces the same uneven material conditions. Instead, taylor's *Confluence Decree* introduces grounds for new political imaginaries to seed new relations and new demands for a transformational infrastructure that binds us to a new world.[6] Considering the invisibility of these complex histories and current conditions, especially against the backdrop of escalating water crises and climate catastrophe, taylor engages the participation of a breadth of St. Louis residents to address the sewage infrastructure as a political and social site. A three-part community-driven newsprint publication, *Confluence Decree* is a series of magical dispatches to and from the St. Louis sewage system that asks: What does this consent decree have to do with our agreements with each other? When we do meet each other, how can consent be found in a city built on such uneven foundations?

Responding to MSD's major commitment to upgrade the metropolitan wastewater management system, Jordan Weber's *Defensive Landscape* connects the violence of the land to the violence of the body and offers a critical intervention into the generational health implications of the intertwined crises of mass incarceration and ecological apartheid. Weber starts first by calling attention to generations of persistent environmental racism in a monumental sculptural installation near MSD's headquarters. At the end of Counterpublic 2023, the work will travel to become part of Weber's *Defensive Landscape*, a regenerative earthwork in northern St. Louis. The permanent wetland will grow in Peace Park, within a neighborhood experiencing outsized impacts of the toxic flooding, and will be an active site for stormwater capture, carbon sequestration, soil purification, community gathering, education, and play.

[5] "Consent Decree," MSD Project Clear, accessed January 21, 2023, https://msdprojectclear.org/about/our-organization/consent-decree/.

[6] Lauren Berlant, "The Commons: Infrastructures for troubling times*," *Environment and Planning D: Society and Space* 34, no. 3 (2016): 393–419, https://doi.org/10.1177/0263775816645989.

Started by civil rights activist Otis Woodard, Peace Park was a community hub with a "share shed" stocked with free food and free tools. Since vacated, a multipartner coalition of city entities and community groups have joined together to rebuild Peace Park in Woodard's honor and transfer ownership into a community land trust, subverting individual ownership into a regional model of community stewardship.

Building on Weber's *All Our Liberations* (2021) presented by the Pulitzer Arts Foundation and his multiyear work with the Sam Fox School at Washington University, local abolitionist group Close the Workhouse, and caregivers The Black Healers Collective, *Defensive Landscape* is in service of ecological liberation. In its uplifting of community caretakers and activists, it offers a place to gather and break bread reoriented toward an abolitionist geography of collective care and self-determined infrastructures of resource distribution and land remediation. It is a place to contemplate the complex and vital role of water in the cultural landscape of St. Louis, or as Woodard envisioned, a refuge for gathering "to talk about the good things, the peaceful things."[7]

Through deep engagement with the geographies of and beyond Downtown West, these three commissions lay bare the undeniable entanglements of infrastructure and Empire. As Downtown West currently undergoes a necessary era of remembering, as demonstrated through St. Louis artist Damon Davis's mile-long Mill Creek Valley monument to the families of the erased neighborhood, these works show us that remembering itself is not redemption. It is but a step toward metabolizing the past to reconstruct a new series of infrastructures. Through a collaborative or participatory approach to public artmaking, these projects consider what is possible when we—individually and systemically—choose otherwise, choose alternative pathways to support more life.

[7] "Otis Woodard, advocate for the poor in north St. Louis, has died," *Fox 2*, February 14, 2015, https://fox2now.com/news/otis-woodard-advocate-for-the-poor-in-north-st-louis-has-died/.

Steffani Jemison

CURATOR:
DIYA VIJ

LOCATION:
UNION STATION

Steffani Jemison's multidisciplinary practice spans time-based, sculptural, and discursive mediums, informed by deep research into movement practices, literature, ethnomusicology, and the history of cinema. Much of Jemison's recent work has explored writing, gesture, performance, and animation, focusing particularly on the relationship between bodies and "things," often working closely with other artists to consider these complex subject-object relationships. This work has led her in several directions, from a multiyear, multipart exploration of pantomime to the production of functional, site-responsive rock and stone tumblers that rotate, erode, and transform local metal debris, found coins and glass, and semiprecious geological materials.

Sky Is the Only Roof, a three-part site-specific installation by Jemison, is inspired by the complex legacy of the Black stage in the Downtown West neighborhood of St. Louis as it intersects with the region's complex legacies of migration, dispersion, and flight. Invoking St. Louis-born performer Josephine Baker as an icon of Black expatriation, the works take root in these themes of loss and longing. Jemison explores the transitory history of Black artists and performers in the city of St. Louis.

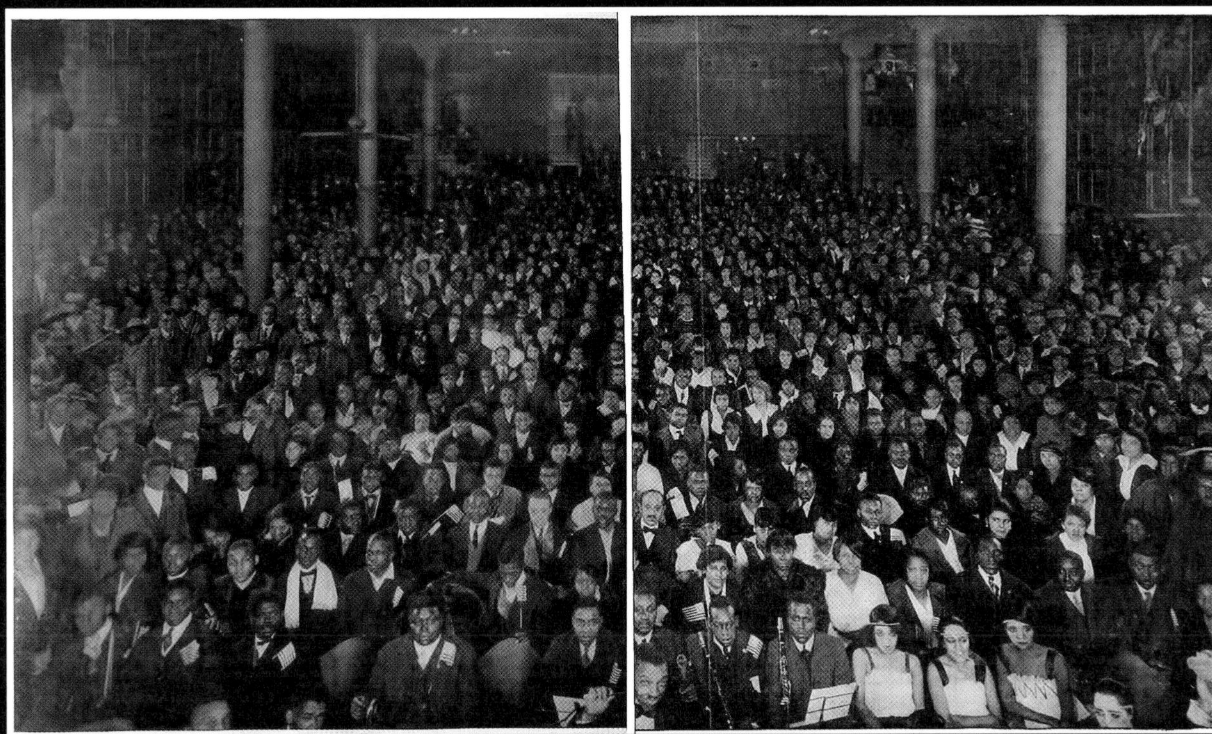

"A Midnight Audience at the Booker T. Washington Theater in St. Louis," *Crisis Magazine,* May 1918

Installed in Union Station, once the biggest railroad terminal in the world and today an indoor-outdoor entertainment destination and hotel, Jemison presents three works: *Sky Is the Only Roof*, a sound installation made in collaboration with St. Louis storytellers and performers Jackie and Papa Wright; *Untitled (Ripple)*, a monumental sculpture of decommissioned theater drapes and scenic canvas flats; and *Untitled (Press)*, a functional penny press with fragments of lyrics invoking freedom sung by Baker ("sky is the only / roof I've ever had").

Baker, who famously said, "I had been suffocating in the United States. I can't live anywhere that I can't breathe freedom," was not the only internationally recognized Black St. Louis performer to sever ties with the city. Born after the Great Migration and raised in the shadow of the white vigilante terror of the East St. Louis Riots of 1917, a massacre that displaced thousands of Black families, artists like Miles Davis, Clark Terry, and Quincy Troupe fled St. Louis in favor of supportive communities in California, the East Coast, and Europe. Many artists associated with the experimental Black Artists' Group likewise moved to Paris and New York.

Baker's early career in vaudeville and dance is associated with many St. Louis venues formerly clustered near Union Station, including iconic Black theaters and cinemas such as Club Riviera, Ruby's Zodiac Lounge, the huge Booker T. Washington Theater, and others, which were subsequently entirely destroyed. For Jemison, the present-day Downtown West neighborhood holds no traces of this vibrant past. It is what happens when a city chooses "no life" over "Black life." The project pays homage to this lost history by producing symbolic and real tokens of change and exchange.

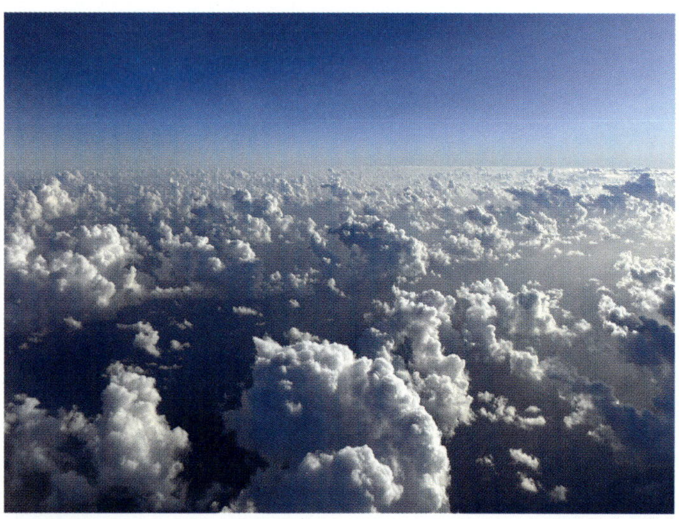

Steffani Jemison
Sky Is the Only Roof research image

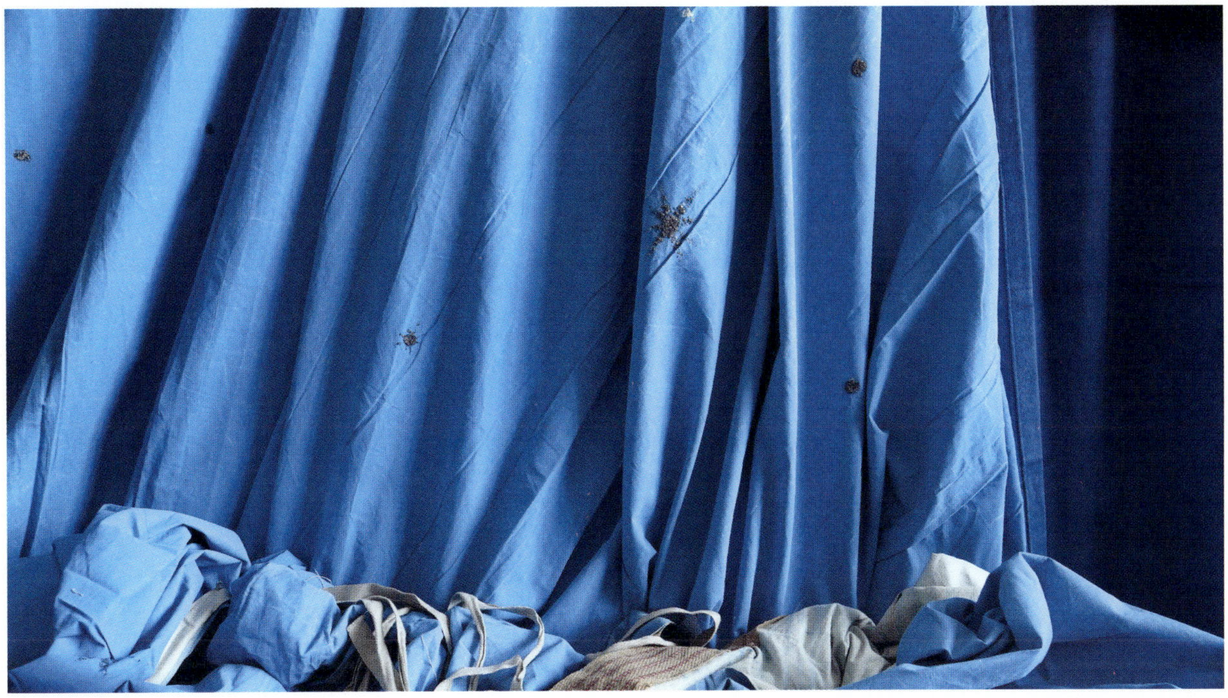

Steffani Jemison
Sky Is the Only Roof research image (*Ripple*)

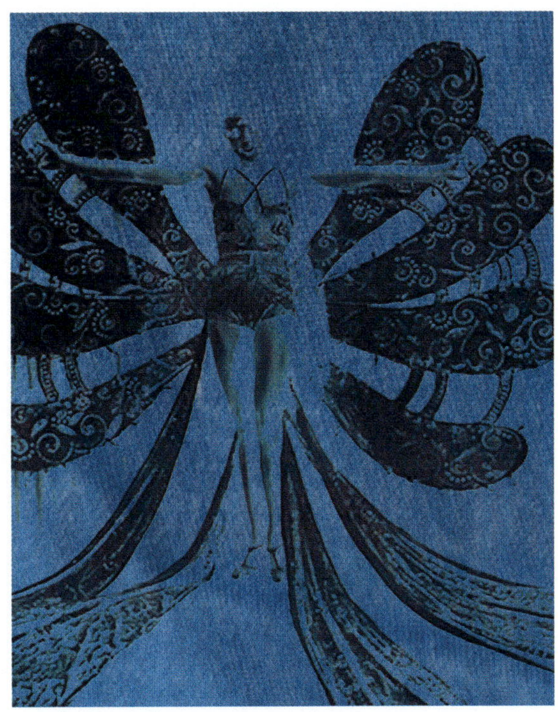

Steffani Jemison
Sky Is the Only Roof research image

IN CONVERSATION

Jackie and Papa Wright with Steffani Jemison

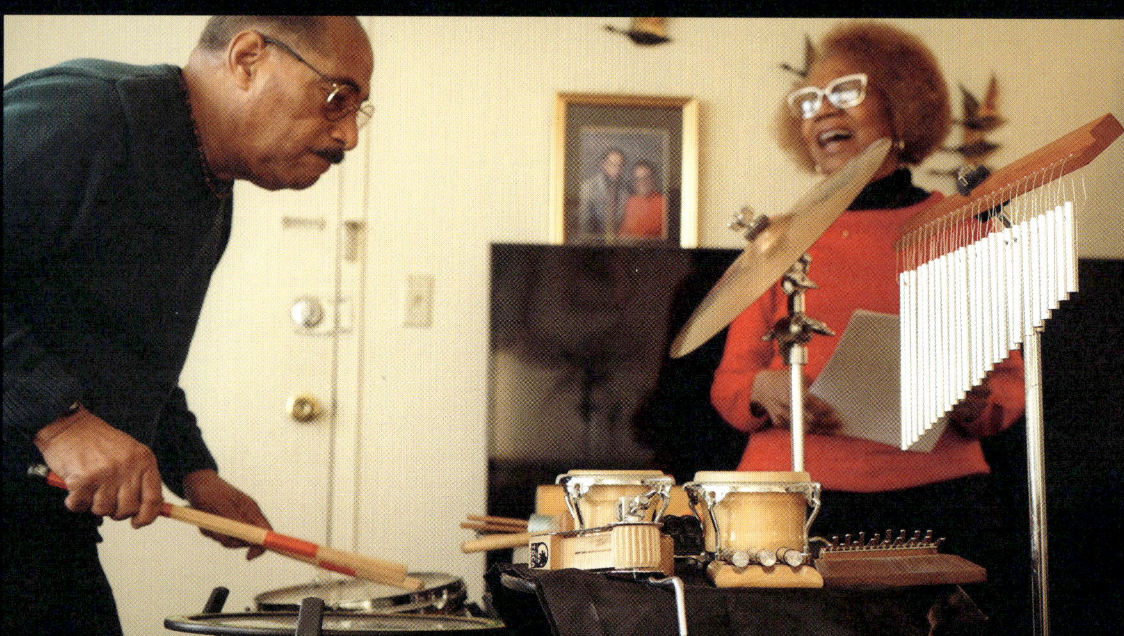

Jackie and Glen "Papa" Wright in rehearsal
Courtesy of Steffani Jemison

Sky Is the Only Roof began as a meditation on movement, travel, and performance in and through St. Louis, a meditation on Black life and the legacy of live performance generated by one of the largest Black communities in the United States in the twentieth century: Mill Creek Valley. When I arrived in town, one of my first tasks was to explore the neighborhood on foot. I came prepared with a spreadsheet and map plotting two dozen Black performance spaces active in the 1930s and 40s—concert and vaudeville halls, nightclubs, theaters—all clustered within a radius of a half mile.

You know how it feels to be the one person walking in a city where everybody drives? People look at you funny, trying to make it make sense—she's dressed too nice to not have a car, they're thinking; you can feel their confusion right through the tinted windows. Meanwhile, what seemed to be a normal street on Google Maps turns out to be a whole highway. You find yourself stuck on a median or tightroping along the skinny "shoulder," cars driving a little too close for comfort, not a crosswalk in sight.

And so I moved on foot from university parking lot to stadium parking lot to bank parking lot, standing where spots like the Vendome, Star, Retina, and Booker T. Washington theaters had once been.[1] I closed my eyes and tried to feel something. Tried my hardest to hear something. Even squinted and tried to see something: an aura, a spirit, a ghost. There was nothing to see.

Systematically destroyed by decades of underinvestment and "urban renewal," few local traces remain of the sparkling, dense network of creativity that produced Miles Davis and Scott Joplin and Josephine Baker in the former Mill Creek Valley. Nearly five thousand buildings were destroyed, including dozens of historical churches and performance spaces. Words like "diaspora" and "migration" feel too stable to evoke this powerful expulsion and explosion; the violence and scatter; the electric radiation of Black creativity from Mill Creek Valley, St. Louis to Harlem and Broadway and Los Angeles and Paris.

In optics, the concept of *diffraction* describes "the spread of light or deflection of its rays," from a Latin root that means "break apart in pieces," the way a community, vibrant and rich, can be broken up into pieces.[2] And yet, diffraction also describes the movement of light *around* obstacles into the shadows, producing visible patterns—not unlike the way that the arc of a life can bend around a barrier, going deeper and further than we might ever imagine.

[1] According to Eric Ledell Smith's *African American Theater Buildings: An Illustrated Historical Directory, 1900–1955* (Jefferson, NC: McFarland, 2003), there were thirty-one African American theaters in St. Louis during those years. For more information, see "African American Theaters of St. Louis," *St. Louis City Talk* (blog), October 23, 2015, http://www.stlouiscitytalk.com/posts/2015/10/african-american-theaters-of-st-louis.

[2] Online Etymology Dictionary, sv. "diffraction," accessed February 5, 2023, https://www.etymonline.com/word/diffraction#etymonline_v_8560.

The way that light moves to transcend even interference—the way it keeps moving and moving and moving—that's the spirit that has guided *Sky Is the Only Roof* in multiple directions. I leaned toward concrete experiences of dispersion and exchange symbolized by a machine that alchemizes the contributions of visitors into real investments in local communities. I gravitated toward decommissioned—but still usable and useful—material relics of theater and performance. And finally, I turned to Josephine Baker, icon of Black emigration, who served as a central source of inspiration for my collaboration with artists and performers Jackie and Glen "Papa" Wright. Indeed, it is Baker's anthem of freedom and flight, "Breezin' Along with the Breeze" (1926), that inspired the title of this body of work, *Sky Is the Only Roof*.

Jackie and Papa Wright are deeply collaborative performers whose lives have, directly and indirectly, intersected with the most important stories in St. Louis. Jackie and Papa have chosen to stay in St. Louis, building deep relationships and roots across the fields of education, storytelling, and experimental music. As a touring musician, percussionist, music educator, and puppeteer, Papa has intersected with many of the city's most significant artistic exchanges, from the St. Louis Conservatory of Music, where he taught percussion, to the Black Artists' Group of St. Louis, an influential interdisciplinary collective.[3] Meanwhile, Jackie's work as a storyteller situates her at the heart of a rich local network of actors, writers, and performers who maintain this tradition, which is passed from the voice of one teller to the next.

As the three of us have worked together to build a sound installation that evokes experiences of departure, flight, and new beginnings, particularly through the lens of Josephine Baker's complex relationship to St. Louis, we've also shared stories about our own trajectories as artists.

[3] "At the peak of the national Black Arts Movement, the Black Artists' Group of St. Louis (BAG) was unique in their interdisciplinary, artistic approach to combating social injustice and exploring the far reaches of experimental performance." See the official website for the 2020 documentary *The Black Artists Group: Creation Equals Movement*, accessed February 5, 2023, https://www.bagstl.com/. "The Black Artists Group (BAG) was a multidisciplinary arts collective that existed in St. Louis, Missouri, from 1968 to 1972. BAG is known for the convergence of free jazz and experimental theater." "Black Artists Group," *Wikipedia*, last modified April 8, 2022, https://en.wikipedia.org/wiki/Black_Artists_Group.

STEFFANI JEMISON:
Jackie and Papa, could you describe your practice in a few sentences? What is it that you do?

JACKIE WRIGHT:
Under the umbrella "The Wright Entertainment," I perform as a storyteller and Papa plays percussion. We also perform puppet shows. Papa is the puppeteer, and I'm the assistant. He's behind stage working all the characters and I'm upfront interacting with the puppets and the audience. Under the same umbrella, we also do percussion workshops. Papa introduces a variety of percussion instruments to children. Sometimes I go along with him and show them how we use percussion with storytelling.

STEFFANI:
How did the two of you meet?

GLEN "PAPA" WRIGHT:
As a kid, I didn't have money to buy instruments. I beat on buckets and tin cans. In the second grade, my mother bought me a snare drum for six dollars at the pawn shop. My friend and I played and won first place. That's when I knew the drums were for me. Later, I became a touring musician, playing drums with a group called Mel and Tim.[4] One night, I went to Club Highlander to see the Oliver Sain Revue. I met a woman (not Jackie) who told me she was part of a social club that needed help with music. We agreed to connect the next day. She didn't come—instead, she sent someone else from her social club. That's how I met Jackie. I had never met a woman that was so nice. I used to call her Miss Jackie, because I had so much respect for her.

[4] "Born in Holly Springs, Mississippi, R&B Soul/Funk balladeers Melvin McArthur Hardin (born November 30, 1948) and Hubert Timothy McPherson (born December 9, 1949), were first cousins and sons of two sisters. They migrated to St. Louis, Missouri, in 1968 then on to Chicago, Illinois, for a music career where they were 'discovered' by legendary R&B performer, Gene Chandler." Otis Alexander, "Mel & Tim (1969–1974)", *BlackPast*, September 4, 2021, https://www.blackpast.org/african-american-history/mel-tim-1969-1974/.

JACKIE:
Of course when you saw me, you melted, right? But I had a boyfriend at the time and I wasn't interested.

PAPA:
Six months later, I was working with a dance group at Greeley Community Center playing conga drums, living with my parents, when Jackie called. I didn't have any money, but at the time, I was a marathon runner, running twenty miles a day. I never missed a day. Anytime she told me that she was free, I put my jogging clothes on and ran to her apartment.

JACKIE:
I had dropped out of college and was out for five years before I went back. In high school, I had been a top student in my class, on the Dean's List all the time. When I went to college at Harris Teachers College, now called Harris-Stowe State University, that was the first time I faced discrimination. There were a couple of teachers that I just couldn't do anything right for. I let them control my life and dropped out of school. I said, if I'm going to get up early every morning, I'm going to make some money. So I left school in 1970 and took a job as a waitress.

PAPA:
Jackie was so kind to me, and I said this is the person I want to live the rest of my life with. This is the person I want to grow together with. I tell people that in order to do things, especially young people, you have to enjoy the journey.

JACKIE:
Papa and I wanted to grow as individuals together. I went back to school in 1975—the teachers who had given me a hard time weren't there anymore. I got my bachelor's degree and master's degree in education with certification in special education. I'm also a reading specialist. I had a wonderful experience the second time around. I went on to graduate with honors. I taught in St. Louis schools for thirty-two years.

PAPA:
Jackie graduated *cum laude* from college. I started studying with Rich O'Donnell, the principal percussionist with the St. Louis Symphony.[5] I studied piano with Bill Romer, and also studied theory and composition. I was the only African American mallet player in St. Louis. I was invited to teach at Saint Louis Conservatory and Schools for the Arts (CASA). After two years, I was teaching applied music students at the junior college level. I always felt that I was a good student, not because I'm a smart man but because I worked so damn hard at it. I've only got a high school diploma.

[5] Rich O'Donnell's career spans sixty-five years as percussionist, improvisor, composer, designer and builder of percussion and electronic instruments, teacher, and writer. He was director of the Electronic Music Studio at Washington University from 1980–2018. He has encouraged and facilitated the growth of independent contemporary music in the community for forty-nine years as music director of the St. Louis New Music Circle, which he left in 2009. He retired in 2002 after forty-three years as principal percussionist of the St. Louis Symphony Orchestra. In 2009, he co-founded HEARding Cats Collective, an artists collective working to keep St. Louis strange and wonderful. More information available at: https://www.richodonnell.com/.

JACKIE:
And when I saw how creative he was . . . I'm the reason he started his percussion workshops.

PAPA:
Being a percussionist, you have to depend on so many other people. I wanted to take control of my own career. Jackie said, you can't depend on people to feed you. You have to create your own opportunities. I said, okay, dang it. I'm going to do it. I began leading percussion workshops for Young Audiences, an organization that sends artists into schools for enrichment programs. I continued the same work with Springboard to Learning.

I always loved puppets but never saw Black men, or any men, who were puppeteers. In 1991, I got up the nerve to connect with the Puppet Guild of Greater St. Louis and they welcomed me with open arms.[6] Once I started, my creativity just kept flowing. I'm the only African American to be the president of the guild; I was president for eleven years. Those puppets have taken us to Europe and around the world. Over the years, I've performed with the Julius Hemphill Ensemble[7] in St. Louis, including saxophonist J. D. Parran and trumpeter Baikida E. J. Carroll. I've also played with Oliver Lake at the Black Artists' Group building.[8] I also formed my own group called the Outer Limits in the 80s, with original music I composed. I'm currently playing with a free improvisation group with Greg Mills and Fred Tompkins. We enjoyed the journey of getting where we're at now, and I'm really excited about the next ten years. I'm busy. Things look bright.

[6] "The Puppet Guild of Greater St. Louis has been in operation since 1939, making it the second oldest puppetry guild in the country. Its members include professional puppeteers, as well as amateurs, families, and people with special needs who use puppeteering as a way to express themselves freely." "The Puppeteers of St. Louis," HEC, accessed February 5, 2023, https://www.hecmedia.org/posts/the-puppeteers-of-st-louis. More information available at: https://www.facebook.com/PuppetGuildStL.

[7] "The work of saxophonist (mainly alto), flautist, vocalist, composer, conductor, arranger, organiser, bandleader, teacher and label founder Julius Hemphill (1938–1995) spans solo saxophone music, brilliantly poised small 'jazz' groups (often setting his alto with cello, drums and trumpet); compositions for chamber ensembles and big band; saxophone quartets, sextets and a saxophone opera; as well as collaborations with poets, dancers and fuller theater works." "A Short Guide to Julius Hill," *Wire*, March 2021, https://www.thewire.co.uk/audio/tracks/a-short-guide-to-julius-hemphill-60791.

[8] "In July 1969, the group obtained, for an annual rent of $1, a building at 2665 Washington Blvd., in the heart of the inner city, which soon housed living quarters, performance/rehearsal space, a painting studio and teaching facilities for dance, theater, music, film, creative writing and visual arts." Liam Otten, "Rediscovering the Black Artists' Group," *The Source*, Washington University in St. Louis, February 2, 2006, https://source.wustl.edu/2006/02/rediscovering-the-black-artists-group/.

STEFFANI:
Tell me about your creative process. How do you create new work?

PAPA:
For puppet shows, I'm the one that's more creative. I will come up with a particular idea about a puppet show, put the beginning and the middle and the end together. Then the rest is a partnership. It's all improvisation: no shows are on paper; everything is in our mind.

JACKIE:
No script. We just know where we're going with the story. And then we feed off the audience as well. I'll find a story that I think is interesting. I choose fairy tales or folktales or fables. Believe it or not, a lot of them aren't very interesting. You kind of have to add a little more to them yourself, you know, because they don't quite end the way you want them to end.

PAPA:
Then we have to add the percussion in with the stories. We can tell if a piece is successful—

JACKIE:
—by the audience, immediate feedback from the audience.

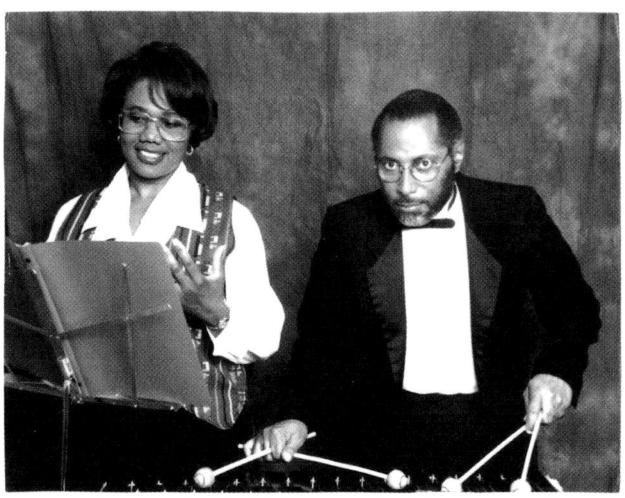

Promotional photo
Courtesy of Nathaniel Warren

PAPA:
It's not *what* we do. It's *how* we do it. The little kids really love what we do. We do 250 puppet shows a year. My percussion workshop is one of the top percussion workshops around the Midwest.

JACKIE:
I had somebody ask for his autograph last night!

PAPA:
I work at what I do. Every day. I practice every day, and whatever I decide to do, I'm going to try to nail it. Nail it!

STEFFANI:
We can feel that. Who are your favorite writers and performers, your favorite artists? Other people in your field that you follow or are inspired by?

PAPA:
Emily Dickinson wrote a poem, "Gifts." I love her. I like Shirley LeFlore, the poet.

JACKIE:
She was one of St. Louis's poet laureates.

PAPA:
Eugene B. Redmond, a great poet. Also the poet Quincy Troupe, who's originally from St. Louis.

JACKIE:
Gladys Caines-Coggswell inspired me to start doing storytelling. She had an organization called By Word of Mouth Storytelling Guild (BWOM).[9] Diann Joy Bank was my storytelling coach. Susan Hinkel was president of Missouri Storytelling (MO-TELL).[10] She gave me the first opportunity to tell at her festival. Joyce Slater, who lives in Kansas City, gave me another big festival opportunity. For the St. Louis Storytelling Festival,[11] Nan Kammann-Judd was the director of the festival at the time. Becky Walstrom was the next director; she's the one who invited me to be on the St. Louis Storytelling Festival Planning Committee.

[9] "By Word of Mouth Storytelling Guild (BWOM) is an organization of storytellers and story listeners who are united in an effort to preserve and perpetuate the awesome oral tradition of storytelling. Our members include professional and non-professional storytellers, teachers, librarians, counselors, retirees, seniors, preachers and others who love to hear and/or tell stories." Dr. Gladys Caines-Coggswell, "By Word of Mouth Storytelling Guild," accessed February 5, 2023, https://www.gladyscstories.com/by-word-of-mouth-storytelling-guild/.

[10] "MO-TELL was established in 1984 as Missouri's leading storytelling group for storytellers and listeners alike with the intention to promote and perpetuate storytelling throughout the state. Throughout our history we have successfully reached Missourians by providing storytelling in the Missouri State Parks. Currently we provide storytellers to 12 state parks and/or historic sites in Missouri." "Missouri Storytelling, Inc. (MO-TELL)," MO-TELL, accessed February 5, 2023, https://www.mo-tell.org/.

[11] St. Louis Storytelling Festival features nationally renowned storytellers and programs for all ages, currently held at the St. Louis County Library. More information available at: https://www.slcl.org/events/st-louis-storytelling-festival.

PAPA:
Joyce Slater, she's instrumental in the Midwest, as far as promoting storytelling. J. D. Parran is the one who gave me my first break, playing creative music. And you [Steffani] inspire me. Jackie and I are busy, we're traveling, but what you're doing to have the confidence in two old folks—you're a young woman—to have the confidence in us that you want us to do this. I don't usually speak this way, but we've built a relationship over a period of time. I feel comfortable talking. We're at that point. This [our collaboration with Steffani] didn't start two months ago or two weeks ago. It started six months ago. Now we're at that spiritual point, that creative point, and ready to explore.

JACKIE:
Steffani, tell us about your background as a writer.

STEFFANI:
Well, I've always been interested in writing. When I was a kid, I used to make up invented languages and write stories and poems. Later, I wrote plays and performed them in my basement. I was a very early reader—I learned to read when I was three—so I was always reading and I was always writing. In junior high, I started writing chapter books, first in a notebook during sleepovers with my best friend, and later by myself on our home computer. I always had one going. My novels were always about girls who were a little cooler than me.

JACKIE:
All your life, then?

STEFFANI:
Yup, all my life. My grandfather was a pastor with a very creative relationship to language and words. My father is retired now; he was an attorney, which is also very verbal, very rhetorical. He's a very good storyteller because he had to develop that skill for his professional work. My mother actually trained to be an English teacher, and she's always been a very good writer. So I was always confident writing and thought I might want to be a journalist or writer.

Later, I began to feel as though I wanted a broader palette. I never knew a professional artist until long after college, but once I learned more about that career, I realized it was a container through which I could explore a lot of different ideas. When I first started making art, I felt that I was relying too heavily on the comfort I felt when writing.

STEFFANI (cont.):
So, for almost ten years I published almost nothing in connection with my creative work because I wanted to strengthen my other tools—like tying your good hand behind your back, so you have to learn how to write with the other hand. I wanted to learn how to work without writing. It's only in the last few years that I've begun writing as an extension of my creative practice.

JACKIE:
Would you also describe yourself as a sculptor?

STEFFANI:
Sometimes I make sculptures. Sometimes I make photographic work. Sometimes I make drawings, and often I make videos and also performances.

JACKIE:
What about the larger project you're making in St. Louis?

STEFFANI:
My research has taken me in a few directions. I've become fascinated with the connection between the penny press—those objects you find at county fairs that produce stretched pennies, like little sculptures—and the history of St. Louis. As part of the exhibition, I'm making a functional press for Union Station, which will collect donations to be redistributed to local performing arts organizations. The pressed pennies evoke dispersion and flight. I've also been researching decommissioned theatrical drapes and canvas backdrops. I've been thinking about the monumental feeling of these drapes, which are often twenty-five feet high, and the way they evoke the living (and lost) histories of theater and performance in St. Louis. Finally, our work together is a pillar of my research. We're developing a sound installation through self-contained episodes, some of which refer historically to Josephine Baker's life and others of which refer to experiences of departure and dispersion.

I'm curious if you could talk about what you hope for the future of storytelling and experimental music, your intersecting fields, especially in St. Louis. I'm also curious to hear what your next steps are as artists.

JACKIE:
Storytelling had a resurgence in the 80s. And now, in my opinion, it seems to be dying out again. So I don't know what storytelling will look like during the next ten years. I just read that the Northlands Storytelling Network is shutting down,[12] and even our St. Louis Storytelling Festival has changed hands this year. I'm hoping that more young people will develop an interest in storytelling so that we can continue, you know, telling tales.

On a personal note, Papa and I created an original story, *Reuben, the Jealous Lion*. We've been performing it for several years and are now developing it as a children's book.

[12] "In 1978, five storytelling friends traveled together to the National Storytelling Festival in the 'Southlands' of Jonesborough, Tennessee. Inspired by and celebrating storytelling, these five friends formed an organization up 'North.' In forty-four years, Northlands has grown a membership, a conference and this website, bringing together a network of storytellers whose feet are planted in the heartlands of Illinois, Iowa, Michigan, Minnesota and Wisconsin but whose hearts reach wherever tales are told. Northlands Storytelling Network closed its membership organization as of December 31, 2022." "Northlands Storytelling Network," Northlands, accessed February 5, 2023, https://www.northlands.net/.

PAPA:
I hate to waste time. During the pandemic, when I had spare time—when I wasn't practicing—I wrote thirty original melodies for children's songs. So far, Carol Watkins, a St. Louis storyteller, has written lyrics for twenty of them. Jackie and I also developed an original puppet show.

I'm planning on phasing out my work as a teaching artist during the next two years. I'm entering the last part of my life, and I want to spend more time being a creative musician. I just want to create. I want to concentrate more on being a musician. After playing a show last night, we stayed up until after four o'clock, because—I like to say, "I haven't got the music; the music's got me"— I couldn't sleep. When I was playing, people were saying, "Boy, you're possessed." A spiritual thing comes over me and it's not me playing; it's something in my body that I created. So it's not that I've got the music, it's that the music's got me. I believe this is what the Creator wants me to do before I die. I'm afraid of that word "regret." I don't want any regrets.

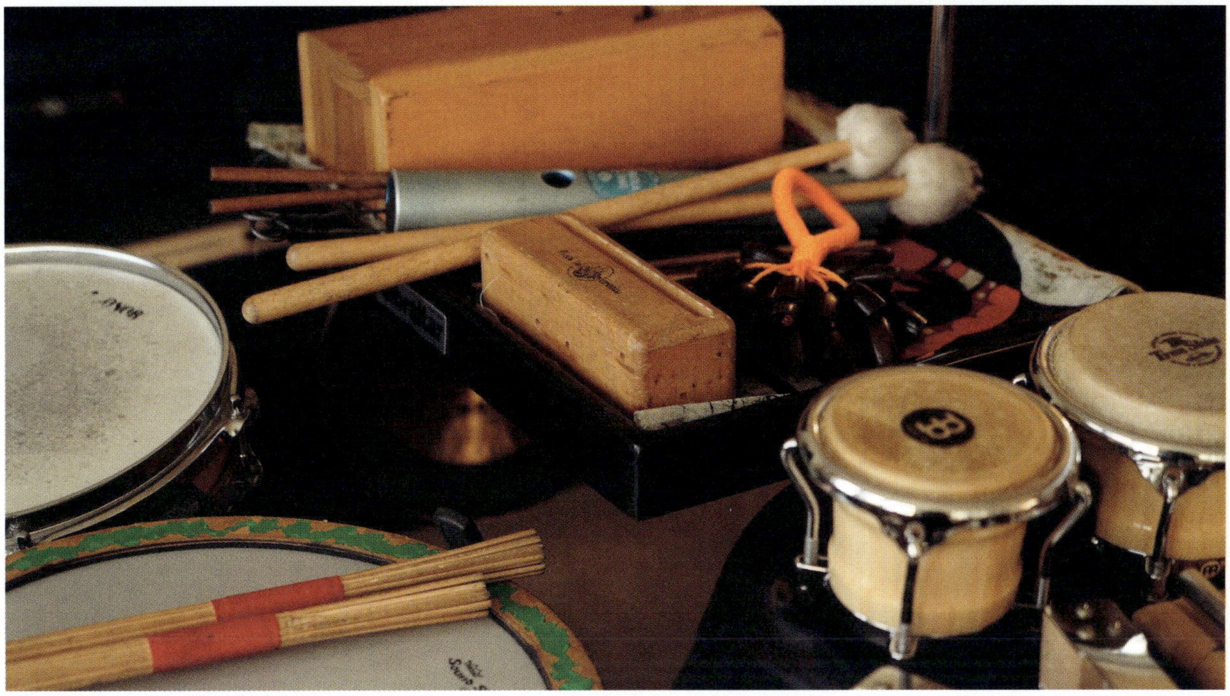

Collection of instruments in Jackie and Glen "Papa" Wright's studio
Courtesy of Steffani Jemison

virgil b/g taylor

CURATOR:
DIYA VIJ

LOCATION:
ASSEMBLED IN WORKSHOPS THROUGHOUT THE CITY

Confluence Decree is distributed primarily at the decommissioned bus stop outside of the Metropolitan St. Louis Sewer District (MSD) Headquarters and at various Counterpublic 2023 sites across the city.

virgil b/g taylor is an artist, writer, and public historian whose work explores histories of care, crisis, exclusion, and toxicity. taylor's recent exploration of public infrastructures unfolds through rigorous research, text-based graphics, and poetic encounters.

For Counterpublic 2023, *Confluence Decree* is a series of magical dispatches from and to the sewer system of St. Louis. Departing from the principle that a great deal of power and potential is tied up in a vast infrastructure shared by more than a million people in the greater St. Louis area, *Confluence Decree* aims to offer the grounds for alternative political imaginary through a reimagination of Greek and Roman *katadesmos*, ritual curse tablets made of lead. These ancient practices of language-based magic are intimately linked to the transformational language of modern contract law, an urgent question in the context of the Metropolitan St. Louis Sewer District's (MSD) current restructuring process under the auspices of the consent decree, an agreement to remedy a legal dispute signed between two or more parties without any admission of guilt. In this instance, the consent decree includes four signatories: MSD, the US federal government, the State of Missouri, and the Missouri Coalition for the Environment.

virgil b/g taylor
GIS map export using data from US government road surveys and MSD to map locations of manholes near a stretch of Jefferson Avenue

Confluence Decree is a three-issue newsprint publication that uses the legal document of MSD's consent decree as its point of intervention. In 2011, the United States Department of Justice issued a consent decree requiring MSD to spend a minimum of $4.7 billion over the next 23 years to update the combined sewer system, which is responsible for ejecting 13.4 billion gallons of untreated sewage into urban streams, lawns, the Mississippi River, Missouri River, Meramec River, River des Peres, and their associated tributaries. The 9,600-mile network of pipes, the oldest in the country, remains largely invisible until something goes wrong—a lawn floods with toxic human waste, a geyser explodes on the street. *Confluence Decree* hones in on the invisible failure of this system, connecting the toxicity of today's sewage infrastructure to regional history and colonial geographies internationally.

The consent decree is between the government of the United States, the State of Missouri, the sewer system, and a nonprofit corporation representing the interests of St. Louis residents, just as MSD represents its ratepayers, the city its residents, the state its voters, the federal government its citizens. Or at least, they are meant to. When these bodies come together in a consent decree, who is agreeing to what and with whom? Are these representative bodies mutually agreeing with each other, endlessly? What does this consent decree have to do with our agreements with each other? When we do meet each other, how can consent be found in a city built on such uneven foundations? If consent is untenable, what about confluence—flowing together through new infrastructure which "binds us to the world in movement"?[1] What forms of social control, interpersonal agreement, violence, and faith hold us to our commitments? What gives a contract power? What is the transformational power that lies within contracts?

Each issue is addressed to a mundane piece of the sewer system—a manhole, a pipe, a drain, etc.—and connects stories of lead, magic, contracts, consent, rivers, history, and presence in St. Louis. Each issue invites local actors to express their wishes for the system and their life to the mutual power, extensive potential, and collective being embodied by the sewer system itself. Throughout the publications, poetic offerings address larger questions about water, earth, and toxicity with invited contributions. The newsprint will be distributed for free from the *Confluence Decree* newsstand at a former bus stop adjacent to MSD Headquarters' green campus as well as several locations in the Counterpublic 2023 footprint. taylor addresses the sewer infrastructure as a social sculpture, a social and political site in which everyone participates. If everyone participates, then everyone should have the power to transform it.

[1] Lauren Berlant, "The Commons: Infrastructures for troubling times*," *Environment and Planning D: Society and Space* 34, no. 3 (2016): 393–419, https://doi.org/10.1177/0263775816645989.

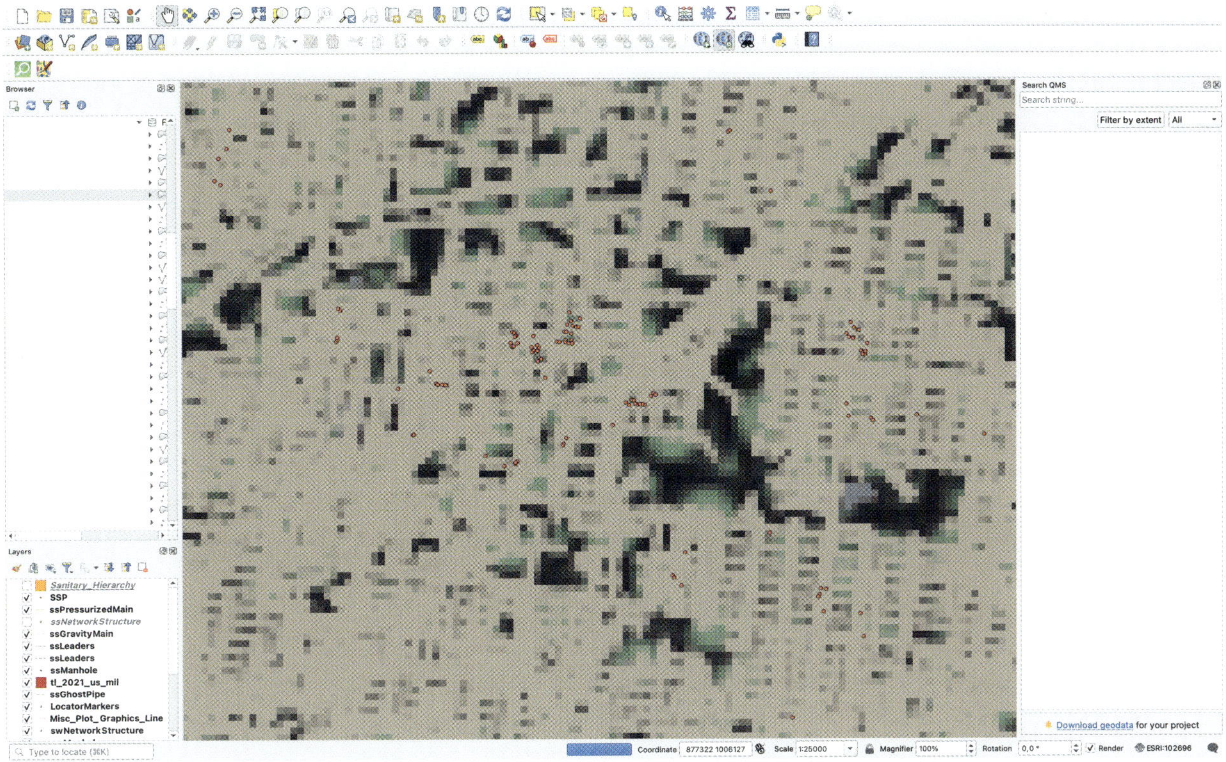

virgil b/g taylor
Screenshot of rendering GIS data from US government road surveys and MSD to map locations of manholes near a stretch of Jefferson Avenue

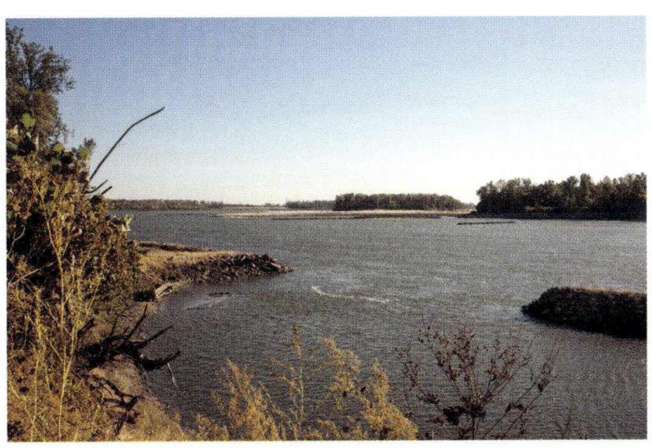

Confluence of Missouri and Mississippi Rivers

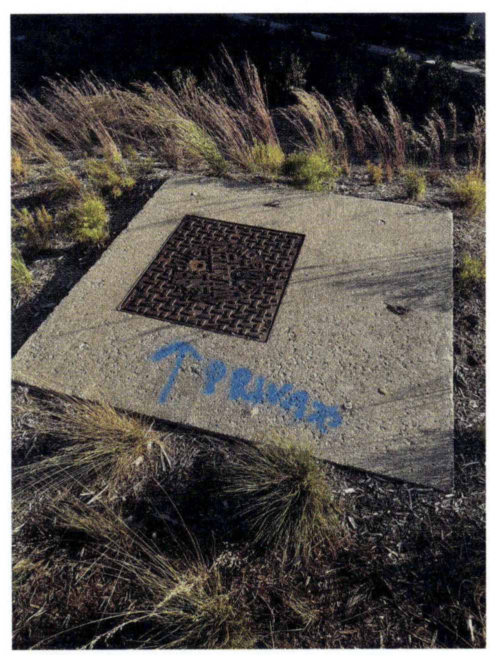

Stormwater inlet to river at MSD Headquarters, St. Louis

Jordan Weber

CURATOR:
DIYA VIJ

LOCATION:
MEMORIAL PLAZA AND PEACE PARK

Jordan Weber is a Midwest-based regenerative land sculptor and activist who works at the cross-section of social justice and environmental racism. Over the past decade, Weber has realized large-scale land works that involve extensive research in the areas of ecological remediation and environmental and racial justice. This includes carbon sequestration and hyperaccumulator plant mitigation strategies, Zazen meditation to address toxic stress in teens/adults, and the mental decompression benefits of "green space" activations in predominantly Black communities. Most recently, Weber was commissioned by the Walker Art Center to create an urban farm in North Minneapolis called *Prototype for poetry vs. rhetoric (deep roots)*, which acts as a countertactic to industrial violence upon biodiverse lands and racially diverse communities. The project was produced in collaboration with North Minneapolis community members during the height of the George Floyd protests in late May 2020.

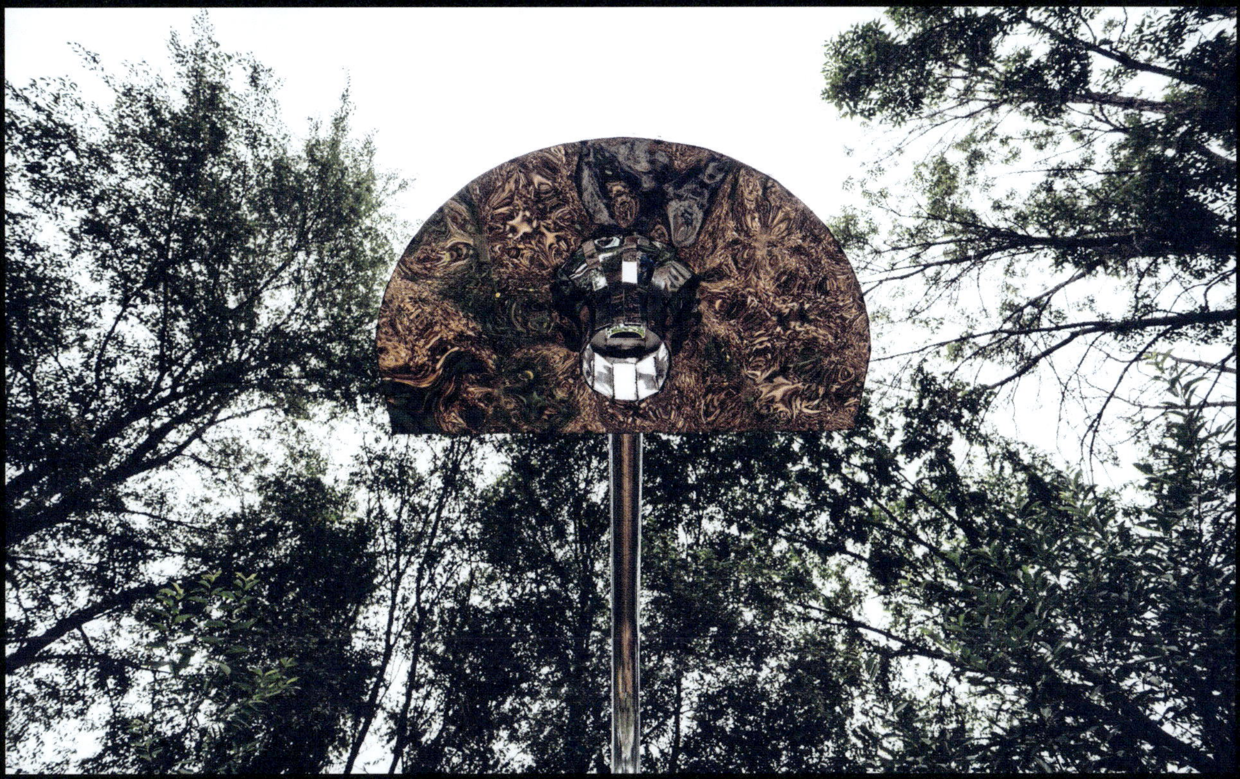

Jordan Weber
Prototype for poetry vs rhetoric (deep roots), 2021
Walker Art Center
Photograph by Aaron Graves

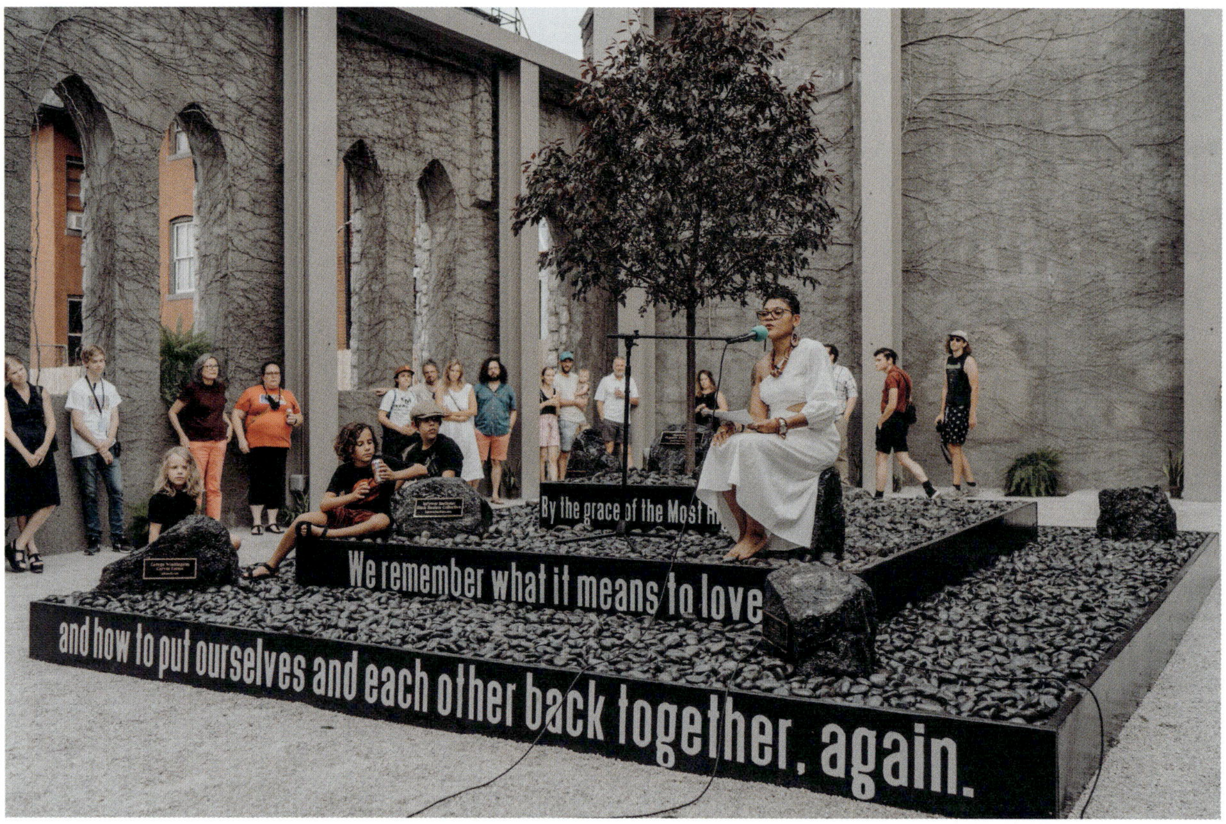

St. Louis-based poet and storyteller Cheeraz Gormon
in Jordan Weber's *All Our Liberations*, 2022
Spring Church, Pulitzer Arts Foundation
Photograph by Virginia Harold
Courtesy of Pulitzer Arts Foundation

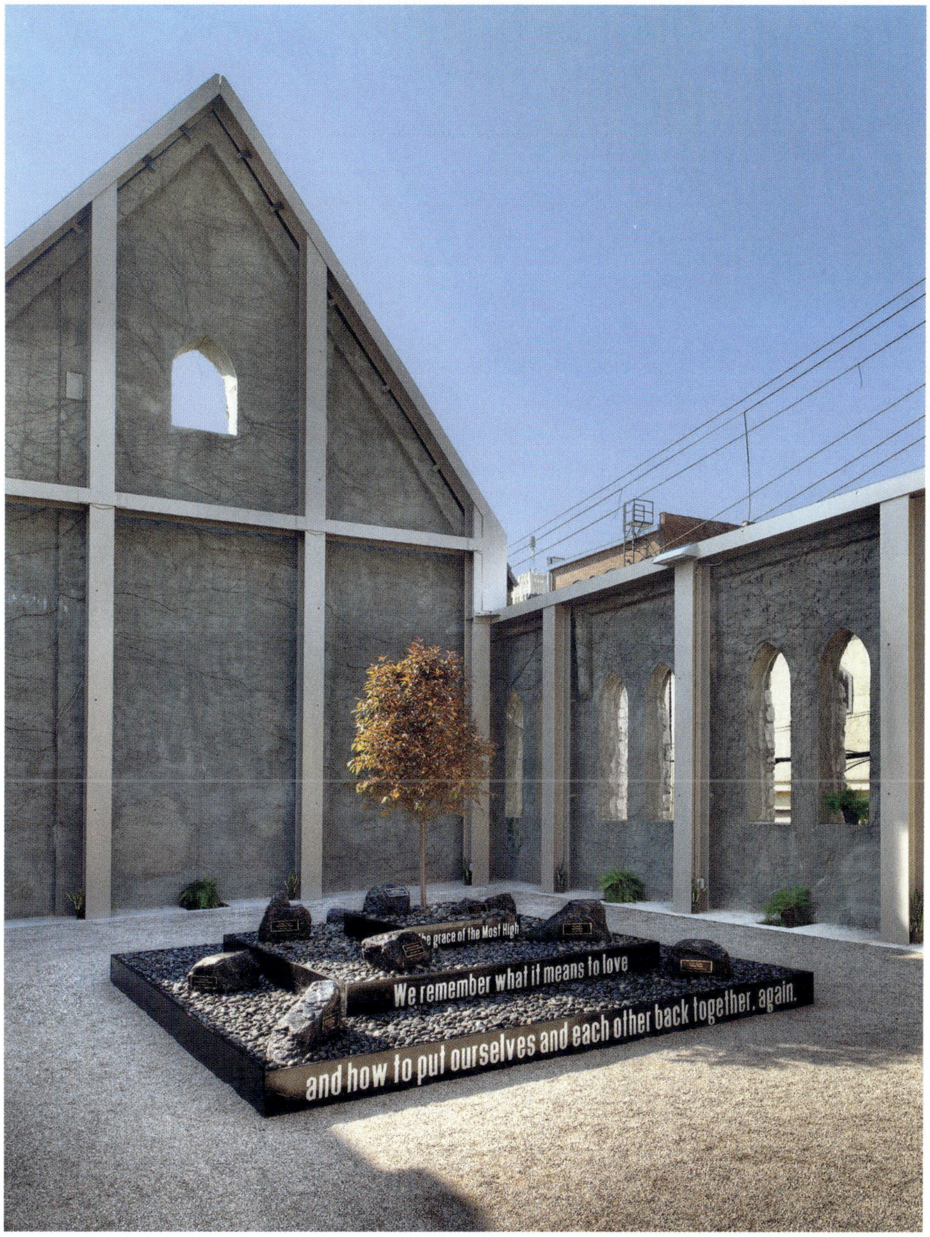

Jordan Weber
All Our Liberations, 2022
Spring Church, Pulitzer Arts Foundation
Photograph by Virginia Harold
Courtesy of Pulitzer Arts Foundation

For Counterpublic 2023, Weber has developed *Defensive Landscape*, a site-specific regenerative earthwork for St. Louis's Peace Park built in collaboration with the site's existing community and institutional partners. A community-engaged rainwater garden, gathering space, and play area responds to St. Louis's major commitment to upgrade the metropolitan wastewater management system while offering a critical intervention into the generational health implications of the intertwined crises of captivity and ecological apartheid.

Peace Park was established by civil rights activist Otis Woodard to offer his community of College Hill, St. Louis a place for sharing space and resources. Woodard's "share shed," a mutual aid site that distributed tools and food to the neighborhood, formed the cornerstone of the park. Today, the park is a community land trust, a regional model for shared ownership of land. Honoring this long history, Weber's multi-sited project features a series of obsidian stone monuments that carry updated and practical information about local abolitionist networks and community support systems available specifically to St. Louis residents of color. *Defensive Landscape* connects violence to the land and violence to the body while platforming alternative economies of care based on collective action and mutualism. The result is a significant educational, sculptural, and gathering site that repairs toxic soils, diverts sewage from the waterways, and furthers life-sustaining community infrastructures.

Defensive Landscape represents the culmination of Weber's ongoing work in St. Louis in partnership with the Pulitzer Arts Foundation, Washington University's Center for the Study of Race, Ethnicity, and Equity (CRE2) and the Sam Fox School of Design and Visual Arts, Green City Coalition, and numerous other collaborators. Jordan's two-year residency centers on social and environmental justice, incarceration, and healing, with this project offering an opportunity to create a permanent site of healing and repair within the landscape of North St. Louis.

To realize this project, Jordan Weber is working with the Metropolitan St. Louis Sewer District (MSD) and community partners to establish this large-scale rain garden in a manner that is ecologically impactful as well as to raise awareness of the crucial role of stormwater management systems to the health and futures of St. Louis residents. Throughout Counterpublic 2023, Weber's sculptures will be on view in a park near the MSD headquarters at 2350 Market Street to act as a gathering space to contemplate the complex and vital role of water in the cultural landscape of St. Louis before returning permanently to Peace Park to culminate the multiyear effort.

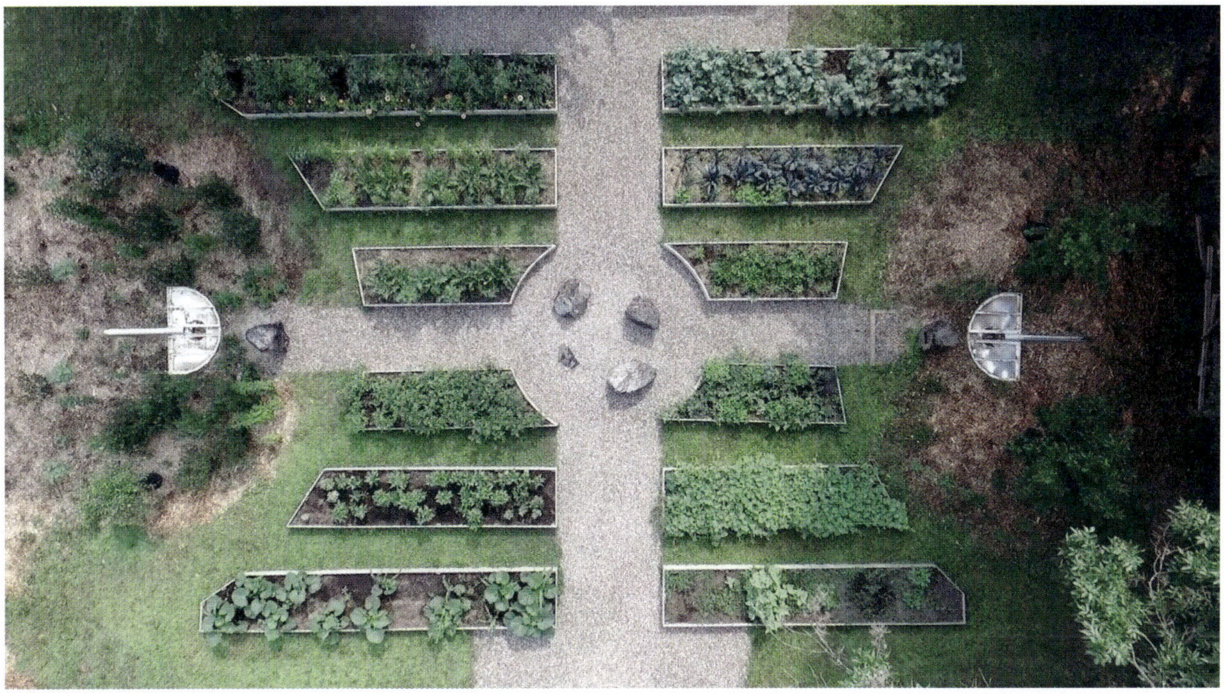

Jordan Weber
Prototype for poetry vs. rhetoric (deep roots), 2021
Commissioned by the Walker Art Center and installed in North Minneapolis in collaboration with Youth Farms
Photograph by Teddy Grimes

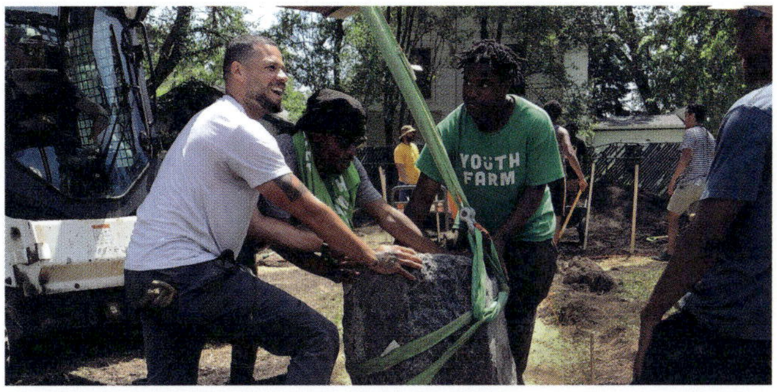

Jordan Weber installing stone sculptures at *Prototype for poetry vs. rhetoric (deep roots),* 2021
Commissioned by the Walker Art Center and installed in North Minneapolis in collaboration with Youth Farms
Photograph by Aaron Graves

Whereas, Between 1845 and 1848 and instrumentalized through the Treaty of Guadalupe Hidalgo the U.S. forcibly seized at least 658 million acres of American lands at a price of 4 cents per acre and subsequently constructed borders to remove present heirs from their lands, through acts of State Terror;

Whereas, Between 1898 and 1917 the U.S. Government invaded Puerto Rico following ten years of independence, forcibly seized 2.25 million acres of Puerto Rican lands, barred present heirs from their lands, and deemed Puerto Rico a U.S. Territory without voting representation in the U.S. federal government through acts of State Terror;

A PROPOSITION FOR ST. LOUIS PLACE

By
Allison Glenn

St. Louis Place is a small neighborhood in the northeast corner of St. Louis, within proximity to the Mississippi River. The St. Louis Place neighborhood and boulevard both derive their name from King Louis IX, the namesake of the city. Through the combination of many factors, including divestment and city planning, the St. Louis Place neighborhood has transformed from being known as "Millionaire's Row" to a neighborhood with a seriously underserved and declining population, reflective of the entropy that was inherently built into the city planning system. The history of the neighborhood, and what remains of it, is a rich place to begin.

Plotted out in the mid-nineteenth century by John O'Fallon, one of the wealthiest men and largest slave owners in St. Louis at the time, the neighborhood was "settled" by Irish and German immigrants in the late nineteenth century.[1] It began as an area for prominent businessmen to build their mansions, earning the street the title of "Millionaire's Row." From the fleur-de-lis in the city flag to the sprawling boulevards lined with magnificent homes, the imprint of colonial influence on the development of St. Louis—and the larger influence that French colonial history had on the region—remains legible to this day.

Shifts in industry in the region, postindustrial decline, the fear and racism that the Great Migration ensued, city planning, and mid-twentieth-century suburban desire were some of the many catalysts that started the neighborhood on its steady decline. Central to my curatorial contribution to Counterpublic 2023 (and this essay) is an interest in the history of this site, place, and landscape, and how the work of David Adjaye, Matthew Angelo Harrison, Maya Stovall, and Mendi + Keith Obadike dynamically intersects, highlights, and expands upon it.

Situated on the southeast corner of St. Louis Avenue and North 25th Street sits The Griot Museum of Black History. Founded in 1997 by Lois Conley as a wax museum, The Griot is dedicated to sharing the impact of Black St. Louisans through narrative and storytelling. In West African traditions, a griot is a storyteller. Griot is also the national dish of Haiti, a country that, under French occupation and colonization, made it possible for the European nation to "develop" and "acquire" the Louisiana Territory, which includes present-day Missouri.[2] The confluence of West African and Caribbean traditions is also symbolized in The Griot's logo, the Adinkra symbol of the Twi word *Sankofa*, which is an image of a bird looking backward that symbolizes the Asante ideology that one must know the past to overcome the future, to retrieve or "go back and get it"—a perfect sentiment by which to reconsider space, site, and the environment.

Looking to the past as a framework to understand the present and the potentiality of a more equitable future, Maya Stovall's *Theorem, no. 3* presents a series of actions in the form of a performance and a text gathered here in the catalog. Each action is a form of reparations, offering a set amount of money to St. Louisans who identify as African American, Black, Indigenous, Chicana/o/x, Latina/o/x, or of mixed ancestry.

[1] Kelly Schmidt and Jeff Ward, "Remembering John O'Fallon," The WashU & Slavery Project, August 11, 2021, https://slavery.wustl.edu/news/remembering-john-ofallon.

[2] The success of the Haitian Independence Movement had an impact on France's financial stability, and Napoleon eventually sold this territory to the United States. The "founding" of St. Louis and the larger Louisiana Purchase are intrinsically connected to real and problematic ideologies of westward expansion that our nation is slowly confronting.

Stovall's work as a conceptual artist and anthropologist engages with power structures and the politics of racial capital. Through a rigorous study of reparations theory and the implementation of reparations within municipal and civic infrastructures, Stovall's project highlights and removes the heavily bureaucratic structures that can impede direct action toward measurable outcomes. Her careful approach considers how to gain the trust of participants while maintaining their anonymity. The performance includes *Resolutions on State Terror*, a series of text-based statements created by Stovall (included in this catalog), where the artist has identified crimes that have been committed against Black, Brown, Indigenous, Chicana/o/x, and Latina/o/x people in the United States by the United States. Included in the performance is a Letter of Apology, where Stovall assumes the position of President of the United States of America and writes an "unauthorized" public apology for the crimes that have been committed. With *Theorem, no. 3* Stovall responds to inequitable histories, proposing alternative methodologies for the ensuing process of reparations unfolding across the United States while responding to histories of inequity in St. Louis.

The building that houses The Griot was constructed in 1916 as a Catholic school as part of the St. Louis Archdiocese. Later, it was converted to the Montgomery Hyde Park Community Health Center as a part of the Model Cities initiative, where it was also the site of dances and a community radio station that operated out of the third-floor ballroom.[3] As a nod to the history of music and rhythm of The Griot and the city, Mendi + Keith Obadike's *SlowDrag* is a sound installation consisting of cars moving through the St. Louis Place neighborhood, simultaneously playing remixed sound. This aural composition takes influence from Scott Joplin's ragtime piano works, referred to as "rags" or ragtime because of their reliance on a syncopated beat. The title *SlowDrag* is a reference to the slow drag dance form, a "slow intimate dance associated with the blues that has continued through R&B."[4] The sonic procession relies on the shape and form of the neighborhood to determine the route. Collaborations with local car clubs and musicians based in St. Louis and New York create a work that engages with the moment, while this temporal activation of the neighborhood evokes the sonic memory of place through the production of Mvstermind—a St. Louis-based performing and recording artist—and local car clubs that speak to sound system culture.

The Griot's position in the neighborhood is a precarious one, due largely to the relocation of the National Geospatial-Intelligence Agency's (NGA) main campus to the area located across the street from the museum, on land acquired by eminent domain.[5] Renewed interest in the neighborhood has caused developers to purchase many of the empty lots in preparation for the changing landscape that the relocation of the NGA's main campus will surely bring. A mere mile away, in an adjacent neighborhood, sits the former site of the Minoru Yamasaki-designed Pruitt-Igoe urban housing project—a public housing project notorious for how quickly promises of progress led to decline due largely to decisions city planners and legislators made to not provide adequate support for the communities that lived there. When developing plans for this triennial, feedback from the community listening sessions included how coded language used by developers and city planners had historically indicated for whom progress was afforded and at what cost.

[3] As told to Counterpublic by Lois Conley in conversation in May 2021.

[4] Email exchange between Keith Obadike and the author, December 7, 2022.

[5] The National Geospatial-Intelligence Agency is a combat support agency within the United States Department of Defense whose primary mission is collecting, analyzing, and distributing geospatial intelligence in support of national security. "National Geospatial-Intelligence Agency," *Wikipedia*, last modified January 12, 2023, https://en.wikipedia.org/wiki/National_Geospatial-Intelligence_Agency.

There is a strong connection between home, storytelling, and architectural history in the recent sculptural work of David Adjaye. The conical forms Adjaye has been investigating were developed during the pandemic, when he returned to his ancestral home in Akwapim, Ghana to build a country home for his family.[6] Inspired by historic African architecture like the Tiébélé Royal Complex in Burkina Faso and the walled city of Agadez in Niger, Adjaye's *Asaase I* (2021) engages with "the temporal specificity of place," simultaneously moving forward and backward along a linear idea of time—or perhaps, thinking cyclically about history—as it relates to Black social spaces for community and family gathering.[7]

After purchasing the building that houses The Griot, Conley also acquired the adjacent lots with the vision to develop a sculpture garden and outdoor event space. To the visionary thinker, the vast, open urban prairies that emerged from the divestment and subsequent architectural decline of the neighborhood become sites of possibility. With *Asaase III* (2023), Adjaye has uniquely disassembled the kaleidoscopic, maze-like shape seen in previous Asaase sculptures, its curving fragments positioned across the outdoor lots adjacent to The Griot. Shifting the form to respond to the site, Adjaye considers the history and potential future usage as an event space. The permanent placement of Adjaye's sculpture on the lot adjacent to The Griot is an intentional response to this reemergent land grab. Although the sculptural form will permanently occupy the land, the materiality of the form has a subtler footprint. *Asaase III* is comprised of stabilized rammed earth, a sustainable and economic alternative to concrete, with roots in Indigenous civilizations around the world.

Farther down the block, between The Griot and St. Louis Place Park, sits the George B. Vashon Museum of African American History, a house museum dedicated to Black material culture that tells the history of prominent St. Louisans and Black experience through the lens of a collection of objects acquired by Executive Director Calvin Riley. Located at 223 St. Louis Avenue, the building that houses the Vashon Museum was originally constructed to be the home of prominent businessman James Meagher and his family, who lived there until his death in 1899. It was converted to a funeral home in 1910 and small additions to the property came about a decade later.[8] Calvin Riley acquired the property and opened the George B. Vashon Museum of African American History in 2015.

[6] David Adjaye, "Social Works: Sir David Adjaye OBE," interview by Antwaun Sargent, *Gagosian Quarterly*, Summer 2021, https://gagosian.com/quarterly/2021/06/16/interview-social-works-sir-david-adjaye-obe/.

[7] "Asaase," Adjaye Associates, accessed January 18, 2023, https://www.adjaye.com/work/asaase/.

[8] Nathan Jackson, "James Meagher Mansion," St. Louis History and Architecture, July 19, 2019, https://www.stlhistoryandarchitecture.com/st-louis-place/epyjh1t5egoy4sdrehscot3wmdzvzm.

Riley named the organization after George Boyer Vashon, New York State's first Black attorney,[9] whose son was a teacher and principal in St. Louis public schools for over thirty years.[10] The museum galleries are a veritable *Wunderkabinett* where Riley has amassed a collection of over 10,000 artifacts of material culture related to Black experience—from patented hair products to family photographs, mammy dolls, clothing, records, books, and more. The present-day vitrines that house Riley's archival collection subtly nod to the practice of preservation that the site was known for in its funerary days. Some areas of the collection contain a deeper dive into the archives and work of prominent St. Louisans, such as Dr. Eugene Mitchell, the first Black student accepted into the medical program at Missouri University, and the *St. Louis Argus* newspaper,[11] a weekly periodical founded in 1912 by brothers Joseph Everett Mitchell and William Mitchell.[12]

Formal and conceptual affinities abound between the work of Matthew Angelo Harrison and Riley's approaches to the exhibition of archival objects. Employing analog and digital technologies, Harrison investigates the relationships between African and African American culture through found objects including African sculptures from the Bambara, Dogon, Makonde, and Senufo tribes, United Auto Workers (UAW) memorabilia, and fossils.[13] Harrison, who was born and currently resides in Detroit, Michigan, traces the relationships between the histories of enslavement and labor unions, automation, and Ford's five-dollar workday, which drove the waves of Black migration from the South to Detroit for work in the factories. To achieve this, he combines material references, imbuing the surfaces of his resin-encapsulated objects with the remnants of material culture. The trace of a Dogon sculpture is cut into the surface of a resin-encapsulated UAW strike poster. Similarly, a sculpture from the Makonde tribe is embedded into resin that bears the imprint of machination. The combination of UAW strike posters, gloves, hard hats, and other personal protective equipment with imprints of 3D-scanned African sculptures makes visual and conceptual connections to Black labor histories in the United States, speaking also to the artist's previous employment at Ford Motor Company.[14] Harrison's vitrine-like sculptures are created from a CNC machine the artist built himself. The objects Harrison chooses to encase come from a variety of sources, intentionally questioning ideas of authenticity, authorship, and translation. The resultant forms are situated within a historical framework designed by Riley, making meaningful connections to history through material culture.

Tuning into the historical threads that bridge this contemporary moment with those that came before, this proposition for Counterpublic 2023 fuses together a set of practices that delicately and intentionally interweave influences, making meaning of history through the development of new works that simultaneously speak to the past and present. The opportunity, and proposition, here is to consider a future that reimagines, recapitulates, and dismantles commonly held narratives and registers upon which this country is built. The dedicated individuals and organizations in St. Louis Place are similarly committed to speaking to, of, and from this unique place in the city and this moment in time; engaging with some of the complex and nuanced narratives that comprise this area of the city to truly understand a way forward.

[9] "George Boyer Vashon: New York's First African American Attorney," Historical Society of the New York Courts, November 20, 2021, https://history.nycourts.gov/george-boyer-vashon/.

[10] "About Us," George B. Vashon Museum of African American History, accessed June 15, 2022, https://georgevashonmuseum.org/about-us.

[11] "Exhibits," George B. Vashon Museum of African American History, accessed June 15, 2022, https://georgevashonmuseum.org/exhibits.

[12] "A Brief History of the St. Louis ARGUS," *St. Louis Argus*, accessed November 16, 2022, https://stlargusnews.com/about/.

[13] MIT List Visual Art Center, "Matthew Angelo Harrison: Robota," YouTube video, 4:31, April 29, 2022, https://youtu.be/ixkFnMPo8Nc.

[14] MIT List Visual Art Center, "Matthew Angelo Harrison: Robota."

Whereas, The U.S.'s moral, ethical, scientific, practical, financial, capital crimes of land seizure; land annexation; human trafficking and genocide; and acts of State Terror result in the U.S. owing direct payments of $744,352 to each present heir;

Resolved *a fortiori*:

1. The U.S. Government has committed and continues to commit massively criminal acts against American humanity at scale and the forms of U.S. State Terror and accumulation by dispossession articulated herein were subsequently applied to subjugate Americans further with increasingly convoluted devices;

2. White supremacy, advanced by the U.S. 1526-present, is an existential threat to humanity at scale;

3. The U.S. Government owes direct compensation payments to persons whose predecessors were harmed by State Terror;

4. That the U.S. Government owes a formal presidential letter of apology with each direct compensation payment;

5. The U.S. Government owes a formal public presidential apology;

6. Given the U.S. Government's ongoing failure to remit the above, the "exclusive representative" will perform the above actions at Counterpublic in the action entitled, *Theorem, no. 3,* to the extent possible with project resources and delivered personally by the "exclusive representative"/artist Maya Stovall and the curator Allison Glenn.

7. A copy of this resolution and the letter of apology be distributed by Counterpublic public relations/communications representatives on behalf of the "exclusive representative" to the Office of the President of the United States; the Office of the Vice President of the United States; U.S. Senators; U.S. Congresspersons; State Senators, State Legislators; The Governor of Missouri; Governors of the United States; The Mayor of St. Louis; Mayors of Cities in the United States; The St. Louis City Council; City Councilpersons of Cities in the United States; Artforum; ARTnews; Artsy; Culture Type; New York Times; Wall Street Journal; CNN; MSNBC; Fox News; St. Louis Post; and Counterpublic attendees, participants, passersby, artists, curators, administrators, representatives, organizers, and staff persons.

SEAL OF THE PRESIDENT OF THE UNITED STATES

EXECUTIVE OFFICE OF THE PRESIDENT OF THE UNITED STATES

This is an original work of art which includes an unauthorized public apology with an unauthorized seal and an unauthorized signature applied by Maya Stovall, the "exclusive representative"/"the artist;" these unauthorized symbols have been combined by the artist to produce a work of art.

David Adjaye

CURATOR:
ALLISON GLENN

LOCATION:
THE GRIOT MUSEUM OF BLACK HISTORY

David Adjaye is an award-winning Ghanaian-British architect known to infuse his artistic sensibilities and ethos into community-driven projects. His largest architectural project to date, the Smithsonian National Museum of African American History and Culture, opened on the National Mall in Washington, DC in 2016. The third translation of an ongoing series of earthen sculptures, and Adjaye's first permanent public sculpture, *Asaase III* is conceived as a contribution to the cultural infrastructure of the city of St. Louis.

With the ambition to encourage social engagement and interaction, *Asaase III* reimagines a world where individuals from disparate walks of life harmonize in shared experiences. Sited outside of The Griot Museum of Black History, the sculpture acts as an invitation, dissolving the perceived social barriers of many museums, to instead embolden individuals and passersby—who may normally shy away from cultural institutions—to engage, explore, and convene with a material that deeply resonates with their collective memory.

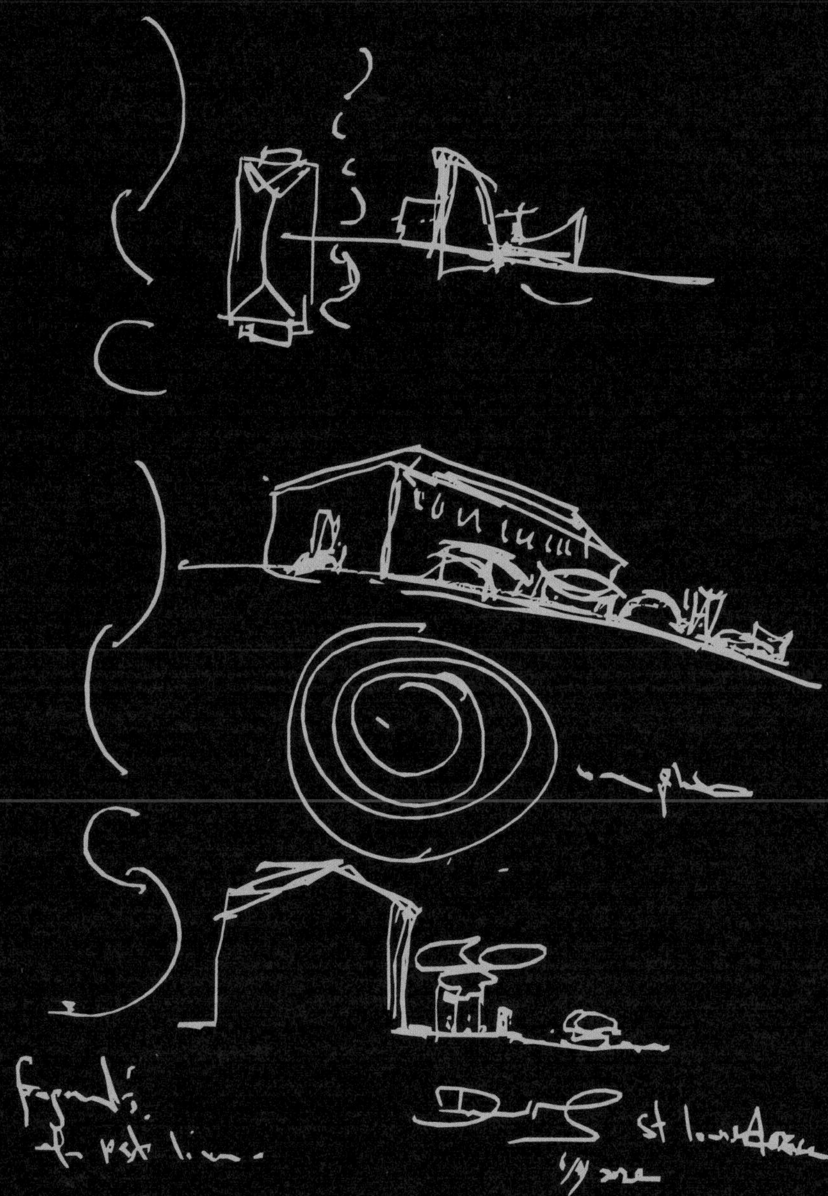

David Adjaye
Asaase III sketch

In this iteration of *Asaase*, Adjaye builds upon the vision of The Griot's founder, Lois Conley, to create and sustain narratives and stories of African Americans. The introduction of *Asaase III* to the landscape of St. Louis Place concretizes and expands the long trajectory of archiving and storytelling that already exists within The Griot, but also adds to this archive by creating direct linkages back to African architectural histories that inform Adjaye's work. *Asaase III* is rooted in deep memory of what a place or a sense of home can mean through fragments of architecture and its geometry. Comprised of rammed earth sourced locally from across Missouri, the structural form and materiality is a nod to the earth-based architecture of West Africa such as the Tiébélé Royal Complex in Burkina Faso and the walled city of Agadez in Niger. Rammed earth creates layers of materials that echo the geological strata of the Earth's crust. In Adjaye's words, "It's a piece of compressed earth with records of climate and geology—our habitation of the world. I wanted to create a different kind of reading of [the] language that one can see—a geological language." Aligned with cosmic notions of renewal and rebirth, earthen walls are both an indicator of the structure's location and an anchor to its surroundings. In symbiosis with its environment, the texture creates a visual backdrop that emphasizes the richness of the landscape beyond and the temporality of the sun—changing color from dusk to dawn—making it a favorable material for secular gathering spaces.

Both a social and terrestrial sculpture, *Asaase III* aims to weave people, place, and time together. Spatially, the elemental curving forms orchestrate a series of outdoor rooms for engagement. With the goal of creating a new site for both informal and formal programming, *Asaase III* allows for a broad spectrum of activities such as daytime workshops for children, evening speakeasies, and musical performances.

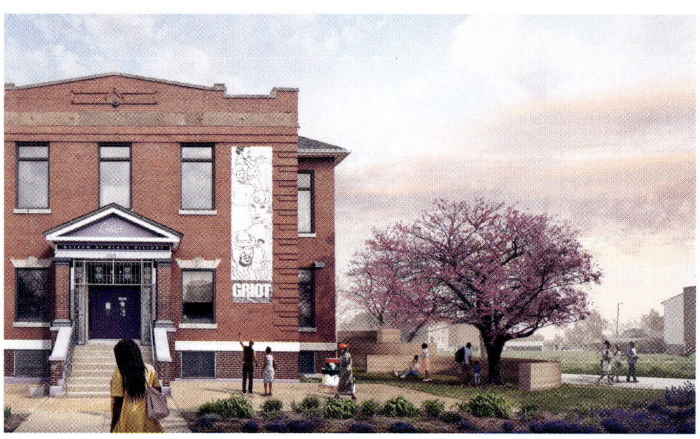

David Adjaye
Asaase III rendering

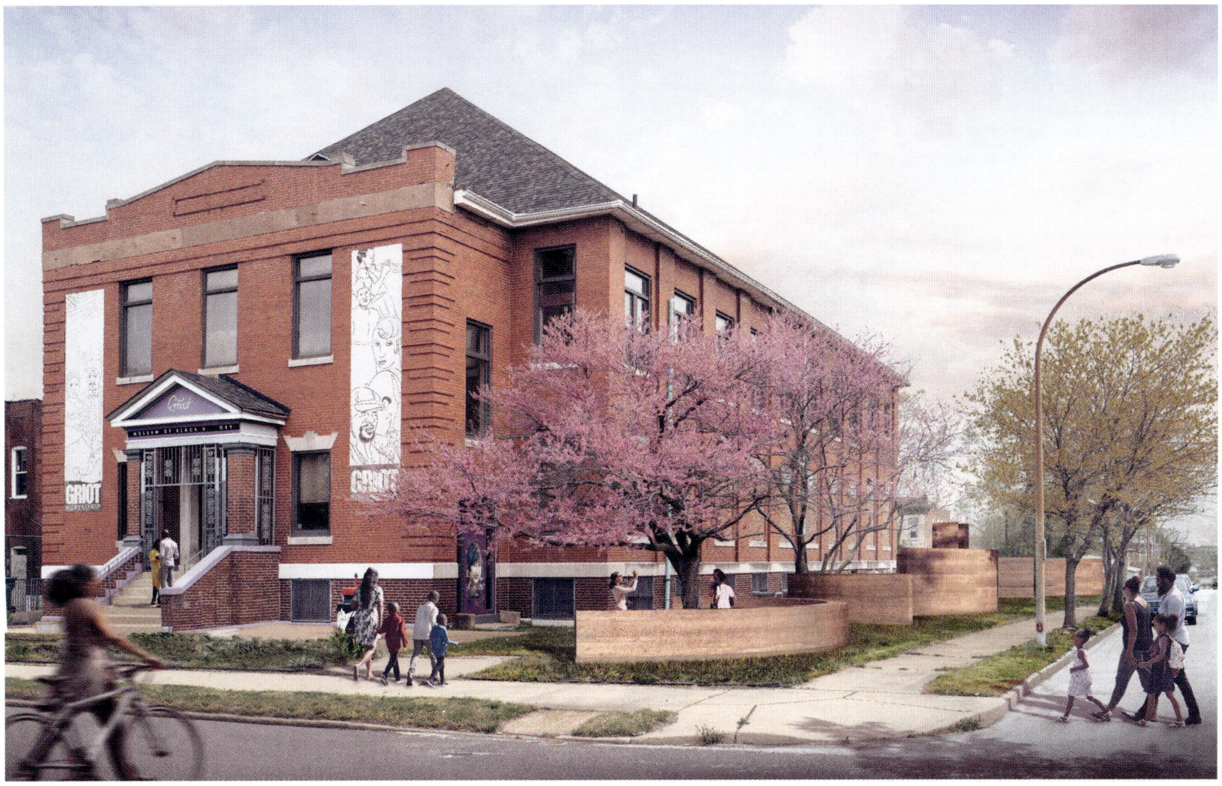

David Adjaye
Asaase III rendering

Matthew Angelo Harrison

CURATOR:
ALLISON GLENN

LOCATION:
GEORGE B. VASHON MUSEUM OF AFRICAN AMERICAN HISTORY

In his sculptures and installations, Matthew Angelo Harrison engages with legacies of racism and colonialism, parsing their contemporary connections to labor in the United States through an evolving visual language. With works that merge manufacturing technologies with the formal concerns of modernism and minimalism, the artist questions ideas of authorship and reproduction. Harrison's sculptures often include found objects—for example, traditional African figurines and auto industry ephemera—encased in resin blocks. Frozen and entombed, these sculptures appear as strangely haunted minimalist objects, both ancient and futuristic.

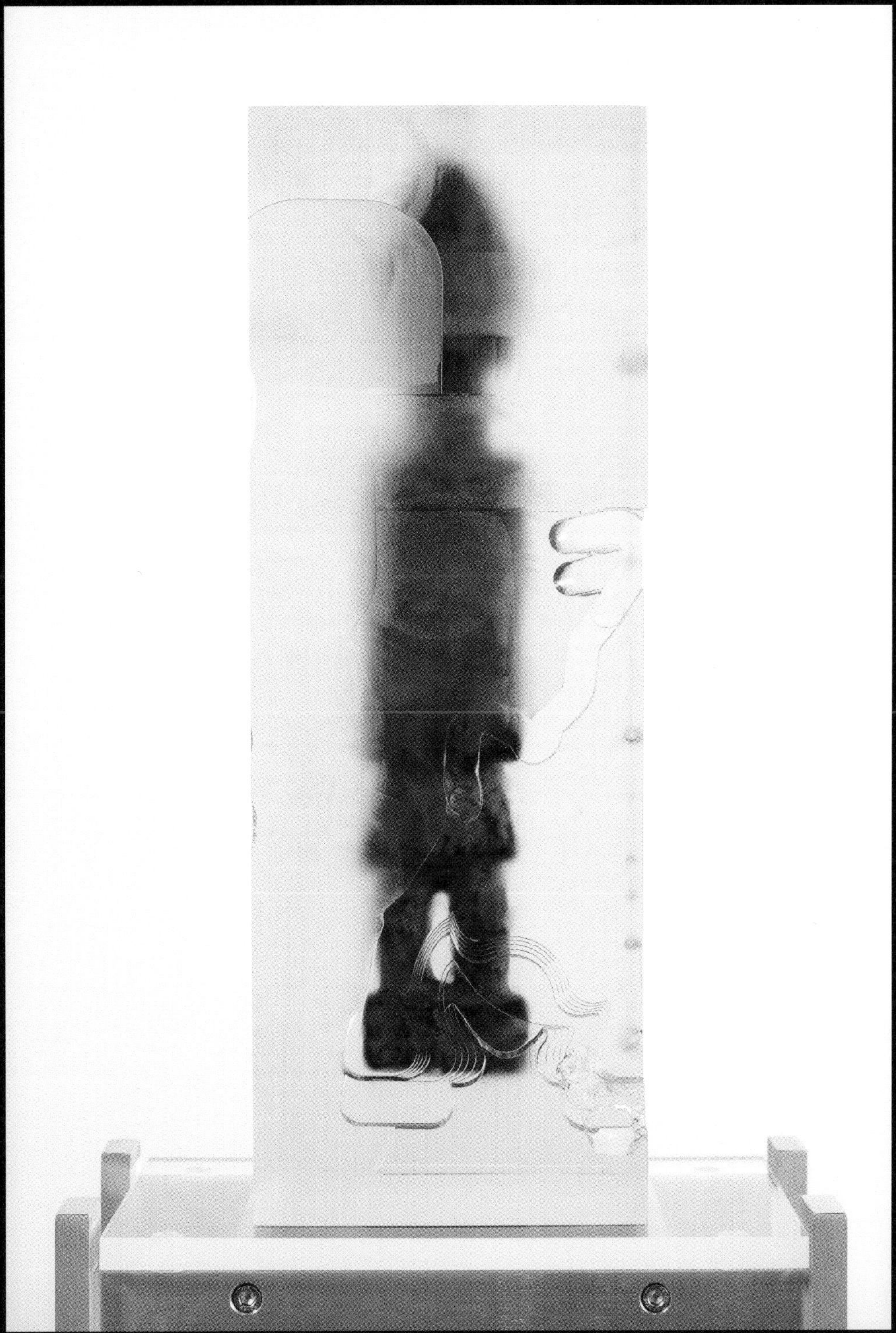

Matthew Angelo Harrison
Lanced Below, 2022
Dogon wood sculpture, polyurethane resin, and aluminum stand
Sculpture: 16″ × 5.625″ × 5″ / 40.6 × 14.3 × 12.7 cm

"I have a strong affinity for sculptures from Ghana and Mali. In the 80s, my uncle always collected wooden figures from these places. He may have not known the specifics of each object he collected, but through them, he curated his own idea of a homeland. When I choose historic African objects from private or museum collections, these intuitive affinities float through my mind."

—Matthew Angelo Harrison

For Counterpublic 2023, Harrison's sculptures nest alongside the dense historic collection of the George B. Vashon Museum of African American History, a house museum founded by Executive Director Calvin Riley that is dedicated to Black material culture and tells the history of prominent St. Louisans and Black experience. The objects Harrison chooses to encase come from a variety of sources—from traditional African figures and objects from the "queen mother of black dance"[1] Katherine Dunham's personal collection to the yearbooks of Black high schools throughout North St. Louis. Situated within a historical framework designed by Riley, the Vashon's collection annotates Harrison's inquiries into authorship, ownership, and presentation while making meaningful connections with Black history through material culture.

[1] Joyce Aschenbenner, *Katherine Dunham: Dancing a Life* (Urbana: University of Illinois Press, 2002).

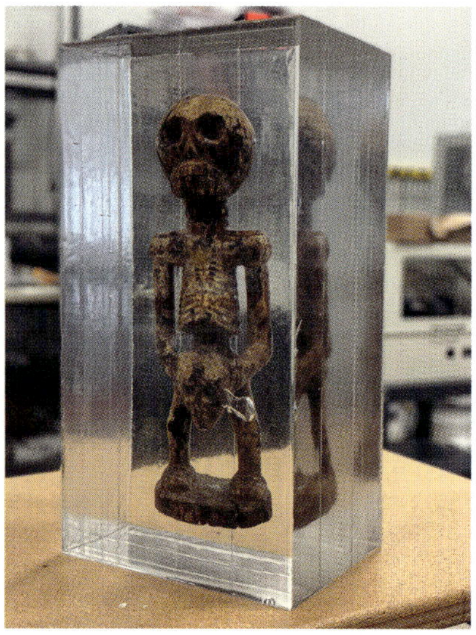

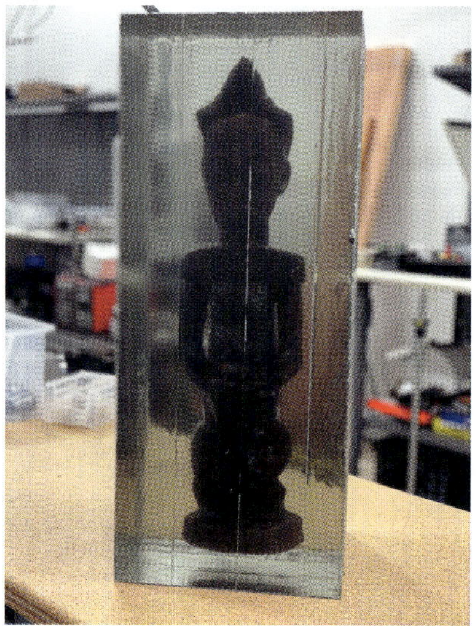

Matthew Angelo Harrison
Work in progress for Counterpublic 2023

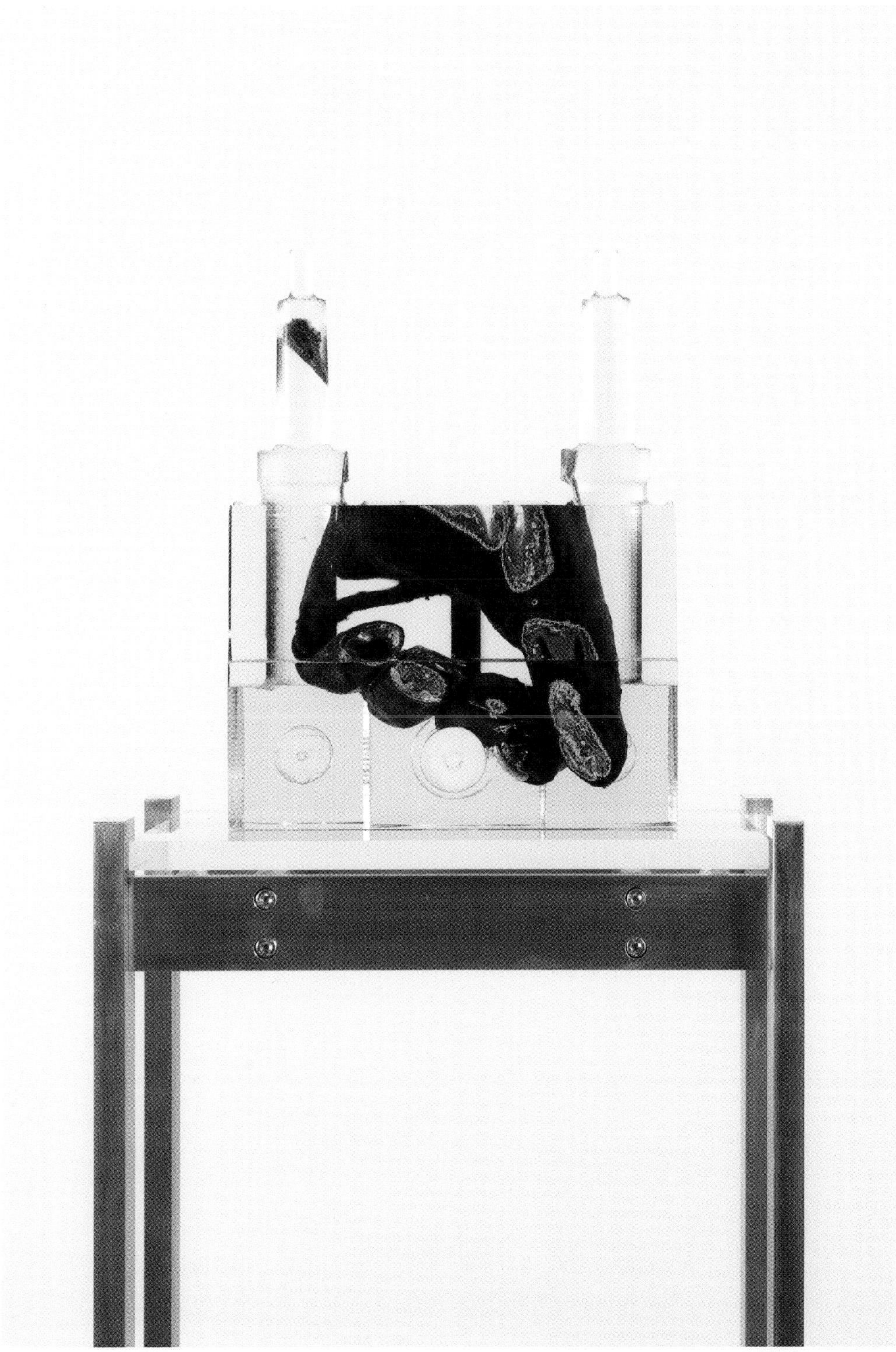

Matthew Angelo Harrison
Bodily Study: Inverted Labor, 2021
Leather glove, polyurethane resin, and stainless steel
Sculpture: 9.875" × 7.5" × 3.375" (25.1 × 19.1 × 8.6 cm)

Mendi + Keith Obadike

CURATOR:
ALLISON GLENN

LOCATION:
ST. LOUIS PLACE

Mendi + Keith Obadike's collaborative practice exists at the intersection of sonic, visual, and literary traditions, often highlighting the resonant histories embedded within the three forms. Through the creation of site-responsive works such as immersive installations and sonic sculptures, the duo considers the effect of time and environment on the body.

Mendi + Keith Obadike's *SlowDrag* is a sound installation consisting of cars moving through the St. Louis Place neighborhood playing numerous simultaneous remixes of a song (an interpolation of "Black Angel Blues") created by the artists. Their sonic procession relies on the shape and form of the neighborhood to determine the route, as evidenced in the adjacent "lyrograph" inscribing the lyrics of "Black Angel Blues" (first recorded in 1930 by Lucille Bogan and later by many other artists including Robert Nighthawk, who lived in St. Louis in the mid-1930s) into the streets of St. Louis Place.

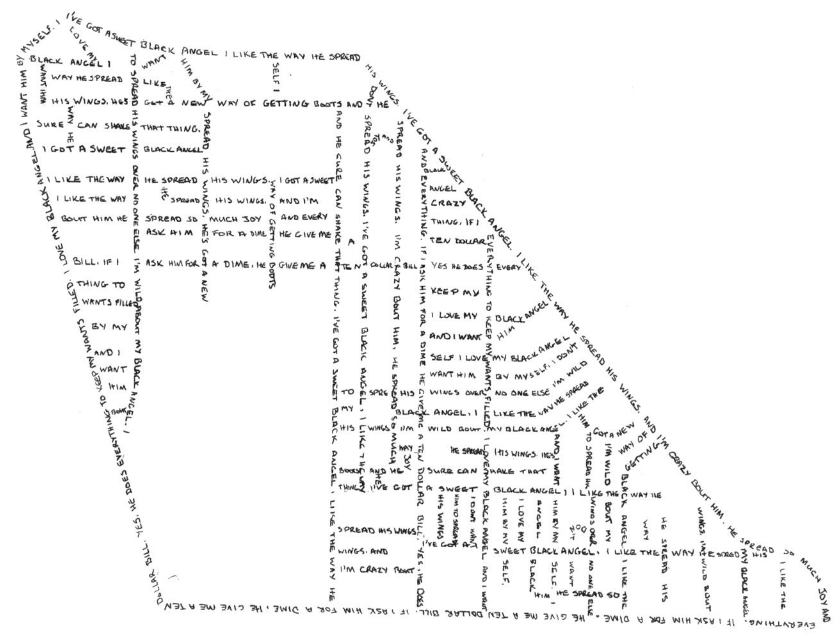

Mendi + Keith Obadike
"Lyrograph" inscribing lyrics of the song "Black Angel Blues" onto the streets of St. Louis Place

Rooted in associations of the intimate slow-drag dance form that has persisted from the early blues through to contemporary hip-hop and R&B, *SlowDrag* starts with a song by the artists that is then reinterpreted and remixed. Contained within the work is a condensed musical history that speaks to its place of performance. Slow drags carry resonance in St. Louis through their popularization by Scott Joplin in his early "rags," or piano pieces, carrying the name and onward into one of the few filmed portrayals of the dance by Bessie Smith and her partner toward the end of the short film *St. Louis Blues* (1929). Through a collaboration with music contractor and event producer Mvstermind, this history is carried forward by St. Louis hip-hop producers and brought from its space of intimacy into new relations with public space.

To open Counterpublic 2023, the work is "performed" by dozens of cars with custom speakers rooted in sound system culture. Drawing participants from local car clubs, the sound installation places a cacophony of sound prominently in public, resisting the silencing and policing of public space. As Xochitl Gonzalez states in *The Atlantic*, "The sound of gentrification is silence."[1] Within a St. Louis Place neighborhood that is actively undergoing the stresses of displacement and vacancy, *SlowDrag* announces itself as a sonic intervention—and celebration—meant to enter into a heightened intimacy and creation of new relations in the public spaces of St. Louis.

[1] Xochitl Gonzalez, "Why Do Rich People Love Quiet?," *The Atlantic*, August 1, 2022, https://www.theatlantic.com/magazine/archive/2022/09/let-brooklyn-be-loud/670600/.

UNIMAGINING AN EXHIBITION:

A Roundtable Discussion with the Counterpublic 2023 Curatorial Ensemble

with Allison Glenn
Zack Khalil and Jackson Polys (New Red Order)
James McAnally
Risa Puleo
and Diya Vij

JAMES MCANALLY:
Wrapping up this publication, it felt like a roundtable reflecting on our process was appropriate since so much of our time together over the last two years has been rooted in conversation. The monthly curatorial ensemble meetings focused our efforts, in which so much of the ideas occurred in discussion—to give the exhibition a title, or not, the meaning of permanence in relation to our commissions, the relation to history and futurity and attention to the land in longer durations. These conversations attuned us to the ways in which we were a group, but not in direct collaboration. The word "ensemble" itself points to the idea that we are parts of a whole, taken together.

The first thing I wanted to call attention to is that the idea of working as a curatorial ensemble is itself distinct. This is not necessarily how our field works, in museums or biennials alike, in which individual authorship is so paramount, but this approach to multiple curatorial voices from disparate fields and carrying distinct expertise is something we embedded in the model for Counterpublic from the outset. The ensemble responds directly to the meaning of a "counterpublic" itself—that both our internal working processes and the publics we engage are not always confluent. Counterpublics are at times overlapping, at times conflicting, at times complimentary publics and opinions. I think this curatorial ensemble really reflects that as well. As a group, I'm curious how this ensemble approach has affected your process and your thinking about exhibition-making, particularly in this kind of forum.

ALLISON GLENN:
What was interesting about this proposition when you [James] first suggested it, was that it moves against the idea of singular authorship and into a third space where there isn't one central voice, but a constellation of voices or a cacophony of voices, which is really appealing in practice and in theory. I have to admit, at first, I happily struggled with the idea of an ensemble—namely, because I really am inspired by and curious about the co-curators and their processes. Your proposition for an ensemble shifted a lot of the registers of understanding that I have around this kind of work, and ultimately I think it was very productive.

DIYA VIJ:
I agree. It's a really interesting model counter to a traditional biennial, which is often focused on that singular, authoritative voice. I think, in practice, I'm used to working around the idea of collaboration, working with artists who use collaboration as their means of practice, and it was definitely challenging for me to be working alongside but not necessarily with or in collaboration with my co-curators. It was a process that actually I've come to really respect. In Counterpublic 2023's formation of this group there are naturally a lot of places where our work overlaps while also showing our own individual approaches to place, people, and this particular kind of institution.

Now that we're coming toward the triennial being realized, it's making so much sense to me in a way that I was still navigating earlier. It still has, at times, felt kind of singular, like, this is my geographic zone and these are my sites and these are my artists—and it's been really cool to talk through that with everyone and learn everyone's experiences—but on that personal level, it could still kind of feel like one author. But now, when I see it coming together, I realize that this ensemble formation allows us to tackle this wide geographic scale with depth and intention. I get how you experience the city differently in this way through these multiple voices, enhanced by the deep local knowledge that the Counterpublic team brings to the table.

JAMES:
Building off that, it has been interesting to see these ideas of collaboration or complimentary practices evolve. This has been an experiment in how to approach a layered, complex context with multiple needs and desires at play without trying to distill it into a single thesis. The city is multiple, a neighborhood is always multiple, at all scales. Why would we try to insist on one way of approaching a place that needs different things? That said, there wasn't an explicit model for us to follow, so we have truly been testing a new way of working.

With this invitation into St. Louis, we didn't come in with a concept but rather a geography and specific historic references— the concepts themselves manifested through the community-engagement process and subsequent report (included in this catalog).

JAMES (cont.):
The thing that remained throughout was an invitation to build something that reached both backward and forward, that encouraged thinking ancestrally and infrastructurally, along much longer timelines than a typical exhibition. I'm curious what that opened up for you, from where the invitation to participate as a curator started to where it ended up.

JACKSON POLYS:
It has been interesting for us to come into this project as those who do not necessarily identify ourselves as curators, and as those whose perspective also runs in some ways counter to the idea of an artist collective. New Red Order is a public secret society. Individually, we are core contributors to this public secret society and our work comes out of our own experience as informants where we, as artists, are often called upon to inform on our own culture—similar to the dynamic of anthropologists calling on Native people to inform on their own culture. So we came in with a degree of apprehension, or at least I did, in terms of what it is that we were being called upon to bring. In this site of intense intentional erasures, how could fulfilling the call for visibility and resurgence lead to extending evasions of realities—a public secret—of Indigenous absence and removals? To what degree do refusals of visibility contribute to further erasures? What moves can we make, through amplifying proxy, perhaps exacerbating it, to scrutinize the risks of speaking for, or to bring others in to do the same? This has been something to continue to negotiate while engaging with the public secret of settler colonialism.

This extends to the ways in which we, as Native artists, have perhaps been or felt operationalized or contained by curatorial forces that want to demonstrate or explain or communicate certain themes which we, as artists, have to contend with, such as artistic freedom, notions of freedom as foundational and borne out of origin stories of the nation, or international progress as presumed to be antithetical to Indigenous values and practices, and then wanting that tension, dynamic, or internal resistance to be something that could be scrutinized through our own work. I'm really excited by the idea of this "cacophony of voices" and moments of potential dissonance, which may, in fact, turn out to allow for other lines of demarcation than we anticipated. For us, as New Red Order, that was just something at a foundational level that we had to wrestle with.

JACKSON POLYS (cont.):
Getting back to your question, James, about the timescales in which this exhibition is operating, we wondered: What is the foundation on which we are being called upon to communicate? What kind of curatorial strategies or tactics or levels of absence might be able to communicate something beyond feeling like we're instrumentalizing other people? What does it mean to curate or care for certain topics that bring in people who are not necessarily artists but may be active in the leveraging of material change brought on by our project, specifically as we try to find instances of giving back or reckoning with the problem of stolen land? And further: How can we work together in ways that might draw out a productive level of dissonance with each other? I'm very excited that it's been able to happen through a lot of these conversations over time.

JAMES:
As we are wrapping up the development of this exhibition, I'm struck by what you're saying and by how much of this process will never be seen or experienced. What is underlying this work but not communicated. I think this is true of many exhibitions, but this particular exhibition has so many levels, not just of research, or even labor, that are not viewable, but truly some of the deepest work is not really able to be understood in a typical exhibition model. There are so many silences in a way, decisions to not disclose, decisions to not display, certainly decisions to not frame both land and people in ways that are instrumentalizing, to not address very concrete communities as a spectacle to be experienced.

A lot of the exhibition will never be viewed as an exhibition. It will not be experienced or moved through in this three-month cycle. That is something that's really landed for me, how much of that knowledge is held within the ensemble and held with our collaborators and held with many different conversations in the community. I think that's been a big part of your process, in particular, Risa, that I know I learned from. And it bled into the whole exhibition.

RISA PULEO:
An ethical question drove my curatorial choices and resulted in imperceptible or even invisible artistic interventions: How to engage with a city that is not mine and yet be true to that city in a way that is both historically and site-specific, to clear space so the city may speak on its own terms? I'll also say that I felt like I got a head start. James, your invitation came to me at a moment that aligned with my research. St. Louis is located geographically as a nexus point between the South and the West, and historically, it is the meeting point of concurrent histories of dispossession and abolition. Mining these histories, as they are specific to St. Louis, reveals a paradox at the core of US-American definitions of freedom: the Free Soil Party headquartered in St. Louis in the mid-nineteenth century worked to make the West a slavery-free zone, where to be recognized as "free" within the structure of the nation-state meant the ability of formerly enslaved people to participate in dispossession and occupation.

Rather than mining these histories, the artists I worked with all present possibilities outside of these entanglements. Oftentimes, I find the answer lies not in acting or intervening, but in withdrawing and removing. In not adding an additional framework or interpretive layer but in helping to unbuild those layers that obfuscate, and work to make visible, if not work toward removing, the very real but invisible social structures that determine how people can and cannot move and live in St. Louis. I'm very committed to refusal and withdrawal as a political act as well as a curatorial one.

ALLISON:
Risa, early on in the process, and we talked about this in our meetings, I really struggled with how the permanence of David Adjaye's work could perhaps be seen in a kind of binary opposition to the real delicate impermanence that has been your curatorial framework. I was not necessarily struggling with the artist's intention, or the work itself, which I fully believe in and which underscores the curatorial framework I have developed in response to ideas from The Griot's founder, Lois Conley, who specifically wanted a permanent artwork for the museum's grounds.

ALLISON (cont.):
The proposition that I have for St. Louis Place is engaged in activism and occupation of land, namely because the communities in that area have been shuffled and reshuffled and positioned and repositioned. The neighborhood has been developed through architectural interventions, including the Pruitt-Igoe housing complex built in the mid-twentieth century and demolished in the 1970s, and the future site of the National Geospatial-Intelligence Agency, which is being developed across the street from The Griot. So, I understood and was really clear on why the proposition for permanence was really important to my curatorial framework, yet still struggled. I wonder if you have anything to offer to that dialogue or if you want to speak more about the impermanence of the way that you're working and the intentionality around it?

RISA:
I also thought about your curatorial interventions often during this process. I think it's also interesting that we're positioned on the two terminal points of the city and the exhibition footprint. So, I do wonder: Are we building in antagonisms or binaries? Maybe that's also not giving our audiences enough credit because they're going to bring their own sophisticated readings of what we are doing as curators, the statement each artist is making within those frameworks and also on their own, and how all these positions mix and intermingle in space.

In particular, I've thought about the ways in which David Adjaye's work functions as both monumentally scaled public art and as a monument. In relation to your work, I've thought about how the move to reclaim the form of the monument in our time is also a way to make space for histories that have been overwritten. As such, monuments function as important markers of legitimation that signal an arrival into a moment in which one's experience of the past is recognized in the present. This is especially important for a space like The Griot Museum of Black History in St. Louis, which has done so much to sediment Black contributions to the city and the nation. As such, Adjaye's work physically insists on recognition and is an important rendering of legibility for North St. Louis communities.

My project aims to bring attention back to the ground on which any monument is built, to recognize how the land and its histories have also been silenced, and the other histories and voices that have been silenced in it.

RISA (cont.):
And this premise presents a complication that is entangled with your concern about what it means for public art as a form of occupation: What does it mean to unthink the nation-state, when so many have worked to be recognized, through forms like the monument, within its frameworks? It's my hope that our contributions, when seen together, will help navigate a path outside of what appears to be a binary.

One book that I've come back to a lot is Jodi Rios's *Black Lives and Spatial Politics: Policing Blackness and Practicing Freedom in Suburban St. Louis* (2022).[1] She talks about how, in the wake of Michael Brown's death in Ferguson, there was a very large, very loud, queer, Black contingent that needed to exercise their presence in a highly visible way. I've thought about them too as a different kind of energy than the one that I'm investigating. This third space outside of the antagonisms of binaries that is created in the spaces in-between our projects is a space where different kinds of registers can exist simultaneously. In this third space, I hope the loud productivity of a protest, or the insistence of a monumental work of public art, can meet the quiet energy of the slow work of dismantling. In my project, that energy is generated through the intimacy of listening to landscapes and people to explore different possibilities for decolonial abolitionist futures. Both registers are interdependent; both are doing the work of liberation.

[1] Jodi Rios, *Black Lives and Spatial Matters: Policing Blackness and Practicing Freedom in Suburban St. Louis* (Ithaca: Cornell University Press, 2022).

ALLISON:
And emancipation, for sure.

DIYA:
They often go together. It's not normally one or the other. It's one process leading to the other and going back again, so it really is the kind of confluence of all those scales of making and scales of being together and navigating geographies that lead to the possibility of an emancipation or abolition. It's in the togetherness of those registers. I don't even necessarily see them as binaries, but as tactics together toward this ultimate idea of what emancipation might be.

JAMES:
I remember the word you, Risa, used a lot early on was "sovereignty," and I think that has remained resonant; sovereignty of community, of land. Speaking for myself, coming into this exhibition as a longtime resident of St. Louis—and moving through its many cycles of resistance work occupying the streets and the quieter groundwork that upholds it or brings rest and repair after for those same organizers—my thinking was strongly informed by these questions that came out of reflections on these cycles of resistance and burnout, and wondering what, if anything, an exhibition could do to propose some other way. In that moment of 2020 and all it contained, I was wondering: What is next? What comes after this cycle of resistance? And through a very specific lens of St. Louis, what more can be done by art and artists specifically? What agency do we have? What can we insert infrastructurally?

These sorts of questions were very intentional in the invitation to this ensemble to think generationally, ancestrally, and infrastructurally. For me, it really was naming a frustration with the art world, with the sort of dead ends we were seeing in mass politics that left the lingering question: What can be done? Frankly, that informed the invitation to each of you in different registers because I felt like we could see in your previous work there were some seeds of possibility to step beyond where at least the art world had been operating in terms of these questions.

ALLISON:
Stepping beyond where the "art world" has been operating, or moving beyond commonly held registers, approaches, and methodologies is so crucial and intrinsic to the curatorial work that I focus on.

RISA:
For me, a starting point is always thinking about the ways in which exhibition-making or the art world is complicit in the problem and enacting a withdrawal from that complicity as a first step that precedes any sort of action or claim to action.

JACKSON:
As New Red Order, we're always feeling like we have to contend with these received possibilities of liberation and then see how we can shift or maybe mesh what seems sometimes like oppositional terminology. For example, freedom.

JACKSON (cont.):
At least from my perspective, freedom, although it maybe doesn't have to be, is often tied to the foundation of the nation through which seeds of reformation or resistance or remediation or correction of a certain model can move.

If we're starting with a foundation of emancipation in which I, as a Native person, am having to contend with legacies and received notions that accept the nation-state as a given, I would prefer not to have to accept that reliance. Instead, I'd love to hold out for the possibility of different kinds of sovereignty. However, I'd also love to feel the freedom to accept models of liberation that might flow with the art world and, as an artist, to be able to utilize those kinds of concepts and foundational ways of thinking for myself. That frustration that you, James, are referring to is one that we've definitely long had to deal with and then think through as New Red Order. What kind of acceptance or embrace is necessary—or advantageous—now, and generations forward?

ALLISON:
I really appreciate you sharing that, Jackson. I often think about what would happen if we unimagined this nation-state. It exists in the imagination, the colonial imagination, right? I know that's why I struggled with the idea of an occupation or an artwork performing a kind of permanence, because the nation-state is assumed *a priori*, right? The existence of David Adjaye's work as a monument registers moments in time but also reimagines that place, reaching back to African architecture, and to the earth itself, moving alongside its site. So, I'm curious: What would it look like to you or your project to unimagine?

JACKSON:
I really appreciate your question. I also thought through the David Adjaye piece and the ways in which it has the potential to shift, in perhaps radical ways, the ways in which the context is felt as a given. I've been very appreciative of that while struggling to think through ways in which any material manifestation or collaboration with other artists might be able to do something similar. That model of a kind of occupation and a kind of placetaking or presence that resuscitates, renews, and subverts histories has been inspirational to me, as I've had to think with it along the way.

JACKSON (cont.):
Back to James's questions, we're thinking about our curation in terms of who might be potential collaborators that are not necessarily connected to an art world at all or would never even think of themselves as artists, around these conversations and negotiations attempting to interrogate the potential pathways for material transfer of land to Indigenous peoples—in a way that might move toward some kind of sovereignty, if not be sovereignty itself—and how those might be, in some way, counter to the idea of curation itself. That's all to say many of these negotiations remain behind the scenes as we push toward what may or may not be materially possible. We continue to aim to enact crimes against reality.

Negotiating with ways in which the land transfers we are working toward are developing necessitates engaging on a longer timescale, with multiple invisibilities, pushing how the efforts manifest in the end but also the ways that those erasures can remain legible; how they can remain felt as absences in this project. This shifts toward something that looks like art, that culminates, at least partially, in film—but the filmmaking process might involve a kind of curation through those relationships with the people who don't think of themselves as artists. What does that reverse capture mean when we're simultaneously trying to move toward material changes over the long term as well as redirect our own material resources given to us through the possibilities afforded by this project for public art?

ZACK KHALIL:
What's been so great about working with you all and the framing of this whole event is that the emphasis, in my mind, has really been on material change and the ways in which the discourses we use can actually facilitate material change as being the core of a lot of these projects, though in different ways. Not to be flippant or to disregard the radical potential of art, but I think it has been important in how we have grounded it more in the reality of people's lives and how resources get spent and what's achieved, and who thinks what and what they actually go out and do afterward. Working with you all has really deeply changed the way I think about how that's possible.

ZACK KHALIL (cont.):
Allison, I appreciated your amazing question about an imagination beyond the nation-state. I really appreciate the directness with which you asked that, because I think it's something a lot of people talk around, myself included, but from a Native American, Indigenous perspective, this is a push for non-metaphorical decolonization, for the repatriation of all Indigenous land and life. I think that's a proposition that's really at the core of a lot of our work, and as part of this project in the future, we really want to un-silo that conversation from a Native American, Indigenous focus to everybody who's on this land right now. What does that actually mean, the repatriation of all Indigenous land and life? And that certainly does mean coming together with new forms of reciprocity and relationship.

I think, for a lot of people, that's a really radical, impossible gesture. But I love your question, Allison, because it almost takes that as a given. If we are going to all move forward together, what's the first step? It's like we have to be able to have a new sort of imagination that isn't rooted in this incredibly racist formation. And I think that's been a lot of the value of working together, but also as an ensemble: allowing those conjunctions and dissonances to arise and develop naturally. I think all the work we're doing will be something that continues to evolve well past the exhibition itself. That's something I don't see often enough, and something I am excited to be a part of.

DIYA:
When I was approaching my geographic zone of Downtown West, I was struggling initially because when you drive up to it, it's kind of hard to even see that you've reached a destination. It is a giant intersection with all these municipal buildings and parking lots, and you have to be told that it was once Mill Creek Valley, a bustling Black neighborhood that there's no trace of. Now there will be a mark, speaking of permanence, through the mile-long permanent monument by Damon Davis marking the addresses and families of that neighborhood. I was really contending with this site framed by the Gateway Arch that marks the westward expansion and all these municipal buildings that mark expansion of infrastructure are also marking the proliferation of a nation logic and a nation-state logic. So, what does it mean to commission art that stems from that?

DIYA (cont.):
I have been working with artists who are thinking about that in really different ways. Jordan Weber's approach is working through the municipal sewer district's reparative grant-making initiative against stormwater contamination to fund other kinds of green infrastructures. He is making a regenerative wetland in College Hill that will be a permanent part of a new park held by a community land trust in relationship to a lot of community activists, organizers, and mutual aid providers in the neighborhood. So, Weber is thinking about material change. Steffani Jemison's work will be in Union Station, which was this soaring success when it was constructed—everything in St. Louis once upon a time was the biggest, the best, the most, the model for engineering, and we now are dealing with the failures of that particular moment in modernity. Jemison's approach is also focused on refusal, looking at Josephine Baker and all these Black artists that have had to leave and have dispersed. Jemison is thinking about Josephine Baker's expatriation as a refusal of participating in the nation. So, what are all these ways that art might do the work of political education or might ask us to think about not melding or fixing or patching to continue the logics of the nation-state, but help to at least make visible to people that the foundational problem shows up in these really mundane municipal ways as well—the concrete parking lots, railroad tracks, sewage pipes? That is something I can see throughout everybody's work in this triennial.

JAMES:
It's interesting to see how the language is carried throughout each of your responses, and that happened in the process of forming this exhibition, which was that the reimagining process has to come after an unimagining. That happened in each of our processes in its own way, and I think it has to happen on a municipal level; it has to happen on an artistic level too, to move through this process of unimagining what is right in front of you in order to even arrive to a reimagining once you see what is left. In my role in the exhibition, I receive the question of our particular emphasis on permanence. That is one of the distinct things we are doing, as we insist on infrastructural and generational change, but our answer to what is permanent within the exhibition is slippery. Intentionally so.

JAMES (cont.):
It might look like Damon Davis's mile-long monument. David Adjaye's piece, of course, and Jordan Weber's. Risa's signage project in relation to Jaune Quick-to-See Smith's painting. They are each permanent in a way, for a foreseeable horizon. It is the shift in scale and resources for The Griot. It is, we hope, the material transfer of Sugarloaf Mound in full to the Osage Nation. The question of what is left after this exhibition is really a provocation. It's not what it appears. That proposition of permanence is something else—it's what will have materially changed because we convened together in these forms, with each of our processes and intent, and with resources to realize something profound. And I think that is an open-ended question that will certainly extend beyond 2023. There's not a single answer to that question, but we are offering some propositions, some provocations, and, yes, some material changes that we will manifest in this time. We use the phrase "generational change" throughout, but that isn't manifest in objects. It is what shifts in the city, what shifts in us, in the viewers who move through this and see that some other reimagining is possible.

Contributor

Bios

Lee Broughton is the co-founder of Counterpublic and the Chief Brand Architect for St. Louis CITY SC as well as a member of the team's ownership group. Broughton worked as a brand marketing professional for more than twenty years. His career spanned both agency/consultancy in London, England, and various leadership roles within the brand marketing department of Enterprise Holdings, including Vice President of Global Brand Marketing. Broughton also founded and runs his own brand strategy practice, Broughton Brand Company (BBC), which worked closely with Greater St. Louis, Inc. and other leading St. Louis business development organizations to create and launch the STLMade movement. A tireless advocate for the city of St. Louis, Broughton serves on the board of directors for the Pulitzer Arts Foundation, the Donald Danforth Plant Science Center, and The Luminary, one of St. Louis's leading contemporary art institutions.

Jennifer Colten is a photographer whose work examines the representation of landscape, embedded cultural geographies, and environmental implications of land use. Colten is part of a team of artists, educators, and researchers recently awarded a Mellon Foundation Humanities for All Times Grant for the project Mississippi River Open School for Kinship and Social Exchange (2022–2024). Past and ongoing projects have received support from a Regional Arts Commission (RAC) Fellowship Grant (2020), Ferguson Academic Seed Grant from Washington University in St. Louis, and Mid-America Arts Alliance. In addition to private collections, Colten's photographs have been included in a number of international public collections, including the Denver Art Museum, Museum für Fotografie, Museum Hundertwasser as well as Museo de Arte Moderno, Museo de Antioquia, and Bellas Artes Instítuto, across Colombia.

Allison Glenn's curatorial work focuses on the intersection of art and publics through public art, biennials, special projects, and major new commissions by a wide range of contemporary artists. Her 2021 groundbreaking exhibition at the Speed Art Museum in Louisville, Kentucky, titled *Promise, Witness, Remembrance* reflected on the life of Breonna Taylor, centered on her portrait painted by Amy Sherald, and was selected by the *New York Times* as one of the "best art exhibitions of 2021." Glenn was previously Senior Curator at Public Art Fund; Associate Curator of Contemporary Art, Crystal Bridges Museum of American Art; and Manager of Publications and Curatorial Associate for Prospect New Orleans' international art triennial *Prospect.4: The Lotus in Spite of the Swamp*. Her writing has been featured in numerous publications, including those produced by Princeton Architectural Press, Los Angeles County Museum of Art, Rebuild Foundation, California African American Museum, and the Studio Museum in Harlem.

Walter Johnson grew up in Columbia, Missouri, and is a member of the Rock Bridge High School Hall of Fame (2006). His prize-winning books, *Soul by Soul: Life Inside the Antebellum Slave Market* (1999) and *River of Dark Dreams: Slavery and Empire in the Cotton Kingdom* (2013), were published by Harvard University Press. His autobiographical essay, "Guns in the Family," was included in the 2019 edition of *The Best American Essays*; it was originally published in the *Boston Review*, where Johnson is a contributing editor. *The Broken Heart of America: St. Louis and the Violent History of the United States* was published in the spring of 2020. Johnson is the Winthrop Professor of History at Harvard University and a founding member of the Commonwealth Project, which brings together academics, artists, and activists in an effort to imagine, foster, and support revolutionary social change, beginning in St. Louis.

James McAnally is the Executive and Artistic Director of Counterpublic 2023. Previously, McAnally was the co-founder and director of The Luminary, an expansive platform for art, thought, and action based in St. Louis. He additionally serves as the executive editor and co-founder of *MARCH: a journal of art & strategy* and as a founding member of Common Field, a national network of independent art spaces and organizers. McAnally has presented exhibitions, texts, and lectures at venues such as the Walker Art Center, Kadist Art Foundation, Pulitzer Arts Foundation, The Artist's Institute, and Gwangju Biennale. McAnally's writing has appeared in publications such as *Art in America*, *Art Journal*, *Bomb Magazine*, *Hyperallergic*, *Terremoto*, and many others, and his publications are in the collections of the Museum of Modern Art, Smithsonian Museum of American Art, Los Angeles County Museum of Art (LACMA), and Brooklyn Museum. McAnally is a recipient of the Creative Capital/Andy Warhol Foundation Arts Writers Grant for Short-Form Writing.

New Red Order (NRO) is a "public secret society" collaborating with self-described "informants" to subversively yet earnestly interrogate desires—individual and collective—for indigeneity. The group deploys elements of time-based media, including video and sound, along with sculpture, installation, and performance in order to shift potential obstructions to Indigenous growth. Core contributors are Adam Khalil (Ojibway), Zack Khalil (Ojibway), and Jackson Polys (Tlingit). Their individual and collaborative work has been presented at the Museum of Modern Art, Sundance Film Festival, Toronto Biennial of Art 2019, Museum of Contemporary Art Detroit, Walker Art Center, Whitney Museum of American Art, Museum of Modern Art, Sharjah Biennial, and more.

Risa Puleo is an independent curator. Her exhibition *Walls Turned Sideways: Artists Confront the Justice System* was curated for the Contemporary Arts Museum in Houston and traveled to Tufts University Art Galleries in January 2020. *Monarchs: Brown and Native Contemporary Artists in the Path of the Butterfly*, curated for Bemis Center for Contemporary Arts, traveled to the Museum of Contemporary Art in North Miami, Blue Star Art Space and Southwest School of Art and Craft in San Antonio, and the Nerman Museum of Contemporary Art in Kansas City. Puleo has written for *Art in America*, *Art Papers*, *Art21*, *ArtPacific*, *Hyperallergic*, and *Modern Painters*.

As a curator and an artist, **Katherine Simóne Reynolds** investigates emotional dialects and psychogeographies of Blackness, and the importance of "anti-excellence." Her work tries to give physical form to emotions and experiences by constructing pieces that include portrait photography, video work, choreography, sculpture, and installation. Reynolds has exhibited and performed work within many spaces and institutions, including the Pulitzer Arts Foundation, Museum of Modern Art, and SculptureCenter. She has exhibited in national and international group and solo shows and has spoken at the Contemporary Art Museum St. Louis, Saint Louis Art Museum, and the Black Midwest Initiative Symposium at the University of Minnesota. Alongside her visual art practice, she has embarked on curatorial projects at The Luminary, SculptureCenter, and upcoming exhibitions for Stanley Museum of Art as well as the Clyfford Still Museum. Reynolds was a 2022 Fellow with the Graham Foundation for Advanced Studies in the Fine Arts.

Diya Vij is the Curator at Creative Time in New York City. Over the past decade, she has held programming, curatorial, and communications positions at the High Line, the New York City Department of Cultural Affairs (DCLA), and the Queens Museum. As the Associate Curator of Public Programs at the High Line, she organized dozens of live events and performances with artists, activists, practitioners, and healers. At DCLA, Vij launched and co-directed the Public Artists in Residence (PAIR) program, a municipal residency program that embeds artists into city agencies to address New York City's most pressing issues.

Jesse Vogler is an architect and educator whose work sits at the intersection of landscape, politics, and performance. His writing and projects address the entanglements between landscape and law and take on themes of work, property, expertise, and memory. Vogler is a MacDowell Fellow, Fulbright Scholar, and, in addition to his art and research practice, is a land surveyor, co-directs the Institute of Marking and Measuring, and teaches across landscape, architecture, art, and urbanism. He is based out of Tbilisi, Georgia, where he is Professor and Head of the Architecture Program at the Free University of Tbilisi.

Artist

Bios

David Adjaye is an award-winning Ghanaian-British architect known to infuse his artistic sensibilities and ethos into community-driven projects. In 2000, David founded his own practice, Adjaye Associates, taking on projects that span the globe. The firm's work ranges from private houses, bespoke furniture collections, product design, exhibitions, and temporary pavilions to major arts centers, civic buildings, and master plans. His largest project to date, the Smithsonian National Museum of African American History and Culture, opened on the National Mall in Washington, DC in 2016 and was named "cultural event of the year" by the *New York Times*.

The Black Healers Collective, an initiative of InPower Institute, is a community of change agents, healers, educators, activists, ministers, artists, therapists, chaplains, organizers, academics, health practitioners, and systems thinkers who work to advance the healing and wholeness of African diaspora peoples. Located in St. Louis, Missouri, BHC members engage in healing practices, programs, and partnerships that support the Black community in (1) "re-membering" itself—repairing that which feels fragmented and broken within its households, families, and neighborhoods; (2) expressing its truths and exercising its power; and (3) creating healed futures that affirm and uplift Black lives. As part of this work, BHC curates healing spaces with other groups, organizations, and initiatives to help them foster deepened states of well-being for their members and communities.

Black Quantum Futurism is an interdisciplinary creative practice between Camae Ayewa and Rasheedah Phillips that weaves quantum physics, Afrofuturism, and Afrodiasporic concepts of time, ritual, text, and sound, creating counterhistories and Black quantum womanist futures that challenge exclusionary mainstream versions of history and future. Black Quantum Futurism has created a number of community-based projects, performances, experimental music projects, installations, workshops, books, short films, and zines, including the award-winning Community Futures Lab and the Black Woman Temporal Portal. The BQF collective is a 2022 Creative Capital Fellow, 2020 CERN Artist Resident, 2020–2022 Vera List Center Fellow, 2021 Knight Arts + Tech Fellow, 2018 Velocity Fund Grantee, 2018 Solitude x ZKM Web Resident, 2017 Center for Emerging Visual Artists Fellow, and 2017 Pew Fellow. BQF has presented, exhibited, and performed at documenta fifteen, Red Bull Arts New York, Chicago Architecture Biennial, Village of Arts and Humanities, Manifesta 13, apexart, MoMA PS1, ICA London, Metropolitan Museum of Art, and more.

Raven Chacon is a Pulitzer Prize-winning composer, performer, and installation artist from Fort Defiance, Navajo Nation. A recording artist over the span of twenty-two years, Chacon has appeared on over eighty releases on national and international labels. Chacon has exhibited, performed, or had works performed at the Los Angeles County Museum of Art (LACMA), Vancouver Art Gallery, Haus der Kulturen der Welt, SITE Santa Fe, Kennedy Center, and more. His artworks are among the collections of the Whitney Museum of American Art, Smithsonian's American Art Museum and National Museum of the American Indian, LACMA, and others.

Juan William Chávez is an artist and activist whose multidisciplinary practice extends across painting and drawing, installation and video, as well as beekeeping and agriculture. He often works collaboratively on social-practice projects that address the environment, sustainability, and urban ecologies. Chávez has exhibited his work at venues such as Artpace, McColl Center, El Museo del Barrio, Contemporary Art Museum St. Louis, and more. His work has gained the support of institutions such as the John Simon Guggenheim Memorial Foundation, Creative Capital, Joan Mitchell Foundation, Andy Warhol Foundation for the Visual Arts, and Art Matters Foundation.

Damon Davis is a post-disciplinary artist who works and resides in St. Louis, Missouri. His work spans a spectrum of creative mediums to tell stories exploring how identity is informed by power and mythology. Davis's work is featured in the permanent collection of the Smithsonian National Museum of African American History and Culture, and he has exhibited at the Museum of Contemporary Art Detroit, Saint Louis Art Museum, Museum of Contemporary African Diasporan Arts, and Museum of Contemporary Art San Diego. He has been a fellow of Firelight Media, Sundance Labs, TED, and the Kennedy Center.

Torkwase Dyson describes herself as a painter working across multiple mediums to explore the continuity between ecology, infrastructure, and architecture. In addition to participating in group exhibitions at the Smithsonian National Museum of African Art, Whitney Museum of American Art, Museum of Modern Art, and California African American Museum, Dyson has had solo exhibitions and installations at Colby College Museum of Art, Graham Foundation for Advanced Studies in the Fine Arts, Schuylkill Center for Environmental Education, and Suzanne Lemberg Usdan Gallery, Bennington College, Vermont.

Jen Everett is an artist from Southfield, Michigan, currently based in St. Louis, Missouri. Her practice moves between lens- and time-based media, installation, and writing. Her work has been shown nationally and internationally at art spaces including the Contemporary Art Museum St. Louis, Krannert Art Museum, SCAD Museum of Art, Kunsthall Stavanger, Seattle University's Hedreen Gallery, and Flux Factory. Everett has been an artist in residence at the Fire Island Artist Residency, Vermont Studio Center, Atlantic Center for the Arts, and ACRE. She was a 2021–22 Duke University DocX Archive Lab Fellow. Her work is in the collection of the Museum of Contemporary Photography (MoCP) at Columbia College, Chicago.

Artist **Anita Fields** and musician **Nokosee Fields**, mother and son, are collaborating on work for Counterpublic 2023. Anita creates clay and textile works that reflect her native Osage culture. Her practice explores the complexities of cultural influences and the intersections of balance and chaos found within our lives. Her work can be found in collections such as the Museum of Arts and Design in New York, IAIA Museum of Contemporary Native Arts, Crystal Bridges Museum of American Art, Smithsonian's National Museum of the American Indian, and more. Nokosee, the great nephew of celebrated Cherokee fiddler Sam O'Fields, began studying orchestral violin at a young age and has recently turned his attention to various forms of traditional American music, performing, teaching, and touring professionally. A quest for balance shapes his work, whether he is reconciling the weight of tradition with his creative impulses or challenging the demands and vacuity of colonialist, capitalist structures and systems with the richness of his experience and upbringing as a member of the Osage, Creek, and Cherokee Nations.

General Sisters is an art collective based in North Braddock, Pennsylvania, founded in 2009 by Dana Bishop-Root and Ginger Brooks Takahashi. Bishop-Root and Takahashi have shared work as General Sisters at John Michael Kohler Arts Center; Jewish Museum, New York; Art Gallery of Ontario, Toronto; Konsthall C, Stockholm; Williams College Museum of Art, Williamstown; and the Japanese American Museum of San Jose. They have participated as collaborators in art, conversation, growing, food production, and commerce in their shared garden and building in North Braddock, Pennsylvania; Whitney Museum, New York; Carnegie Museum of Art, Pittsburgh; and the Hammer Museum, Los Angeles.

General Sisters are additionally collaborating with Dail Chambers, Dustin Gibson, Basmin Nadra, and Xochitl Plancarte:

Dail Chambers is an ethnographic artist, grower, mother, and educator. She is the founder of Yeyo Arts Collective and Mississippi Mermaid, as well as a member of Sibyls Shrine, Civic Arts Development, and Women's Earth Alliance. Chambers works in communities to develop authentic organizing and art practices for the public through nativity, ancient civilization, and Afrofuturism. Chambers stewards an educational homestead, farm, and orchard in North St. Louis.

Dustin Gibson is the Director of Access, Disability and Language Justice at PeoplesHub. He is a peer support trainer with disABILITY LINK in Georgia and a board member with Straight Ahead and HEARD. He is also a founding member of the Harriet Tubman Collective, Us Protecting Us in Atlanta, Georgia, and the Policing in Allegheny County Committee. He has worked on the ground with Centers for Independent Living (CIL) in Southwest Pennsylvania with a focus on deinstitutionalization and youth self-determination. His work in the national CIL networks supported youth peer-support networks and the abolition of policing and prisons. He teaches courses about abolition and disability justice in communities, high schools, universities, and law schools.

Basmin Nadra is a daughter of all relations extending her life practice as a generous art practice into streets, rivers, nightclubs, and homes. Nadra brings her lived experience as a native St. Louisan of diverse experience and versatile expression in all of her offerings: performance for film, stage, music, or theater productions; administration in media; and as an activist for social justice, food sovereignty, the environment, and caregiving and advocacy for Elders. As a character innovator and vocalist, her unique and memorable presence has been commissioned by writers, directors, and producers to illuminate and activate visions.

Xochitl Plancarte weaves lineage, migration, present tense locations, and the capacity to expand into garments of celebration and everyday being. Plancarte's practice invites and enters gatherings of differences with shared glances and tender time. Plancarte has made home growing up in St. Louis venturing through the city's parks, bookstores, and performance spaces.

Robert E. Green's artistic practice combines physical artmaking (assemblage, sculpture, painting, photography, and video) with acts of social justice that take the form of cultural festivals and events, creating a kind of *Gesamtkunstwerk*. His works and actions celebrate Black Pride and foster economic success within the Black community. Green's artistic practice has also included the rescue and collection of African/African American historical and cultural artifacts. He uses the collection and the community events he organizes as catalysts for education and the advancement of Black Pride. Across these initiatives, Green speaks to the spatial displacement of lives and communities fractured by the politics that have fostered years of systemic oppression of African Americans in St. Louis. A recipient of an artist grant from the Regional Arts Commission (RAC), Green has also shown his work at The Sheldon Art Galleries, 10th Street Galleries, The Griot Museum of Black History, 14th Street Artist Community Gallery, and Webster University, among others.

Matthew Angelo Harrison creates sculptures that combine organic found objects he then sculpts using machinery. The resulting forms investigate the subtle politics of mass production, authenticity, metamorphosis, and abstract ancestries. He has been awarded grants and fellowships by the Los Angeles County Museum of Art (LACMA), United States Artists, and Kresge Arts. He has enjoyed solo shows in the following public institutions: Broad Art Museum (East Lansing, Michigan); Atlanta Contemporary; and the Museum of Contemporary Art Detroit (MOCAD). His work is in many permanent collections, including the de Young Museum, San Francisco; Detroit Institute of Arts; Galeries Lafayette Foundation, Paris; Institute of Contemporary Art, Miami; Musée d'Art Moderne de la Ville de Paris; Museum of Contemporary Art Chicago; and the Whitney Museum of American Art, New York, among others. Harrison lives and works in Detroit. He is represented by Galerie Eva Presenhuber and Jessica Silverman Gallery.

Steffani Jemison is an interdisciplinary artist based in Brooklyn, New York. Her work has been exhibited at the Stedelijk Museum Amsterdam, Jeu de Paume, CAPC Bordeaux, Museum of Modern Art, RISD Museum, LA><ART, Guggenheim Museum, the Whitney Biennial, and more. Jemison has completed artist residencies with the Skowhegan School of Painting and Sculpture; Core Program at the Museum of Fine Arts, Houston; Project Row Houses; Studio Museum in Harlem AIR; and others. She has been an Art Matters grantee, Louis Comfort Tiffany Biennial Foundation awardee, NYFA Fellow in video/film, Mildred Londa Weisman Fellow at the Radcliffe Institute for Advanced Study at Harvard University, Guggenheim Fellow, and a recipient of the Herb Alpert Award in Visual Art.

Artist and advocate **Seitu Ken Jones** has been tending the soil of community through art for more than forty years. Throughout his career, he has harnessed the tools of visual art, infrastructure, and civic engagement to create work that links history to the present and honors the community's assets—from its historic figures to natural resources to cultural traditions. In his public art and events, His large-scale sculptural installation *Turnip Greens* was dedicated in 2019 at the Nashville Farmers Market, inspired by the city's bounty of food and Black culture. First enacted in St. Paul in 2014, *A Community Meal* convened two thousand people over dinner at a table half a mile long. Jones is a recently retired faculty member of Goddard College in Washington State. He holds a BS degree in Landscape Design and an MLS in Environmental History from the University of Minnesota. He has been a Senior Fellow in Agricultural Systems in the College of Food, Agricultural and Natural Resource Sciences at the University of Minnesota and is a member of the Board of Managers for the Capitol Region Watershed District. He resides in St. Paul, Minnesota with his partner, the poet Soyini Guyton.

Ralph Lemon is a dancer, choreographer, writer, and visual artist who generates interdisciplinary modes of artistic expression as he strives to communicate stories, emotions, memories, and identities that do not conform to standard categories of representation. He incorporates sensibilities and approaches gleaned from endeavors beyond the arts, such as ethnographic and historical research, into a diverse and complex body of work that includes choreography, books, paintings, and experimental stage and lecture performances. Lemon's work has been exhibited at the Studio Museum in Harlem, Zilkha Gallery at Wesleyan University, Hayward Gallery in London, Nasher Museum of Art at Duke University, and more. Lemon was a 2013–14 Annenberg Fellow at the Museum of Modern Art and was named a MacArthur Fellow in 2020.

Born on the Standing Rock Reservation in North Dakota, **Cannupa Hanska Luger** is an enrolled member of the Three Affiliated Tribes of the Fort Berthold Reservation. Through monumental installations, Luger interweaves performance and political action to communicate stories about twenty-first-century Indigeneity. Luger has received numerous awards, such as the United States Artists Fellowship, Creative Capital Fellowship, and the Native Arts and Cultures Foundation Fellowship, and has been the subject of solo exhibitions at venues such as the Princeton University Art Museum, Denver Art Museum, Crystal Bridges Museum of American Art, Gardiner Museum, and the Museum of Arts and Design.

New Red Order, a public secret society of rotating membership, including core contributors Adam Khalil, Zack Khalil, and Jackson Polys, collaborates with informants to create exhibitions, videos, and performances that question and rechannel subjective and material relationships to indigeneity. Orienting their work through the paradoxical conditions of Indigenous experience, NRO explores the contradictions and missteps that embody, in their own words, "the desire for indigeneity in the myths, dreams, and political foundations of the so-called Americas." NRO's work has been exhibited at the Audain Gallery at Simon Fraser University, Museum of Contemporary Art Detroit (MOCAD), Toronto Biennial of Art, EFA Project Space, Artists Space in New York, Walker Art Center, 57th New York Film Festival, Whitney Museum of American Art, Museum of Modern Art, Sharjah Biennial, and more.

Mendi + Keith Obadike are creators of music, art, and literature. Their work has been shown at the Studio Museum in Harlem, New School in New York, Metropolitan Museum of Art in New York, and more. They have received numerous awards including a Rockefeller New Media Arts Fellowship, Pick Laudati Award for Digital Art, New York Foundation for the Arts Fellowship in Fiction, and the Louis Comfort Tiffany Biennial Foundation Award.

Yvonne Osei is a Ghanaian multidisciplinary artist with a global creative practice characterized by public interventions that address beauty, memory, and the eradication of history, racism, colonialism, and the politics of clothing. Osei received her MFA from Washington University in St. Louis. Her practice has been supported by several artist residencies including Cité internationale des arts in Paris, Fountainhead in Miami, and the Fine Arts Work Center in Provincetown. She is the recipient of the 2022 Stone & DeGuire Contemporary Art Award and the 2022 Great Rivers Biennial Award by the Contemporary Art Museum St. Louis.

Digital artist **Tim Portlock** creates postapocalyptic urban landscapes. He has mastered a variety of digital platforms and employs them to make art that depicts worlds in which industrial culture has come and gone, leaving certain classes and communities blighted in its wake. Portlock lives and works in St. Louis and Philadelphia and is an Associate Professor at the Sam Fox School of Design and Visual Arts at Washington University. A recipient of a Pew Fellowship, Portlock has exhibited work at Georgetown University in Washington, DC; Contemporary Art Museum St. Louis's Great Rivers Biennial; Institute of Contemporary Art in Philadelphia; Tate Modern in London; and more.

Jaune Quick-to-See Smith has been creating complex abstract paintings and prints since the 1970s, grounded in themes of personal and political identity. Quick-to-See Smith has received the Academy of Arts and Letters Purchase Award, a Joan Mitchell Foundation Painters Grant, the Women's Caucus for Art Lifetime Achievement Award, and more. She has been an ArtTable Artist Honoree, was elected to the National Academy of Design in New York, received the Living Artist of Distinction Award at the Georgia O'Keeffe Museum, and has received four honorary doctorates. Her work is included in the collections of the Museum of Modern Art in Ecuador, Museum of Mankind in Austria, Walker Art Center in Minneapolis, Smithsonian American Art Museum, Museum of Modern Art, Brooklyn Museum, Metropolitan Museum of Art, and Whitney Museum of American Art.

Will Rawls is a multidisciplinary artist working with choreography, performance, video, sculpture, works on paper, and installation. He uses performance as a vehicle for reformulating perceptions and embodiments of Blackness in contemporary life. Rawls has received grants, fellowships, and residencies from the Guggenheim Foundation, Herb Alpert Foundation, Creative Capital, MAP Fund, New England Foundation for the Arts, National Performance Network, Foundation for Contemporary Arts, United States Artists, Rauschenberg Foundation, MacDowell, and several universities and museums. He lectures widely and publishes his writing in academic and community contexts.

Vincent Stemmler is a mixed-media artist who uses various forms of collage to explore a world in constant flux. Investigating issues of individual and social identity, fragmentation, and loss, Stemmler employs materials with social and political connotations. The material focus of Stemmler's work is often derived from bringing disparate pieces together to form a whole while addressing ideas of labor, class, and multiculturalism. Born and raised in St. Louis, Missouri, Stemmler holds an AA from Florissant Valley Community College, a BFA from the School of the Art Institute of Chicago, and an MFA from Southern Illinois University Edwardsville. Stemmler is currently artist in residence at the Kranzberg Arts Center in St. Louis.

Maya Stovall is an American conceptual artist, anthropologist, and author. Stovall is known for her use of ballet and public space in her art practice. She is an Assistant Professor at California State Polytechnic University, Pomona, and lives and works in Los Angeles. Her work has been featured in the Whitney Biennial and the Studio Museum in Harlem F-Series. It is held in public permanent collections including the Los Angeles County Museum of Art (LACMA), Studio Museum in Harlem, Cranbrook Art Museum, Kalamazoo Institute of Arts, and the Whitney Museum of American Art.

Simiya Sudduth is a mother, multidisciplinary artist, and art educator who maintains a fluid creative practice that explores the intersections of healing, wellness, ecology, social justice, and spirituality. Their practice is a provocation for collective healing and expansion serving as a vessel to explore their personal mental and emotional healing, as well as a space to journey through the realms of spirituality. Sudduth's practice is one of integration, a way to explore and connect multifaceted interests and influences. In addition to maintaining their creative practice, Sudduth is a full-time K–6 art educator.

jackie sumell is a multidisciplinary artist and abolitionist whose work is fueled by her relationship to the natural world and gratitude for her elders. Anchored at the intersection of activism, social practice, ritual, and mindfulness for nearly two decades, she has shared this work extensively throughout the world. sumell has been the recipient of residencies and fellowships including a Marguerite Casey Foundation Fellowship, S.O.U.R.C.E. Studio Fellowship, A Blade of Grass Fellowship, Robert Rauschenberg Artist as Activist Fellowship, Soros Justice Fellowship, Eyebeam Fellowship, Headlands Center for the Arts Residency, and Schloss Solitude Residency. sumell's long-term collaboration with Herman Wallace was the subject of the Emmy Award-winning documentary *Herman's House* (2012) and the driving force behind her abolition-centered practices. She is based in New Orleans, Louisiana.

virgil b/g taylor is a New York faggot living in Germany. He makes *fag tips*, an online speculative zine. He is one half of sssssssssSsss, a study-friendship with Ashkan Sepahvand, and a member of What Would An HIV Doula Do?, a collective of artists, writers, caretakers, activists, and more gathered in response to the ongoing HIV/AIDS pandemic. His work explores histories of care and crisis, magic and toxicity.

Jordan Weber is a regenerative land sculptor and activist who works at the cross-section of social justice and environmental racism. Weber was most recently commissioned by the Walker Art Center to create an urban phytoremediation farm in North Minneapolis. Weber was recently in residence at the Pulitzer Arts Foundation; the Center for the Study of Race, Ethnicity & Equity (CRE2) in St. Louis, Missouri; Yale University as part of the inaugural Environmental Humanities Artist Residency; and Harvard University as the inaugural LOEB/ArtLab Fellow. Recent awards and fellowships include the 2022 United States Artist Award, Joan Mitchell Foundation Award, Creative Capital, and A Blade of Grass Fellowship.

X is an Indigenous futurist, multidisciplinary artist, and architect specializing in land, architectural, and new media installation. His work illuminates the liminal space between the ancestral plane and our accelerating posthuman world. X is a 3Arts Award Winner, a 2020 New City Top 50 Artist, and the first Native American contributor to the Chicago Architecture Biennial. His work has been exhibited and collected internationally by the IAIA Museum of Contemporary Native Arts, Ars Electronica, and the Museum of Contemporary Art Chicago. In 2020, X was commissioned by the US State Department as the lead artist of the American Arts Incubator Brazil.

STAFF
James McAnally
Executive + Artistic Director

Aja Corrigan
Managing Director

Jessi Mueller
Director of Exhibitions

Katherine Simóne Reynolds
Associate Curator

Melisa Sanders
Community Engagement Strategist

Kristen Oyer
Communications Coordinator

Marianne Laury
Installation Manager

Alexis Rivierre
Project Coordinator

Micah Mickles
Sam Fox School of Design & Visual Arts Fellow

CURATORIAL ENSEMBLE
Allison Glenn
Risa Puleo
New Red Order
Diya Vij

SUPPORTERS
This publication is supported by:

LEAD SPONSORS
Andrew W. Mellon Foundation
Lee + Chrissy Broughton
Regional Arts Commission
VIA Art Fund

SUPPORTERS
The Andy Warhol Foundation for the Visual Arts
Arts and Education Council
Clayco
Dan + Sarah Wessel
Edward Jones
Emily Rauh Pulitzer
Graham Foundation for Advanced Studies in Fine Arts
William T. Kemper Foundation

PARTNERS
Angad Arts Hotel
Brown School Evaluation Center
City of St. Louis
Cortex STL
Great Rivers Greenway - Brickline Greenway
Griot Museum of Black History
MARCH
Mildred Lane Kemper Art Museum
Opera Theatre of Saint Louis
Osage Nation
Pulitzer Arts Foundation
Saint Louis Art Museum
Sam Fox School of Design and Visual Arts
STLMade
St. Louis CITY SC
The Luminary

MEDIA PARTNERS
Once Films
Orange Barrel Media
Outfront Media

Colophon

EDITOR
James McAnally

MANAGING EDITOR
Sarrita Hunn

COPY EDITOR
Bonnie Begusch

Designed by Visitor Assembly

Printed by KOPA

Published by MARCH
march.international

COVER IMAGES
(from top to bottom)

The Griot Museum of Black History
Photo courtesy of Nyara Williams and Counterpublic

Damon Davis
Pillars of the Valley installation view, 2023
Courtesy of St. Louis CITY SC

Jennifer Colten and Jesse Vogler
From the Heckenberg Family Scrapbook
Courtesy of Joan Heckenberg

Counterpublic
2701 Cherokee Street
St. Louis, MO 63118
www.counterpublic.org